A GUIDE TO ISLAMIC
PSYCHOLOGY PROGRAMS

In the Name of Allāh
the Most Gracious, Most Merciful

DEDICATION

The editor would like to dedicate this book to his deceased parents

SYED FAZAL & SAFIA HAQUE

May this work be a source of perpetual charity.

A GUIDE TO ISLAMIC
PSYCHOLOGY PROGRAMS

Edited by

Amber Haque, Ph.D.

Professor of Psychology

Riphah International University

Islamabad, Pakistan

This book first published 2025
Department of Psychology
Riphah International University
Islamabad, Pakistan
Copyright © 2025 belongs to the author Dr. Amber Haque, Department of Psychology, Riphah International University

All rights for this book reserved. No part of this book may be reproduced, stored in a retrieval system, or transmitted, in any form or by any means, electronic, mechanical, photocopying, recording, or otherwise, without the prior permission of the copyright owner.

CONTENTS

FOREWORD v

Anis Ahmad

Vice Chancellor, Riphah International University, Islamabad, Pakistan

Abdallah Rothman

President, International Association of Islamic Psychology (IAIP). xix

ACKNOWLEDGMENTS xxiii

LIST OF AUTHORS xxv

INTRODUCTION 1

Amber Haque

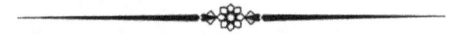

CHAPTER ONE 17

An Overview of the Global Interest in Islamic Psychology

Amber Haque

CHAPTER TWO 47
Doctorate Program in Islamic Psychology, Universitas Muhammadiyah Surakarta, Central Java, Indonesia

Taufik Kasturi

CHAPTER THREE 63
Traditional Islamically Integrated Psychotherapy (TIIP) and its accompanying Certificate, Diploma, and Degree Programs Worldwide

Khalil Center (US), Ibn Haldun University (Turkiye), Hamad Bin Khalifa University (Qatar)

Sena Aycan, Hooman Keshavarzi, & Fahad Khan

CHAPTER FOUR 81
Master's Degree in Islamic Psychology and the First Graduate School of Islamic Psychology in the United States, The Alkaram Institute, Virginia, USA

Carrie M. York

CHAPTER FIVE 89
Revitalizing the Science of the Soul: Psychology from an Islamic Perspective Bachelor of Human Sciences in Psychology (Honors), International Islamic University Malaysia, Kuala Lumpur, Malaysia

Jamilah Hanum Abdul Khaiyom, Mohd Ferdaus Harun, Usman Jaffer, Jusmawati Fauzaman, & Shukran Abdul Rahman

CHAPTER SIX 123
Postgraduate Diploma in Islamic Psychotherapies for Mental Health Riphah International University, Islamabad, Pakistan

Mifrah Rauf Sethi, Anis Ahmad, & Mujeeb Bhatti

CHAPTER SEVEN 137
Postgraduate Certificate in Islamic Psychology, Cambridge Muslim College, Cambridge, UK

Abdallah Rothman, Armaan A. Rowther, Samir Mahmoud, & Khalid Sharif

CHAPTER EIGHT 159
Graduate Certificate in Islamic Psychology, Charles Sturt University, Sydney, Australia

Hanan Dover

CHAPTER NINE   171

Psychology as the Science of Human Soul, Cognition, Emotion, and Behavior, Avicenna Academy, Yogyakarta, Indonesia

Bagus Riyono

CHAPTER TEN   179

Al Balagh Academy's 4 Year Online Islamic Psychology and Counseling Program with Ongoing Continuing Professional Development in Islamic Psychology and Psychotherapy, Bradford, UK

G. Hussein Rassool

CHAPTER ELEVEN   205

Islamic Psychology Certificate

Islamic Psychology Counselor Certificate, Académie Islam & Psychologie, Paris, France

Ali Habibbi

CHAPTER TWELVE   225

Certificate in Islamic Counseling, Aligarh College of Education, Aligarh, India

Akbar Husain

CHAPTER THIRTEEN   233

An Islamic Approach to Islamic Psychology and Psychological Therapies, Islamic Therapeutic Services, Bradford, UK

Rasjid Skinner

CHAPTER FOURTEEN   239

Islamic Psychology at Stanford University, Stanford University Muslim Mental Health and Islamic Psychology Lab, Palo Alto, CA, USA

Huda Naeem & Rania Awaad

CHAPTER FIFTEEN   251

Unifying Perspectives: Merging Contemporary and Islamic Psychology in University Curricula in Pakistan, Shifa Tameer-e-Millat University, Islamabad, Pakistan

Muhammad Tahir Khalily, Neelam Ehsan, Fatima Khuram, & Tamkeen Saleem

CHAPTER SIXTEEN   267

Introducing Islamic Psychology Courses at Two Iranian Centers of the Islamic Psychology Association and the Comprehensive Center for Counseling, Growth, and Empowerment in Qom and Mashad, Iran.

Hamid Rafiei-Honar & Masood Azarbayejani

CHAPTER SEVENTEEN   283

Certificate in Islamic Theoretically Oriented Counseling, Graduate level Courses in Islamic Psychology, Istanbul Sabahattin Zaim University, Istanbul, Türkiye

Ayse Kaya Goktepe

REFERENCES   299

APPENDIX   319

LIST OF TABLES

		Page No.
Table 1	Curriculum Map Matrix of Doctorate Program in IP	54
Table 2	Details of the faculty involved in Islamic Psychology Diploma	131
Table 3	Key publications of faculty members during RIU tenure	134
Table 4	CMC IP Diploma Cohort Demographics by Year	143
Table 5	CMC IP Program Modules	146
Table 6	Student Enrolment in the Graduate Certificate in IP Program	168
Table 7	Admission to Program	169
Table 8	Islāmic counselling and psychology (Level 2): Aims, learning outcomes, contents, course team and duration	186
Table 9	Addiction Counselling: Islāmic Model – Level 1. Aims, learning outcomes, contents, course team and duration	188
Table 10	Child Psychology: Western Insights and Islāmic Perspectives. Aims, learning outcomes, contents, course team and duration	189

Table 11	The Fiqh of Psychology, Psychiatry, and Counselling	190
Table 12	Organization of the courses	230
Table 13	Curriculum Development of IP across Educational Levels	260
Table 14	Overview of CCIP Courses: Titles, Syllabi, and Suggested Resources	269
Table 15	Overview of SSIP Courses: Titles, Syllabi, and Suggested Resources	272
Table 16	Titles of the specialized and elective syllabus in IP	278
Table 17	Role, ability and general competence expected from graduates	279
Table 18	Role, ability and special competence expected from graduates	279
Table 19	IZU Graduate Course Structure and Outcomes in Islamic Psychology	288

LIST OF FIGURES

		Page No.
Figure 1	Curriculum Flow 1st to 6th Semester	55
Figure 2	The Sejahtera Academic Framework	91
Figure 3	Country Wise of Islāmic	196
Figure 4	Gender ratio	197
Figure 5	Effort and Learning Outcomes	197
Figure 6	Course Content and Structure	198
Figure 7	Instructor Performance	198
Figure 8	Satisfaction and Overall Course Experience	199
Figure 9	Course content [helped boost your career or CV]	199

LIST OF ABBREVIATIONS

Islamic Psychology	(IP)
Aligarh Muslim University	(AMU)
Universiti Teknologi Malaysia	(UTM)
King Saud University	(KSU)
Ibn Haldun University	(IHU)
Cognitive-Behavioral Therapy	(CBT)
Government College University	(GCU)
Hamad Bin Khalifa University	(HBKU)
World Islamic Association for Mental Health	(WIAMH)
Islamization of Knowledge	(IOK)
International Institute of Islamic Thought	(IIIT)
Higher Education Commission	(HEC)
International Islamic University Islamabad	(IIUI)
Association of Islamic Psychology	(API)
Australian Society of Islamic Psychology	(ASI)
Universitas Muhammadiyah Surakarta	UMS)
Doctorate Program in Islamic Psychology	(DPIP)
Systematic Literature Review	(SLR)
Traditional Islamically Integrated Psychotherapy	(TIIP)
Cambridge Muslim College	(CMC)
International Islamic University of Malaysia	(IIUM)
International Association of Islamic Psychology	(IAIP)
Research in Understanding the Heart in Islamic Psychology	(RUH-IP)

CONTRIBUTORS

Post Graduated Certificate	(PGCert)
Continuing Professional Development	(CPD)
Psychology from an Islamic Perspective	(PPIG)
Heart Over Mind Institute	(HOME)
Doctorate Program in Islamic Psychology	(DPIP)
Riphah International University	(RIU)
International Association of Islamic Psychology	(IAIP)
Charles Sturt University	(CSU)
Islamic Studies Research Academy	(ISRA)
Memorandum of Understanding	(MOU)
International Association of Muslim Psychologists	(IAMP)
Continuous Professional Development	(CPD)
Académie Islam & Psychologie	(AIP)
International Students of Islamic Psychology	(ISIP)
Spiritual Counseling and Guidance	(SCG)
Philosophy and Religious Sciences	(PRS)
International Students of Islamic Psychology	(ISIP)
Islamic Psychology and Psychotherapy	(IPP)
Master of Arts	(MA)
Community-based Participatory Research	(CBPR)
Board of Studies	(BOS)
Malaysian Qualifications Framework	(MQF)
Post-graduate Certificate of Higher Education	(PgCert HE)
International Association of Muslim Psychologists	(IAMP)
Centre for Islamic Studies and Civilization	(CISAC)
English Language Proficiency	(ELP)
Australian Association of Islamic and Muslim Studies	(AAIMS)
Australian Counselling Association	(ACA)
Psychotherapy and Counselling Federation in Australia	(PACFA)
Markfield Institute of Higher Education	(MIHE)

FOREWORD

Anis Ahmad

Viability of a holistic ethical intelligence: A Qur'anic perspective

The study of human behavior from a psychological perspective involves understanding how individuals behave in specific situations over time, utilizing research methodologies and empirical data gathered from clinical studies. Employing empirical research methods helps organize valuable insights into how our cognitive brain responds in stressful situations. Scholars in modern psychology and management also emphasize the importance of emotional intelligence in making critical decisions and forming quick judgments.

Daniel Goleman, in his bestselling book "Emotional Intelligence," references the work of Paul Ekman and Seymour Epstein from the University of California, San Francisco, and the University of Massachusetts, respectively. He notes, "The emotional mind is far quicker than the rational mind, springing into action without pausing for even a moment to consider what it is doing. Actions that arise from the emotional mind carry a powerful sense of certainty. It is only after we have responded to the situation that we think, 'What did I do that for?'" (Goleman, 1996, pp. 334–335).

Psychological and physiological research suggests that the roots of emotional intelligence can be traced back to the amygdala, which, independent of the neocortex, triggers all emotional decisions. This means that in many personal, national, and international decisions and judgments, it is often our emotional responses—rather than our cognitive mind—that prevail. According to Goleman, our heart usually guides our first impulses in emotional situations, rather than our mind (Goleman, 1996, pp. 336). Additionally, Goleman and Ekman (2007) note that the full intensity of an emotion is very brief, lasting only a few seconds at most. Emotional memory plays a crucial role in our snap judgments. The process of matching an experience, stored in emotional memory, with a new situation occurs extremely quickly, often resulting in a judgment being made in twelve thousandths of a second.

According to Goleman's findings, the rational mind takes longer to respond. Cognitive thinking, which is rooted in the neocortex, analyzes situations in black-and-white terms. Since emotions arise before cognitive thinking, developing emotional literacy can facilitate conflict resolution and help prevent embarrassment after an incident has occurred. In other words, the challenge we face is primarily one of managing emotions and fostering emotional stability.

The behavioral issues of individuals are typically understood through the lens of the theoretical framework that a researcher, psychologist, or psychotherapist follows. For instance, behaviorists rely on the fundamental principles of their approach. Consequently, the analysis and comprehension of a person's personality by a clinical psychologist largely depend on the clinician's own theoretical orientation and professional training. This complexity increases in cross-cultural contexts. Observations are often interpreted based on the social constructs specific to a culture. While the values of a given culture may be relevant to those raised within it, they might not necessarily apply to individuals from entirely different cultural backgrounds.

This foreword to the book suggests that in a multicultural global village, a Euro-centric empirical understanding of an object may not be appropriate due to its particularistic nature. Holistic ethical intelligence, with its transcendent and universalistic qualities—not tied to any specific time or place—can aid in making more responsible, real-time ethical judgments. Holistic ethical intelligence transcends emotional responses; its ethical foundation enables individuals to think beyond personal likes or dislikes when making ethical decisions.

In both contemporary Western and Eastern thought, ethics is understood as a social construct rooted in specific local traditions. For instance, the values and ethics found in Japanese, Chinese, or African cultures are often believed to stem from the social constructs of their respective communities. Many sociological, anthropological, and psychological studies support this view. A notable example is the research conducted by European anthropologists and sociologists on African cultures and values. What may be considered natural within native African culture is often perceived by non-African anthropologists as "primitive," "heathen," "uncivilized," or even "unethical." Consequently, since much of the psychological research on non-Western individuals relies on a Eurocentric worldview, data, and prevalent empirical research methodologies, the findings may not accurately reflect the true nature of those cultures.

The Particularism of the Eurocentric Epistemic

As we know, the Eurocentric epistemic paradigm is based on an "intellectual trinity" of individualism, materialism, and hedonism. The empiricist mindset, along with existentialist and postmodernist thought, assigns authority to the individual experience of a phenomenon and due to its particularism, the Eurocentric worldview and research methodology reduces a phenomenon to its psychological, social, economic, or political dimensions. Common sense tells us that a holistic view of reality cannot be achieved through a reductionist approach.

When we talk about a paradigm shift, or the need for a holistic ethical approach, we mean that the existing Eurocentric methodology of the social sciences falls short of providing a comprehensive understanding of human situations. The empiricist epistemic tradition arose historically as a reaction to the theocratic dominance of the Christian church. It took intellectual inspiration from Auguste Comte's (1789-1857) theory that human thought has evolved through three stages: the age of faith or dogma, leading to the age of speculative philosophy, and culminating in the age of positivism and scientism.

Comte's positivism, along with the individualism of William James (1842-1910) and John Dewey (1859-1952), laid the groundwork for a modern, liberal, and postmodern age characterized by a strong emphasis on individual autonomy. These assumptions warrant a critical review.

Twentieth-century Muslim scholars Iqbal (1877-1938) and Mawdudi (1903-1979) not only critique European thought but also present a holistic perspective on Islamic ethics and culture. Mawdudi questions the relevance of the Eurocentric epistemic paradigm, arguing that it is too particularistic. He advocates for a comprehensive understanding of Islam and humanity, drawn directly from the Qur'an and the Prophetic sunnah (conduct). Mawdudi elaborates on the universality of the ethical principles in Islam, which are rooted in these two non-variable sources: the Qur'an and sunnah (Ansari, 2006).

One simple example can illustrate the universality of the ethical principles found in the Qur'an and the sunnah. Tawhid, one of the fundamental themes in the Qur'an, signifies the Oneness, Uniqueness, and Transcendence of the Creator God (Allah) s.w.t. While it is often viewed as a matter of faith, and thus associated with theology and metaphysics, Mawdudi highlights that the concept of Allah's Sovereignty in the Qur'an extends far beyond His supremacy within sacred spaces like mosques, churches, or synagogues. His Sovereignty encompasses all spaces and times.

It would be illogical to assert that the Creator God holds Sovereignty only within places of worship but has no authority in public realms such as parliaments, courtrooms, or marketplaces. This perspective does not advocate for a return to the institutional dominance of the church or the establishment of a theocratic order led by ordained priests. Instead, it supports the rule of law and the adherence to fairness, truth, and honesty—universal ethical values that should govern both personal and public life. The ethical values of Islam transcend any specific cultural origin, whether Asian, African, or European.

Decolonization of Psychology

In this context, there is a need for decolonization of psychological thought and the introduction of a more holistic approach to studying human behavior. Current psychological theories largely reflect social constructs rooted in a Eurocentric worldview. This perspective reduces human beings to mere aggregates of specific individual needs, desires, and appetites—both physically and emotionally. In other words, humans are often portrayed as social animals, driven primarily by economic interests, power struggles, greed, and sexual pleasures.

Holistic Ethical Intelligence

The holistic ethical intelligence we suggest, makes a departure from the current Eurocentric, colonial approach. It is more than what is commonly called "integration of knowledge" (Ahmad, 2012, 2009). It stands for, first, a reconstruction of our concept of ethical values as universal, absolute, and not situational or relative. Both Western and Eastern perspectives consider ethical values within the context of specific times and places. Therefore, in both the Western and Eastern mindsets, ethical values and norms are viewed as products of a social evolutionary process. This means that specific social local traditions, customs, concepts and views gradually gain the status of authentic ethical practices, eventually evolving into maxims and laws. This simply means that norms and values are deemed authentic, within a particular time and context. However, because they are specific to their milieu, they can become obsolete and irrelevant over time, necessitating the adoption of new norms and values.

Universal Values

When we discuss universal ethical values, we are not referring to a specific set of values and principles that have developed over time within a particular culture or civilization, such as those found in Rome or Arabia. Instead, universal values originate from their objective and divine nature, upheld by all Prophets of Allah (SWT). More specifically, these were introduced by the Prophet Ibrahim (Abraham) (may Allah's peace be upon him), who serves as a common link among Judaism, Christianity, and Islam.

The worldview he presented was not merely a product of his own intellect, but rather a revelation received from God (Allah). This revelation teaches that true success for all humanity lies in following the guidance of the Creator (Allah) and embracing tawhid, which can be understood as the unity of life, the universe, and society. If human life becomes fragmented into separate, uncoordinated segments of behavior, it is destined to result in imbalance, contradictions, conflicts, etc.

Conversely, when a person adheres to a single ethical path, their conduct and behavior become integrated and synergized. The Abrahamic principle of a unified or tawhidic life is the foundational principle of universal Islamic values. Additionally, changes in space and time do not render this principle archaic, irrelevant, or outdated.

The second universal value of adl, which means fairness, balance, moderation, and justice, is another fundamental theme and principle found in the Divine messages received by the Prophet Ibrahim and the Prophet Muhammad (S.A.W.S.). This principle remains relevant today for promoting mental health and achieving balance in life. We believe that the modern psychological and moral crises can be transformed into a balanced and fulfilling life by developing a holistic understanding based on these first two principles from a sevenfold scheme of universal values.

This can be accomplished by first decolonizing the existing social sciences, including psychology, and freeing ourselves from the Eurocentric, particularistic epistemic paradigm that has dominated both the West and the rest of the world for over two hundred years. Below are some preliminary ideas intended to elaborate on a holistic ethical approach that can aid in achieving mental health.

Why a New Paradigm?

The ongoing moral and psychological crisis, along with a significant rise in substance use and constant changes in social constructs, norms, and values, has led to a persistent crisis in society. The universal ethical values of unity in life and fairness (adl) have the potential to replace the current set of values and the reductionist perspective on human beings and behavior.

Universal and holistic ethical values offer a solid foundation for achieving human dignity, security, well-being, sustainability, and self-understanding. These values go beyond race, color, gender, economic status, or ethnicity. Ethical literacy, rooted in holistic ethical intelligence and informed by seven global values or principles, can provide a universal ethical framework. This framework encourages a unified, creative, proactive, and socially responsible approach to meaning and life.

The seven global values are as follows:

1. Unity in Life (Tawhidic) - Emphasizing the oneness and interconnectedness of all life.

2. Realization of Social Justice - Ensuring fair and just conduct in all affairs (Adl).

3. Preservation and Promotion of Life - Valuing and safeguarding human life (Nafs).

4. Practice of Reasoned and Ethical Conduct - Upholding reason and ethics in our actions (Aql).

5. Respect for Religious and Cultural Freedom - Acknowledging and honoring diverse beliefs and traditions (Din).

6. Protection of Legitimate Human Relations and the Sanctity of Lineage - Valuing human relationships and the sanctity of heritage (Nasl, Nasb).

7. Protection of Property - Safeguarding individuals' rights to their property (Mal).

For brevity reasons, lets discuss only two of these seven values that are inherently applicable regardless of time, place, race, color, faith, or ideology. They serve to build and uplift human society, fostering the development of a holistic and sustainable healthy environment essential for mental well-being. The first global value, Unity in life or Tawhidic principle entails the removal of contradictions and dualism in human behavior and conduct. A dualistic and conflicting personality, when critically examined, is unlikely to lead to a peaceful life or a healthy social order. In contrast, a tawhidic or unified personality, characterized by the absence of moral and ethical contradictions, forms a solid foundation for socially responsible behavior and the creation of a just and compassionate society. The concept of a unified personality is not exclusive to Muslims, despite the terminology that may suggest otherwise. Any individual, regardless of faith or culture, can achieve inner peace and harmony with the external world by adhering to consistent ethical and moral standards. Likewise, a Muslim who upholds double standards will struggle to find the solace and peace associated with a unified personality. A unified personality liberates a person from pride, ego, individualism, materialism, racism, gender injustice, and the divides between religious and secular life.

The second global value of fairness, or adl, equity, and justice, should not be confused with the conventional concept of quantitative equality. Fairness, or adl, means giving individuals what they deserve. If one person deserves more than another, it is only fair to provide them with what is due. This value transcends gender, color, ethnicity, material status, authority, and power; in short, it calls for a complete conceptual transformation. We often fail to realize that we are generally born into environments shaped by gender, race, ethnicity, capitalism, and secularism, and we tend to blindly follow the social constructs that are deeply embedded in our society.

The first and second global values are inherently connected. Tawhid, or unity, demands adl, which means fairness; thus, no one should be denied what they deserve. adl, or justice, implies that the Creator of humanity has a right to be acknowledged by His creation—to be thanked for His countless favors and blessings. Consequently, it is only natural to serve Him alone.

The opposite of adl is zulm, or transgression, which signifies an attitude of ungratefulness toward the true Sovereign and Lord of the Universe. This intrinsic relationship between the two principles, when deeply understood, liberates an individual from local social constructs and ethically empowers them to serve both the Creator and humanity, as the Creator desires.

The Role of Mind and Heart in the Holistic Ethical Paradigm

The Qur'an emphasizes the importance of cognitive engagement by stating: "Behold, We have revealed this Qur'an as a discourse in the Arabic language so that you might comprehend it with your reason" (Yusuf 12:2). The phrase "La'allakum ta'qilun" encourages individuals to use reason or 'aql. This message is reiterated in various passages: "Thus Allah makes His injunctions clear to you so that you may understand (ta'qilun)" (al-Baqarah 2:242), as well as in al-Muminun (23:78-80).

The Qur'an invites its readers, both Muslims and non-Muslims, to reflect: "...in this way Allah clearly expounds His injunctions to you so that you may reflect (tatafakarun) upon them" (al-Baqarah 2:219). Furthermore, the Qur'an encourages its readers to question and think critically: "Then ask them, are the blind and the seeing alike? Do you not reflect?" (al-Zumar 39:9). It urges contemplation of every statement within the Book: "Do they not ponder (yatadabbaru) about the Qur'an? Had it been from anyone other than Allah, they would surely have found it to be full of inconsistencies" (al-Nisa 4:82).

The Qur'an criticizes those who read or listen without engaging in critical and deep thinking (tafaqquh), saying, "The truth is that they understand little" (al-Fath 48:15). It commands the Muslim community to prioritize serious research and investigation. "It was not necessary for all the believers to go forth together (to fight); rather, from each group among them, some should devote themselves to acquiring tafaqquh (a deep knowledge of the faith), so that they may warn their people when they return" (al-Tawbah 9:122).

On nearly every page of the Qur'an, readers are encouraged to think critically, reflect, and use their faculties of vision, hearing, and introspection to understand the continuous and abundant favors and blessings of Allah (SWT), the Creator of all that exists in the universe. For instance, the Qur'an states, "He has subjected for you the night and the day, and the sun and the moon; the stars have also been made subservient by His command. Surely, there are signs in this for those who use their reason" (Al-Nahl 16:12). Additionally, it emphasizes, "Surely, the hearing, the sight, and the heart—each of these will be called to account" (Bani Israel 17:36).

The Role of Heart

The Qur'an emphasizes the importance of fostering a culture of knowledge, learning, reason, and wisdom (hikmah). It also highlights the role of the heart (qalb) as the seat of emotions, kindness, tenderness, love, and consolation. As stated in Al-Imran 3:159, "(O Prophet) it was thanks to Allah's mercy that you were gentle with them. Had you been rough and hard-hearted, they would surely have scattered away from you."

The concept of the heart in the Qur'an reflects both positive and negative attributes. For instance, it is described as the source of inner peace: "He it is who bestowed inner peace (sakinah) on the hearts of the believers so that they may grow yet more firm in their faith" (Al-Fath 48:4). However, it also refers to the heart as a seat of unethical attitudes and behaviors. In

Al-Baqarah 2:10, it states, "There is a disease (hypocrisy) in their hearts, and Allah has intensified the disease."

A significant reason for not responding to the call of Truth and becoming true servants of Allah, as the Qur'an explains, is the hardening of the hearts of the polytheists and those who oppose Islam and the Prophet. Al-Baqarah 2:74 describes this hardening metaphorically: "Then your hearts hardened and became like stones, or even harder. For surely there are some stones from which streams burst forth and some that split apart, causing water to flow out, and some that fall down in fear of Allah. Allah is not heedless of what you do."

The Qur'an symbolically explains this hardening of the heart as a sealing of hearts: "Do they not reflect on the Qur'an? Or are there locks on their hearts?" (Muhammed 47:24).

Synergy of Mind and Heart in Holistic Ethical Intelligence

The Qur'an critiques the unwavering behavioral patterns of unbelievers, stating: "They have hearts with which they fail to understand, eyes with which they fail to see, and ears with which they fail to hear; they are like cattle – indeed, even more misguided, as they are utterly heedless." (Al-A'raf 7:179). This verse highlights the synergy between emotional (heart) and cognitive (mind) intelligence, suggesting that both have limitations.

The Qur'an aims to align cognitive and emotional intelligence within the framework of universal ethical principles, such as halal (permissible) and haram (prohibited), ma'ruf (good) and munkar (evil), adl (fairness) and taghut (oppression) and zulm (injustice). While rational or emotional responses may lead to quick reactions, these ethical guidelines of halal and haram serve as immediate filters that guide individuals toward making ethical judgments.

For example, consider a situation where a person commits theft and attempts to escape, only to fall into a river or lake. The aggrieved party may feel compelled by their cognitive mind to allow the thief to drown as punishment for the theft. Simultaneously, their emotional mind might urge them to let the thief suffer as a lesson for their wrongdoing. However, ethical intelligence takes precedence, prompting the aggrieved individual to save the thief's life, recognizing that preserving life is a universal value. In this moment, they set aside their feelings of anger and judgment. Later, they may choose to report the thief to the authorities for appropriate action, but the ethical obligation to save a life comes first.

The process of developing ethical awareness (ethical literacy) can be better understood through the Qur'anic perspective on human nature (nafs), which represents different types of personalities.

The Qur'an describes a certain personality type that is driven by immediate gratification, material gain, and short-term benefits. This is referred to as nafs ammarah, or the self that inclines a person toward wrongdoing. As stated in Yusuf 12:53, "I do not seek to acquit myself; for surely one's self prompts to evil, except for the one to whom my Lord may show mercy."

Another aspect of the human self is called nafs lawwamah, or the reproaching self. This inner voice encourages a person to avoid wrong and evil actions. This is supported by the verse in al-Qiyamah 75:2: "Nay, I swear by the self-reproaching nafs." This dynamic can be understood as a struggle between cognitive and emotional intelligence.

The third type of personality is the nafs mutma'innah, or the serene self. This type represents a person who is fully convinced, satisfied, content, ethically oriented, and committed. This "self" acts as an ethical filter, known as holistic ethical intelligence, in crisis situations. The Qur'an refers to this serene self in al-Fajr 89:27-30: "O serene soul, return to your Lord, well pleased (with you) and well pleasing (to your Lord), so enter among My servants and enter My Paradise."

Ethical intelligence, or khulq, is a capacity that can be developed as a person internalizes seven global values that we previously mentioned. These values shape human responses in various situations where quick ethical judgments are necessary to resolve crises.

The three states of nafs, or personality, are not completely exclusive or static; rather, they are dynamic. A person's nafs can respond in different ways depending on various factors. Holistic Ethical Intelligence, which stems from the ethicalization of the mind and heart—also referred to as ethical literacy—guides our actions through the concepts of halal (permissible) and haram (prohibited), as well as ma'ruf (good) and munkar (wrong).

Actions rooted in holistic ethical intelligence are immediate, confident, resolute, and more authentic compared to those driven solely by cognitive or emotional intelligence. This ethical orientation creates a synergy between the cognitive and emotional realms, aligning the responses of the brain and heart with the principles of halal and haram, tayyib (pure/good), and khabith (impure/bad).

FOREWORD

In Islam, the ethical terms "halal" and "haram" encompass a vast range of human conduct and behavior. Almost every activity a person engages in or intends to engage in falls within the scope of these categories. This includes thoughts, feelings, physical actions, and even considerations related to auditing, touching, tasting, strategy, economic policies, education, culture, media, love, hate, and compromise. Each of these is classified as halal (ethically good and permissible) or haram (ethically bad, harmful, and therefore not allowed).

The global Islamic ethical values consist of seven key principles: tawhid (the oneness of God), adl (justice), nafs (the self or soul), 'aql (reason), din (religion), nasl or nasb (lineage), and mal (wealth). These values are further complemented by concepts such as ma'ruf (what is known to be good), birr (virtue), khayr (goodness), itqan (perfection), wasatiyah (moderation), and taqwa (ethical behavior). Together, these principles form an Islamic worldview that encourages all of humanity to embrace unity in life and to free themselves from the divisive influences of dualism, ethnic or racial nationalism, egotism, and similar concerns.

The Holistic Ethical Intelligence integrates the qalb (heart), 'aql (mind, reason), nafs (self), and ruh (soul) in a unified manner under the concept of tawhid (unity, unification, and the elimination of all dualisms). This holistic ethical intelligence provides guidance that helps individuals transcend emotional and biologically driven responses, which are rooted in the amygdala and transmitted throughout the nervous system. It also goes beyond purely cognitive responses.

Holistic Ethical Intelligence allows a person to pre-qualify and judge a situation more swiftly than the amygdala, enabling them to make prompt, ethically grounded decisions. For instance, consider a scenario where a driver witnesses a motorcycle skidding and sees a person hurt and bleeding on the roadside. The cognitive mind may caution against involvement, fearing that if they assist, they could be suspected of causing the accident. Emotional intelligence might suggest simply calling the police to report what happened and leaving the injured person on the road. However, ethical intelligence compels the individual to prioritize saving the person's life by taking them to the nearest hospital, even at the risk of being wrongly accused.

The Qur'an references the story of Prophet Yusuf (Joseph) to illustrate how the nafs lawwamah (the self that blames) and nafs mutma'inah (the peaceful self) operate in such situations. In Yusuf's case, both cognitive and emotional intelligence were informed by his holistic ethical intelligence, which recognizes the distinction between halal (permissible) and haram (forbidden) actions. This enabled him to make an immediate and correct judgment to protect himself from the advances of the ruler's wife.

Holistic ethical intelligence, grounded in universal ethical values, can play a crucial role in conflict resolution, anger management, and alleviating depression and phobias. It also contributes to restoring socio-psychological health and well-being. Furthermore, it can aid in making strategic national and international decisions related to defense, the economy, and geopolitical conflicts. Since the ethical values outlined in the Qur'an are inherently transcendent and global, any group can adhere to these values to make responsible and meaningful judgments. This approach fosters fairness, inner peace (nafs mutmainnah), consolation (sakinah), and freedom from guilt and psychological complexes.

The field of IP examines human nature through the lenses of the Qur'an and Sunnah, employing Holistic Ethical Intelligence. It is encouraging to see that this discipline has experienced consistent growth in recent decades across many parts of the world, as demonstrated by the following chapters. This book offers valuable insights, as the authors outline and discuss programs from which readers can benefit. We hope it enhances the understanding of IP and encourages institutions to integrate this field into their learning and educational programs. Additionally, we aspire to facilitate a paradigm shift in the mindset of the Muslim community. We also anticipate increased collaboration among various institutions to enhance and advance the study of IP.

With the founding of the AMSS at the Illinois Institute of Technology in Chicago in 1972, the association began organizing its annual gatherings at various university campuses across the U.S. The goals and objectives included assisting members in developing an Islamic perspective on contemporary issues and applying such a vision to studies and research. The researchers involved faculty members from various universities as well as PhD students from different disciplines in the social sciences. The main purpose was to generate Islamic thought through critical and scientific inquiry and to disseminate it through various means of communication.

The papers presented at these conventions were compiled into proceedings. The first volume contained the proceedings of the third national seminar held in Gary, Indiana, and was published in 1974. The proceedings of the fourth annual conference were published in two volumes: the first volume in 1975 and the second volume in 1976. Subsequent volumes included papers presented in the conventions of 1977 and 1978. It is important to note that during each convention, the group on IP presented research papers. For example, in 1975, Rashid Hamid presented a paper titled "Reflections on a Balanced Islamic Personality"

FOREWORD

(Hamid, 1977). In the 1976 proceedings, Malik Badri's paper "Muslim Psychologists in the Lizard's Hole" was included. The 1978 proceedings featured Malik Badri's "The Muslim Alcohol Dependent: Can Islam Help Him?" as well as a joint paper titled "An Islamic Mental Health System: An Operational Model" by Rashid Hamid, Muhiyudin, Shakoor, and Allia Swilliam (Badri, 2020).

These were the early beginnings. Alhamdulillah, the ongoing movement to approach social sciences from an Islamic perspective has evolved into a vibrant hub for generating Islamic thought. I had the privilege of being the Founding Secretary General of the AMSS in 1972 and continued to serve in various capacities within the organization until 1979, including as President from 1978 to 1979. After moving to the International Islamic University Islamabad in 1981, I had the honor of organizing an International Conference in 1982, where Professor Isma'il Raji al-Faruqi presented his paper on the "Islamization of Knowledge," which was later delivered in Kuala Lumpur.

My association with this dynamic movement for over 55 years has led me to believe that, in light of contemporary intellectual challenges, our focus should be on the ethicalization of social sciences based on global holistic ethical principles, which I have summarized as seven universal values (Ahmad, 2009).

I am pleased that Professor Amber Haque, has produced groundbreaking work to assist Muslim psychologists in studying human psychology from an ethical Islamic viewpoint. This work will serve as a foundation for the systematic development of discipline. I appreciate this unique achievement deeply. At the same time, I believe that since Islam is a universal faith with principles that promote a wholesome life for anyone who adopts them, our research and development efforts should reach a broader audience, not just Muslims. This is why I advocate for the ethicalization of psychology rather than the integration of Islamic knowledge.

I hope this edited book will offer practical guidance to academics and practitioners in psychology and mental health on a global level.

FOREWORD

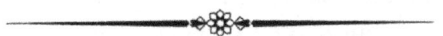

Abdallah Rothman

Over the past two decades, the field of Islamic psychology has undergone a profound shift, from a small set of courageous initiatives to a recognizable, global discipline with its own institutions, standards, and scholarly communities. In the early 2000s there were, quite literally, only one or two programs from which a student could learn psychology in a way that meaningfully engaged with the Islamic tradition. A landmark among these was the program established at the International Islamic University Malaysia under the leadership of Professor Malik Badri (may God have mercy on him), which integrated Islamic sciences into psychology and helped lay the groundwork for everything that has followed. When Dr. Amber Haque and I published Islamic Psychology Around the Globe (2021) through the International Association of Islamic Psychology (IAIP), the country chapters collectively showed how sparse formal offerings still were, and how the prevailing model in the early development of the field globally tended to "Islamize" existing psychology curricula rather than build an Islamic psychology from the ground up.

What has changed, dramatically and very recently, is the emergence of programs that begin with the Islamic paradigm of the human being and then construct their pedagogy, research agendas, and clinical training upon that paradigm. Only in the last five years have a growing number of institutions designed full programs explicitly rooted in an Islamic psychology worldview. And in just the past one to two years we have witnessed a genuine acceleration: multiple new programs, across regions and languages, now teaching Islamic psychology as Islamic psychology, not as an add-on or elective, but as a coherent, primary framework.

This volume documents that turning point. Each chapter presents a program from a different institution and part of the world. Collectively, they chart a transition from a period of isolated pioneers to an era of institutional plurality: online and hybrid delivery alongside in-person study; degree-granting and validated programs alongside professional certificates; local cohorts alongside international enrollments. For students and practitioners entering the field today, this diversity of pathways is not merely convenient, it is historic. Whereas my mentors, colleagues and I had to train in secular frameworks and conduct our study of the Islamic tradition in parallel, today's learners can be formed from the outset within a Qur'anic and Prophetic anthropology of the self.

From its inception in 2017, the International Association of Islamic Psychology, founded by Professor Malik Badri, was created to support precisely this maturation of the field: to disseminate knowledge responsibly, to uphold academic and professional rigor, and to steward a certification process that protects both the integrity and the breadth of Islamic psychology. Our vision has never been to impose a single school; rather, it is to articulate parameters within which a plurality of "Islamic psychologies" can flourish, diverse in method and emphasis, yet unified by fidelity to the Qur'an, Sunnah, and the verified tradition of the scholars. IAIP's standards of scholarship and practice have been developed through our network of Senior Fellows representing different institutions, countries, and schools of thought who deliberate in a collegial and transparent way. Within that framework, programs may seek IAIP certification; many represented in this book already have, and others are in process. Graduates of IAIP-certified programs that incorporate practitioner training are then eligible, through their supervised training, to become IAIP-certified practitioners, creating a clear pathway from study to ethical, competent practice.

Why does this matter? Because the paradigm from which one learns psychology shapes what one can see and, ultimately, how one can heal. Islamic psychology begins with a holistic metaphysic of the human person: the nafs (self), ʿaql (intellect), qalb (heart), and rūḥ (spirit) stand in ordered relation, animated by fitrah (innate natural disposition), oriented toward meaning, and responsive to moral and spiritual cultivation. When students are formed within this anthropology from the outset, they are better equipped to engage contemporary mental-health challenges not as isolated disorders of cognition or behavior, but as disruptions within a unified soul-body-mind-spirit ecology. The implications are practical and far-reaching: from theory development, case formulation and therapeutic method to prevention, community mental health, and education.

Crucially, the significance of these developments is not limited to Muslim communities. As coherent curricula, research programs, and clinical placements multiply, the field can generate new textbooks, shared terminology, and robust data, resources that invite the wider discipline of psychology into constructive dialogue with Islamic intellectual and practical wisdom. Our hope is that this encounter will enrich psychology as a whole, just as it equips practitioners to serve Muslim populations with competence and cultural-spiritual attunement.

The programs collected here represent real leadership. They show how universities, institutes, and training centers, often in partnership with scholars of the tradition and senior clinicians, are building governance, pedagogy, assessment, and supervision aligned with Islamic first principles while remaining conversant with contemporary science. They also demonstrate that standard-setting and innovation are not opposites: IAIP's certification provides guardrails without stifling creativity, ensuring that what bears the name "Islamic psychology" genuinely reflects the tradition and meets professional expectations.

As President of the IAIP, a role that I take on as an amanah to honor the legacy of Professor Badri, it is both humbling and joyful to introduce a book that maps this new landscape. I am grateful to Dr. Amber Haque for once again leading on a landmark contribution to literature, to the chapter authors for documenting these programs with clarity and candor, and to the institutions that have invested in building something worthy of future generations. May this volume serve students discerning their path, faculty designing curricula, and leaders committed to the flourishing of their communities.

We are, by God's grace, witnessing the pioneering years give way to an era of consolidation and growth. From one or two programs a decade ago to a tapestry of offerings today, the story of Islamic psychology has entered a new chapter. I pray that the efforts represented here continue to be guided, protected, and made of enduring benefit, to Muslims and to the broader human family.

ACKNOWLEDGMENTS

The editor wishes to express heartfelt gratitude to all the chapter authors of this book. Your contributions, both in writing your chapters and in your commitment to teaching courses in Islamic Psychology, are genuinely appreciated.

I extend my sincere thanks to Professor Dr. Anis Ahmad, Vice Chancellor of Riphah International University in Islamabad, Pakistan, for writing the foreword. He was the first Dean of the Kulliyyah of Islamic Revealed Knowledge and Social Sciences at the International Islamic University Malaysia when it was established in the 1980s. I also thank Dr. Abdallah Rothman, President of the International Association of Islamic Psychology (IAIP), for contributing the second foreword.

I want to express my sincere gratitude to Dr. Mifrah Rauf Sethi, Head of the Psychology Department, as well as Dr. Mujeeb Bhatti and Khirman Khadija from Riphah International University, for their invaluable assistance with typesetting and copy editing the manuscript and special thanks to my daughter, Raabia Haque, for her support throughout the publication process in the U.S. I have relied on her assistance for my last five books, as well as numerous other academic projects.

The publication of any book is a collaborative effort, and this project would not have been possible without the support and cooperation of everyone involved. Thank you all very much!

Dr. Amber Haque

Editor

LIST OF AUTHORS

Abdallah Rothman is the Head of Islamic Psychology at Cambridge Muslim College, Founder and Director of Dar al-Shifaa, co-founder and President of the International Association of Islamic Psychology. He holds an MA and a PhD in psychology and is a Licensed Professional Counselor (LPC) and a Board-Certified Registered Art Therapist (ATR-BC).

Akbar Husain has been retired from the Department of Psychology, Aligarh Muslim University, Aligarh after serving more than 41 years of service. He was Chairman, Department of Psychology and the Dean, Faculty of Social Sciences, Aligarh Muslim University, Aligarh. After retirement he is engaged in writing books, monographs, articles, psychological tests standardization, and executing research projects in the fields of Islamic Psychology, Positive and Spiritual Psychology. Professor Husain is writing books for the Readers Paradise and Institute of Objective Studies: Genuine Publications Pvt. Ltd. New Delhi. He is associated with the Institute of Objective Studies, New Delhi and Centre for Study Research, Hyderabad in different capacities.

Ali Habibbi, a clinical psychologist, and support worker with over twenty years of experience helping individuals facing difficulties and suffering, has consistently aimed to connect Western psychology with the Muslim faith. Trained in religious sciences from the age of nine, he grew up in a religious learning environment. Later, he studied traditional therapy (Ruqiyah) before pursuing formal studies in psychology. His goal was to bridge the gap between Western therapeutic approaches and faith. Through his research and work, he has sought to integrate belief and faith into psychotherapy, which led him to develop his own model of the self, centered around the heart. He named his approach HEART, which stands for Healing and Empowerment through Active Religious Therapy.

Amber Haque is a psychologist and the National Director of Muslim Family Services at ICNA Relief USA. He is full professor of psychology at Riphah International University in Islamabad, Pakistan and affiliated with the Muslim Mental Health Consortium, Michigan State University and as a nonresident research scholar at Cambridge Muslim College. Previously, he held the position of full professor and director of clinical psychology programs in Qatar and the UAE and led the psychology department at International Islamic University Malaysia. Dr. Haque also practiced psychology in Michigan for over a decade. He earned his Ph.D. in psychology from Western Michigan University and master's in clinical psychology from Eastern Michigan University. He has been a visiting scholar at Cornell University and the University of Pennsylvania, taught in Bosnia, and is involved with the editorial boards of several international journals, reviewing for over forty peer-reviewed journals and several international institutional review boards. Dr. Haque has published extensively on mental health and Islamic psychology.

Anis Ahmad is a renowned social scientist and the founding Vice-Chancellor of Riphah International University. He holds a Ph.D. from Temple University in Pennsylvania, USA. Throughout his career, he has held numerous academic leadership positions both nationally and internationally. He served as the Vice President of the International Islamic University in Islamabad and was the founding Dean of the Faculty of Revealed Knowledge and Human Sciences at the International Islamic University in Malaysia. Dr. Ahmad is also a former President and Secretary-General of the Association of Muslim Social Scientists in the USA and is a Fellow of the University of Sains Malaysia. He writes extensively on contemporary social, political, and cultural issues affecting the Muslim Ummah. His articles have been published in various prestigious works, including the Oxford Encyclopedia of the Modern Muslim World (New York), the Encyclopedia of Islam (Istanbul, Turkey), the Encyclopedia of Islamic Economy (London), the Muslim World Book Review (UK), and several other professional journals.

Armaan Ahmed Rowther is a Resident Physician in the Department of Psychiatry at the Harbor-UCLA Medical Center in Torrance, California. He holds a Doctor of Medicine and a Doctor of Philosophy in Social and

LIST OF AUTHORS

Behavioral Interventions. Dr. Rowther received a Postgraduate Diploma in Islamic Psychology at the Cambridge Muslim College in Cambridge, UK, in 2023.

Ayse Kaya Goktepe is an assistant professor of psychology of religion at Istanbul Sabahattin Zaim University and the founder of Endulus Counseling. advisory board member of ISIP Türkiye. She holds an MA in Clinical Psychology and Musicology, and a PhD in psychology of religion, and a postgraduate diploma in Islamic Psychology at Cambridge Muslim College. She is a clinical psychologist, Board-certified schema therapist (ISST), and co-psychodramatist (FEPTO).

Bagus Riyono is a senior lecturer in psychology at the Faculty of Psychology, Universitas Gadjah Mada in Indonesia. His areas of expertise include Islamic psychology and I/O Psychology. He serves as the President of the International Association of Muslim Psychologists (IAMP), an organization that connects Muslim psychologists worldwide. Dr. Riyono earned his master's degree from Hofstra University in the US and his doctoral degree from Universitas Gadjah Mada. His research focuses on topics such as tazkiya therapy, motivation, personality, leadership, and organizational development. He has developed several theories related to motivation and personality, including the Theory of Motivational Sources, the Theory of Motivational Force, and the Anchor Personality Theory. Additionally, he created the Theory of Human Basic Potentials. His research reflects a deep commitment to advancing Islamic psychology. He has been a visiting lecturer and international speaker at universities around the globe, including those in Australia, Russia, Germany, the Netherlands, Japan, India, and Pakistan. He has authored numerous articles and books, with his most recent work, titled "Tazkiya Therapy in Islamic Psychotherapy", providing both conceptual and practical guidance for promoting mental health and addressing psychological challenges.

Carrie M. York is founder and president of the Alkaram Institute – the first graduate school of Islamic psychology in the United States. Her areas of interest include Islamic psychology and spirituality, spiritually integrated health, healing and wellness, and virtue and character development. Over the past twenty years, she has researched, taught, and published extensively on these and related topics at the intersection of psychology and religion. Having lived outside of her native United States in various countries for nearly 17 years, she now lives with her family in Great Falls, Virginia, where she is the caretaker of the Great Falls Zawiya. In her free time, she enjoys jogging, traveling, and spending time with loved ones. She is also a licensed real estate agent and works in the property industry as a side hobby.

Fahad Khan is a Licensed Clinical Psychologist with a Doctorate of

Clinical Psychology and a Master's degree in Biomedical Sciences. He has also been a student of religious studies, beginning with his memorization of Qur'an at the age of 16. He currently serves as the Deputy Director at Khalil Center, providing psychological services while supervising clinical and research work. He also teaches undergraduate as well as graduate courses in various academic institutions. His research and writing interests includes Muslim mental health and Islamic psychology. He is a fellow of the International Association of Islamic Psychology and serves as a reviewer and editor for various peer-reviewed journals in the United States and Pakistan. He is actively involved in professional organizations and has served on many committees and divisions of the American Psychological Association (APA) as well as Illinois Psychological Association (IPA). For his work and dedication, the APA awarded him the 2021 Early Career Psychologist Champion and 2020 Early Career Achievement Awards.

Fatima Khurram is a medical doctor by training and has a passion for Islamically integrated, holistic mental health care practice, and service delivery. She has a broad based experience of 9 years in clinical, teaching, community, administrative and management work in mental health at public and private institutions in Pakistan and currently serves as a lecturer in the Department of Clinical Psychology, Shifa Tameer-e-Millat University, Islamabad, Pakistan.

G. Hussein Rassool is a professor at the Center for Islamic Studies and Civilization (CISAC). He also serves as the Director of Studies for the Department of Islamic Psychology, Psychotherapy, and Counseling at Al Balagh Academy. Previously, he was the Director of the Riphah Institute of Clinical and Professional Psychology in Lahore, Pakistan, and the first Head of the Department at Islamic Online University, where he later became the Dean of the Faculty of Liberal Arts and Sciences. He has published extensively in the field of Islamic Psychology.

Hamid Rafiei-Honar is an Assistant Professor at the Islamic Sciences and Culture Academy and a former Vice President of the Islamic Psychology Association (IPA) in Iran. He graduated from the Hawzah Elmiyyah of Qom, the Islamic Theological Seminary in Qom, Iran, with degrees in Fiqh and Usul al-Fiqh (Methodology of Ijtihad). He holds a BA in Psychology and Islamic Studies, an MA in Clinical Psychology, and a PhD in General Psychology from the Imam Khomeini Education and Research Institute (IKERI) in Iran. Dr. Rafiei-Honar has authored three books and published 40 articles on topics related to Islamic Psychology, Psychotherapy, and Psychometrics. Additionally, he has supervised the development of 50 treatises that focus on creating Islamic psychological scales and educational interventions, particularly in the areas of self-control and self-regulation.

LIST OF AUTHORS

Hanan Dover is the Islamic Psychology Lecturer at Center for Islamic Studies and Civilisation (CISAC) and she has published in areas related to psychology and Muslim communities, refugee communities and developed a validated scale that aims to assess Muslim religious reflection. She is also the founder and clinical director of Mission of Hope since 2001, Founding member and former Convenor of the Islamic from an Islamic Perspective Interest Group of the Australian Psychological Society (APS). Hanan has been the elected Vice President of IAMP since 2016 and is a on the Board of Trustees of IAMP. She is invited to present various keynote addresses in Islamic Psychology internationally, since 2004. Hanan works professionally and clinically as a clinical and forensic psychologist in private practice and integrates Islamically-congruent values in the psychological and therapeutic practices when working with Muslim clients.

Hooman Keshavarzi is a licensed clinical psychologist in the state of Illinois; he holds a Doctorate and Masters in Clinical Psychology and a Bachelor's of Science – specialist psychology track/minor in Islamic Studies. He currently serves as the program director for the Masters in Counseling Islamic Psychology Program in Doha, Qatar, is a visiting scholar for Ibn Haldun University (Istanbul, Turkey) and adjunct faculty at the Hartford Seminary. He is the founding director of Khalil Center – the first Islamically oriented professional community mental wellness center and largest provider of Muslim mental healthcare in North America. He is also a senior fellow at the International Association for Islamic Psychology (IAIP), conducting research on topics related to Islam, Muslims and Mental Health. Hooman Keshavarzi is an international public speaker and trainer providing education on the intersection of Islamic studies and behavioral health.

Jamilah Hanum Abdul Khaiyom is an Associate Professor and Clinical Psychologist in the Department of Psychology at the International Islamic University Malaysia (IIUM), where she also provides clinical services through the university's Psychology Services Unit. She has secured numerous international and national research grants and authored over 50 refereed journal articles and 10 books/modules, including works on integrating Islamic spirituality with Acceptance and Commitment Therapy (i-ACT for Life) for the prevention of psychological distress. The i-ACT for Life program, now digitalized through the SELANGKAH app, has reached thousands of Malaysians under the Selangor Mental Sihat initiative. Recognized with awards such as the Highest Citation in Indexed Journal Award (Social Sciences) and the Mental Health Advocator Award, Dr. Jamilah's work emphasizes the integration of cognitive-behavioral approaches, mindfulness, and spirituality to advance holistic mental health.

Jusmawati Fauzaman is an academic at the Department of Psychology, International Islamic University Malaysia. She read her masters in the field of Industrial and Organizational Psychology and a PhD in Psychology. Her research areas include identification of personality taxonomy via lexical study; personality correlates of performance; development and validation of psychological instruments, and recently she is interested in venturing in the context of rejuvenating the study of soul in psychology to attain a more comprehensive understanding of human being.

Khalid Sharif is a Licensed Alcohol and Drug Counselor based in Saint Paul, Minnesota. He holds an M.A. in Counseling and Psychological Services and a Graduate Certificate in Addiction Studies. Khalid completed a Postgraduate Diploma in Islamic Psychology at the Cambridge Muslim College in 2023.

Masoud Azarbayejani is a professor at the Research Institute of Hawzah and University (RIHU) and serves as the Director of the Institute of Behavioral Sciences at RIHU. He is a former president of the Islamic Psychology Association (IPA) in Iran. Masoud graduated from the Hawzah Elmiyyah of Qom, where he studied Fiqh, Tafsir, Philosophy, and Mysticism. He holds a master's degree in Islamic theology and a master's degree in clinical psychology from RIHU, as well as a PhD in Philosophy of Religion from Tarbiat Modares University in Iran. He has authored or co-authored 25 books and 60 articles across the fields of Psychology of Religion and Spirituality, Islamic Psychology, Philosophy of Psychology, and Islamic Ethics and Education. Additionally, he has supervised 50 master's and doctoral dissertations and has contributed to the development of three educational programs focused on psychology and Islam.

Mifrah Rauf Sethi, currently serving as Associate Professor and Head, Department of Psychology at Riphah International University, has made significant academic, research, and institutional contributions in the field of psychology. With over 29 research publications in esteemed national and international journals including *PLOS One, BMC, Reproductive Health, JPMA,* and *JPMI,* her work reflects a strong commitment to advancing mental health research and evidence-based practice. Beyond research, she had played a pivotal role in curriculum design and academic innovation, successfully initiating new academic programs such as the Postgraduate Diploma in Islamic Psychotherapy for Mental Health and the BS in Clinical Psychology. Her leadership extends to mentoring and supervising undergraduate and postgraduate students at Riphah International University, as well as medical and dental students at Peshawar Medical College, Peshawar. She also actively contributed to the broader academic and ethical landscape as a Member of the World Association of

LIST OF AUTHORS

Cultural Psychiatry, Secretary of the Ethical Review Board, and Member of the Institutional Review Board at Prime Foundation. Additionally, her service as a Senate Member at Shaheed Benazir Bhutto Women University underscores her ongoing role in shaping academic policy, promoting ethical research practices, and strengthening the field of mental health education and research in Pakistan.

Mohd Ferdaus Harun is an Assistant Professor in the Department of Psychology at the International Islamic University Malaysia (IIUM), where he aspires to integrate modern psychology with Islamic scholarship. He holds a bachelor's degree in Islamic studies, a Master of Human Sciences, and a PhD in Industrial and Organizational Psychology. He specializes in psychometrics, organizational change, and organizational culture and actively involved in lectures, research, and consultation. In 2022, he represented Malaysia as a delegate for the Australian-ASEAN Muslims Exchange Program (AAMEP). Currently, he leads the Islamization of Knowledge Committee at IIUM's Department of Psychology, promoting the integration of Islamic perspectives into psychological practice, research, and education.

Muhammad Tahir Khalily currently serves as the Vice-Chancellor of Khushal Khan Khattak University, Karak (KKKUK) Pakistan. He brings with him over three decades of distinguished national and international experience in teaching, research, clinical practice, academic leadership, administration, and service development. Prior to his appointment at KKKUK, Prof. Khalily held several key academic and administrative positions. He served as Professor of Clinical Neuropsychology and Dean, Faculty of Social Sciences at Shifa Tameer-e-Millat University, Islamabad. He was also Chair of the Department of Psychology and Vice President (Academics) at the International Islamic University, Islamabad (IIUI). He worked as Senior Clinical Psychologist at Roscommon Mental Health Services Republic of Ireland for more than a decade. He has special interest in Islamic psychology.

Mujeeb Bhatti is currently serving as an Assistant Professor at the Department of Psychology, Riphah International University, Islamabad. He is also a Research Fellow at the NIHR Centre for IMPACT project, based at the Institute of Psychiatry, Rawalpindi. Dr. Mujeeb holds a PhD in Health Sciences from the University of York, UK, along with an MSc in Psychology and an MS in Clinical Psychology. He has over five years of experience teaching research methods and data analysis to undergraduate and postgraduate students at renowned universities in Rawalpindi and Islamabad, including the International Islamic University Islamabad, Riphah International University, and Foundation University Rawalpindi.

His research primarily focuses on access to mental health care and the management of common mental disorders. Dr. Mujeeb has worked on multiple national and international research projects, gaining expertise in systematic reviews, research protocol development, randomized controlled trials, and quantitative and qualitative data analyses. Known for his meticulous attention to detail and strong analytical skills, he is recognized for his commitment to research excellence, critical inquiry, and academic integrity.

Neelam Ehsan is a Professor in the Department of Clinical Psychology at Shifa Tameer-e-Millat University, Islamabad, Pakistan. Dr. Ehsan is an academic, researcher, and clinical psychologist with an extensive career spanning over 18 years during which she has served at leading institutions. She has successfully supervised and continues to mentor numerous MPhil, MS, and PhD scholars in Social Psychology, Clinical Psychology, Educational Psychology, Psychological Testing & Measurement, and Islamic Perspectives in Psychology. She has authored numerous national and international publications which reflect her research excellence and dedication to advancing psychological science.

Samir Mahmoud is Academic Director of Usul Academy and Lecturer on the Diploma in Islamic Psychology at Cambridge Muslim College. He holds a BA (Hons) in Anthropology & Politics, an MA in Architectural History, Theory & Urban Design, an MPhil in Theology & Religious Studies, and a PhD in Islamic Studies.

Sena Aycan is a licensed clinical psychologist and serves as a Research & Content Development Fellow at the Khalil Center, where she integrates her expertise in psychology with a commitment to advancing Muslim mental health. She holds a master's degree in clinical psychology, a bachelor's degree in psychology, and is currently pursuing a bachelor's in Comparative Islamic Studies at Usul Academy. Sena's postgraduate research focused on developing an Islamically-integrated model of psychological wellbeing, and she continues to center her work on integrating Islamic perspectives into mental health paradigms and practices.

Shukran Abd Rahman is a Professor of Industrial and Organizational Psychology in the Department of Psychology, AbdulHamid Abu Sulayman Kulliyyah of Islamic Revealed Knowledge and Human Sciences, International Islamic University Malaysia. His research areas include career development, change and development of higher education institution, organizational behavior, academic culture, and Islamic work ethic.

Tamkeen Saleem is a clinical psychologist, researcher, and academic leader with over 18 years of experience in clinical psychology. She currently serves as the Head of the Department of Clinical Psychology at Shifa Tameer-e-Millat University (STMU). Her research interests encompass clinical psychology, psychological interventions, art therapy, psychology of religion, family psychology, emotion regulation, social competence, and cross-cultural psychology. She has contributed extensively to these fields, with numerous publications in national and international journals.

Taufik Kasturi is a professor at the Faculty of Psychology, Universitas Muhammadiyah Surakarta (UMS), Indonesia. He completed his Ph.D. at Tilburg University, The Netherlands, building a strong academic foundation in psychological sciences. His research interests lie at the intersection of psychology, spirituality, and human well-being, with particular emphasis on quality of life, spiritual well-being, happiness, empathy, and the cognitive and emotional processes involved in memorizing the Qur'an. Taufik has taught a variety of interdisciplinary subjects, including Islamic Psychology, Islamic Worldview, Positive Psychology, Philosophy of Science, and Research Methodology. In addition to his teaching and research, he is actively involved in academic collaboration, particularly in research and scholarly publication. He has also served as an external examiner for doctoral candidates at several reputable institutions, including the University of Malaya, International Open University, Universiti Malaysia Kelantan, Gadjah Mada University, Airlangga University, Syarif Hidayatullah State Islamic University, and Universitas Muhammadiyah Surakarta.

Usman Jaffer is an Assistant Professor of Neuropsychology in the Department of Psychology, AbdulHamid Abu Sulayman Kulliyyah of Islamic Revealed Knowledge and Human Sciences, International Islamic University Malaysia, and holds a Doctor of Neuroscience,, a Master's in Clinical Psychology, a Master of Arts in Islamic and Other Civilizations, plus dual bachelor's degrees in Psychology and Islamic Jurisprudence. His research areas include neuro-psycho-spiritual frameworks, mental health in marginalized communities, neurobiological correlates of Islamic practices, digital addiction and youth resilience, and biopsychospiritual approaches to education and well-being.

INTRODUCTION

Amber Haque

The emergence of Islamic Psychology (IP) as a distinct discipline is relatively recent, yet it is beginning to influence modern psychology worldwide. This trend is evident in more than a dozen countries that have established IP programs, as well as in others where elements of IP are incorporated into psychology courses. The growth of IP is driven by an increasing demand from clients and clinicians who find modern psychological theories inadequate for fully explaining and addressing the issues faced by people of faith.

There is also a notable interest among younger people, including students and aspiring clinicians, who have contacted the author over the years to inquire about which IP programs to join for degrees, diplomas, certificates, or simply for education in IP. Many people are seeking knowledge in IP for personal growth and self-improvement, rather than for professional reasons.

Interestingly, some IP programs consider themselves pioneering without being aware of other contemporary or earlier programs offered globally. These scenarios underscore the need for this book, as there is currently no comprehensive guide available on the subject. Furthermore, awareness of existing IP programs worldwide can assist students, provide necessary context, expand curricula, document historical developments in modern times, and encourage collaboration among researchers, all with the goal of advancing the IP discipline on a global scale.

The Arabic equivalent of IP is *ilm-al-nafs*, which early Muslim scholars explored within the domains of theology and Islamic philosophy. However, terms that are more commonly used in Muslim spiritual and intellectual circles include *nafs, ruh, qalb, aql,* and *fitrah*, all of which frequently appear in the Qur'an. By repeatedly mentioning these terms, the Qur'an and Hadith provide deep insights into human nature, which can lead to a better understanding of human behavior, promoting self-discipline, and inner peace. Terminologies related to IP can also be found in the theological writings of other Abrahamic religions. In recent decades, there has also been a growth in spiritual and multicultural psychologies that aim to promote culturally sensitive education and training in the Western world.

From the 7th to the 10th century, early Muslim scholars extensively explored the concept of *ilm-al-nafs*, or the science of self. Sufism, the mystical dimension of Islam, also played a crucial role in developing this field, particularly through the writings of Imam Al-Ghazali and Ibn Arabi. For over a thousand years, Muslim intellectual contributions expanded globally, delving into the inner dimensions of the self and emphasizing the significance of self-knowledge and purification of the soul to achieve spiritual enlightenment and closeness to God.

However, the decline of traditional IP began in the 19th and 20th centuries with the rise of Western scientific psychology. This new approach often neglected moral and spiritual phenomena and led to the development of deterministic theories that disregarded human volition. The uncritical adoption of secular thought by Muslims further weakened their faith and contributed to a decline in their civilization and culture, resulting in an intellectual crisis within Muslim communities (AbuSulayman, 1993). This crisis is particularly evident in the social sciences, where concepts are often followed blindly without a clear understanding of Western philosophy, which is typically shaped by an atheistic worldview, historical contexts, and social circumstances.

This background provides insight into the challenges faced by Muslim scientists and scholars, including psychologists, over the past several centuries. A survey of contemporary Muslim psychologists would show that nearly all of them were trained in secular approaches, as IP did not exist as an independent discipline until recently. IP is now emerging in academic settings and is working to gain recognition within the field of psychology. It is important to understand that IP is beneficial not only for

INTRODUCTION

Muslims but for everyone, as its epistemology and ontology are rooted in divine principles.

Despite the relatively brief history of modern IP, it is encouraging to see its rapid development around the globe. Since the 1970s, there has been a growing effort to cultivate a more holistic and culturally relevant understanding of human behavior that incorporates Islamic perspectives. This resurgence of *ilm-al-nafs* or IP offers a rich and multifaceted view of human existence, emphasizing the integration of spiritual, emotional, and intellectual dimensions of life. It promotes a synthesis of knowledge and experience that benefits all of humanity. While this paper will introduce various IP programs around the world, the next section will provide a brief history of IP from the late 20th to the early 21st century.

The Growth of Modern Islamic Psychology

The concept of *ilm-al-nafs* has existed for centuries, but there has been a noticeable resurgence in interest in this topic starting in the 1970s. During this period, scholars in various Muslim countries began to write textbooks on the subject, particularly in the English language. Previous research indicates that texts related to IP were produced in Turkey during the Ottoman era and by Muslim scholars in British India in the early twentieth century, as well as in other countries, although mostly in local languages.

In Malaysia, the first book on IP was published in 1956, followed by several publications in Indonesia during the 1970s. This trend illustrates the growing interest in IP beyond Arabic-speaking countries, where the discipline was not traditionally included in psychology programs.

While some contemporary scholars (Rothman et al., 2022) credit Malik Badri (1932-2021) as the father of modern IP, Uthman Nagati is recognized for coining the term "*ilm-al-nafs al-Islami*" in the 1940s (Elzamzamy, Bader, & Bilge Bircan, 2024; Rassool & Luqman, 2022). Among many contributions of Nagati to IP, his book, *madkhila Ilm al-nafs al Islami*, was published posthumously in Arabic in 2001. Both Badri and Nagati were originally from Sudan and taught IP in Khartoum during the 1970s. In my 17 years of teaching experience in the Arabian Gulf, I found that Nagati was well-known among Arab students as a prominent figure in IP. In contrast, Badri gained popularity primarily in countries with a Muslim majority that have an interest in IP and where psychology is taught in English.

Malik Badri introduced the undergraduate course on IP in English at the International Islamic University of Malaysia (IIUM) in the 1990s. This initiative was part of the Islamization of Knowledge (IOK) Project that flourished at IIUM. The IOK movement was initiated in the 1980s by Ismail

Raji Al-Faruqi (1921-1986), who authored the "General Principles and Work Plan for IOK," published by the International Institute of Islamic Thought (IIIT) in Virginia, USA (Al-Faruqi, 1989).

To provide historical context for the development of IP during the 1970s, it is important to note that Malik Badri was invited to a conference organized by the Association of Muslim Social Scientists (AMSS) of North America in the mid-1970s. This invitation came from Professor Anis Ahmad, who is a founding member of the AMSS. When Malik Badri joined IIUM, Professor Ahmad served as the founding dean of the Faculty of Humanities and Islamic Revealed Knowledge. He is also the founder and current Vice Chancellor of Riphah International University, which has been established in Islamabad, Pakistan, since 2003.

Malik Badri's influential paper, presented at the American conference, was later published under the title "Dilemma of Muslim Psychologists." In this work, he argued that many Muslim psychologists were often adopting Western psychological approaches that may not align with Islamic principles (Badri, 1979).

As the IOK movement spread across various countries, Malaysia emerged as a leader in incorporating Islamic perspectives into multiple disciplines, including psychology. During this period, many prominent Muslim international social scientists were affiliated with IIUM, where I served as an Associate Professor and Head of the Psychology Department from the late 1990s to early 2000s. While the foundations for modern IP and other social sciences were being established in Malaysia, similar efforts were underway in other parts of the world. Providing readers with context about the emergence of the IOK movement and the role of IIUM, in which Malik Badri and many other scholars played significant roles, would be beneficial.

To go back a bit more into how the IOK concept developed, we need to know about the First World Conference on Muslim Education, held in Mecca in 1977 that focused on modern Muslim society, the rise of modernity, and the conceptual challenges facing Muslim education. Modernity refers to the post-traditional, capitalist, and secular (non-theistic) beliefs that shape our worldview and influence academic disciplines such as the humanities and social sciences. Secularization involves the disenchantment of the divine, the desacralization of politics, and the de-sanctification of values, which means removing faith and ideals from educational contexts.

Discussions at the Mecca conference among more than 300 scholars from various disciplines across the Muslim world resulted in numerous recommendations, culminating in a conference proceeding published in 1979. The proceedings emphasized the importance of integrating acquired knowledge with Islamic revealed knowledge, across all disciplines. This integration was deemed relevant to curriculum development, mass media, architecture, city planning, environmental considerations, teacher recruitment and training, female education, youth development, and more.

The conference aimed to promote the development of intellectual organizations and academic institutions while advocating for educational reform in the Muslim world. As a result of this conference, the IIIT was founded in Virginia, USA, in 1981, and the first International Islamic University was established in Malaysia in 1983. Following this, several other institutes and International Islamic Universities were created worldwide, encouraging an integrative thought process among Muslim scholars and inviting them to reassess and rewrite their disciplines from an Islamic perspective. This context led Malik Badri to Malaysia and facilitated efforts toward knowledge integration at IIUM.

Another significant aspect is the influence of Sayyid Abul Ala Maududi's writings (1903-1979) on both Ismail Raji Al Faruqi and Malik Badri. Maududi discussed the contrasting views of traditional and modernist Muslims regarding the educational system in his Urdu work, *Talimat* (1936) and argued that Islamic Thought represented a critical analysis of Western humanities and sciences to recast them in accordance with the teachings of Islam. It is likely that Ismail Faruqi encountered this concept during his two years of sabbatical at the Central Institute of Islamic Research in Pakistan from 1961 to 1963 that led him to establishing the IOK movement (Haque, 2018). Malik Badri often mentioned to this author the impact of Maududi's writings on him; he even traveled from Beirut to Pakistan to meet Maududi in Karachi.

Author's Interest in Islamic Psychology

My interest in IP developed from various experiences, the most significant being my work with a White American Christian patient at a psychiatric hospital in Michigan, where I worked as a psychologist in the 1990s. This patient did not respond well to the reinforcement-based behavior modification treatment plans I implemented. He challenged my beliefs as a Muslim and expressed disappointment that I did not address his suffering from a spiritual perspective. He requested that I take him to a local pastor or the masjid, believing he could find guidance through sermons held there. Unfortunately, I was unable to comply with his request because he was housed in a locked unit at the state hospital.

A decade earlier, I read Malik Badri's book, "The Dilemma of Muslim Psychologists," which reinforced my belief in the need to reassess modern psychology and its relevance for people of faith. Growing up in a traditional Muslim home, I had previously questioned whether psychology was the right field for me. However, I found it difficult to leave, as I had invested several years in my psychology career.

In my search for answers during the 1980s, I interviewed B.F. Skinner (Haque, 1983), the father of modern behaviorism. He criticized religion as a man-made construct that brought more harm than good to humanity. I disagreed with him, and despite facing struggles with my academic supervisors in a heavily behaviorally oriented graduate program, I pursued my Ph.D. in psychology. I graduated in 1993, a decision I consider one of the best of my life, as it opened opportunities for teaching and allowed me to work and travel around the world to various academic institutions.

For personal and family reasons, I eventually accepted an academic position at IIUM, where I was immersed in psychology, not just as a professor but also as a student of IP. It was a wonderful learning experience, as my colleagues also had backgrounds in secular psychology, and we were all learning to incorporate Islamic perspectives into the curriculum. My engagement with the IOK philosophy and insights from various scholars at IIUM deepened my belief in IP and my desire to explore the contributions of early Muslim scholars to the field, which I continue to cherish (see e.g., Haque, 2004; 2023). I taught my first master's-level IP course at IIU Malaysia from 2001-2004, after developing, the first English-based IP syllabus anywhere.

My first significant contribution to IP was the edited book titled "Psychology of Personality: Islamic Perspectives" (Haque & Muhammad, 2022a). It was first published in 2005 by Cengage Learning and reprinted by International Association of Islamic Psychology (IAIP) in 2022. This book has become a key resource for IP in several countries. A paper I published on "Psychology from Islamic Perspective: Contribution of Early Muslim Scholars and Challenges to Contemporary Muslim Psychologists" became a key resource for many readers, including over 25,000 views on my academic website (Haque, 2004).

After relocating from Malaysia to the UAE in 2004 and then to Qatar in 2018, I was not surprised by the secular nature of psychology programs offered in the Gulf countries. There was an influx of globalization of knowledge even in the social sciences that led me to study local identity (Haque, 2007). While the youth showed love for local culture there was an overall leaning towards western thought. I encountered resistance when advocating for IP primarily because it did not fit the globalization agenda. Despite this, my passion for the subject remained strong, and I continued to publish work in this area, finding intrinsic satisfaction in my efforts. Even after two decades away from Malaysia and the IOK culture, its influence remained strong. I strongly believe that Muslim psychologists should draw knowledge from Islamic epistemology and ontology and encourage the younger generation to do the same.

Islamic Psychology Field Construction

I outlined five key areas on the topic during my talk at the 12th Annual Convention of Muslim Mental Health in 2020, which took place in the U.S. I would like to include these points here for later evaluation of IP programs.

Theoretical Foundations

The concepts of *ruḥ* (spirit), *nafs* (self), *aql* (intellect), and *fitrah* (natural disposition) are essential elements of IP. Some critics argue that because abstract ideas are difficult to study, a person's *aamal* (actions) can serve as the subject matter of IP. Topics such as Qur'anic theories of personality, the dimensions of *fitrah*, the concept of humans as a microcosm, and Islamic spirituality are important areas of study. Additionally, the lives of the prophets can provide valuable insights into Islamic perspectives. The works of early Muslim scholars remain invaluable resources, with many contemporary psychological theories tracing their origins back to their insightful contributions. Examples include Islamic models of mental health, child development, interpersonal relationships, and the differentiation between cultures and religions.

Research Methodology

Various research methodologies can be employed in this field, including grounded theory, qualitative content analysis, critical ethnography, and methodologies grounded in revealed knowledge. The Islamic sciences can yield valuable insights, and *ijtihad* (independent reasoning) is crucial for adapting scientific methodologies that align with Islamic values and principles.

Research Integration

It is essential to develop an integrated mindset when studying areas such as religious growth in children, conflict resolution in Islam, positive youth development, spirituality measurement scales, religious coping, stem-cell research and psychoethics. Initiatives like student capstone courses and publications can enhance the quality, reach, and effectiveness of IP.

Intrapersonal Integration for Psychologists

Intrapersonal integration involves achieving greater personal congruence between one's *nafs* or the self, and religious beliefs. This process includes reflecting on one's theological and psychological viewpoints and analyzing one's own personality. Reviewing the stories of the prophets and deriving lessons from them, along with self-analysis, are key components of intrapersonal integration. For example, my chapter addressing the Qualities of a Muslim Therapist (Haque, 2023) as outlined by Thanvi provides insights into this area. An earlier paper, "Cognitive Restructuring of Muslim Psychologists: A Prerequisite for Islamization of Psychology" (Haque, 1996), highlighted the need to reflect on one's own theological and psychological beliefs and explore how one's personality and theology can work together harmoniously.

Integration in Training

Utilizing religious-based assessments, therapies (such as *Tazkiya*), and supervision from an integrated perspective is crucial for effective training. Treatment methodologies should only be applied if they are congruent with Islamic principles. Case studies and treatment plans must form an essential part of training programs. Integration in clinical training can occur in areas such as religious-based assessments, therapies, supervision of students from an integrated perspective, and through integrated symposiums and seminars on various topics.

A Guide to Islamic Psychology Programs

The book consists of seventeen chapters. The first chapter, written by the book's editor, provides a brief overview of the growth of IP programs worldwide. The remaining chapters are authored by program heads or coordinators from various institutions and programs across the globe.

In a preliminary survey (Haque et al., 2024), five key themes were identified in IP programs at ten institutions. These themes included an introduction to psychology, Islamic perspectives on mainstream psychological concepts, the restructuring of psychological constructs, the Islamic model of the self, and digital education. Although these themes were present in all programs, the specific subthemes varied significantly. For instance, while all programs introduced the concept of IP, the specific topics covered differed. Some programs placed an emphasis on philosophy and Sufism, while others focused on *Fiqh* and *Shariah*. The survey also revealed several challenges within these programs, including issues related to clinical placements, accreditation, and the employability of graduates. The author is grateful to the contributors of this initial survey, which was presented at the First Islamic Psychology Conference, held in Doha, Qatar,

INTRODUCTION

on Feb. 7-8, 2024.

Upon reviewing full chapters including syllabi of most of the existing programs received from various institutions offering IP, we notice considerable variations. This includes differences in the vision and mission of programs, their philosophical foundations, educational focus, duration, curriculum structure, and content emphasis. Moreover, the reference materials used in these programs vary significantly, depending on the availability of resources in local languages. Notably, some programs place a strong emphasis on developing writing skills, requiring students to publish articles to graduate, a requirement more commonly found at the postgraduate level.

Degree Programs

IP has been offered in Indonesia at the undergraduate and graduate levels since the 1994, and it launched at the doctoral level in 2023. In Iran, undergraduate-level courses began in 2003, with a PhD program in Qur'an and Psychology starting in 2007. Master's degrees in different specializations of IP were introduced at various universities in 2010, 2011, 2012, 2013, 2016, and 2020.

Admission requirements typically include passing an entrance examination that assesses proficiency in several areas, including specialized Arabic language skills for interpreting religious texts, an understanding of the Qur'an and Hadith, psychology, psychological teachings found in the Qur'an and Hadith, and the philosophy of psychology. The curriculum features specialized courses, electives, and thesis requirements. Degrees are conferred by public universities, and there is recognition of these degrees, enhancing employability in various fields.

In 2021, Ibn Haldun University introduced Traditional Islamically Integrated Psychotherapy (TIIP) as a concentration within its clinical psychology PhD program. This program includes specialized TIIP courses, clinical training, thesis requirements, and symposiums offered at the Süleymaniye Research Center within the historic Darul Shifa, as well as the summer intensive program at the Ozbeki Spiritual Lodge in Istanbul, Turkey, which attracts students from around the globe.

IP education expanded to Qatar with the introduction of a master's program in Counseling Psychology in 2024 at the College of Islamic Studies at Hamad Bin Khalifa University.

The introduction of a master's degree in counselling psychology within the College of Islamic Studies is also a significant advancement, emphasizing the integration of knowledge. An interesting aspect of this program is the teaching of IP from a traditional perspective, using principles of *Fiqh* and *Shariah*. While these programs primarily address the needs of Muslim communities, some authors reflect on their personal life experiences as the impetus for these offerings. In my experience, this personal interest and passion can serve as intrinsic motivation for program growth.

Alkaram institute in the US is starting its first master's program in 2026 but has been offering a certificate course since 2021. While their master's is a 2-year program with a thesis and internship component, the graduate certificate is a 1-year program and was created primarily for professionals who are already working in a field related to psychology or Islamic studies and would benefit by expanding their knowledge base of IP due to its relevance to their work. Alkaram Institute prides itself on having instructors and research fellows from highly esteemed institutions in the United States, while also offering both certificates and master's degrees. Most programs now provide easy access through online registration and classes.

A bachelor's degree in psychology at IIUM was introduced in 1983 and the program emphasized the integration of heart, with body, mind, soul, and spirit, promoting a holistic understanding of human existence. Master's and PhD program within the Islamic paradigm but not called IP per se, also started in the 80s and continued to grow in strength and numbers. Many students from these programs graduated over the years and sowed the seeds of IP in their countries. IIUM hosted many international scholars from the early 1990s to the early 2000s and the IOK movement played a major role in developing and shaping the Islamic thought and a desire to develop programs with Islamic perspectives. Instead of IP, the phrase "psychology from Islamic perspectives" is used at IIUM and new courses called "Science of Soul I and II" were introduced to delve deeply into Qur'anic perspectives on human nature and its implications. A significant advantage of these degrees is their accreditation at the government level.

Diplomas and Certificates

Several postgraduate certificates are offered around the globe. In 2015, Riphah International University (RIU) in Islamabad launched a one-year postgraduate diploma in Islamic psychotherapies for mental health, in collaboration with its sister program in Lahore. However, the progress of this program was halted for reasons to improve the administration. The program is now offered from the Riphah campus in Islamabad.

Charles Sturt University (CSU) in Australia in collaboration with the Islamic Studies Research Academy (ISRA) launched an accredited

INTRODUCTION

Graduate Certificate in IP in 2020 and the courses were designed as part of the existing subjects taught in the Master's program in Islamic Studies at CSU.

Another Postgraduate Certificate in Islamic Psychology is offered by the Cambridge Muslim College in the UK. This program has transitioned from the previous Diploma in IP, introduced in 2021, reflecting practical considerations and emphasizing its foundation in indigenous Islamic knowledge of the soul. It serves as a pathway for healing and personal development. The admission process for this program is quite competitive, with 25 to 30 students accepted each year from an applicant pool of approximately 200. Students come from various parts of the world, and their ages range from their early 20s to 60s.

Although a certificate in Islamic Counseling was introduced through the Department of Islamic Studies at Aligarh Muslim University in India, this program requires a master's degree for enrolment, making it a post-master's program that started in 2024. The shift of IP courses offered as Islamic Counseling indicates various challenges, including a lack of acceptance of IP in the field of psychology, limited support from the broader community, and a scarcity of qualified staff to teach the courses. It's ironic that, despite the presence of numerous Muslim institutions in a country as large as India, only AMU showed some interest in IP. This initiative was largely driven by a one-man team who has since retired but continues to publish work in the field. There is now a pressing need to cultivate a team that can maintain the same level of enthusiasm and dedication to the subject.

The Al-Balagh Academy in UK offers a Certificate in Continuing Professional Development (CPD) through its Department of IP, Psychotherapy, and Counseling. Al-Balagh Academy has formed strategic partnerships with various academic and clinical institutions. On the clinical side, it collaborates with Ihsaan, a dedicated Islamic psychological therapy service, to provide an innovative online course in IP and Counseling. A distinctive feature of Al Balagh Academy is its integration of Islamic principles with contemporary psychological practices. This fosters a culture of research, innovation, and personal growth among professionals through a vertically and horizontally integrated curriculum model of IP.

The certificates offered at Académie Islam & Psychologie are in French. The program provides two certificates; the first program lasts one year and is designed for mental health professionals who wish to specialize in IP. The second spans two years and is intended for non-mental health professionals seeking training in this field. Both programs are offered in partnership with the International Students of IP (ISIP) and the Al-Balkhi Institute. Additionally, a program titled "Awareness of Mental Health" was specifically developed for Imams and religious leaders.

Courses in Islamic Psychology

Ihsaan Therapeutic Services in the UK has played a crucial role in raising awareness of IP, responding to the needs of local Muslim clinicians and therapists by offering two IP courses. The first course, called Part One, was taught in 2001 and has been running 1 to 3 times a year. It is primarily theoretical in nature. In contrast, Part Two, which was introduced in 2017, is more practice-focused and addresses a specific area of clinical work. The courses are structured as short modules, with the potential to be developed into more formal courses and programs under an accredited institution. The alumni from this program since its inception in 2001 can serve as a valuable resource for enhancing the program further.

The introduction of the IP course at Stanford started in 2020 as part of their undergraduate program and is held annually in the Spring quarter. It is jointly provided by the Department of Psychiatry within the School of Medicine and the Center for Comparative Studies in Race and Ethnicity (cross-listed as CSRE 144A) under the School of Humanities and Sciences. This innovative course could pave the way for similar course and program developments at other institutions in the US.

In Pakistan, several universities have made efforts to integrate Islamic perspectives into psychology, with the International Islamic University Islamabad (IIUI) being a leader in this initiative. The course in IP was optional at the undergraduate level but became mandatory for master's and doctoral programs. In 2007, IIUI introduced the course as "Muslim Psychology," offering it as a three-credit-hour class. The Riphah Institute of Clinical and Professional Psychology was established in Lahore, and the Center of Islamic Psychology was founded in Islamabad in 2015. Other initiatives include a certificate course launched in collaboration with the IAIP in 2019 and the Traditional Islamically Integrated Psychotherapy (TIIP) course, introduced in 2022.

In Iran, the establishment of the Islamic Psychology Association (IPA) in 2004 attracted hundreds of students with backgrounds in Islamic studies. Islamic Psychology in Iran aims to explore and establish principles that ensure mental health and well-being, fostering a fulfilling life for individuals, families, and society in alignment with the divine principles set forth in the Quran and Hadith.

Istanbul Zaim University (IZU) now offers graduate-level courses in IP within its programs in Spirituality and Guidance, as well as Philosophy and Religious Sciences. These programs provide a certificate in Theoretical Oriented Counseling. These initiatives began in 2020, leading to the establishment of a Psychology of Religion and Spirituality Lab in 2025, which focuses on research projects related to IP.

Challenges and Solutions

It is interesting to observe that different programs express their concerns in various ways. Some newer programs emphasize the need for clarity regarding the field of IP, as scholars hold differing opinions about its definition. This uncertainty ultimately impacts the course content. While it is essential for IP to clarify what constitutes the field, it is unlikely that a consensus on a standard definition will be reached. Perhaps a more practical approach would be to educate students about the various definitions and rationales, allowing them to choose the definition they wish to adhere to.

A common concern among these programs is the lack of resources, including English-language textbooks. Additionally, some programs may be unaware of the books and materials used in other regions, as many of these resources exist in indigenous languages, but their translations are not readily available. The responsibility for selecting key textbooks for translation into English falls on scholars proficient in the native languages who can assess whether the book includes sufficient IP content and qualifies for translation. An international body could take the lead on translation efforts, or a local organization could handle it, provided that the quality of work is not compromised.

The shortage of qualified instructors with expertise in psychology and relevant Islamic knowledge poses a significant challenge that does not have a simple solution. Graduates of IP programs could be strong candidates to teach these courses, provided they hold at least a master's degree in psychology or a related field. It would be counterproductive to have these courses taught by individuals without a psychology background, except in cases where the course focuses on Islamic studies, spirituality, or philosophy, which should be taught by scholars trained in those disciplines.

To address this issue, offering continuing education in areas where individuals may lack skills, along with potential certifications for those skills, is likely to be beneficial. Moreover, integrating lectures from and forming partnerships with Islamic scholars and institutes is essential for enhancing the overall educational experience.

A key issue in IP is the need for a standard textbook that addresses essential topics such as cognition, emotions, motivation, personality, intelligence, and social development. Currently, there is no comprehensive resource available. Compiling the works of early Muslim scholars on these subjects could serve as a good starting point. However, we must acknowledge that these works may not fully address today's circumstances.

To bridge this gap, we can expand upon the insights of early Muslim scholars while integrating contemporary knowledge from psychology that aligns with Islamic beliefs and practices. For example, cognitive-behavioral therapy (CBT) can be adapted within an Islamic framework, but its underlying theories must be rooted in Islamic principles. This is an area where we are significantly lacking and need to address seriously.

An interesting observation is the potential for integrating this field with other disciplines. For example, could it be offered as a combined program with Islamic studies, chaplaincy, or counseling? Although the number of publications in this area is increasing, there remains a lack of research output and articles in well-known journals. Additionally, many of these resources are not easily accessible to all, particularly students. Such topics can be addressed in IP conferences and discussions as appropriate.

Another concern is the excessive focus on mental health needs, which often leads to the neglect of other areas in psychology where integration and IP practice could be beneficial, such as work, school, and family dynamics. Muslim psychologists specializing in non-clinical areas can assess and incorporate Islamic perspectives into their courses. For instance, organizational psychology is an important discipline where Islamic ethics can be integrated.

A challenge for many programs is ensuring student satisfaction and the utility of the courses offered. For students in IP, securing paid employment after graduation is a major concern, especially in non-Muslim countries. It's also important to consider whether the program promotes personal growth, which includes both intellectual and spiritual development.

To address these issues, IP programs should regularly review and update their curricula to include relevant learning materials. Conducting ongoing student surveys to assess satisfaction and gather recommendations is crucial. Graduates of these programs can also provide insights and suggestions for enhancing program utility.

It's worth noting that IP programs attract individuals who may not intend to practice professionally but are eager to understand and improve themselves. This audience can strengthen the programs, and their feedback is invaluable for improving overall quality.

While there is some digital accessibility, it is crucial to incorporate the latest technologies. Furthermore, developing strong writing skills and fostering creativity in research are necessary so that students can publish their papers in international journals. This is important not only for students but also for faculty members, particularly those whose native language is not English. Collaborating with academics and practitioners—especially those who have graduated from Islamic studies programs—can help apply this knowledge in psychological practice.

Additionally, there is a significant need to create an international IP Journal for academics, as well as a student-run journal that publishes articles based on theses, dissertations, conference abstracts, conference reports, book reviews, and more.

The issue of accreditation is crucial, as it significantly impacts opportunities for further studies and job prospects. It is essential for scholars and administrators within the IP community to take this matter seriously. While accreditation may not pose a challenge in most Muslim countries, addressing it requires creativity and hard work.

We should consider whether it is possible to offer programs from accredited institutions so that degrees are recognized. I suspect that the marketing of IP utility has been slow, which could explain the lack of awareness and demand. Therefore, educating stakeholders about the benefits of accreditation and publication is vital. The role of IP program alumni cannot be underestimated.

The lack of universally accepted guidelines in IP risks misrepresentation. Without clear standards, some may mistakenly broaden IP to encompass all spirituality or religious discourse, overlooking key psychological theories vital to the discipline. This undermines the field's integrity and complicates the development of a strong academic framework. To gain accreditation in IP, individuals must have a solid psychological foundation, as the field integrates established psychological science with Islamic knowledge rather than serving merely as a spiritual or cultural add-on.

An important issue is the need for students and teachers to unlearn non-Islamic theories, contents, and approaches, replacing them with perspectives grounded in Islamic and spiritual principles. Therefore, courses in IP at the undergraduate level, as well as for teachers seeking to reorient their perspective to an Islamic worldview, are essential. IP cannot simply be a capstone course, as previously practiced by IP scholars; it should instead be the very first course in psychology to help shape young minds.

Moreover, despite advancements in technology, there remains a communication gap among scholars from different regions of the world. This gap may stem from cultural differences, language barriers, or other factors that ideally should not hinder academic pursuit and excellence. We have yet to see collaborative publications in IP authored by scholars from diverse global backgrounds. Senior and experienced authors could play a vital role by guiding and co-authoring articles with younger colleagues and dedicated students.

It is essential for the IP community to build meaningful connections, even when there are conceptual or philosophical differences. Collaboration on seminars, conferences, teaching, and research initiatives is crucial. These ideas can be further developed and addressed by individual programs, either independently or in partnership with others. Establishing a strong platform in both the public and private sectors for consultancy, training, and cooperation can significantly strengthen IP programs on a global scale, enhancing the field overall.

The good news is that IP programs have made significant progress over the past few decades, and there is great potential for the future, thanks to the scholars and passionate graduates eager to advance the field. In addition to the dedicated efforts of IP program administrators, the establishment of an international IP alumni association could help elevate the field further and create a legacy that benefits both current and future generations.

Conclusion

The growth of modern IP is relatively recent, but various programs have emerged around the world. This book presents a collection of international program descriptions and curricula designed to promote mutual learning and collaboration, with the goal of advancing psychology as both an academic and practical discipline. For Muslims, the study of human behavior is considered a religious obligation, which adds particular significance to this field. Early Muslim scholars delved into the concept of *ilm-al-nafs* (the science of the soul), and contemporary Muslim psychologists are now tasked with developing and adapting curricula and training that address all aspects of human nature from both scientific and Islamic perspectives. While some countries may lack established psychology programs, scholars have produced valuable works in their native languages that could greatly benefit the field if translated into English.

CHAPTER ONE

AN OVERVIEW OF THE GLOBAL INTEREST IN ISLAMIC PSYCHOLOGY

Amber Haque

The term "Islamic Psychology" may be unfamiliar to many, especially those who do not speak Arabic or are not familiar with the phrase "ilm-al-nafs," which translates to "the science of the soul." Early Muslim scholars used this terminology to explore various aspects of human psychology. Many modern psychological theories can be traced back to these early concepts (Haque, 2004).

Before the widespread influence of the English language and Western thought in various regions around the world, much of the writing in the Muslim world was done in Arabic and other indigenous languages. While many of these writings still exist today, only a small fraction has been translated into English.

To demonstrate that Islamic Psychology (IP) is not a new discipline and has developed in various parts of the world, the author invited over twenty international scholars in 2020 to contribute chapters on IP as it exists in their respective countries. This collaborative effort resulted in the edited book titled "Islamic Psychology Around the Globe," from which many references are sourced (Haque & Rothman, 2021). Interestingly, although IP has its roots in the Muslim world, it has also gained significant traction in the Western world.

The increasing popularity of Indigenous psychologies in recent decades stems from a growing dissatisfaction with mainstream psychology, particularly among non-Western populations (Haque, 2002; 2005; 2008). This trend is not limited to Muslims; the indigenization of mainstream psychology has taken place in various regions around the world. For Muslims, Indigenous psychology is particularly significant because it is grounded in Islamic ontology and epistemology. Similarly, Christian psychology began to appear as a formal discipline in the mid-20th century and is now taught in faith-based institutions in the US and UK. The degrees offered in this field are accredited and can lead to professional licensure. For further insights, see the author's earlier articles on the integration of psychology and religion in the Western world (Haque, 2001a; 2001b; Haque & Keshavarzi, 2014).

Although this overview is brief, it provides a concise summary of the development of IP across various continents, organized alphabetically. The author has highlighted initiatives from different countries to keep the information concise. Interested readers can find added details from other sources, including the scholars and programs referenced in this book. The invitation to contribute a chapter for this book is included in the appendix.

Asia

The Subcontinent

The significant Muslim population in the Indian subcontinent can be attributed to the influential Sufis in British India, who guided and educated Muslims throughout undivided India. Notable figures in this movement include Shah Muhammad Ghaus (1703-1759), Shah Waliullah (1703-1762), and Ashraf Ali Thanvi (1873-1943). These scholars played a vital role in promoting Islamic mysticism in the region. However, the educational institutions in India at that time, and still largely today, are dominated by a secular and Western approach to education, which often contrasts with Islamic ideology and worldview.

The writings of these Muslim scholars were primarily in Urdu or Persian, rendering them largely unknown to the English-speaking world. They produced hundreds of manuscripts that explored human nature from Islamic perspectives. Due to his personal interest in these topics and his native language being Urdu, the author published academic articles on the works of two prominent personalities: Ashraf Ali Thanvi and Shah Waliullah Dehlavi (Haque, 2023; Haque, 2025).

India

The only institution in India known to the author that offers IP as a subject at the university level is Aligarh Muslim University (AMU). In 2016, the University Grants Commission approved a master's level specialization titled "Islamic Perspectives in Psychology." The curriculum committee at AMU subsequently approved four Master's level courses for the second year: IP, Psychology and Sufism, Human Nature and Personality, and Islamic Practices, Counseling, and Psychotherapeutic Intervention. The final semester of the Master's program included a practicum.

Interestingly, instead of the proposed Master's level courses from the psychology department, a Certificate in Islamic Counseling was introduced in 2024 through a collaboration between the Department of Psychology and the Department of Islamic Studies. Over the years, the Psychology Department has organized numerous activities, and its faculty members, especially Akbar Hussain, have published papers and developed psychological tests related to IP.

Additionally, the Institute of Objective Studies (IOS), established in 1986 in New Delhi, has made significant contributions to this field by publishing important works, including "Quranic Concepts of Human Psyche" by Z.A. Ansari (1992), "Psychology and Society in Islamic Perspective" by M.G. Husain (1996), "An Introduction to Islamic Psychology" by A.A. Vahab (1996), and "Psyche in Islam," edited by Shamim Ahmad Ansari (2018). The IOS also collaborated with AMU to organize a joint conference in 2009 focused on "The Concept of Psyche in Islam."

Indonesia

The first book on IP in Indonesia, titled "Psychology of Religion," was authored by Zakaria Darajat in 1970. The Muslim Psychology Student Organization was established in 1991, followed by the launch of the IP Journal *KALAM* in 1992. Several universities began offering IP courses, and the first national symposium on IP was held in 1994, followed by a second symposium in 1996.

In 1999, the National Dialogue of IP Leaders took place, with additional symposiums occurring in 2000 and 2001. The Association of Islamic Psychology (API) was formed in 2003, and an international IP conference was organized in 2016.

Between 2000 and 2020, 18 books and 12 journals were published related to IP. By 2021, twenty universities were offering courses in this field, and various institutions had organized 22 conferences. Additionally, ten major points are planned as future directions and research priorities in IP. While individual names are not specified, Bagus Riyono is the current President of the International Association of Muslim Psychologists (IAMP),

Iran

Many early Muslim scholars, such as Al-Tabari, Al-Farabi, Al-Majusi, Ibn Miskawayh, Ibn Sina, and Al-Ghazali, who extensively studied IP, were from Persia. Their writings were primarily in Arabic, as it was the lingua franca of the time. Numerous Persian scholars also authored manuscripts that explored various topics, including the semantics of nafs (self) and aql (intellect), the psychospiritual strengths and weaknesses of individuals, the religious education of children, the connection with God, spiritual self-supervision, and interpersonal and social relations.

Some notable works include Shaikh Al Kulayni's (836-907) manuscript "Al-Kafi" (The Sufficient), the "Sermons of Musadaqat Al-Ikhwan" and "Al-Mawaiz," Shaikh Al-Saduq's (883-959) "Al-Khisal," which discusses human traits, Al-Sharif Al-Radi's (837-984) "Nahj Al-Baligha" (The Way of Eloquence), and Sayyid Ibn Tawus's (1167-1242) "Muhasabah Al-Nafs" (The Spiritual Monitoring of the Self).

Early pioneers between the 12th and 19th century

- Yahya Suhrawardi (1154-1191): In his book *Hayaakil-al-Noor*, he considers the human soul as a heavenly truth imprisoned by the earthly body and returns to its original truth after acquiring virtues and perfections. In Book *Fi Haqiqat al-Ishq*, he describes the human soul with cognition and emotion that includes knowing God and self-knowledge.

- Nasir al-Tusi (1201-1274): In his book, *Akhlaq-I. Nasiri* believes in the longitudinal pyramid of perfection and considers the health of the Nafs as the first level of human perfection. The other part of the book discusses *Moalaja Amraaz al-Nafs*, referring to Kindi's explanations of depression and proposed *ilaj-al-huzn*.

- Mulla Sadra (1571-1640): Originator of the theory of substantial motion and transformation *(al harakat al-jawhariyya)* as a result of self-flow. Also wrote the Transcendent Philosophy of the Four Journeys of the intellect. Three thousand articles on Mullah Sadra's ideas are registered in the database in the Noor specialized journals in Iran. His writings on Nafs are detailed, explaining that Nafs is eternal and if it reaches perfection, it can be spiritual in timeless existence (ruhanniyat al-baqa). The Nafs also has different degrees, from its formation until it reaches its end or returns to God.

- Fayz Kashani (1585–1669) wrote *Al-Mahajjatal-bayda'fitahdhib al-ihya* to explain and refine Ghazali's *Ihya-Ulum-al-Din*. He presented a cognitive-motivational theory to explain behavior. He stated that resolving or not resolving conflicts will place Nafs in one of the four levels: Nafs and mulhama (inspired), Nafs al-mutmainnah (nafs at peace), nafs al-lawwamah (self-accusing soul), and nafs al-ammara (inciting nafs). He provided strategies for conflict resolution.

- Mahdi al-Naraqi (1771-1829). *Miraj al-Saada* (Ladder of Happiness) explains the psychological characteristics, pathologies, and their corresponding treatments. He is a pioneer in Islamic positive psychology, explaining the human psyche as a mountain with only one peak, which is good, but difficult to climb and easy to fall. Those who ascend or descend use the forces of lust (shahwa), anger (ghazab), and intellect (aql). He wrote about *Tazkiya al-Nafs* and divided mental disorders into seven categories and three subtypes.

The 20th century

The first article in Iran that examined modern psychology from a Quranic perspective was "Human Personality in terms of Modern Psychology and Religion" (Saeedi, 1950, quoted by Rafei-Honar in Haque & Rothman, 2021), followed by many other books. In the 1960s, a series of articles entitled IP were written by scholars at the Hawzah or Theological Seminary in Qom, including Fitrah by Ahmadi (1983), Islam and Psychology (Riaazi, 1981), Principles of IP (Hosseini, 1985), and Islam and Psychology (Ale-Ishaaq, 1990). References to these and other Iranian publications can be found in the chapter by Rafei-Honar in Haque & Rothman (2021).

2000-2020

In the past 20 years, according to Rafei-Honar in Haque & Rothman (2021), there have been 14 professional journals that published articles related to IP. Additionally, 13 conferences were organized, and various universities began offering courses related to IP, including one that offers a PhD in Islam and Psychology, as well as several institutions providing master's and undergraduate degree programs. A certificate in IP has been available since 2018.

In total, 73 books have been published covering 12 areas of IP, and six religiosity scales have been developed. Many of these materials originate from the Hawzah Center and are authored by theological psychologists based in Qom. The psychologists in Iran established the IP Association in 2004 and introduced a specialized discipline, known as Positive-Oriented IP, in 2010. However, the exploration of contributions from Iran has been limited due to reasons including the publication of works in the Persian language.

Malaysia

The development of IP in Malaysia can be divided into three distinct eras:

a. Early contributions from the 1950s to the 1980s,
b. Establishment of discipline from 1990 to 2000, and
c. Growth of IP from 2000 to 2020.

During the first era, several notable books were published, notably by Yusuf Zaky Yacob, a Malay Islamic scholar. He released "Saikologi Remaja" (Adolescent Psychology) in 1956, which was based on his notes written in Arabic while studying at the Faculty of Education at the American University of Cairo. Initially, the book used the traditional Malay spelling, but it was republished in 1977 with updated spelling. Throughout his career, Yacob published several articles, including "Secrets of Happiness" (1957), "Insan Kamil" (1958), "The Tears of the Servant" (1958), "Child Psychology" (1960), "Human Psychology" (1970), "Psychology of Fear" (1976), and "Searching for Psychological Tranquility" (1988). He also compiled a collection of articles titled "1001 Psychological Problems Faced by Humans," which was published in 1986 in various Malay magazines. In 1996, he translated Qutb's book "*Darasat Fi Al-Nafs Al-Insania*" (Studies in Human Psychology), which is considered one of the earliest Islamic critiques of Western psychology. Since these works are in Malay, they are not widely recognized in the English-speaking world.

In the 1980s, Hasan Langgulung contributed to the field with two notable books: a) "Theories of Mental Health: Between Modern Psychology and Islamic Education" (1983), and b) "Research in Psychology: An Ummatic Paradigm" (1989).

During the second era of establishing IP in Malaysia, the Department of Psychology at the International Islamic University Malaysia offered two courses focused on the subject: 1) Islam and Psychology and 2) Contributions of Early Muslim Scholars to Psychology. From the 1990s until 2000, all psychology majors were required to minor in subjects such as Islamic Revealed Knowledge and Heritage, the Science of the Quran, Islamic Ethics, Aqidah, Fiqh, and the Biography of the Prophet Muhammad (S). During this period, the Faculty of the Psychology Department published extensive research, producing over 100 papers on topics related to IP (Alyas, 2021). Additionally, two major seminars were held between 1996-97, and a review article published by this author on Islamic perspectives in psychology (Haque, 1997; Haque, 1998a; 1998b). However, starting in the early 2000s, the nationalization movement in Malaysia led to many international faculty members leaving the country, as Malay faculty members returned home after completing their doctoral studies in psychology.

Beginning in the third era, spanning from 2000 to 2020, a curriculum review was first conducted in 2005 to integrate Islamic perspectives throughout the curriculum. A follow-up review was conducted in 2009 to ensure that learning Islamic perspectives became an integral part of the learning outcomes. From 2005 to 2018, the book "Psychology of Personality: Islamic Perspective" by Haque and Yasien (2005) was required reading for the Islam and Psychology course.

Noraini Noor's edited book, "Psychology from Islamic Perspectives: A Guide for Teaching and Learning" (2009), has played a crucial role in teaching introductory psychology courses at IIUM. This book is a compilation of chapters written by departmental lecturers, featuring their published journal articles.

In addition to the International Islamic University Malaysia (IIUM), several other institutions have begun offering courses in IP. These include Universiti Teknologi Malaysia (UTM), Kolej Universiti Islam Selangor, Kolej Universiti Islam Melaka, and Universiti Kebangsaan Malaysia (UKM). Notably, the General Studies Centre at UKM has published a book titled "Islamic Psychology: Philosophy, Theory, and Application." Another significant publication is "Psychology of Dawah," released in 2020 by the University of Malaya, among others.

Pakistan

Psychology in Pakistan was primarily taught in philosophy departments until the 1960s, following British colonization. Muhammad Ajmal (1919-1994) played a pivotal role in establishing the psychology department at Government College University (GCU) in Lahore. He emphasized the importance of Muslim psychology in his work (Ajmal, 1968). In the late 1970s, Syed Azhar Ali Rizvi (1936-2004) introduced a course on Muslim Psychology and founded the Society for the Advancement of Muslim Psychology. Additionally, Rizvi developed three indigenous personality tests and established the Institute of Muslim Psychology in the early 2000s. Notable contributors to indigenous psychology in the 1980s and 1990s included Shahabuddin Muhammad Moghni, Farhana Jehangir, and Mahnazir Riaz, who authored several papers on the subject. Interestingly, all these psychologists were affiliated with the University of Peshawar in Pakistan.

After the establishment of the Higher Education Commission (HEC) in Pakistan in 2002, which was restructured from the original

University Grants Commission, the Muslim psychology course was introduced as an optional subject in the Master's program. In some departments, such as at the International Islamic University Islamabad (IIUI), it was made a core subject at the doctoral level.

In 2007, Malik Badri served as the head of the Psychology Department at IIUI for one year. He introduced the Muslim psychology course as an optional subject at the bachelor's level, while it remained a requirement at both the master's and doctoral levels. In 2019, Muhammad Tahir Khalily organized a certified course on Islamic Approaches to Psychology and Psychotherapy in collaboration with the International Association of IP.

The Riphah Institute of Clinical and Professional Psychology in Lahore and the Center for IP in Islamabad were established in 2015 under the leadership of Anis Ahmad. Additionally, the IP Certificate Course was launched in 2019 by G.H. Rassool.

From 1995 to 2019, 16 IP-related conferences were held in Pakistan, including one in partnership with IIU Malaysia in 2019. Additionally, there have been numerous books and peer-reviewed publications over the decades.

Saudi Arabia

The Islamic Rooting Movement started in Saudi Arabian universities with the emergence of psychology departments in the 1960s. IP was applied in various ways.

Islamic Guidance for Psychology

The terminology mentioned was utilized in two universities around 2006-2007: Imam Mohammad Bin Saud Islamic University and King Saud University (KSU). They offered courses such as Islamic Guidance for Psychological Studies. This perspective suggests that a psychologist has a responsibility before God to guide individuals according to Islamic principles for living. Additionally, it is the duty of specialists in Shari'ah sciences to ensure that the content of these courses aligns with Islamic law. Other courses included topics on the psychological heritage of Muslim scholars, personality from an Islamic perspective, and the Islamic direction of psychology.

The Islamic Rooting of Psychology began in the 1980s as an invitation to return to early Islamic origins, which served as a primary source for many scientific disciplines. It is important to note that this approach would not contradict scientific progress, as long as it aligns itself with Islamic principles that promote knowledge and inquiry.

These efforts continued until 2020, when the three original courses were consolidated into one, titled "Islamic Rooting for the Science of Self." Additionally, there is a course focused on Islamic Perspectives on Deviation and Crime.

At KSU, a seminar was held in 1978 that featured 23 papers discussing the intersection of Islam and psychology. Between 2000 and 2019, 26 theses and 36 books were published on the subject, along with the development of eight Islamic-based psychological measurement scales from 1984 to 2014.

Overall, there has been a decline in the Islamic rooting of psychology, partly as a result of the pandemic in 2019, and no significant changes are noted from KSA after Covid-19.

Türkiye

During the late Ottoman Period, Hoca Tahsin (d. 1881) wrote the book Ilm-i-ruh, which is considered the first psychology textbook in Turkey. Additionally, Hakikat-ul-Insan or ilm-i-ahval-ruh was published by Yusuf Kemal in 1878. The first psychology conference in Türkiye took place in 1869 at Darul-Funun, Istanbul University, where the types of personality were discussed.

Following the establishment of the modern Turkish Republic, the influence of Islamic intellectual traditions declined, and this trend continued for decades, hindering the development of psychology from Islamic perspectives. However, interest in this field resumed after the year 2000, as evidenced by an increase in publications and the introduction of new academic programs.

2000 to Present

Mustafa Merter authored "Nafs Psychology" (2014) and "Nine Hundred Layers of a Human" (2016). He developed a psychotherapy model that combines Islamic mysticism with modern psychology. Currently, he is working on a project regarding Quranic exegesis from a psychological perspective.

Medaim Yanik established reading groups and research teams focused on IP. He served as the Chair of the Psychology Department at Ibn Haldun University (IHU). Yanik also initiated various forms of media engagement, including newspaper articles, radio discussions, and TV shows centered on IP topics. Notably, he hosted a series of seven-week discussions with Recep Senturk, the former Rector of IHU.

Mustafa Ulusoy is a psychiatrist known for his novels that discuss

IP and psychotherapy within the framework of the Quran. He has written academic articles on the effects of Quranic ontology on psychotherapy and how Aqeedah influences emotions.

Taha Burak Toprak introduced the 4T model into psychotherapy, specifically cognitive-behavioral therapy (CBT), based on Said Nursi's *"Vesvese Risalesi."* This model serves as a psychoeducational process for treating obsessive-compulsive disorder (OCD) and consists of four components: *Tahayyul* (imagination), *Tasayyur* (conception), *Taakkul* (reasoning), and *Tasdik* (confirmation). Additionally, he established an Islamic Thought Platform that facilitates reading groups and symposiums focused on Islamic perspectives.

Hooman Keshavarzi, originally from Türkiye, is the founder of Khalil Center in the USA, where he utilizes the Traditional Islamically Integrated Psychotherapy (TIIP) Model. He currently leads the Master's program in counseling at Hamad Bin Khalifa University (HBKU) in Qatar. Additionally, he played a key role in developing the IP Program at IHU in Istanbul, Türkiye.

Radio and TV Programs

An intriguing program titled "Sufism and Human Psychology," hosted by Suleyman Derin, explores the psychological insights of Imam Ghazali's *Ihya Ulumuddin*, Jalaluddin Rumi's Mathnavi, and *Balkhi's Masalihul Abdan Wal'anfus*. In another program called "Fihi Ma Fih," Dr. Faik Ozdengul discusses Sufi psychology on TRT Avaz, focusing primarily on Rumi's contributions to psychology and the benefits of transcendental therapy (Haque, 2025).

Africa

Egypt

One of the earliest organized efforts in the field of IP was established by Gamal Atiyya in 1974, when he founded the *Jamiyyat Al-Muslim Al-Muaser* (The Modern Muslim Forum), which served as an educational and research platform, facilitating discussions on the Islamic roots of various sciences, including psychology.

The clinical application of IP was first introduced by the World Islamic Association for Mental Health (WIAMH), which was founded in 1983. They published a bimonthly magazine called *Al-Nafs Al-Mutmainnah* (The Peaceful Soul), showcased on their website, Oasis of the Soul | World Islamic Society. It also features the Reassuring Soul Magazine and a Psychological Encyclopedia.

AN OVERVIEW OF THE GLOBAL INTEREST IN IP

An Egyptian scholar, Amir Al-Najjar, wrote *Al-Tassawuf Al-Nafsani* (2002), presenting the views of three Sufi scholars from the third century. Al-Sharqawi published *Nahw Ilm-Al-Nafs Al-Islami* (1976), (Towards an IP), and authored Foundational Psychological Concepts in the Quran and The Question of Terminology (1989), advocating for the use of Islamically informed psychological language in Muslim research. Uthman Nagati's book, An Introduction to IP, was published posthumously in 2001, while Muhammad Omar published Characteristics of IP (1983). Mahmoud, a former Head of the Psychology Department at Cairo University, published Towards an Operational Definition for Muslim Psychologists (1990). Abu Halab from Ain Shams University authored Towards an Islamic Paradigm for Psychology (1992), identifying six directions for the field of IP.

While Nagati and Qutb (1919-2014) were teaching at Umm Al Qura University, Qutb's writings had a significant impact on Malik Badri. Mohammad Qutb was the younger brother of Sayyid Qutb (1906-1966), who was tried for treason and executed in Egypt. In the author's personal communications with Badri, the latter frequently mentioned the names of two individuals who shaped his thinking: Sayyid Qutb from Egypt, and Syed Abul Ala Maududi from Pakistan (1903-1979).

Qutb critiqued modern psychological theories, particularly psychoanalysis and behaviorism. Additionally, other scholars, such as Sayyid Abdulhamid Morsi (1983), Sa'd Riyad (2004a; 2004b), and Elmahdi (2002), have also contributed to an Islamic understanding of human nature.

In 1989, the International Institute of Islamic Thought (IIIT) held a conference in Egypt, which resulted in 34 research papers emphasizing the need for the field of IP and the establishment of precise terminology and curricula. However, by 2021, IP had not yet been incorporated into Egyptian universities.

A significant collaborative effort was initiated by the IIIT to explore, survey, summarize, and present over 400 classical treatises authored by more than 100 Muslim scholars from the first century to the 14th Hijri century. This extensive work resulted in the publication of four volumes titled *"Ilm al-Nafs fi al-Thurath al-Islami"* (Psychological Sciences in the Islamic Heritage), led by Nagati and a team of scholars from Egypt (Majariyya et al., 2011).

In addition, Elmahdi (1990) published "Psychotherapy in Light of Islam," and Abu Hindi (2002) released "Towards an Islamic Psychiatry." Meanwhile, Salem (2009; 2010) proposed an Islamic theory of the mind and developed therapy models that integrate Islamic principles.

Nigeria

The Islamic perspectives on knowledge can be traced back to the Sokoto revivalist literature of the 19th century, which initiated an intellectual reform. In the late 1700s, Shaikh Usman Dan Fodiyo wrote extensively on topics related to psychology, including works such as "*Ilm al-Suluk*" (Science of Behavior) and "*Husn al-Khulq*" (Good Moral Conduct). In "*Bayan Wujub al-Hijrah ala al-Ibad*," he explained people's psychological dispositions, traits, and tendencies, providing advice to rulers on how to interact with their subjects. This marked the beginning of political psychology as a distinct field.

As a result of the contributions from such intellectuals, Wazir Junaid of Sokoto, in his acceptance speech for an honorary doctorate at Ahmadu Bello University in 1971, asserted that knowledge is universal but influenced by sociocultural factors driven by one's worldview. He emphasized that Muslims should be guided by the Tawhidic paradigm. This discourse facilitated the entry of the Islamization of Knowledge (IOK) movement in Nigeria, paving the way for the development of Islamic-based curricula and related research. Wazir Junaid encouraged academics to reclaim knowledge by reevaluating imported philosophies, course content, and educational orientations. Consequently, he is recognized as the first advocate for a paradigm shift aimed at promoting the Islamic worldview and value system in Nigeria.

Three scholars are credited with initiating IP in Nigeria during the 1980s: Danjuma Abubakar Maiwada, Musa Ahmad (deceased), and Muhammad Kabir Younus, all from Bayero University in Kano. The first two professors taught in the Department of Education, where psychology was housed, while the last taught in the Department of Islamic Studies.

It was at Bayero University that IP courses were introduced in 1997, which included an undergraduate course titled "Introduction to IP" and a graduate course called "Advanced IP." Additionally, two elective courses—"Counseling in Islam" and "Contributions of Muslim Scholars to Guidance and Counseling"—are offered in the Postgraduate Diploma in Guidance and Counseling Program.

The IIIT Office in Nigeria has also promoted IP through three main channels: Al-Ijtihad, a local journal; monthly seminars related to the IOK movement, which began in 2000 or earlier, where numerous papers on IP have been presented by psychologists including Salisu Shehu, Sani M. Ayagi, Rabiu I. Garba, and Mustapha Auwal. In addition to these scholars, articles on IP topics have been published by Mohammad Ibn Abdullahi and Abdul Kadir Ismail.

Sudan

In 1977, the University of Khartoum established its first Department of Psychology within the Faculty of Education. Malik Badri joined as a professor and introduced a capstone course titled "Islam and Psychology" at the undergraduate level. In this course, students reviewed all their previous coursework from an Islamic perspective.

There are several key terms associated with this field, including the Islamization of Psychology, Islamic interpretations of behavior, Islamic guidance in psychology, the Islamic authenticity (Taseel) of psychology, and the concept of IP, which was adopted by Badri.

Prominent Books

- Psychology in the Arab-Islamic Heritage (Bashir Taha, 1995)
- Experimental Psychology in the Arab-Islamic Heritage (Omar Khalifa, 2001)
- Introduction to Psychology: Islamic perspectives (Khatib & Shannan, 2003)

In three years between 2015-2018, five universities had 240 master's and PhD theses submitted on topics related to IP: Uni of Khartoum, Islamic Uni of Omdurman, International Uni of Africa, Uni of Gezira, Al Neelain University, and Sudan Uni for Science and Technology.

Psychological Scales

- Islamic Religious Observance Scale (IROS) based on a local sample (Shennan, 2002).
- Intelligence test based on Ibn Qayyim al-Jawzi's book on intelligence by Najda Abdul Rahim (2005). 60 items over six axes with known validity and reliability.

Research published from 2015 to 2020

- Psychological dimensions of facial expressions in the Quran
- The effectiveness of Quranic stories in behavioral education for children
- Psychological aspects associated with walking in the Quran

Australia

Interest in IP in Australia began in 1996 when the Federation of Australian Muslim Students invited Malik Badri to their conference in Sydney. The topic was first explored at the School of Psychology at Western Sydney University (formerly known as the University of Western Sydney) in 2001. This exploration led to the inaugural IP Conference in 2002, which featured speakers Malik Badri and Amber Haque from Malaysia. At that time, Western Sydney University was at the forefront of research in the psychology of religion.

After the 2002 conference, the UWS School of Psychology sponsored and partnered with the newly established Australian Society of Islamic Psychology (ASI), marking the first formal IP association outside of Muslim-majority countries. This collaboration sparked a growing interest in IP in Australia, resulting in numerous conferences and seminars, primarily held in Sydney. In 2004, an interest group was formed, initially called the IP Interest Group, which later changed its name to Psychology from an Islamic Perspective (PPIG). Since its inception, PPIG has hosted ongoing seminars and professional development workshops that integrate Islamic principles with psychological practices.

In 2003, an organization called Mission of Hope was established by Muslims studying psychology and other health fields to address mental health issues within Muslim communities. In 2007, a research group developed the Muslim Spiritual Attachment Scale. This scale was utilized in a large-scale study conducted in Australia in 2013. A significant advancement occurred in 2019 with the introduction of a Graduate Certificate in IP from Charles Sturt University (CSU). This was followed by the HOPE Muslim Mental Health Conference, organized in 2020.

Europe

United Kingdom

The voice of clinicians to look beyond Western psychology was the main push behind the development of IP in the UK and Rasjid Skinner in a chapter mentions three factors in developing his interest in IP: a) Dilemma of Muslim Psychologists by Malik Badri (1979), b) Islamic Anthropology by Akbar S. Ahmed (1984), and c) Islamic Medicine by Hakim Salim Khan (1986) and Mohsin Clinic where Islamic counseling is provided from Tibb perspective. The following timeline is indicative of how IP developed in the UK (Haque, 2025).

- Late 70s: Nafsiyat Clinic in North London was opened by Jafar Kareem. However, the primary focus here was psychoanalysis from a cultural lens rather than IP.

- 1985: An-Nisa Society was established by sisters Khalida and Humera Khan for an Islamically compatible counseling service.

- Mid-90s: Islamic counseling courses started by Abdullah and Sabnam Maynard, husband and wife, and these courses were accredited by the National Health Service.
- Late 90s: Hanif Bobat and Abul Hussain ran conferences under the Ethnic Health Initiative (EHI), and from 2008 onwards, they included IP, inviting international scholars. Unfortunately, EHI ended in 2015 due to funding cuts.
- 2000: Rabia Malik developed Islamic therapy based on the ninety names of Allah (SWT) and the Quranic narratives at the Marlborough Cultural Therapy Center.
- 2008: UK clinical psychologists, Abul Wali Wardak, Rukhsana Arshad, Rasjid Skinner, created the first IP Syllabus called "Al-Ghazali Model" for local Imams, but it shifted to training the mental health clinicians and was later called Approaches to IP and Psychotherapy.
- 2009: Rasjid Skinner gave three talks on "Race and Culture" under the British Psychological Society Clinical Division roadshow.
- 2011: Sabnam Dharamse introduced an Islamic counseling module at Cambridge Muslim College (CMC), which later turned into a nine-month diploma course.
- 2015: Nasima Khanom established the IP Professionals Association, with monthly seminars on IP topics.
- 2015: INAYET was established by Yasser Ali to train Muslim therapists in the Islamic way of arbitration.
- 2016: Attempts by Rabia Malik, Shahnawaz Haque, and Rasjid Skinner to create a UK Association for IP, but did not materialize. Talat Baig established Inspirited Minds Counseling Services based on Islamic principles.
- 2017: Al Balagh Academy was established by Dr. Rafaqat Rashid based on Fiqh and medicine. Currently, Ihsaan Therapeutic Services and Al Balagh Academy are partnering to develop more IP courses.
- 2020: Cambridge Muslim College (CMC) started the IP Diploma course with Abdallah Rothman as principal and then later head of program.

Germany and the Netherlands

The psychologists in Germany and the Netherlands proposed in their chapter (Kaplick, Loucif, & Ruschoff, 2021) a top-down vs. bottom-up approach. In the top-down approach, Islamic elements are integrated into scientifically validated psychotherapies as opposed to the bottom-up approach, which involves therapies based on Islamic intellectual tradition. The top-down approach requires the use of scientifically sound and evidence-based methods, rather than constructing a new school.

In 1988, the Islamic Association of Social and Educational Professions, a platform to discuss culturally and religiously sensitive psychotherapy, was founded. This association organized 15 professional conferences between 1988 and 2019, during which there was consistent development of Islamically Integrated Psychotherapy (IIP). This included publications on the top-down approach in IP and attempts to build an international network between IP and Muslim mental health professionals. A few notable articles from this endeavor are as follows:

- Islamic Approaches to Psychology, Murken & Shah (2002).
- Medicine, Psychology, and Counseling in Islam, Ulrike Eldorfer (2007).
- Psychology, Psychotherapy, and Islam: Building an IP Theory, Shiva Khalili (2008).
- Islam and Psychology, Ruschoff & Kaplick (2018).

There are three distinct groups in Germany consisting of Muslim psychologists and psychotherapists, Islamic theologians and Imams, and psychologists of religion and their IIP Intervention focuses primarily on religious anamnesis (recollection), Amanah as a therapeutic principle, Quranic verses and hadith, the connection between image of God and image of parents, and effective use of mosques.

North America

USA

Two key factors primarily influenced the development of IP in the United States. The first was the series of annual conferences organized by the Association of American Muslim Social Scientists (AAMS), where Malik Badri presented his paper, "Dilemma of Muslim Psychologists," in 1976. The second factor was the IOK Movement, led by the IIIT in Virginia. IIIT played a crucial role in promoting Islamic perspectives across various social sciences. In 1998, their publication, the American Journal of Islamic Social Sciences, released a special issue focused on *Psychology from Islamic Perspectives*, which included a chapter by this author (Haque, 1998), titled

"Psychology and Religion: Their Relationship and Integration from an Islamic Perspective."

Several prominent names, such as Laleh Bakhtiar, Lynn Cox, and Vilayat Inayat Khan, also resonate with IP, primarily for their promotion of Sufi Psychology. A few IP-related publications in the US are as follows (Haque, 2025):

- Introducing Spirituality into Counseling and Therapy, Vilayat Inayat Khan (1982)
- Quranic Theory of Personality, Article published in Journal of Muslim Mental Health (Hisham Abu-Raiya, 2012)
- Sufi Enneagram: Secrets of the symbols unveiled (Bakhtiar, 2013)
- Principles of Islamic Psychology (Farid Yunus, 2017)
- Islamic Theoretical Orientation to Psychotherapy (Abdallah Rothman, 2018)
- Islamic Psychology: Towards a 21st Century definition, (Carrie York, 2018)
- Quranic Psychology of the Self: Islamic Moral Psychology (Laleh Bakhtiar, 2019)
- Sufi Psychology (Lynn Cox, 1997)

The Khalil Center was established in 2010 by Hooman Keshavarzi, who has published several books and articles, including "Traditional Islamic Integrated Psychotherapy" (Keshavarzi et al., 2020). One of the more recent chapters published by another scholar from Khalil Center is titled "Islamic Psychology: The Missing Link in Muslim Mental Health" (Khan, 2025). The International Association of Islamic Psychology (IAIP) was registered in Seattle, WA, in 2017; however, it does not have a physical office in the United States. IAIP offers certification courses in IP and hosts international conferences.

The Alkaram Institute, founded by Carrie York in 2018, provides a certificate program in IP and will begin offering a master's degree in this field starting in Fall 2025. Additionally, the Heart Over Mind Institute (HOME), founded by Marwa Assar in 2019, promotes IP-based psychotherapy, along with related articles and lectures.

A Synopsis of Programs

The following list includes programs that offer a variety of qualifications, ranging from doctoral and master's degrees to certificates and shorter courses. Detailed descriptions and information about each program can be found in different chapters of this book. A guideline for developing the chapters was provided to the authors by the book editor (Appendix). Readers will notice that some chapters are more comprehensive than others. Additionally, since some programs are new, not all the questions posed by the editor were included in the chapters.

Universitas Muhammadiyah Surakarta

Central Java, Indonesia

The Doctorate Program in Islamic Psychology (DPIP) was established under the Minister of Research, Technology, and Higher Education Decree No. 808 in 2022, and its first cohort was launched in 2023. The Faculty of Psychology at UMS is the first academic institution in Indonesia to formally embrace and advance IP, having hosted the 1st National Symposium of IP in 1994, followed by another in 1998, which included both psychologists and Islamic scholars. IP courses were first started in some Indonesian universities in 1994. After the 2nd National Symposium, the Faculty of Psychology redefined its vision in 1999 to further the development of IP by introducing it as a mandatory course in the undergraduate curriculum.

In 2003, UMS hosted the 1st National Congress of the Islamic Psychology Association (API) and established the Center for IP and the Center for Indigenous Psychology, which serve as platforms for research and community engagement, emphasizing the integration of Islamic and Indigenous perspectives in psychological practice.

The DPIP program focuses on three main areas: IP, educational psychology, and mental health. A key requirement for all students is the publication of articles, which is part of the curriculum. The program aims to establish IP as a reference point for the development of mental and behavioral sciences in Indonesia, a predominantly Muslim country.

Khalil Center, Usul Academy, Ibn Haldun University, Hamad Bin Khalifa University

USA, Turkiye, Qatar

The Khalil Center (KC) in the United States launched a certificate program in 2013 called TIIP. This program is based on the article by Keshavarzi and Haque (2013), titled "Outlining a Psychotherapy Model for Enhancing Muslim Mental Health within an Islamic Context." KC serves as the birthplace and primary hub for IP initiatives in the US. Additionally, it has expanded its reach to Turkey and, more recently, to Qatar.

A comprehensive publication from the center provides a detailed description of the development of TIIP, discussing the epistemological and ontological foundations of the model, as well as its practical applications in clinical mental health practice. Since the program's inception, students from multiple countries have participated in TIIP training programs held internationally. The TIIP training program is structured into three levels, designed to enhance expertise in Islamically Integrated Psychotherapy progressively.

IHU in Türkiye is a leading institution for advancing the field of IP through its Ph.D. program in Clinical Psychology. This program includes a specialization in Islamically integrated psychotherapy, which offers a comprehensive academic and clinical foundation in TIIP. Students in this concentration can develop advanced expertise in IP.

IP education expanded to Qatar with the introduction of a master's program in Counseling Psychology in 2024 at the College of Islamic Studies at HBKU. Additionally, a graduate certificate in IP and Psychotherapy, a one-year program derived from the three-year master's program in counseling psychology, also commenced in 2024. The curriculum integrates Islamic teachings with contemporary psychological studies, along with rigorous practical training.

The program is modeled after the clinical approach established at the Khalil Center and aims to serve as a key educational and clinical resource for the region. Over the next decade, the newly established department plans for significant growth, including the introduction of the region's first PhD program in Clinical and Counseling IP. Additionally, the department intends to offer a specialization in IP within the PhD in Islamic Studies, designed for individuals with theological backgrounds who wish to study in a non-clinical setting while contributing to the field of IP.

Usul Academy and the Foundations in Islamic Sciences, based in Chicago, offers an online IP Diploma Program that lasts one year and is divided into three terms. The program also includes a summer intensive session at the Süleymaniye Madrasah and the Ozbeki Spiritual Lodge in Istanbul, Türkiye. This structure allows students to participate in both academic and experiential spiritual learning. It features options for live sessions as well as additional asynchronous components, providing flexibility in the learning process.

Alkaram Institute

Virginia, USA

The Alkaram Institute is the first graduate school of IP in North America. Established as a 501(c)(3) non-profit organization, its mission is to advance

IP for the benefit of Society and to improve lives. This institute has been offering a certificate course since 2021 and starting its first master's program in 2026. While their master's program is a 2-year program with a thesis and internship component, the graduate certificate is a 1-year program created primarily for professionals already working in a field related to psychology or Islamic studies who would benefit from expanding their knowledge base of IP due to its relevance to their work. The institute's foundation is built on the personal and professional interests of its founder, exploring various definitions of IP within the context of the field.

This course was introduced in 2017 by Carrie York, the founder of the Alkaram Institute. The Master's program has a two-year curriculum that includes a thesis and an internship component. In contrast, the graduate certificate program is designed for professionals already working in fields related to psychology or Islamic studies and lasts for one year. Before the two programs at this institute, there was a course titled "Introduction to Islamic Psychology" (RELS 2570), which was the first and only class on IP at the University of Iowa.

A significant strength of the institute is its collaboration with Faculty from several prominent universities, such as George Washington University in Washington, D.C. Additionally, the program partners with institutions where its research fellows are enrolled, including Columbia University, Yale University, HBKU, IIUI, and the University of Wisconsin. The institute also has a Memorandum of Understanding (MOU) with Effat University in Jeddah, Saudi Arabia, which was signed in 2019.

International Islamic University Malaysia

Kuala Lumpur, Malaysia

The philosophy of IIUM is rooted in the Tawhidic paradigm, which emphasizes that the pursuit of knowledge should be viewed as both a continuous act of worship ('Ibadah) and a sacred trust (Amanah). The Bachelor of Human Sciences in Psychology (Honors) program was launched in 1990 and aligns with the Malaysian Qualifications Framework (MQF; 2024), ensuring that its learning outcomes are grounded in Islamic principles. Master's and PhD programs are offered within the Islamic paradigm but are not called IP. Many international students also graduated from these programs over the years and now teach IP in their countries.

The department collaborates with public and private universities, government bodies, and non-governmental organizations across Malaysia, as well as institutions in Indonesia, Thailand, Pakistan, and other countries. However, the exploration of the "Science of the Soul" within psychology faces significant resource gaps. Despite the increasing interest in integrating spiritual, metaphysical, and psychological perspectives, there is a lack of comprehensive academic references and scholarly literature on this topic, particularly in English. As part of its long-term strategy, the Department of Psychology at IIUM is launching a significant project aimed at developing authoritative reference materials for this field.

Graduates of IIUM's psychology program are highly regarded and sought after by leading organizations nationwide. They consistently receive top ratings, including a 6-star rating from Malaysian employers in terms of employability. This outstanding recognition reflects their excellent preparedness and well-rounded qualities.

Riphah International University

Islamabad, Pakistan

The Riphah Institute of Clinical and Professional Psychology (RICPP) was established in 2015 in Lahore, Pakistan. Its objective is to develop a comprehensive educational program for psychologists in response to the need for enhanced cultural sensitivity in mental health care, the integration of faith and therapy, and the addressing of gaps in professional training.

Riphah International University (RIU) in Islamabad offers a postgraduate diploma in Islamic psychotherapies for mental health. This program defines Islamic psychotherapy (IP) as a spiritually grounded and theologically consistent approach to mental health that incorporates Islamic concepts of the self and healing along with evidence-based psychological practices. The key conceptual pillars of the program include spiritual anthropology, Tazkiyah an-nafs (purification of the self), therapeutic ethics, and the use of integrated methods.

The one-year diploma is designed to provide advanced education and clinical training for individuals with a background in psychology. The program collaborates with RICPP in Lahore and the Tarbiyah Department at RIU in Islamabad. While this program is the first of its kind in Pakistan, developed by a multidisciplinary team of academicians, clinicians, and Islamic scholars, there remains a limited availability of Faculty with dual expertise in Islamic scholarship and mental health, a common challenge across many institutions.

Additionally, there is a need for culturally validated measurement tools, as well as skepticism within mainstream academic circles regarding faith-based therapies. Insufficient funding to develop the program and challenges related to program accreditation continue to be obstacles.

Despite these challenges, the program aims to expand into a full master's and doctoral program within the next decade, gain accreditation, promote the publication of faculty research in academic journals, develop multilingual training resources in Arabic, Urdu, and English, and strengthen the alum network to enhance employment outcomes.

Cambridge Muslim College

Cambridge, UK

With the fifth cohort of students, CMC started the Postgraduate Certificate of Higher Education (PgCert HE) in January 2025, in Islam and Psychology. This certificate was previously known as the Diploma in IP, which was started in 2021. The program is a training initiative rooted in an indigenous Islamic understanding of the soul. As the authors explain in their chapter, it has been "formulated from the ground up," rather than replicating prior intellectual Islamization projects. The admission process for these programs is quite competitive, with 25 to 30 students accepted each year from an applicant pool of approximately 200. Students come from various parts of the world, and their ages range from their early 20s to their 60s.

A significant focus of the program is not only to provide a comprehensive understanding of human psychology but also to create a pathway for self-healing and soul development. The training approach emphasizes a process of cultivation that begins with *takhliyya* (the cleansing or emptying of the self) before *moving on to taḥliyya* (the adorning or beautifying of the self).

The program is currently validated by the Open University (OU) as a Postgraduate Certificate (PGCert) in Higher Education in Islam and Psychology. This academic award falls within the discipline of Theology and Religious Studies and adheres to the QAA benchmarks. The certificate is conferred by the Open University.

During the validation process, the program's original title, IP Diploma, was changed to the Certificate in Islamic and Psychology to better align it with its focus on Theology and Religious Studies. The program has expanded the applicant pool by eliminating the previous requirement for a professional qualification in psychology or a related field, as well as the focus on practitioner training.

With this shift away from practitioner training, subsequent cohorts, starting in the academic year 2025-26, will no longer be eligible for certification as practitioners by the IAIP.

Charles Sturt University

Victoria, Australia

In partnership with CSU, the Islamic Studies Research Academy (ISRA) launched the Graduate Certificate in IP in 2020, making it the first accredited program of its kind in the Western world. The program was designed to align with CSU's guidelines for the Graduate Certificate, utilizing existing courses from the Master's program in Islamic Studies. IP integrates Islamic teachings with psychological practices, viewing human behavior as a complex interplay of various dimensions.

Through a MoU between ISRA and the IAMP, the program enhances the student experience by offering guest lectures, networking opportunities, and collaborative research. It has consistently attracted international students, becoming the only comprehensive accredited certificate in IP in Australia. However, the program's four-subject format limits entry-level accreditation from professional counseling bodies. To address this issue, the program plans to expand and offer a Graduate Diploma in IP and Counseling.

Avicenna Academy

Yogyakarta, Indonesia

The program is titled "Psychology as the Science of the Human Soul, Cognition, Emotion, and Behavior." It emphasizes that IP aims to promote the well-being of the human soul, viewing human life as a journey towards returning to Allah in the hereafter. Additionally, IP employs a multimethod approach that combines observations, psychodynamics, and teachings from the Quran to develop its theories.

The curriculum acknowledges the limitations of conventional psychology and redefines the discipline in alignment with the nature of human beings as creations of Allah. Although the program consists of only nine credit hours, it offers ten in-depth courses, referred to as discussions. These cover various topics, including the philosophy of science, history of science, principles of science, the dynamics of the human soul, lessons from classical scholars, and critical evaluations of major mainstream theories.

Al Balagh Academy

Bradford, United Kingdom

The IP program offers specialized courses and training designed to give students a comprehensive understanding of both Islamic teachings and modern therapeutic techniques. As the mental health needs of the Muslim community evolve, Continuous Professional Development (CPD) allows professionals to improve their skills to meet these changing demands continually. Al Balagh Academy has formed strategic partnerships with various academic and clinical institutions to facilitate professional development.

The curriculum is designed to equip students with the skills needed to support individuals facing psychological disorders from an Islamic perspective, thus contributing to the growing field of Islamic mental health. The courses employ a variety of instructional methods, including live online sessions, recorded video lectures, live webinars, discussion forums, and practical assignments, to effectively convey the material. Students also have access to the ILM Portal, which serves as a central hub for course materials, announcements, and progress tracking. A summary of the patterns and findings indicates that most students entered the course with a moderate level of knowledge and demonstrated significant improvement by the end of the training.

Académie Islam & Psychologie

Paris, France

The Académie Islam & Psychologie (AIP), in collaboration with the International Students of Islamic Psychology (ISIP) and the Al-Balkhî Institute, is dedicated to promoting IP. Their mission focuses on educating and training individuals interested in this field.

In 2023, the AIP launched two certification programs in IP. The first program is one year long and is designed for mental health professionals who wish to expand their knowledge in this area. The second program covers two years and is intended for individuals who are not mental health professionals. Additionally, the AIP has developed a program called "Awareness of Mental Health" specifically for Imams and religious leaders.

The teaching team comprises 15 international experts from diverse fields. The program offers flexible learning options, including live classes on weekends and access to recorded sessions.

Aligarh Muslim University

Aligarh, India

The Department of Psychology in collaboration with the Department of Islamic Studies, introduced an Islamic Counseling certificate in 2024. This certificate course requires a master's degree for enrolment in the program, and it emphasizes education and training in today's context, offering an integrative and practical model for the field of IP suitable for both research and training purposes.

The course explores how psychologists, counselors, social workers, and scholars of Islamic Studies who specialize in IP can assist individuals in coping with physical and psychological illnesses. The introduction of this certificate highlights the evolving nature of IP as a professional field in

India.

The program is unique in that its admission requirements include a mental ability test, academic performance scores, self-report inventories, and interviews.

Ihsaan Therapeutic Services

Bradford, UK

The program offers two parts of IP courses. The Part 1 course was first introduced in 2001 and has been offered one to three times a year since then. It was developed in response to requests from Muslim therapists who felt a disconnect between their understanding of fitra and the principles of mainstream Western psychology. In 2017, the Part 2 course was launched, featuring a significantly revised syllabus that emphasizes practical skills and specific areas of clinical work.

The ultimate goal of combining Parts 1 and 2 is to train psychological therapists who are proficient in working within an Islamic framework for both diagnosing and treating psychological disorders, serving both Muslims and non-Muslims.

While the courses are not accredited by a government entity—which is not a requirement in the UK—they were accredited by IAIP during Prof. Badri's lifetime. Additionally, the courses are expected to receive accreditation from the UK Association for IP, which is currently being established.

There are no examinations, essays, or assignments in this program. Instead, the emphasis is on developing case studies in small groups. The author acknowledges that the courses could reach a broader audience and be more cost-effective if offered online. However, he believes that high-quality clinical training can only be effectively delivered in person.

Stanford University

Palo Alto, USA

The IP course at Stanford University started in 2020 and is the first of its kind offered in a Western psychology program. It is taught annually as part of the mainstream undergraduate curriculum at a secular university by a core faculty member. It is jointly provided by the Department of Psychiatry within the School of Medicine and the Center for Comparative Studies in Race and Ethnicity (cross-listed as CSRE 144A) under the School of Humanities and Sciences. The course aims to incorporate Muslim voices and perspectives from Islamic heritage into the field of psychology.

Unlike typical psychology courses that focus primarily on psychological principles and psychopathology from a Western perspective, this course integrates elements from the Quran, the Sunnah, and principles of historical Islamic philosophy and tradition. A significant focus is the comparison of Islamic and Eurocentric methodologies and the exploration of the ontological structure of the human psyche within both frameworks.

A key feature of this course is its engagement with leading scholars and practitioners in the fields of Muslim mental health and IP.

Shifa Tamir Millat University

Islamabad, Pakistan

The Muslim Psychology course has been taught in several Pakistani universities since 1991, with almost the same content, and was later approved by the HEC in 2006. The contents contained the works of early Muslim scholars on understanding human nature, personality, and other psychological concepts. It was in 2007 that the International Islamic University Islamabad (IIUI) first offered the Muslim Psychology course as an option at the undergraduate level, and it became a required course in master's and doctoral programs. While this course remained at the university level, a five-day IP certificate course was offered jointly with the International Association of Islamic Psychologists (IAIP).

The authors of this chapter examine the integration of IP with modern psychology and discuss the views that suggest complete separation between the two disciplines or merging Islamic principles with contemporary psychology. The findings from their qualitative study of faculty members in two universities suggest the need for an inclusive curriculum that reflects diverse human experiences. They emphasized the advantages of incorporating IP into university programs, which can enhance cultural sensitivity, promote ethical responsibility, and contribute to the development of well-rounded psychologists.

To establish IP as a well-respected field, the authors recommend introducing IP courses at both undergraduate and postgraduate levels, integrated within mainstream psychology programs. The undergraduate course in IP introduces students to the historical roots of psychological knowledge. It highlights the contributions of classical Muslim philosophers to *ilm-al-nafs*, or the science of the soul.

Postgraduate programs aim to deepen students' understanding of Islam's cosmological framework and its connections to scientific human psychology. They also stress the importance of applying an Islamic perspective in clinical practice. For instance, the Clinical Psychology

Institute at Shifa Tameer-e-Millat University offers IP as a foundational course within its Master of Science in Clinical Psychology (MSCP) Program. This includes courses such as Islamic Perspectives in Psychopathology and Psychotherapy. Furthermore, for the PhD in Clinical Psychology, courses like Islamic Perspectives of Integrated Psychotherapy and Islamic Perspectives in Mental Health and Psychopathology have been offered since Fall 2022.

Islamic Psychology Association

Iran

The undergraduate-level courses in IP began in 2003, with a PhD program in Quran and Psychology introduced in 2007. Master's degrees in different specializations of IP were introduced at various universities in 2010, 2011, 2012, 2013, 2016, and 2020. IP programs are currently available at a minimum of nine universities, which include two undergraduate programs, six master's degrees, and one doctoral degree. Additionally, two seminaries offer programs that specifically focus on the intersection of Islam and psychology, providing both master's and doctoral degrees.

Admission requirements typically include passing an entrance examination that assesses proficiency in several areas, including specialized Arabic language skills for interpreting religious texts, an understanding of the Quran and Hadith, psychology, psychological teachings found in the Quran and Hadith, and the philosophy of psychology. The curriculum features specialized courses, electives, and thesis requirements. Public universities confer degrees, and these degrees are recognized, thereby enhancing employability in various fields.

The field of IP was developed at the Master's level by a group of Islamic psychologists within the Psychology Commission of the Specialized Council for the Development and Promotion of Human Sciences. The Ministry of Science, Research, and Technology officially recognizes this discipline. The main objective of the IP curriculum is to ensure mastery of the fundamentals, teachings, and concepts of IP as outlined in primary Islamic texts and by Muslim scholars. Three key factors emphasized in IP programs are addressing theoretical gaps, enhancing mental health, and integrating science with religion.

IP was first offered at Shahed State University in Tehran. Currently, Baqir al-Uloom, a private university in Qom, is also seeking approval for its IP programs. Public universities typically offer these programs free of charge, while private universities usually charge around $3,000.

IP presents various career opportunities both now and in the future.

Potential job positions include roles at research and investigation centers, employment in government organizations focused on mental health, welfare, and social services, as well as involvement in cultural and social development programs that promote Islamic values.

Istanbul Zaim University

Istanbul, Turkiye

IP courses are available through the Master's program in Spiritual Counseling and Guidance (SCG), as well as the Master's and PhD programs in Philosophy and Religious Sciences (PRS) departments. The SCG program aims to train professionals with both theoretical and practical knowledge in psychology, enabling them to integrate spirituality into therapeutic settings. Although IP is not a standalone program, the Psychology of Religion and Spirituality Lab was established in 2025 in collaboration with the ISIP student club and the ISIP community. IZU offers a variety of graduate-level courses in IP, and the therapeutic strategies seek to cultivate inner harmony and moral excellence in alignment with the ethical and spiritual vision of the Qur'an and Sunnah.

In 2019, IZU launched the "Counseling from an Islamic Theoretical Orientation" Certificate Program in collaboration with the IAIP, under the leadership of Malik Badri, who worked there from 2017 to 2021. Notable publications from the IZU program include Badri's (2021) *Emotional Aspects in the Life of the Prophets*, his compilation on *Cultural Adaptation and Islamization of Psychology*, and the coauthored *Trilingual Dictionary of Psychiatry and Psychology* (Dictionary Annafssany). Dr. Kaya-Göktepe also translated Malik Badri's commentary on Abu Zayd al-Balkhî's *The Sustenance of the Soul*.

A significant issue with IP in Turkey is that the term "psychology of religion" is often associated solely with Islamic content, thereby preventing the establishment of an independent field of IP. For IP to be recognized as a distinct field, well-structured Master's and doctoral programs are recommended.

Conclusion

IP has intrigued Muslims for centuries and has experienced significant growth in recent decades across various parts of the world. A key reason for this surge is the dissatisfaction with mainstream methodologies that often conflict with the Islamic worldview. Additionally, scholars in many regions have made notable efforts towards this discipline. Indigenous psychologies have emerged globally, emphasizing both cultural and religious perspectives, even in the West. This chapter aims to provide readers with an overview of the developments occurring in many parts of the world, which may not be widely known. Citations not listed in the references can be found in the book by Haque & Rothman (2021). Additionally, a summary of expanding international programs in IP highlights a promising future for both the field and its students.

CHAPTER TWO

DOCTORATE PROGRAM IN ISLAMIC PSYCHOLOGY

Universitas Muhammadiyah Surakarta

Central Java, Indonesia

Taufik Kasturi

Introduction

Muhammadiyah is the largest reformist Islamic organization in Indonesia, established on November 18, 1912, in Yogyakarta province. Its influence has since expanded globally, with branches in 29 countries. Muhammadiyah engages in various sectors, notably health, education, and social services. In the health sector, it manages numerous hospitals throughout Indonesia, while in education, it oversees thousands of institutions, including 170 universities both domestically and internationally. One notable institution is Universitas Muhammadiyah Surakarta (UMS).

Located in Surakarta, Central Java, UMS has evolved into a significant educational institution with 12 faculties and 73 departments, serving an active student body of approximately 40,000. The Faculty of

Psychology, founded in 1983, plays a crucial role within this framework, offering four academic programs: a Bachelor's in Psychology, Professional Psychology, Master's in Psychology, and a Doctorate in Psychology, with a collective student enrolment of about 1,850.

The Faculty of Psychology at UMS has been pivotal in pioneering IP in Indonesia, recognized as the first academic entity to formally embrace and advance this discipline. This commitment is highlighted by several key historical milestones, such as hosting the 1st National Symposium on IP from November 11–13, 1994. The symposium's theme—"The Concept of Psychology with an Islamic Insight as an Alternative Approach to Modern Psychology" (Thoyibi & Ngemron, 1996)—attracted scholars from psychology, religious studies, philosophy, and education, as well as participants from various universities, social organizations, and religious institutions across Indonesia (Bastaman, 2005).

Four years later, on February 12–13, 1998, the faculty organized the 2nd National Symposium on IP, themed "Sharia Principles in Islamic Psychology." This gathering once again assembled leading psychologists and Islamic scholars to explore the integration of Sharia principles into psychological research methodologies. The symposium notably discussed how traditional research methods could be adapted to comply with Sharia. For instance, in observational studies, Sharia mandates avoiding morally objectionable contexts; therefore, studying a naturist community would require non-participatory observation to uphold these principles.

Additionally, the symposium critically evaluated qualitative research techniques, such as verstehen analysis, suggesting that while this method is useful for interpreting data, its application must align with Sharia principles depending on the research's thematic content. These discussions emphasized the importance of crafting a framework for IP that respects both academic standards and Sharia guidelines.

Following the 2nd National Symposium on IP, the Faculty of Psychology at UMS redefined its vision to further the development of IP. This strategic initiative was formalized in 1999 with the introduction of IP as a mandatory course in the undergraduate curriculum. Additional courses, such as *"Mu'amalah in Psychological Perspective"* and *"Islamic Character Development,"* were later incorporated to deepen the integration of Islamic principles into psychological education. However, the extent of this integration in other courses largely depended on individual lecturers' approaches and interpretations.

Five years later, on October 12–13, 2003, the Faculty of Psychology at UMS hosted the 1st National Congress of the IP Association

(API). This congress brought together experts in psychology, health, and Islamic studies from across Indonesia. It served as the founding moment for the IP Association, which has since expanded its reach to numerous provinces throughout the country. API convenes every five years to elect new leadership and establish increasingly progressive visions for the advancement of IP.

In 2022, UMS launched the Doctorate Program in Islamic Psychology (DPIP), reflecting its longstanding commitment to this field. This program is the first doctoral level offering in psychology in Central Java and the only one in Indonesia dedicated exclusively to Islamic Psychology. The inauguration of DPIP marks a significant shift from merely hosting conferences and workshops to establishing advanced academic studies in this specialized discipline. To further promote the growth of Islamic Psychology, UMS has also created the Center for Islamic Psychology and the Center for Indigenous Psychology. These centers serve as platforms for research and community engagement, focusing on the integration of Islamic and Indigenous perspectives in psychological practice. In November 2024, the Center for Islamic Psychology published a pioneering book titled *"Pillars of Islam in the Perspective of Psychology,"* authored by faculty members and doctoral students. This publication underscores UMS's ongoing efforts to enrich academic discourse and contribute to the global advancement of IP.

Profile

The DPIP was officially established under the Minister of Research, Technology, and Higher Education Decree No. 808/E/O/2022, dated November 2, 2022. The program initially focused on two primary areas: IP and Educational Psychology, both of which were in high demand among prospective students, primarily academics from various Islamic universities. Recognizing the evolving needs of the field, DPIP introduced a third area of interest—Mental Health—in its second year.

In its inaugural year (2023), 18 individuals applied to the program, with 7 being accepted. All students in the first cohort were female, representing diverse professional backgrounds, including lecturers, employees of educational institutions, and authors. By the second year (2024), the program received 25 applications, again accepting 7 students, who included lecturers, researchers, and hospital staff. The program benefits from the expertise of scholars in IP, Educational Psychology, and Mental Health from across Indonesia.

DPIP graduates are expected to advance the conceptual and theoretical frameworks of IP through original research. It is anticipated that their findings will be disseminated through scholarly publications in prestigious international journals.

Vision

To become a leading center for doctoral education in IP that drives changes.

Aim

To be a department that nurtures doctoral scholars proficient in integrating psychology with Islamic principles, fostering inter, multi, and trans-disciplinary research, which will be disseminated through national and international scientific publications.

Strategy

Enhancing the program's reputation at national and international levels by promoting research and scholarly publications in IP.

Curriculum

Philosophical Basis

The curriculum of the DPIP is based on integrating psychology with Islamic principles, viewing this endeavor as an act of worship to Allah *Subhanahu Wa Ta'ala* (SWT). This philosophy is encapsulated in the "Discourse of Science and Islam," with the aim of cultivating scholars who serve Allah SWT and positively contribute to the world.

The values promoted by DPIP are "transcendence, liberation, and humanization."

Transcendence encompasses the principles of monotheism and worship. Monotheism involves recognizing Allah SWT as the sole and ultimate object of worship, embodying all His unique attributes (Utsaimin, 2004). Worship requires submission, obedience, and humility before Allah SWT, in accordance with the guidance of the Prophet Muhammad PBUH (Al Qardhawi, 1979).

Liberation involves the pursuit of knowledge and *istishlah*, or the seeking of goodness. In this context, knowledge is characterized as systematic, rational-transcendental, impartial, critical, innovative, creative, and open, and is considered an act of devotion to Allah SWT.

The third value, humanization, includes concepts such as trust, justice, and caliphate (stewardship). Trust is linked to honesty and responsibility, justice emphasizes fairness and the promotion of human welfare, and the idea of caliphate represents the elevation of human nature and dignity.

Sociological Basis

The curriculum development for the DPIP is shaped by extensive consultations with various stakeholders, including members of psychology associations, academic faculty, potential employers, and the wider community. This curriculum addresses a significant societal demand in Indonesia for the application of IP in key areas such as personal development, institutional management (particularly in Islamic schools and boarding schools), and community development. As the country with the largest Muslim population in the world, Indonesia demonstrates a strong cultural preference for values rooted in Islam over other contemporary frameworks.

Psychological Basis

The development of the DPIP curriculum considers the needs, interests, and competencies necessary for advancing Psychology from an Islamic Perspective Interest Group (PPIG). This process involves a thorough evaluation of the expertise of available human resources, the program's internal capabilities, and the aspirations of the Muslim community for an Islamic framework in psychology.

Legal Basis

The legal foundation for the curriculum of the DPIP is based on several key regulations. These include:

1. Regulation of the Minister of Education and Culture Number 73 of 2013, which addresses the implementation of the National Qualification Framework (KKNI) in higher education.

2. Regulation of the Minister of Research, Technology, and Higher Education Number 44 of 2015, which sets forth the National Standards for Higher Education.

3. An amendment to the previous regulation, found in the Regulation of the Minister of Research, Technology, and Higher Education Number 50 of 2018.

Furthermore, the curriculum is in line with the Regulation of the Minister of Education and Culture Number 3 of 2020, regarding National Standards for Higher Education (SNDIKTI), and the 2018 Guidelines for Developing Higher Education Curriculum in the Industrial Era 4.0.

To ensure alignment with national and institutional standards, the Curriculum Development Team (CDT) reviewed the Decree issued by the Association of Indonesian Psychology Higher Education Providers (plate number 1) Number 03/Kep/(plate number 1)/2019. This decree amended the Core Curriculum for Doctoral Psychology Study Programs outlined in SK (plate number 1) Number 03/Kep/(plate number 1)/2014.

The curriculum also complies with the Internal Quality Assurance System (SPMI) at the university level, which consists of eight Quality Standards (SM). Specifically, the curriculum is guided by SM-UMS-01 on Graduate Competency Standards and SM-UMS-02 on Learning Content Standards. This ensures that the program meets institutional expectations for academic quality and student outcomes.

Values developed

The fundamental values guiding the development of the DPIP are rooted in Islamic teachings as outlined in the *al-Qur'an* and *al-Sunnah al-Maqbulah*. The program emphasizes core values, including *tawheed* (the oneness of God), *'ilm* (knowledge), *amanah* (trust), *'adl* (justice), caliphate, and worship. These values are integrated within a framework of belief, values, and character.

As part of UMS, the Faculty of Psychology has shifted from an input-based educational model to an outcome-based education framework. In this novel approach, the graduate profile serves as the foundation for designing the curriculum and related activities. This graduate profile is articulated into a set of learning outcomes that encompass attitudes and values, knowledge, and skills. Within this framework, essential values for program development include *tawheed*, *worship*, *caliphate*, *isti'marah* (stewardship), *shiddiq* (truthfulness), *amanah*, *tableegh* (communication of truth), and *fathonah* (wisdom).

Tawheed is a fundamental belief that underpins all aspects of the academic community. It represents the belief in the oneness of Allah SWT in His names, deeds, and attributes (Utsaimin, 2023). This belief acknowledges that Allah SWT is the creator and sustainer of the entire universe and the only being deserving of worship. Additionally, it encompasses the belief in the Day of Resurrection and the afterlife, as reported by Allah SWT in His books through the intermediaries of His messengers and angels (Asy Syaikh, 2015).

Worship, *caliph*ate, and *isti'marah* represent the essential functions of human existence, which include relationships with Allah SWT, fellow humans, and the natural world. *Worship* signifies devotion and submission to Allah SWT; *caliph*ate entails the responsibilities of human leadership and stewardship; *and isti'marah* emphasizes efforts to sustain and prosper the Earth. These three functions are inherently interconnected and inseparable (Mustaqim, 2024).

All academic and institutional activities aim to develop the attitudes, values, knowledge, and skills necessary for fulfilling essential roles in society. Initiatives focused on advancing science, technology, and human resources are consistently aligned with these fundamental aspects of human existence (Sobron et al., 2017). To effectively support these roles, individuals must embody key virtues such as fairness, honesty, reliability, empathy, and a commitment to helping others—qualities that are deeply rooted in Islamic teachings.

Interest and Research Focus

Islamic Psychology

This area of research allows students to examine psychological concepts and theories that are derived from the *Qur'an*, *Sunnah*, and other Islamic literature. Key themes include the development of ideas such as *akhlaqul karimah* (noble character), *ridho* (contentment), *ikhlas* (sincerity), and the aspect of *tawakkal* (trust in Allah) as strategies for coping with stress (Taufik, Dumpratiwi, & Ramadhanti, 2023; Taufik & Ibrahim, 2019), among others.

Educational Psychology

This research area focuses on helping students understand the dynamics of teaching and learning within educational environments. It explores learning capacities in relation to developmental stages and incorporates Islamic values, such as *tarbawi* learning methods, the *fitra* (innate human nature) paradigm, *aqeel baligh* education (education for intellectual and spiritual maturity), the Islamic concept of human development, and the dynamics of Qur'anic memorization (Taufik et al., 2023), among others.

Mental Health

This area focuses on research related to assessment, diagnosis, and intervention aimed at understanding and treating psychological disorders. It also seeks to improve self-adjustment skills and foster personal development based on Islamic values. Key topics include the connection between prayer and mental health (Suseno, 2024; Rahmanto et al., 2024), the development of the concept of *tazkiyatun nafs* (purification of the soul), and the *fitra* paradigm. Additionally, it explores Islamic perspectives on what it means to be "healthy" or "sick," among other subjects.

Graduate Profile

1. Educators. Graduates are expected to become educators and lecturers in psychology, proficient in developing and teaching contemporary PPIG.
2. Supervisory Researchers. Graduates are equipped to serve as research supervisors, coordinating projects in IP on both national and international scales.
3. Scientists. Graduates are prepared to become distinguished psychologists, producing scholarly work that integrates contemporary psychology with Islamic values.

Curriculum Map Matrix

Table 1

Curriculum Map Matrix of Doctorate Program in IP

No	Semester	CH	Code	Subjects
MK1		3	DPS3231301	Islamic Worldview
MK2	I	3	DPS3231302	Research Method: Mixed Methods & Systematic Literature Review
MK3		3	DPS3231303	Article Writing
MK4		3	DPS3231304	Islamic Psychology: A Critical Analysis
MK5	II		DPS3231305	Contextual Educational Psychology
MK6			DPS3231312	Mental Health
MK7		5	DPS3231306	The Proposal Seminar
MK8		3	DPS3231307	Instrument Seminar
MK9	III	4	DPS3231308	Collecting Data Data Analysis
MK10	IV	10	DPS3231309	Article Publication
MK11	V	5	DPS3231310	Research Results Seminar Thesis Eligibility Assessment
MK12	VI	10	DPS3231311	Viva Voce

DOCTORATE PROGRAM IN ISLAMIC PSYCHOLOGY

Curriculum Flow Diagram

Figure 1

Curriculum Flow 1st to 6th Semester

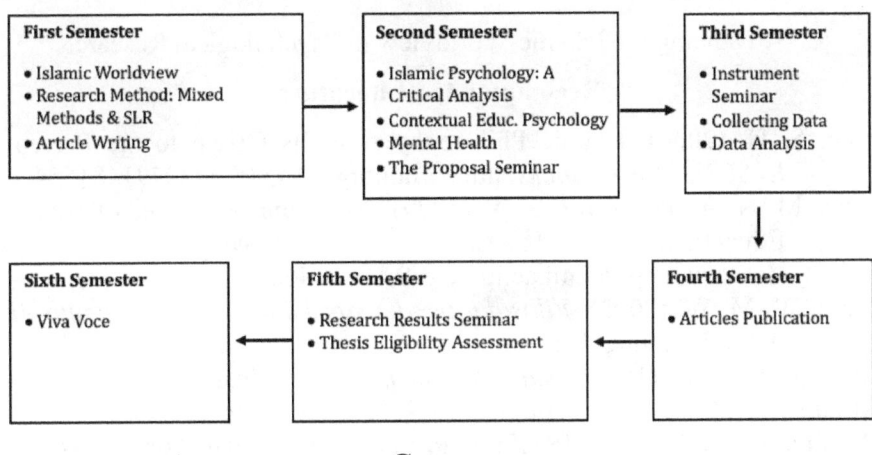

Courses

Islamic Worldview

Description. The Islamic Worldview represents a Muslim's perspective on reality, offering a comprehensive and holistic understanding of existence. Unlike views that rely solely on empirical observation or rational experiences, the Islamic Worldview goes beyond these limitations. It encompasses both al-dunya (the temporal world) and al-akhirah (the eternal hereafter), highlighting their interconnectedness and inseparability. The afterlife is of profound significance, representing humanity's ultimate and eternal destination.

This course encourages students to critically reflect on various psychological concepts and analyze them through the lens of authentic religious understanding, grounded in the Qur'an and the Sunnah. By engaging in this analysis, students will learn to integrate psychological principles within a framework based on Islamic teachings.

Content

1. The Tradition of Knowledge within the Civilization of Tawheed
2. The Historical Evolution and Emergence of the Concept of Worldview
3. Characteristics of Islamic and Western Worldviews
4. The Conceptual Framework of the Islamic Worldview

5. The Transition from Worldview to Scientific Paradigm
6. The Role of Sharia in the Development of the Human Soul
7. A Comparative Analysis of Western and Islamic Psychological Worldviews
8. Advancing the Islamic Worldview in Psychological Research

Recommended Literature

Nasr, S. H. (2006). Islamic Philosophy from Its Origin to the Present. In *SUNY Press eBooks*. https://doi.org/10.1515/9780791481554

Attas, M. N. A., & Ashraf, S. A. (1979). Aims and objectives of Islamic Education. In *Medical Entomology and Zoology*. http://ci.nii.ac.jp/ncid/BA37764662

Daud, W. M. W. (2003). *Filasafat pendidikan Islam Syed M. Naquib Al-Attas.* Bandung: Mizan.

Al-Attas, S. M. N. (1995). *Islam dan filsafat sains*. Mizan.

Al-Attas, S. M. N. (1981). *Islam dan sekularisme*. Pustaka.

Husaini, A. (2013). Filsafat Ilmu: Perspektif Barat dan Islam. *Jakarta: Penerbit Gema Insan.*

Al-Attas, S. M. N. (2001). *Risalah untuk Kaum Muslimin.* Kuala Lumpur: ISTAC.

Muslih, K. (2021). *Worldview Islam.* Gontor: Unida

Daud, W. M. N. W. (2019). *Budaya Ilmu: Satu Penjelasan.* Singapura: Pustaka Nasional Pte Ltd.

Islamic Psychology: A Critical Analysis

<u>Description</u>. The IP course covers a wide range of topics, exploring psychological concepts and theories based on the al-Qur'an and al-Sunnah, while also critically analyzing contemporary psychological theories. The course aims to identify the similarities and differences between modern psychological paradigms and the core principles of Islam. Its primary objective is to develop students' critical thinking skills for evaluating Western psychological theories through an Islamic perspective. A key component of the course will be for students to write book reviews of works authored by experts in IP.

Content

1. Islamic Psychology: Past, Present, and Future
2. Human Potential as Viewed Through the Fitra Paradigm
3. The Delusion of Science
4. Islamic Psychological Critique of Established Psychological

Schools
5. Maqasid Qur'ani
6. Qur'anic Perspectives on Cognition, Emotion, and Behavior
7. Islamic Personality: Structure, Dynamics, and Typology
8. Personality Disorders in Islam

Recommended Literature

Badri, M. (2016). *Dilemma of Muslim psychologists.*
Haque, A. & Mohamed, Y. (2021). *Psychology of Personality: Islamic Perspectives* (Kindle Edition). Washington: International Association of Islamic Psychology.
Badri, M. (2024). *Abu Zayd al-Balkhi's Sustenance of the Soul: The Cognitive Behavior Therapy of a Ninth Century Physician (7th edition).* Washington: International Institute of Islamic Thought.
Al Ghazali, I. (2021). *The Alchemy of Happiness.* Mumbai: Grapevine India
Utz, A. (2013). *Psychology from the Islamic Perspective.* Riyadh: International Islamic Publishing House.
Taufik, T., Prihartanti, N., Daliman, D., Karyani, U., & Purwandari, E. (2023). Be alone without being lonely: Strategies to improve quality of life for an elderly Muslim living in nursing homes. *Current Psychology, 1,* 1-7.
Taufik, T., Kurniawan, R., Abdullah, H., Ibrahim, R. (2019). Preserving Qur'an through Blinds' Eyes: Self-Regulation of Blind People in Memorizing the Qur'an. *Journal of Disability and Religion, 1,* 1-12.

Contextual Educational Psychology

Description. The Contextual Educational Psychology course provides students with a thorough understanding of contextual theories and perspectives, enabling them to analyze contemporary educational issues in depth. These issues range from challenges within family dynamics to those impacting broader societal contexts in Indonesia and the global community. The course takes a multidisciplinary approach, integrating Islamic, indigenous, and Western perspectives to examine educational challenges. By the end of this course, students are expected to propose alternative solutions to these issues, using a framework that harmonizes Islamic principles with indigenous values.

Content

1. Introduction to Contextual Educational Psychology
2. Western Psychological Theories and Their Implications for

Contextual Education
3. Indigenous Psychology and Its Implications for Contextual Education
4. Islamic Psychology and Its Implications for Contextual Education
5. Current Educational Contexts: The Digital Era, E-learning, Artificial Intelligence, and Their Implications for Learning Processes
6. Educational Challenges and Contextual Alternative Solutions
7. Literature Review of Educational Challenges and Analytical Solutions

Recommended Literature

Bronfenbrenner, U. (1979). The ecology of human development: Experiments by nature and design. *Harvard university press.*

Neal, J. W., & Neal, Z. P. (2013). Nested or networked? Future directions for ecological systems theory. *Social development, 22*(4), 722-737.

Stevens-Fulbrook, P. (2020). *Vygotsky, Piaget and Bloom: The Definitive Guide to their Educational Theories with Examples of How they can be Applied.* Paul Stevens-Fulbrook.

Iqbal, N., & Skinner, R. (2021). Islamic psychology: Emergence and current challenges. *Archive for the Psychology of Religion, 43(*1), 65-77.

Kirschner, S. R. (2019). Indigenous psychology compared to what? Some complexities of culture, language, and social life.

Quin, D. (2017). Longitudinal and contextual associations between teacher–student relationships and student engagement: A systematic review. *Review of educational research, 87*(2), 345-387.

Research Methods: Mixed Methods & Systematic Literature Review

Description. The Research Methods course offers a solid foundation for students to engage in research using systematic, objective, sustainable, and contemporary methodologies. The course emphasizes Mixed Methods and SLR, covering quantitative (both experimental and non-experimental), qualitative, and integrated mixed-methods approaches. Students will gain both theoretical knowledge and practical skills essential for conducting rigorous research that meets the standards of academic inquiry.

Content

1. Quantitative Approaches
2. Qualitative Approaches

3. Mixed Methods
4. SLR
5. Protocol Development for SLR
6. Applications of SLR in Islamic Psychology
7. Critical Appraisal of Research Studies

Recommended Literature

Creswell, J.W., & Creswell, J.D. (2020). *Research Design: Qualitative, Quantitative, and Mixed Methods Approaches (5th Edition)*. London: Sage

Shaughnessy, J.J., Zechmeister, E.B., & Zechmeister, J.S. (2014). *Research Methods in Psychology (10th Edition)*. New York: McGraw Hill

Boland, A., Cherry, M.G., & Dickson, R. (2017). *Doing a Systematic Review: A Student's Guide, Second Edition*. Washington DC: Sage

Booth, A., Sutton, A., Clowes, M., & Martyn-StJames (2022). *Systematic Approaches to a Successful Literature Review, Third Edition*. London: Sage

Gough, D., Oliver, S., & Thomas, J. (2017). *An Introduction to Systematic Reviews, Second Edition*. London: Sage

Writing Articles

<u>Description</u>. The Writing Articles course offers a thorough overview of the scientific writing process. It covers essential steps such as identifying research reports, generating ideas, drafting, revising, submitting, and publishing manuscripts. The course places a strong emphasis on ethical standards and established guidelines for scientific writing, equipping students to contribute scholarly articles to reputable national and international journals. By the end of this course, students are expected to have successfully submitted articles to prestigious scientific journals.

Content

1. Concept, Scope, and Purpose of Scientific Writing
2. Types of Scientific Publications
3. Ethics in Scientific Writing
4. Characteristics of a Scientific Writer
5. The Recognition Process in Scientific Publication
6. Plagiarism: Definitions, Forms, and Prevention
7. Understanding the Role of Editors and Reviewers

8. Stages of the Scientific Writing Process
9. Drafting Scientific Manuscripts
10. Submission of Scientific Manuscripts

Recommended Literature

Belcher, W. L. (2009). *Writing Your Journal Article in Twelve Weeks: A Guide to Academic Publishing Success.* London: Sage Publication Ltd

Shon, P. C. H. (2015). *How to Read Journal Articles in the Social Sciences: A Very Practical Guide for Students (Student Success) (2nd Edition).* London: Sage Publication Ltd

Sutanto, L. (2020). *Kiat jitu menembus jurnal internasional terindeks scopus.* Jakarta: Gramedia

Tim Penulis. (2023). *Panduan penulisan proposal disertasi, disertasi, dan publikasi artikel ilmiah.* Surakarta: MUP 3.

Taufik, T., Dumpratiwi, A. N., Ramadhanti, D. H. (2022). From suffering to thriving: Faith In destiny as a resilience strategy of Muslims with post-accident physical disabilities. *Cogent Psychology, 9*: 2045806.

Taufik, T., & Ibrahim, R. (2019). Making sense of disaster: Affinity to God as a coping strategy of Muslim refugees in Central Sulawesi. *Journal of Loss and Trauma, 1,* 1-13

Taufik, T., Dumpratiwi, A.N., Prihartanti, N., & Daliman, D. (2021). Muslim elderly well-being: Participation in religious activities, family support, and happiness. *The Open Psychology Journal, 14,* 76-82

Discussion

The DPIP aims to develop concepts and theories in IP through research and scientific publications. This development is intended to create psychological theories that align with the values of the Qur'an and Sunnah. Currently, the field of Psychology is predominantly influenced by Western perspectives, which may not fully align with Islamic values (Badri, 2016). Therefore, it is essential for Muslims to formulate psychological theories and concepts that are harmonious with Islamic teachings (Al Attas, 2001).

The program involves students and lecturers in various activities, including discussions, lectures, research, and the publication of scientific works. These activities are designed to generate new concepts and theories that contribute to the advancement of IP.

The DPIP has several strategic goals for developing IP. One primary goal is to create new theories in IP based on a series of discussions, literature reviews, and empirical research. Another objective is to encourage the rise of Muslim scholars who are dedicated to studying and advancing IP. Additionally, the program seeks to increase the number of reference materials in IP, including books and articles.

To achieve these goals, the DPIP focuses on developing psychological theories that are aligned with the Qur'an and Sunnah, which are regarded as the firm foundation for scientific development stemming from Allah SWT. While human research and opinions may contain errors, the Qur'an and authentic Sunnah are considered unequivocally true. Thus, research findings that align with the Qur'an and Sunnah can be accepted and further developed, while those contradicting these sources should be rejected or disregarded.

Another important aspect is supporting the development of IP by ensuring that students master the Islamic worldview. This course aims to cultivate the understanding that Muslims should embrace perspectives consistent with the Qur'an and Sunnah. This awareness forms the basis for developing concepts and theories through research and scientific publications, enabling students to prioritize and evaluate how accurately Islamic sources address human life problems.

Furthermore, the research conducted by both lecturers and students aims to integrate psychology with Islam. Based on these findings, new theories of IP will emerge that correspond to Islamic values and the needs of contemporary society.

Conclusion

DPIP offers a Ph.D. program for psychology scholars to actively contribute to the advancement of IP at the doctoral level. The development of IP aims to provide guidance for the progress of psychological practices that align with the values of the Qur'an and Sunnah. This initiative seeks to position IP on par with, or even above, other branches of psychology, establishing it as a key reference for the entire field of mental and behavioral sciences.

This program highlights that IP has been developed at all educational levels, including undergraduate, master's, and doctoral programs. In contrast to other psychology schools, where theoretical frameworks dominate, IP can stand as an independent academic discipline while also serving as a meaningful discourse. In a country with the largest Muslim population in the world, such as Indonesia, the role of IP is crucial for the growth and development of Muslim individuals, families, institutions, and even the nation's character.

CHAPTER THREE

---·❀·---

TRADITIONAL ISLAMICALLY INTEGRATED PSYCHOTHERAPY (TIIP)
and its accompanying Certificate, Diploma, and Degree Programs Worldwide

Sena Aycan, Hooman Keshavarz, & Fahad Khan

Introduction

This chapter offers an overview of the origins and development of TIIP along with its associated academic programs. The TIIP model, first published in 2013, was designed to create a framework for integrating Islamic principles into psychological practice. Since its inception, the model has evolved and is now taught in various forms around the world. These developments have resulted in a three-level certification program for Muslim mental health practitioners, an online diploma program offered by Usul Academy, and the first graduate program in Counseling (Islamic) Psychology at the College of Islamic Studies, Hamad bin Khalifa University (HBKU). This paper will detail the curricula, course study plans, and objectives of these programs.

TIIP: Origin and Development

TIIP was first introduced in 2013 in a seminal article by Keshavarzi and

Haque, titled "Outlining a Psychotherapy Model for Enhancing Muslim Mental Health within an Islamic Context." This publication established the basis for an Islamically integrated approach to psychotherapy, drawing on the contributions of early Muslim scholars. The article addressed the pressing need for a culturally sensitive and religiously congruent model of mental health care for Muslims, a need that had long been overlooked in mainstream psychology.

The Khalil Center in the United States serves as the birthplace and primary hub for the development and application of TIIP. Building on their 2013 publication, Keshavarzi and Khan further refined the model and officially named it "TIIP." The use of the term "traditional" underscores its foundation in Sunni theology and its connection to the longstanding Islamic intellectual tradition (Keshavarzi & Khan, 2018).

In 2020, TIIP released its first comprehensive publication in the form of a book. This book provided an in-depth discussion of the model's epistemological and ontological foundations, as well as its practical applications in clinical mental health practice (Keshavarzi et al., 2020). It became a cornerstone for practitioners and scholars, offering valuable insights into how TIIP integrates Islamic spiritual teachings with contemporary psychotherapy techniques. The publication featured contributions from various experts in the field of IP, further enhancing its scope and impact. In recent years, several publications have contributed to the development and dissemination of TIIP. Among them are The Islamic Workbook for Managing Anxiety (Keshavarzi et al., 2024) and The Islamic Workbook for Religious OCD (Keshavarzi et al., 2022), both of which apply the TIIP model to specific psychological disorders through the integration of Islamic spiritual practices and evidence-based therapeutic techniques. Additionally, peer-reviewed chapters and journal articles have further explored the application of TIIP in clinical contexts, solidifying its place within the field of IP (Khan et al., 2023a; Khan et al., 2023; Khan & Keshavarzi, 2023).

At Khalil Center, the TIIP model has become the primary therapeutic approach for treating a variety of psychological disorders, such as trauma, depression, anxiety, OCD, and relational problems. Its unique integration of Islamic spirituality and contemporary psychology makes it particularly effective in addressing the mental health needs of Muslim communities. A year-long clinical outcome study involving five clinicians and 107 patients across 420 sessions demonstrated the empirical utility and validity of TIIP for use with Muslim patients (Khan et al., 2023b).

Launch and International Expansion of TIIP Training Programs

The recent revival of IP has led to a growing recognition of the importance of spirituality and its integration into psychotherapy. This increased interest has spurred the development of Islamically integrated approaches. In response to this demand, the Khalil School of IP & Research, which serves as the research and training arm of Khalil Center, launched a structured three-level TIIP training program.

The first TIIP training session took place at the Khalil Center's facility in the United States, involving practitioners associated with the center. This initial training established the foundation for a structured approach that combines Islamic spiritual teachings with modern psychological practices.

In 2021, following its success in the United States, TIIP began its international expansion with its first overseas training held at the historic Suleymaniye Madrasah, built in the 16th century in Istanbul, Türkiye. This marked a significant milestone in bringing TIIP to an international platform and strategically situating its trainings within a historic spiritual and health complex in the former capital of the Muslim world.

Since its inception, students from 25 different countries—including the United States, Canada, the United Kingdom, Germany, the Netherlands, Uzbekistan, Singapore, Pakistan, the United Arab Emirates, Sweden, India, South Africa, Qatar, Palestine, Argentina, Australia, Switzerland, and Belgium—have participated in TIIP trainings held in the United States, Türkiye, Qatar, Pakistan, and Australia. The program has attracted participants from diverse professional backgrounds, including graduate students, psychiatrists, private practitioners, chaplains, social workers, and doctoral-level psychologists, highlighting its broad applicability across mental health settings.

To enhance accessibility, 10 scholarships are awarded annually to support underprivileged practitioners and students, particularly from lower-income countries, so that they can benefit from this unique training.

The program's flexibility and adaptability are further emphasized by its multilingual delivery. For example, in Türkiye, TIIP training has been conducted in both Turkish and English, while in Pakistan, training was delivered in Urdu and English. The availability of the program in multiple languages highlights its cultural and linguistic accessibility, greatly enhancing TIIP's role as a globally recognized framework for Muslim mental health care.

Through its comprehensive curriculum and the efforts of the Khalil Center, TIIP has established itself as a respected approach in the United States, Canada, Türkiye, Pakistan, Australia, Qatar, and beyond. This expansion reflects the increasing demand for culturally grounded mental health solutions that integrate Islamic teachings with modern psychology.

Overview of the TIIP Training: Structure, Requirements, and Course Schedule

The TIIP training program is organized into three levels, designed to gradually enhance expertise in Islamically Integrated Psychotherapy.

> *Level 1* introduces the foundational concepts of TIIP, emphasizing the integration of Islamic spirituality with therapeutic practices. This level is aimed at mental health professionals who are new to Islamically integrated approaches, particularly TIIP. The curriculum includes modules on the core tenets and principles of the model, including a discussion of Islamic epistemology—providing a framework for reconciling empirical, rational, and scriptural sources of knowledge within an Islamic context. In addition, trainees are introduced to treatment interventions targeting the elements of TIIP's ontological framework of the human psyche, as well as the role and responsibilities of the TIIP practitioner.
>
> *Level 2* builds on this foundation by deepening therapeutic applications through advanced interventions. It focuses on applying the model to specific clinical problems and patient populations, while also introducing specialized topics such as the role of dreams within TIIP and the integration of mental health medications from an Islamic ethical perspective.
>
> At *Level 3,* trainees complete 200 hours of supervised clinical practice online, which requires them to submit video recordings of their sessions. This level provides hands-on experience in real clinical settings under the guidance of experienced TIIP professionals.

TIIP Level 1 Core Curriculum Highlights

Foundations of TIIP. This module introduces the foundational principles of TIIP, focusing on Islamic epistemology and ontology and their relationship with mental health practices.

Role of the TIIP Practitioner. This module explores the roles and competencies required for TIIP therapists, including ethical conduct and comparisons with other Islamic and clinical disciplines.

Case Conceptualization in TIIP. This module covers the process of case conceptualization, teaching students to apply both qualitative and quantitative assessment techniques within culturally sensitive contexts.

Empathy Techniques. This module focuses on prophetic empathy as a core value in therapeutic relationships, incorporating practical role-play exercises to enhance empathic communication.

Intake Processes. In this module, students learn how to conduct effective intake sessions, emphasizing rapport-building and information gathering in accordance with TIIP principles.

Emotion-Oriented Interventions (Ihsas). This module provides students with a theoretical foundation of a model of emotions within the context of TIIP. It introduces key emotion-oriented interventions and techniques, equipping students to facilitate emotional regulation and transformation in therapy.

Chairwork Group Exercises. Following the theoretical basics of emotion-oriented work learned in the previous module, this module allows students to apply core interventions through role play. Students are divided into groups of 2-3 to practice client-therapist interactions, with instructors offering guidance and feedback throughout the process to help refine their skills.

Cognitive Theories in Islam ('Aql). This module examines the concept of 'aql (cognition) and its application in cognitive restructuring within the Islamic tradition.

Behavioral Interventions in TIIP (Nafs). This module introduces the concept of behavioral reformation within the Islamic tradition, providing students with foundational knowledge of behavioral principles as applied through TIIP. It focuses on integrating Islamic teachings to facilitate behavioral change in therapeutic settings.

Spiritually Oriented Interventions (Ruh). This module demonstrates the effectiveness and power of practices such as prayer, supplication, dhikr (remembrance of God), muraqabah (meditation), and other spiritual exercises in clinical settings, aimed at enhancing psycho-spiritual well-being.

Islamic Virtues and Psychotherapy. This module introduces the foundational role of Islamic virtues in psychotherapy, focusing on how they can be conceptually integrated into therapeutic interventions to support both psychological and psycho-spiritual well-being.

TIIP Level 2 Core Curriculum Highlights

TIIP. This module offers an overview of the model, focusing on case studies and clinical applications to enhance students' therapeutic skills.

Ethical Considerations and Dilemma. Students will explore the ethical challenges that arise at the intersection of Islamic values and mental health practice, utilizing real-world case studies for better understanding.

Role of Mental Illness in Islamic Law. This module examines mental illness from the perspective of Islamic law, investigating how mental health conditions are addressed within Islamic jurisprudence.

Advanced Process Experiential Modalities (Ihsas). This module centers on advanced emotion-oriented techniques within the TIIP framework, involving hands-on practice in simulated therapy scenarios that aim to refine clinical application skills.

Medication and Islamic Consideration. Students will learn how to approach the use of medication through an Islamic ethical lens, emphasizing the balance between spiritual and medical considerations.

Advanced Cognitively Oriented Psychotherapy ('Aql). This module provides comprehensive training in cognitive restructuring, incorporating role plays and practical applications of cognitive techniques within the TIIP context.

Islamic Virtues-Based Intervention. This module emphasizes advanced clinical applications of Islamic virtues. Students engage with case studies and role-play exercises to develop practical strategies for incorporating virtues into therapy, fostering deeper psycho-spiritual growth in clients.

Advanced Behavioral Interventions (Nafs). This module focuses on advanced behavioral strategies for addressing behavioral issues, featuring practical case studies and interventions specifically tailored for Muslim clients.

Advanced Spiritually Oriented Interventions (Ruh). This module offers experiential learning in spiritual interventions, integrating Islamic practices into therapeutic settings. It also addresses bereavement and coping with loss, equipping students with TIIP-based approaches to support clients through grief and spiritual healing.

TIIP Integrative Dreamwork. This module teaches students how to apply dream interpretation in therapy, utilizing Islamic teachings about the significance of dreams.

Training Assignments and Readings

Throughout the program, students engage in various assignments and projects designed to integrate Islamic frameworks with contemporary psychological approaches. Each module includes assignments that promote critical thinking and synthesis, allowing students to explore the intersections between Islamic spirituality, traditional therapeutic methods, and modern therapeutic practices. Reflective assignments, case-based exercises, and integration-focused projects enhance students' understanding and provide practical opportunities to apply TIIP principles.

To progress through Levels 1 and 2 of the programs, trainees must pass a qualifying exam, which consists of a multiple-choice test covering core concepts and practical applications. Additionally, they are required to write a detailed case conceptualization based on TIIP methodology, demonstrating their ability to synthesize theoretical knowledge with practical skills.

In Level 3, practitioners complete 200 hours of supervised clinical practice, during which they must submit video recordings of their sessions for review and feedback from experienced TIIP professionals. Trainees are expected to apply TIIP within their existing treatment settings during supervision, and biweekly supervisory sessions are held online to provide feedback and review the cases in which TIIP is being implemented.

The curriculum includes a variety of resources, such as a core textbook, published articles, and an assortment of handouts and visual aids like mind maps. These materials enhance the learning experience and serve as essential tools for classroom discussions, role-play exercises, and experiential learning sessions. Through practical training opportunities, including role plays and case simulations, students improve their therapeutic skills. Additionally, the program incorporates research-based projects to prepare students for real-world applications and to encourage their contributions to the field of IP.

Türkiye Initiatives: Ibn Haldun University (IHU) and the Concentration in Islamic Psychology

In Türkiye, IHU has established itself as a key institution for the advancement of IP through its Ph.D. program in Clinical Psychology, which features a concentration in TIIP. This concentration offers a comprehensive academic and clinical foundation in TIIP, enabling students to specialize in IP at an advanced level.

Requirements and Components of the Islamic Psychology Concentration at Ibn Haldun University

Core Curriculum and Specialized TIIP Courses.

<u>PSY 670E - Introduction to Islamically Integrated Psychotherapy: Theory and Practice.</u> This foundational course introduces the TIIP model, covering Islamic epistemology and ontological perspectives on the human psyche. Students gain practical skills to conceptualize and treat psychological disorders using TIIP, grounding them in a distinctly Islamic approach to

mental health.

<u>PSY 671E - Advanced Islamically Integrated Psychotherapy: Theory and Practice.</u> Building on the introductory course, this advanced course reinforces the Islamic epistemological and ontological foundations of TIIP. Students delve deeper into the model's core principles, applying TIIP across various therapeutic contexts and complex psychological disorders, enabling them to address diverse clinical challenges within an Islamic framework.

<u>Clinical Training at IPAM</u> (Ibn Haldun University Psychotherapy Application and Research Center). A distinctive feature of the program is the IHU Psychotherapy Application and Research Center (IPAM) with two locations, one in Basaksehir, a suburb of Istanbul and another in the Fatih district housed within the historic Darul al-Shifa of the Suleymaniye Madrasah and Masjid complex. This is the only center in Türkiye where TIIP is offered as a formal therapeutic choice. Students fulfill their required clinical hours specifically in TIIP at IPAM, where they work under the supervision of certified TIIP therapists.

<u>Thesis Requirement.</u> To complete the concentration in IP, students must conduct a thesis on a topic related to IP. This research component encourages in-depth exploration, allowing students to contribute original knowledge to the field of TIIP and gain expertise in a specialized area.

<u>Suleymaniye Research Center and TIIP Symposiums.</u> In partnership with the Khalil Center, IHU has established the Suleymaniye Research Center within the historic Darul Shifa, which hosts annual TIIP symposiums and reading groups. These events, covering both introductory and advanced levels, bring together scholars, practitioners, and students to discuss the latest developments in IP and TIIP, fostering a global intellectual community dedicated to the field.

Through these structured components, IHU has positioned itself as an international hub for IP, offering a unique blend of academic rigor, clinical training, and community engagement in the study of TIIP.

Expanding Islamic Psychology Education in Qatar: The World's First Applied Islamic Psychology Master of Arts Degree (MA) and a Diploma in Islamic Psychology & Psychotherapy (IPP)

Building on the global momentum in IP, HBKU in Qatar has introduced the world's first applied IP Master's degree program. This pioneering program, the master's in Counseling (Islamic) Psychology (MA), is designed to equip students with the skills to integrate Islamic principles directly into clinical mental health practice. HBKU's program represents a key milestone in formalizing IP within higher education, aligning with the Khalil Center's TIIP framework while adapting it to address the unique needs of Muslim communities in Qatar and beyond.

Housed within the College of Islamic Studies, the program curriculum combines both Islamic and contemporary psychological studies with rigorous practical training. Modeled after the clinical approach established at the Khalil Center in the United States, this program is intended to serve as a central educational and clinical resource for the region. In the future, HBKU also plans to develop a Ph.D. program in Applied IP to offer further research and professional development opportunities.

As part of its vision, HBKU is working to establish an IP clinic within Education City in Doha. This clinic, modeled after the Khalil Center, will serve the mental health needs of the community and function as a teaching facility where graduate program students can receive supervised training. The program emphasizes ethical and culturally responsive counseling that aligns with Islamic values, promoting an approach that is both professionally and spiritually enriching.

This initiative is the first of its kind in Qatar and the broader region, where the integration of IP into formal education is still in its early stages. By offering a structured curriculum that combines Islamic and contemporary psychological frameworks, HBKU is providing a vital resource for mental health professionals seeking to enhance their cultural and religious competencies.

For trained mental health practitioners with a graduate degree, the College of Islamic Studies offers a one-year diploma in Islamic Psychology and Psychotherapy (IPP).

The Master of Arts (MA) program

This is a three-year graduate program that consists of coursework, 700 hours of clinical training, and the option to complete either a thesis or a clinical research project.

The faculty members guiding this program include:

- Dr. Hooman Keshavarzi, Psy.D., Executive Director of the Khalil Center and Program Director of the Counseling Psychology Master's program at HBKU.
- Dr. Fahad Khan, MS, Psy.D., Deputy Director at the Khalil Center and Assistant Professor at HBKU.
- Dr. Vahdet Gormez, MD, Child Psychiatrist and Full Professor at Hamad Bin Khalifa University.

- Dr. Khalid Elzamzamy, MD, MA, Research Faculty at Johns Hopkins University and the Khalil Center, specializing in the integration of Islam and mental health.
- Dr. Abdallah Rothman, PhD, Co-Founder and Executive Director of the International Association for Islamic Psychology (IAIP).

These faculty members provide students with in-depth expertise in IP. Additionally, the Islamic Psychology Program (IPP) diploma is a one-year certification program that includes six courses in total—four core courses and two elective courses—sourced from the MA program.

These programs are accredited by Qatar's Ministry of Education and are currently seeking international accreditation from the International Association of IP and AQAS. They are open to admissions to individuals from around the world. All communication and instruction are conducted in English; however, proficiency in Arabic is also required. Students who do not meet the Arabic proficiency requirement must enroll in a mandatory one-year Arabic preparatory program. Applicants to the program are required to hold a degree in a related field within mental health and have some foundational knowledge in Islamic studies.

Curriculum Highlights

The following four courses from the graduate curriculum are required for the completion of the IPP diploma:

Introduction to Psychology in the Islamic Tradition (PSYC600). This course explores classical Islamic scholarly traditions, focusing on psychological topics and questions found within classical Islamic sources such as medicine (tibb), philosophy (falsafah), Islamic spirituality (tasawwuf), theology (kalam), and Islamic law (fiqh). It provides students with exposure to the rich Islamic intellectual heritage.

Introduction to Psychotherapy & Counseling Theories (PSYC604). This course begins with an overview of mainstream counseling theories for the first five weeks. It then transitions into an Islamically integrated approach based on TIIP for the remaining ten weeks. Through this structure, students are introduced to cognitive, behavioral, spiritual, and emotion-oriented therapeutic techniques.

Ethics, Professional & Legal Issues in Psychology (PSYC607). Students learn about Islamic and international ethical guidelines, developing skills to navigate ethical complexities where Islamic values intersect with global standards.

Advanced Techniques & Interventions (PSYC702). This advanced course emphasizes applied skills and case-based learning, refining students' abilities to integrate Islamic frameworks into therapeutic settings. It delves deeply into specialized techniques in TIIP, allowing students to apply these methods in diverse clinical contexts.

Electives Courses

Additionally, the following four courses are electives for the IPP diploma program. Enrolled students must complete at least two electives to fulfill the six-course requirement for the diploma program:

Group Therapy (PSYC606). This course explores the fundamental principles of group dynamics and their application in group therapy through various theoretical approaches. It examines the formation, sustainability, and dynamics of groups, as well as how change is facilitated by the group leader.

Career & School Counseling (PSYC608). This course introduces career and school counseling, covering theories, assessment tools, and their application in various educational and vocational settings. It includes discussions on career development theories, vocational counseling, decision-making models, career planning, and sources of educational and occupational information.

Substance Abuse & Addictions (PSYC609). This course creates a supportive environment for developing counseling skills related to substance use and addictive behaviors. It covers the physiological and psychological effects of drugs, diagnostic criteria, treatment planning, and diverse therapeutic strategies, including individual, group, and family counseling for behavior change and relapse prevention. Students will also explore models of etiology and treatment approaches.

Marital & Family Therapy (PSYC700). This course explores the development and key theories of marital and family therapy, focusing on various schools of thought and current trends in the field. It emphasizes the Muslim family, examining Islamic models of family and marital therapy, and integrates Islamically based strategies and interventions to strengthen marriages and family values.

Other Courses

Other courses in the full graduate program include:

Foundations of Islamic Sciences (PSYC601). This course introduces the foundations of Islamic sciences, focusing on their aims, scope, and methods for building a foundational understanding. Core topics include the Quran, sayings and actions of the Prophet Muhammad, peace and blessings be upon him (hadith), fiqh, kalam, and tasawwuf. Discussions will also cover auxiliary sciences such as falsafah, logic (mantiq), and tibb, with an exploration of the connections between these disciplines and psychology (*ilm-al-nafs*).

Psychopathology & Diagnosis (PSYC602). This course covers the assessment, diagnosis, and treatment of mental disorders using the DSM-5. It includes differential diagnosis, etiology, prevention, and treatment of various psychopathologies. Additionally, it provides a basic survey and review of spiritual diseases of the heart that relate to psychopathology.

Appraisal & Psychological Assessment Methods (PSYC603). This course introduces students to psychological and cognitive assessment techniques, including both standardized and non-standardized testing, behavioral observations, and clinical interviewing. It covers methods such as norm-referenced and criterion-referenced assessments, environmental and performance assessments, as well as individual and group tests. Students will learn how to integrate data to address diagnostic and referral questions from courts, schools, and healthcare providers, and will develop effective report-writing skills.

Cross-Cultural Psychotherapy (PSYC605). This course explores client diversity by addressing ethnographic, demographic, and socioeconomic variables while challenging culturally biased stereotypes in mental health services. It examines multicultural psychotherapy models, cultural identity development, and the impact of culture on psychopathology, health, and service delivery. Students will develop skills in cultural attunement, intervention adaptation, and the incorporation of cultural factors into diagnosis and assessment.

Human Growth & Development (PSYC703). This course investigates human development across the lifespan, examining physical, cognitive, social, emotional, spiritual, and moral growth within various contexts such as family, schools, and cultures. It covers life phase transitions, key developmental theories from developmental psychology and IP, and research-based, culturally appropriate interventions and assessments for psychotherapy. Practical applications relevant to helping professions are integrated through readings and in-class discussions.

Research & Program Evaluation (PSYC707). This course introduces students to both quantitative and qualitative research methods, statistics, and program evaluation in counseling psychology. It covers needs assessments, data collection through surveys and interviews, and statistical analysis. The course also incorporates Islamic epistemology to help students evaluate and interpret rational, empirical, subjective, and scriptural data, focusing on how to assess self-report data and its contexts and applications.

Research Project/Master's Thesis (PSYC695/690). The Research Project or Thesis focuses on enhancing knowledge or contributing to the field. Potential projects may include community programs (e.g., stigma reduction, mental health awareness), educational workshops, program development (e.g., school character education, youth initiatives), program evaluations, community-based participatory research (CBPR), focus groups, or needs assessments within the mental health and counseling domains. Alternatively, students may opt for a thesis project on a topic related to IP or Muslim mental health.

Practicum/Internship (PSYC697/691). The practicum and internship are designed to provide mental health counseling students with opportunities to apply the knowledge, concepts, and skills acquired throughout their graduate program. Interns will take on the role of a counselor at their placement sites, engaging in a full range of activities, including intake, assessment, diagnosis, and both individual and group counseling.

Strengths and Challenges

The IP programs (MA and IPP) at HBKU are exceptional in their ability to address a critical gap in the education of mental health professionals, especially those working in Muslim-majority contexts or with Muslim populations. Several factors contribute to the uniqueness of these programs:

Cultural and Religious Integration

The programs incorporate Islamic teachings at every level, from foundational psychological theories to advanced therapeutic interventions. Courses such as "Introduction to Psychology in the Islamic Tradition" and "Ethics, Professional & Legal Issues in Psychology" provide students with a unique opportunity to learn about mental health care from both modern and Islamic perspectives. This ensures they are well-equipped to navigate the complex cultural dynamics of working with Muslim clients.

Focus on Islamic Ethics in Mental Health Practice

Unlike other programs that offer general ethics training, HBKU's curriculum explores Islamic ethical guidelines and their relationship to global professional standards. This focus is especially important for practitioners facing ethical dilemmas at the intersection of Islamic values and international mental health practices.

Addressing Unique Muslim Family Dynamics

The "Marital & Family Therapy" course is designed to meet the specific needs and challenges of Muslim families by incorporating Islamic family values into therapy. This course is distinctive because it offers culturally and religiously tailored interventions, helping students apply Islamic teachings to real-world family dynamics.

Flexibility and Professional Relevance

The elective structure of the IPP diploma allows students to customize their studies according to their professional needs, whether they are school counselors, addiction specialists, or family therapists. This flexibility ensures that the program is adaptable to various fields of mental health while integrating Islamic frameworks.

However, the programs face several key challenges as they establish themselves within the field of IP. A primary obstacle is the scarcity of comparable IP programs in the region, which limits local benchmarks and collaborative opportunities. Additionally, there is a shortage of faculty specializing in IP worldwide, which is crucial for the program's growth, sustainability, and credibility. Ensuring consistent integration of cultural and religious values into clinical practice remains a continuous focus, along with the challenge of attracting a diverse international student body.

To address these challenges, several targeted solutions have been proposed. Building partnerships with local and international organizations such as the Khalil Center, the International Association of IP, the ISIP, the CMC, and IHU will broaden the program's reach, enabling collaboration and resource sharing. Currently, all courses are taught face-to-face with no online options. However, by offering hybrid or online courses for the IPP diploma, the program can increase accessibility and attract global students who might otherwise be unable to attend in person. Strategic collaborations and recruitment efforts are underway to develop faculty specialization, thereby enriching the teaching staff and expanding the range of expertise available. The curriculum emphasizes cultural and religious sensitivity, equipping practitioners to meet the specific needs of Muslim communities. To attract a global audience, international marketing efforts are being strengthened to highlight the unique offerings of these programs.

A Road Map for the Next Ten Years

In the coming decade, the newly established department envisions significant growth, with plans to establish the region's first PhD program in Clinical/Counseling IP. Additionally, there will be a concentration in IP within the PhD in Islamic Studies program, designed for those with theological backgrounds who wish to study in a non-clinical setting while contributing to the field of IP.

This concentration will offer students the opportunity to explore advanced research, thereby enriching the academic foundation of IP. Further plans include expanding the master's curriculum with advanced training modules aimed at strengthening IP on a global scale, as well as hosting bi-annual symposiums to share knowledge and advancements.

These initiatives align with HBKU's mission to develop culturally competent and ethically grounded professionals equipped to address global mental health needs from an Islamically integrated perspective. Through continuous development, the program aims to set new standards in IP, positioning these initiatives as cornerstones for future academic growth and excellence.

Usul Academy and the Foundations in Islamic Sciences: Islamic Psychology Online Diploma Program

To meet the growing demand for practitioners with a solid foundation in Islamic knowledge, Usul Academy offers an Online Diploma Program in IP. This program is designed for researchers and practitioners in psychology and related fields, providing them with access to the rich Islamic heritage of psychology. In partnership with the Khalil Center, Usul Academy delivers an education that addresses key concerns and questions within the field of psychology through the lens of Islamic traditions.

Dr. Hooman Keshavarzi, a board member of Usul Academy and the founder of the Khalil Center, ensures that the principles and philosophy of TIIP are central to the program's curriculum.

The IP Diploma Program spans one year and is divided into three terms. It also includes a summer intensive program at the Suleymaniye Madrasah and Ozbeki Spiritual Lodge in Istanbul, Türkiye. This format allows students to engage in both academic and experiential spiritual learning, with options for live sessions and additional asynchronous components to provide flexibility in learning.

Core Curriculum Highlights

Introduction to Islamic Psychology

This course introduces students to the historical development of IP, surveying key eras from classical times to contemporary developments in the last 40–50 years. Students explore significant contributions to health sciences within the Islamic tradition.

Psychology in the Tibb and Tasawwuf Tradition

Focused on contributions from tibb and tasawwuf, this course covers the conceptualization of the psyche and soul within these disciplines, including classical approaches to mental health treatment.

Models of Islamic Psychotherapy & Community Psychology

This course provides a foundational survey of mainstream counseling theories and introduces Islamically integrative psychotherapy models, with emphasis on TIIP. It includes Islamic epistemological and ontological frameworks, conceptualizing the psyche's core elements—'aql (cognition), nafs (behavioral inclinations), ruh (spirit), and ihsas (emotions). Students learn skills for applying these models in therapeutic settings.

Contemporary Issues in Islamic Psychology

This course reviews the development of the contemporary field of IP, including emerging trends, challenges, and opportunities. Students will explore new models, research, and literature on various contemporary issues in IP and its applications across different settings, such as education, society, and community.

Comparative Theories & Methods

This course examines the conceptual foundations and assumptions of major methodological schools in the social sciences through a genealogical approach. By comparing diverse worldviews, the course encourages dialogue among various schools, highlighting both strengths and limitations. Islamic schools of thought—falsafah, kalam, tasawwuf, and fiqh—are presented alongside social science perspectives, offering alternative insights into contemporary questions.

Character Development in Islamic Tradition and Positive Psychology

This course explores Akhlaq al-'adudiyya (al-Ījī & Taşköprizade, 2018), a foundational text on virtues in the Islamic tradition, supplemented by classical commentaries. It also examines parallels with positive psychology, identifying ways Islamic principles of character development can inform contemporary practices in areas like parenting, education, and workplace development.

Psychology in Hadith

A selected study of forty hadith related to psychology, covering topics such as human nature, character development, and cognitive restructuring of beliefs. Commentary from classical hadith sources provides insights into how these themes can inform modern psychological practice.

Islamic Mental Health Ethics

This course explores ethical and legal issues in mental health practice from an Islamic perspective, addressing reconciliatory strategies for Islamic values and international ethical standards. Students develop a professional identity as mental health providers within an Islamic ethical framework.

Classical Readings in Islamic Psychology

This course offers an unfiltered exposure to primary Islamic texts across disciplines like falsafah and fiqh, facilitating a deep engagement with Islamic intellectual heritage.

Admission Requirements

The program is designed for students with a background in psychology or a related field, with additional requirements for Islamic foundational knowledge. Mental health practitioners enrolled in the program are also required to complete Khalil Center's TIIP training, available in multiple regions, including United States, Türkiye, Pakistan, and Australia.

Impact and Global Reach

Usul Academy's program addresses the increasing demand for IP education that is not only grounded in classical Islamic sciences but also applicable to modern clinical practice. The curriculum directly supports TIIP's evolution by training practitioners who can apply Islamic principles in therapeutic contexts, aligning with the Khalil Center's mission to offer Islamically grounded mental health services.

Through its collaboration with the Khalil Center, Usul Academy ensures that TIIP-based orientation is foundational to all courses, reinforcing a cohesive, Islamically integrated framework. This partnership enables a dynamic learning environment for practitioners worldwide, fostering a community of mental health professionals dedicated to applying Islamic traditions within psychology.

Interconnection with Khalil Center: The Evolution of TIIP

All the programs mentioned above are connected by a shared orientation and philosophy grounded in TIIP. Khalil Center has been the driving force behind the evolution and spread of TIIP, with its influence seen in programs at IHU, Hamad Bin Khalifa University, and Usul Academy. Each of these institutions has adopted the TIIP framework, ensuring that the philosophy and principles of TIIP continue to guide the development of IP programs around the world.

CHAPTER FOUR

MASTER'S DEGREE IN ISLAMIC PSYCHOLOGY and the First Graduate School of Islamic Psychology in the United States

The Alkaram Institute; Virginia, USA

Carrie M. York

This chapter provides an overview of a Master's degree and a graduate certificate in IP at the Alkaram Institute – the first graduate school of IP in the United States. The chapter begins by discussing the impetus, rational, and development of the institute and then provides an overview of the programs, their curriculum, as well as some reflections on our strengths, challenges, and some solutions. As founder and president of the institute and primary developer of our programs, I was asked to speak to these specific details using the format below and from my own personal experience and vantage point at the time of the chapter's writing, which is June 2025.

Introduction

The Alkaram Institute is the first graduate school of IP in the United States and indeed North America. Founded in 2018 by Dr. Carrie York, it is a 501c3 religious nonprofit institution whose mission is to advance IP to benefit society and improve lives. The institute houses a number of initiatives including the first and only programs in IP in the United States, experiential programs in applied IP and spirituality, an IP research fellowship, and Alkaram Press, which publishes books on IP, spirituality, mental health, healing, and wellness. For more information about the institute and the scope of what we are involved in, visit www.alkaraminstitute.org.

In terms of rationale and impetus for the establishment of the institute and our IP programs, both are linked to my personal and professional interests and experiences over the past twenty years in religion and spirituality within the context of psychology and the need for Muslim and Islamic perspectives within these domains. I have written more about these developments elsewhere (York, 2021; 2024) as well as about my background, including an article the American Psychological Association asked me to write about how I integrate who I am as a Muslim with what I do as a psychologist (York, 2024).

I am the sole person responsible for the vision and establishment of the institute as well as our IP programs, but I certainly have not done it alone. In addition to my own efforts, the expertise and contributions of our world-class faculty bring our programs to life and the guidance of our board of directors moves the institute forward. Everyone at Alkaram carries out functions vital to who we are and what we do, and it is truly a collaborative effort.

In terms of how the Alkaram Institute defines or conceptualizes IP, a core aspect of our programs is to examine this question in depth – what is IP? However, there is no requirement for anyone at the institution - whether students, faculty, or administrators - to subscribe to a particular definition. There are many definitions of IP that exist, and we examine them all (for example, see York Al-Karam, 2018).

Lastly, the mission of the Alkaram Institute is to advance IP to benefit society and improve lives. In our programs, this is done through various course assignments, a final research project on an IP topic where it is used to solve a problem or be of benefit in some way, as well as a service project/internship where the student's area of research is applied. In short, students advance IP though academic and experiential projects and integrate

MASTER'S DEGREE IN ISLAMIC PSYCHOLOGY

it into their own personal development.

Nature of Programs

The Alkaram Institute currently offers two programs in IP – a Master's degree and a graduate certificate. Our graduate certificate began in 2021, and our Master's program begins Fall 2026. Our programs' precursor was a class entitled Introduction to Islamic Psychology RELS 2570 which was the first and at that time only class in IP to be offered at a university in the United States that I developed and taught in 2017 at the University of Iowa (York, 2025).

Our Master's is a 2-year program with a thesis and internship component. It could be considered a terminal degree for someone wanting to use IP in various contexts including a mosque or community center, Muslim non-profit, an Islamic school, social care, as well as newer or emerging professions like coaching or spiritual guidance and care. It could also be considered a "bridge" degree in that it is also ideal for someone looking to continue their studies at the doctoral level in either psychology, Islamic studies, or a related field. This program does not prepare for any kind of licensure.

Our graduate certificate is a 1-year program and was created primarily for professionals who are already working in a field related to psychology or Islamic studies and would benefit by expanding their knowledge base of IP due to its relevance to their work. It is also a good fit for someone interested in IP but who doesn't necessarily want to commit to the rigors of a whole master's program and thesis.

In the following sections, further information about our programs is provided. Please note that such information changes over time and might only be accurate at the current point in time, which is June 2025.

Admission Requirements

Admission requirements for our Master's program include needing to have successfully completed a bachelor's degree, fluency in English, appropriate technology to attend online (computer, stable internet connection etc.), statement of purpose and research interests, which also serves as a writing sample, transcripts, and a letter of recommendation.

Admission requirements for our graduate certificate include needing to have successfully completed a bachelor's degree, fluency in English, appropriate technology (computer, stable internet connection etc.), an application letter describing the applicant's educational and professional background and why they want to enroll in the program.

Duration of Programs

- The master's degree is a two-year part-time program.
- The graduate certificate is a one-year part-time program.

Modes of Instruction

Both programs are fully online and are comprised of synchronous and asynchronous components. There are copious amounts of course readings. The graduate certificate has a final research paper and volunteer project. The master's program has research papers for each class, a thesis, and an internship connected to the thesis project.

Fees

The cost of our graduate certificate has changed from year to year. The cost of our master's program has not yet been set by our board, but our intention is to make it affordable, at least as this is understood within a US context. For more on this see the section in this chapter on "strengths/affordability".

Financial Assistance

Students will not be able to use federal student loans until we are accredited. In the meantime, students have the option of applying for various private Islamic funding and scholarship opportunities such as A Continuous Charity, American Muslim Community Foundation, and the like. We also offer limited financial aid on a case-by-case basis.

Graduation Requirements

Students in both programs need to have regular attendance and must have successfully completed and passed all components of their program to graduate.

Faculty Credentials

All our faculty have terminal degrees, with most of them being at the doctoral level, and all are renowned experts in the topics they teach.

Partnerships with Other Programs or Institutions

The first year we offered our graduate certificate in 2021, we partnered with George Washington University in Washington, DC. We also consider partners to be institutions where our IP research fellows are enrolled such as Columbia University, Yale University, Hamad bin Khalifa University, IIUI, University of Wisconsin, and others. We also have a MOU with Effat University in Jeddah, Saudi Arabia, signed in 2019.

Curriculum

Our master's degree is a 2-year program comprised of five semester long classes, a master's thesis, and an internship related to the thesis. Our graduate certificate is a 1-year program comprised of modules, a final paper, and a volunteer service project.

We also offered an Islamic meditation class for one academic year and although that program is not currently being offered, we do plan on offering other experiential programs, including possible travel programs outside the US.

Without getting too granular as readers can check our website for the most current information about our curricula, both programs cover roots and branches of IP, but the master's program does so in more depth and breadth. Content covered includes context of IP, definitions and conceptualization of IP, philosophical roots such as epistemology, ontology, and cosmology, the Islamic sciences, Islamic spirituality, research methods, Islamically integrated psychotherapy, counseling, coaching, Islamic medicine and healing, psychological topics from an Islamic perspective like human development, personality, psychopathology, and learning. Neither program leads to any kind of clinical practice or licensure (such professions are highly regulated in the United States, specific to each state, and specific to individual professions like psychology, social work, professional counseling, marriage and family counseling etc.). Our Master's program is unique and prepares students to work in fields related to their thesis and internship project.

Strengths

Identifying strengths or weaknesses of a program is a highly subjective endeavor. That said, from my subjective view, our IP programs have four important strengths worth mentioning. In no particular order, they are the following:

First, our programs are comprehensive in depth, breadth, and diversity in terms of what is covered. This statement is based on direct student feedback. Students often say how amazed they are with just how much we cover. Other feedback consistently given is how the program has positively impacted their life, with many having said it "changed their life".

Related to this is our second strength: our world-class faculty and scholars. If you look at our website to see who they are and their bodies of work, it's nothing other than impressive!

A third strength is accessibility. Our Students are located all over the US and the world. Being fully online removes many barriers to seeking knowledge such as hassle and costs associated with moving to where the school is located, of having to regularly get to campus, potential visa issues for international students, and the like. Being online also keeps costs down because we do not have the overhead of a physical location.

Related to this is a fourth strength: affordability. Although at the time of this writing our board has yet to set the cost of the Master's program, what we do know is that it will be relatively affordable. The average cost of Master's programs in the United States today is around $60K (Hanson, 2025). We anticipate ours costing below $20K for the 2-year program. This is done intentionally to keep IP as accessible as possible and to help address the skyrocketing and oppressive student loan debt crisis in this country. Lastly, I was asked to share a few key IP publications by our faculty and/or affiliates. Some of them include but are certainly not limited to the following:

Elzamzamy, K., & Keshavarzi, H. (2019). Navigating ethical dilemmas in mental health practice between professional ethics and Islamic values. *Journal of Islamic Faith and Practice, 2*(1), 40-71.

Faruque, M. (2021). *Sculpting the Self: Islam, Selfhood, and Human Flourishing.* Ann Arbor: University of Michigan Press.

Haque, A. & Rothman, A. (2021). *Islamic Psychology Around the Globe.* International Association of Islamic Psychology.

Keshavarzi, H., Elzamzamy, K., Ansari, B., and Zaidi, A. (2025). *Psychological Themes in Classical Islamic Literature: A Primary Source Reader.* Brill.

Mohr, S. (2022). *Loving the Present: Sufism, Mindfulness, and Recovery from Addiction and Mental Illness.* Wipf and Stock Publishers.

York Al-Karam, C. (2018). *Islamically Integrated Psychotherapy: Uniting Faith and Professional Practice.* Templeton Press.

York Al-Karam, C. (2018). Islamic Psychology: Towards a 21st Century Definition and Conceptual Framework. *Journal of Islamic Ethics.* Brill Publications.

York Al-Karam, C. (2020). Islamic Psychology: Expanding Beyond the Clinic. *Journal of Islamic Faith and Practice. Volume 3.*

York Al-Karam, C. (2021). Islamic Psychology in the United States. Book chapter in *Islamic Psychology Around the World.* Haque and Rothman (editors). International Association of Islamic Psychology.

York, C. (2023). *The Way of Love: Towards an Islamic Psychology of Virtues and Character Development.* Alkaram Press.

York, C. (2024). *Heartfulness: Islamic Spiritual Practices for Health and Well-being.* Alkaram Press.

Challenges

From the perspective of program development, the primary challenge I see is related to IP being a new field. There still lacks clarity as to what this field is about, what kind of jobs one can get if one were to have a degree in it, as well as how IP relates to or is relevant to existing fields, degrees, and professions like psychology, counseling, chaplaincy etc. Such fields have recognized academic degrees, training programs, and professions but IP does not.

Another challenge is not having enough scholars who are doing work in IP. There are many people who have expertise in topics relevant to IP, but not many of them are positioning their discourse within IP explicitly so the advancement of the field is somewhat truncated.

Lastly, one of the challenges we have faced at the Alkaram Institute is that we are a newer non-profit, a new graduate school, and we specialize in an emerging field – all very challenging issues. The fact that we are carrying all three combined at the very same time makes what we are doing more challenging.

Solutions

One solution to the above-mentioned challenges is to educate stakeholders and the public on what IP is and ways it can be used to benefit society and improve lives. This can be done in myriad ways, particularly through community outreach and engagement.

Another solution is to come up with new professions where IP is the preferred or required degree. For example, Muslims have many criticisms about existing professions like psychology because aspects of it are antithetical to Islam. Instead of trying to fit into a box someone else created, how about we create our own? For example, the catholic tradition has a profession called spiritual direction. The purpose of this profession is to help people navigate and strengthen their relationship with God. Those working in this profession are neither priest, nuns, counselors/therapists, or spiritual guides, but elements of each of these professions are found in this profession. As this relates to an Islamic context, Imams often complain that counseling is outside the scope of their training, and Muslim psychologists and counselors often complain they aren't rooted enough in Islamic knowledge. So how about we create "new" profession that a degree in IP prepares for? Muslims would not stop being psychologists or counselors or Imams or social workers or what have you – that would continue. But the (re)-emergence of the field of IP creates opportunities to serve humanity in fresh ways without having to contort into someone else's existing structures that may or may not be in alignment with an Islamic worldview.

Another solution to the above-mentioned challenges is that the field of IP needs heartfelt connections amongst those in the field. Nobody can grow or advance the field on their own. It requires all interested parties to work together and to value and uplift the unique work each person and institution brings to the table. What we do is not a competition – there is space and a need for everyone.

Discussion

For this section, I have been asked to provide details regarding admission rates, graduations, drop-offs, alumni feedback, surveys on knowledge utilization, employment, internal and external reviews, accreditation, and other. I am not able to provide details on these items at this time.

Conclusion

This chapter has provided a brief overview of the IP programs at the Alkaram Institute, some of the challenges we have faced, and possible solutions for them. Future directions include leveraging partnership with existing institutions, clarifying to the public, regulatory bodies, and other stakeholders what IP is and is not, it's scope and application, and all the various ways it can be used to benefit society and improve lives.

CHAPTER FIVE

REVITALIZING THE SCIENCE OF THE SOUL: PSYCHOLOGY FROM AN ISLAMIC PERSPECTIVE
Bachelor of Human Sciences in Psychology (Honors), Department of Psychology

International Islamic University Malaysia

Kuala Lumpur, Malaysia

Jamilah Hanum Abdul Khaiyom, Mohd Ferdaus Harun, Usman Jaffer, Jusmawati Fauzaman, & Shukran Abdul Rahman

Introduction

The International Islamic University Malaysia (IIUM) represents a significant vision of Malaysian Muslim scholars, aimed at establishing a leading Islamic institution in the country. Officially founded by the Malaysian government on May 20, 1983, IIUM was inspired by the 1977 First World Conference on Muslim Education held in Makkah. The university's core philosophy integrates Islamic principles into a comprehensive curriculum that spans the humanities, sciences, and technical disciplines, aligning with its motto, "The Garden of Knowledge and Virtue." IIUM seeks to reclaim the historical role of Muslims in the advancement of education and knowledge, contributing to the overall well-being of humanity. Alongside its focus on academic excellence, IIUM places strong importance on cultivating good character, or Budi, in its students, ensuring they develop strong moral values. This emphasis aligns with Islamic teachings, which prioritize the nurturing of good moral conduct as a core part of education (International Islamic University Malaysia [IIUM], 2024a).

At the heart of IIUM's philosophy is the Tawhidic paradigm, which underscores the belief in the Oneness of Allah SWT as the foundation of all knowledge. The university's philosophy is grounded in the conviction that knowledge must be pursued as both a continuous act of worship ('Ibadah) and a sacred trust (Amanah) granted to humanity by Allah SWT. The pursuit of knowledge should lead to the recognition of Allah SWT as the ultimate Creator, Sustainer, and Lord of all. This philosophy, based on the first five verses of Surat al-'Alaq (Quran: 96), emphasizes the importance of seeking, internalizing, and sharing knowledge in the name of Allah SWT. It highlights the integration of divine revelation and reason, asserting that only through this harmony can knowledge truly elevate individuals. In contrast, knowledge pursued solely through human reasoning, without revelation, is considered incomplete and less beneficial to humanity (IIUM, 2024b).

IIUM is dedicated to embodying a holistic and comprehensive approach to education, rooted in the Islamic worldview. As stated in its vision: "Inspired by the worldview of tawhid and Islamic philosophy of the unity of knowledge as well as its concepts of holistic education, the University aims at becoming a leading international center of excellence in education, research and innovation which seeks to restore the dynamic and progressive role of the ummah in all branches of knowledge for the betterment of human life and civilization" (IIUM, 2024c).

In alignment with this vision, IIUM's mission emphasizes several key objectives that are directly relevant to the development of Bachelor of Human Sciences in Psychology (Honors). First, IIUM aims to reform the contemporary mindset of Muslims by integrating Islamic knowledge with the human sciences in a way that is constructive and holistic. This integration bridges the gap between revealed knowledge and empirical inquiry. Secondly, the university promotes the Islamization of human knowledge, ensuring that teaching, research, and consultancy reflect Islamic values while striving for academic excellence. Thirdly, IIUM fosters holistic excellence by embedding Islamic spiritual and moral values across its educational, research, and administrative endeavors. Finally, the university is committed to creating a lifelong learning environment that nurtures social responsibility among both staff and students, encouraging them to contribute meaningfully to society (IIUM, 2024c).

In 2021, after over 37 years of its establishment, IIUM began a systematic initiative to reformulate and re-strategize its academic programs, marking a significant shift in the institution's educational outlook. The introduction of the Sejahtera Academic Framework (SAF) (refer Figure 2) further reinforced IIUM's ethos as a "Garden of Knowledge and Virtue." In response to the increasing pace of global disruptions, including technological advancements like IR4.0 and challenges such as the COVID-19 pandemic, SAF was developed to enable IIUM to not only manage these changes but to lead proactively. The framework emphasizes the importance of anticipating future disruptions, creating innovative solutions, and remaining aligned with IIUM's core mission of serving Allah and contributing positively to society (Rahmatan lil-'Alamin) (Borhan et al., 2021).

Figure 2: *The Sejahtera Academic Framework*

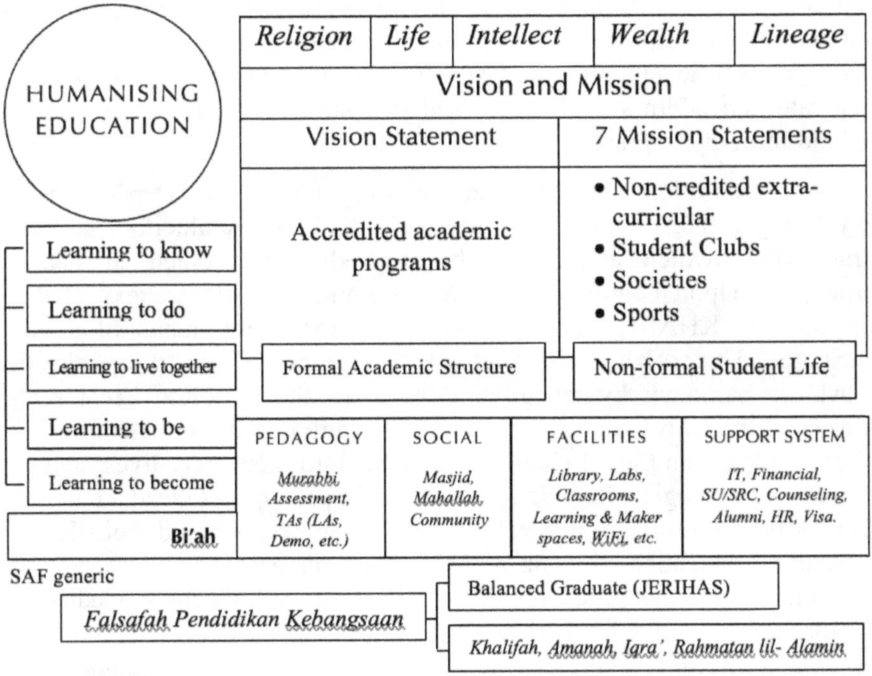

Psychology program: Bachelor of Human Sciences in Psychology (Honors)

The Bachelor of Human Sciences in Psychology (Honors) at IIUM is an academically rigorous program that integrates both conventional psychological theories and Islamic perspectives, guided by the Tawhidic paradigm. This paradigm emphasizes the Oneness of Allah SWT, serving as the foundation for all knowledge and its application. This program is designed to provide students with the essential knowledge and skills to address the psychological needs of diverse communities, in a culturally and religiously sensitive manner. The curriculum incorporates a blend of psychology from Islamic perspectives by revitalizing the Science of the Soul ('Ilm al-Nafs), alongside mainstream psychology courses, preparing graduates to contribute effectively to local and global contexts.

The program aligns with the MQF (Malaysian Qualifications Agency, 2024), ensuring that graduates possess the following learning outcomes: (i) knowledge and understanding of psychological principles; (ii) cognitive skills to critically analyze and interpret information; (iii) practical skills for professional applications; (iv) interpersonal skills to foster effective collaboration; (v) communication skills for clear and impactful expression; (vi) digital skills to navigate and utilize technology efficiently; (vii) numeracy skills to apply quantitative reasoning; (viii) leadership, autonomy, and responsibility to guide and manage projects; (ix) personal skills for self-development and adaptability; (x) entrepreneurial skills to innovate and address challenges; and (xi) ethics and professionalism to uphold integrity in practice.

In addition, the Program Learning Outcomes (Department of Psychology, 2023a) are aligned with IIUM's Sejahtera Academic Framework, which emphasizes holistic education rooted in Islamic principles. Upon completion of the program, students are expected to demonstrate KHAIR (Khalifah- Amanah - Iqra - Rahmatan lil-alamin) attributes. Under Khalifah, graduates are expected to (i) uphold the Tawhidic paradigm by recognizing Allah as the Absolute Creator and Master of the Universe, thereby integrating faith (iman), knowledge ('ilm) of psychology, and good character (akhlaq) into their daily lives; and (ii) possess psychological knowledge and Islamic principles to lead a balanced and harmonious life (Insan Sejahtera), rooted in values-based, holistic, and integrated education for sustainable development. For Amanah, the program ensures that graduates (iii) manifest psychological knowledge and comprehension of the fundamental principles of the field of study and other generic knowledge. The principle of Iqra' emphasizes that graduates (iv) apply independent study skills with a high degree of autonomy and function effectively in a team while practicing good interpersonal skills, essential for thriving in academic, social, and professional settings by utilizing psychological knowledge and Islamic principles; and (v) demonstrate techniques and capabilities to search for and use psychological knowledge and data to make decisions and solve problems, while considering social, scientific, and ethical issues. Finally, under Rahmatan lil Alamin, graduates are expected to (vi) use psychological knowledge and skills in workplace and family settings to reflect professionalism and relevance within society; and (vii) communicate and convey information, ideas, principles, and solutions effectively to diverse groups of stakeholders, utilizing psychological knowledge to promote well-being and harmony.

Rationale and Impetus

Need for integration: Revitalizing the Science of the Soul in psychology

The integration of Islamic principles into psychology is essential not only for addressing the specific needs of Muslim communities but for revitalizing the study of the soul (psyche) within the discipline itself. Modern psychology, influenced by secularism and empiricism, has largely distanced itself from the exploration of the soul, focusing instead on observable mental processes and behaviors, similar to how physical sciences like physics operate. The quest for scientific objectivity, particularly during the behaviorist era, often led to a fragmented understanding of human experience. This narrow focus neglects the holistic understanding of human beings, particularly the spiritual and metaphysical dimensions that are fundamental to overall well-being. As Roger Smith argues in The Norton History of the Human Sciences, psychology lacks the methodological unity of the natural sciences and is inherently interpretive rather than strictly empirical. This recognition opens the door for approaches that prioritize cultural and spiritual dimensions alongside empirical observations. Such perspectives allow psychology to evolve into a discipline that not only explains but also deeply understands human existence (Smith, 1997). By embracing these insights, the integration of Islamic principles into psychology aligns with a broader historical acknowledgment of the discipline's diverse roots and interpretive nature.

At IIUM, our program aims to reclaim the soul's central place in psychology by incorporating Islamic teachings, specifically the Science of the Soul ('Ilm al-Nafs), into our curriculum. This not only serves Muslim communities but also underscores the universality of the soul as a core element of all human life. By restoring a balance between spiritual and psychological, we provide a more comprehensive, culturally relevant, and effective approach to promoting well-being in a manner that acknowledges the spiritual essence of all individuals, regardless of their religious background.

The global rise and contemporary impact of psychology from Islamic perspectives

There is a growing global interest in psychology from Islamic perspectives, as scholars and practitioners increasingly recognize the importance of culturally sensitive approaches to mental health. Psychology from Islamic perspectives provides unique insights into the understanding of human beings (i.e., man) through an Islamic worldview, contributing significantly to the broader field of psychology. This relevance is evident in academic research and applied professional practices, such as clinical psychology and industrial and organizational psychology.

IIUM's program, the Bachelor of Human Sciences in Psychology (Honors), stands at the forefront of this movement, serving as a model for integrating Islamic principles with contemporary psychological practices. The program's global significance underscores the importance of culturally grounded and spiritually informed approaches in all branches of psychology. Graduates of IIUM's program play an essential role in advancing psychology on a global scale by bridging the gap between modern psychological understanding and Islamic worldview.

In addition to IIUM's contributions, several academic institutions worldwide are promoting Psychology from Islamic perspectives. For example, the CMC offers a one-year online program Islam & Psychology (formerly known as the Diploma in Islamic Psychology), providing students with theoretical and practical perspectives of psychology and the Islamic sciences (CMC, 2025).

These initiatives highlight the global relevance of psychology from Islamic perspectives in fostering culturally and spiritually sensitive understanding and practices. The increasing recognition reflects its critical role in addressing the unique psychological needs of Muslim and other faith communities worldwide.

Brief History and Key Founders of the Program

The Bachelor of Human Sciences in Psychology (Honors) program at the IIUM was established in 1990, marking a significant milestone in the development of PPIG. The program was founded with the vision of integrating Islamic principles with contemporary psychological theories, aiming to offer a culturally grounded and spiritually informed approach to the study of psychology.

The first cohort of students graduated in 1994, consisting of 26 students (7 males and 19 females), among whom one female student achieved first-class honors. The initial leadership of the program was under Dr. Shamsur Rehman Khan, the first Head of Department (HoD), who played a pivotal role in shaping the early curriculum and laying the foundation for the program's unique integration of Islamic principles into psychological education.

In its formative years, the program attracted a diverse group of faculty members from various countries, enriching the academic environment with their international expertise. Notable early lecturers included Dr. Abbas Hussein Ali from Sudan, Prof. Dr. Zafar Afaq Ansari from Pakistan, Prof. Dr. Mahfooz Alam Ansari from India, Dr. Mumtaz Fatima Jafri, Prof. Dr. Syed Ashiq Ali Shah, Assoc. Prof. Dr. Syed Sohail Imam from Pakistan, Assoc. Prof. Dr. Amber Haque from USA, Dr. Nizar Al-'Ani from Iraq, Dr. Abdur Rashid from Bangladesh, and Dr. Mustapha Achoui from Algeria. These pioneering educators contributed diverse perspectives that were integral to the program's early development.

Additionally, faculty members from the local university, Universiti Kebangsaan Malaysia (UKM), played an important role in the early stages of the program. Dr. Muhamed Awang taught an introduction to psychology and Dr. Mohammad Hj. Yusuf contributed to teaching statistics. Their contributions helped strengthen the academic foundation of the program during its initial years.

In 1992, Dr. Malik B. Badri, a prominent scholar in IP and referred to as the "Father of Modern Islamic Psychology" (Rothman et al., 2022), joined the program. His expertise and research further enhanced the program's academic rigor and global recognition, helping to solidify IIUM as one of the leading institutions offering PPIG. The program continued to evolve under the leadership of various department chairs from 1990 until 2025. Under their guidance, the program grew in stature and expanded its influence, attracting students and scholars from across the globe who sought to blend modern psychology with Islamic teachings.

Today, the Bachelor of Human Sciences in Psychology (Honors) program at IIUM stands as a leader in the field, continuing to honor the vision of its founders while adapting to the changing needs of psychology education and practice worldwide.

Defining Psychology from Islamic Perspectives: Foundations and Rationale

The Bachelor of Human Sciences in Psychology (Hons) program at the IIUM defines Psychology from Islamic Perspectives as the study of human psyche grounded in Tawhidic Epistemology—the principle of Tawhid (Oneness of Allah), which unifies all knowledge and understanding. This framework integrates divine revelation (wahy) and reason ('aql), offering a comprehensive and spiritually aligned approach to understanding the human being or man (insan). Central to this perspective is the role of the qalb (heart), which occupies a pivotal position in Islamic thought as the seat of intellect, emotion, and moral consciousness. The qalb is not merely an organ but a metaphysical entity that reflects the spiritual state of a person, guiding their actions and decisions (Al-Ghazali, 2010). Its purification and alignment with the divine will are seen as essential for achieving well-being and harmony, as underscored in the Qur'an: "Indeed, in that is a reminder for whoever has a heart (qalb) or who listens while he is present [in mind]" (Qur'an 50:37).

The program emphasizes the integration of the heart (qalb) with the body (jism), mind ('aql), soul (nafs), and spirit (ruh), promoting a holistic understanding of human existence. This comprehensive approach not only addresses the physiological and psychological dimensions but also situates human behavior within a spiritual and ethical framework, aligning psychological practices with the ultimate purpose of servitude to Allah. By grounding its epistemology in the principle of Tawhid, the program bridges divine and empirical sources of knowledge, reflecting their complementary nature.

Furthermore, the program intentionally refrains from using the term IP, opting instead for Psychology from Islamic Perspectives, Islam and Psychology, or more recently, Science of the Soul (a direct translation of 'Ilm al-Nafs) to avoid reductionist interpretations and potential limitations. The term IP risks being perceived as analogous to other frameworks such as Buddhist Psychology or Christian Psychology, which are often seen as narrowly tied to specific religious doctrines and practices. While these traditions offer valuable insights within their contexts, the Tawhidic epistemology guiding IIUM's program is inherently universal and comprehensive, extending beyond religion-specific frameworks to address the human condition as a whole.

By adopting the term Science of the Soul ('Ilm al-Nafs), the program consciously ties its approach to the rich, traditional sources and wisdom of Islamic thought, which has long emphasized the exploration and understanding of the soul, its purification, and its alignment with the divine. This term evokes the classical Islamic sciences that have historically provided profound insights into human nature.

The decision to use Science of the Soul ('Ilm al-Nafs) reflects a commitment to returning to these foundational Islamic texts and teachings, ensuring that the program's approach is rooted in a holistic, timeless framework that acknowledges the nature of the soul. By adopting terminology that emphasizes integration rather than exclusivity, the program underscores the capacity of Islamic perspectives to critically engage with contemporary psychological paradigms. This approach ensures that the insights drawn from an Islamic worldview contribute meaningfully to psychology as a global discipline, resonating with diverse communities. The term reflects IIUM's commitment to advancing an integrated, holistic, and universal approach to psychology, harmonizing spirituality, ethics, and scientific rigor for the betterment of humanity.

Vision, Missions, and Program Educational Objectives

The Department of Psychology at the AbdulHamid AbuSulayman Kulliyyah of Islamic Revealed Knowledge and Human Sciences (AHAS KIRKHS), IIUM, has designed its curriculum, activities, and environment guided by a clear vision, mission, and imperative statements. The department envisions becoming a key player in revitalizing the science of the soul within academia. Its mission focuses on fostering caliber academic activities that revive the science of the soul to advance the ummah and humanity holistically. To achieve these goals, the department is committed to strengthening mindful academic collegiality, revitalizing the science of the soul, and nurturing holistic learners who embody the principles of integrated and balanced education.

The Bachelor of Human Sciences in Psychology (Honors) program aims to achieve five key educational objectives that guide its curriculum and outcomes.

i. Analyze theories, research, and practice in psychology.

ii. Apply a range of leadership and entrepreneurial skills to perform effectively and responsibly in different organizations.

iii. Apply science of the soul knowledge via the use of a wider range of digital applications, empirical-based evidence, and numeracy skills in diverse work tasks imbued with amanah to ensure sustainable development.

iv. Demonstrate interpersonal, communication, creativity, and innovation skills that can nurture well-being in the world and hereafter through intercultural understanding and interaction.

v. Pursue life-long learning in education and career in various settings within Islamic ethical and professional standards.

Nature of Program

Program Structure, Delivery, and Graduation Requirements

The Bachelor of Human Sciences in Psychology (Honors) program is a full-time undergraduate degree designed to provide a comprehensive education in psychology while integrating Islamic principles. It is accredited at MQF Level 6 under the National Education Code (NEC) 0313 (Psychology) and is recognized as an Honors Degree for public service equivalency (Malaysian Qualification Agency, 2025).

The program requires completion of 125 credit hours for local students and 127 credit hours for international students. This credit structure reflects the academic rigor and breadth of the curriculum, ensuring graduates meet the high standards expected of psychology professionals.

The mode of study is full-time, with a flexible study duration ranging from a minimum of four years to a maximum of six years. Each academic year comprises two semesters: long semesters, spanning 17 weeks each, and short semesters, spanning 7 weeks each (Malaysian Qualifications Agency, 2025). However, diligent students may be able to expedite their completion to three years by taking heavier course loads each semester.

The mode of delivery for the Bachelor of Human Sciences in Psychology (Honors) program is conventional, offering in-person, interactive learning experiences that foster direct engagement between students and faculty members. This approach creates a rich educational environment that integrates theoretical knowledge and empirical research while promoting practical applications and collaborative learning. Taught primarily in English, the program adopts an outcome-based, student-centric pedagogical model featuring interactive lectures, seminars, group exercises, and community outreach projects.

This structure supports the program's objective to produce graduates equipped with the skills, knowledge, and ethical grounding necessary to address contemporary challenges in psychology within diverse cultural and professional contexts.

Admission Requirements

IIUM has established specific admission criteria for both Malaysian and international applicants to ensure that prospective students possess the necessary academic foundation and personal qualities to thrive in this intellectually demanding and ethically grounded program (Academic Management and Admission Division, 2024a).

Malaysian applicants

Prospective Malaysian students—whether holding the Malaysian High School Certificate (Sijil Tinggi Persekolahan Malaysia, STPM), a Diploma, or the Malaysian Higher Religious Certificate (Sijil Tinggi Agama

Malaysia, STAM)—must fulfil the following requirements:

- Attain a minimum CGPA (CGPA) of 3.00 or Jayid Jiddan (Very Good) in STAM.
- Secure at least Band 3.0 in the Malaysian University English Test (MUET) for examinations taken from 2021 onwards (or Band 3 for earlier test sittings).
- Achieve at least a grade B in Mathematics/Additional Mathematics and a Science subject (e.g., Biology, Physics, Chemistry) at the Malaysian Certificate of Education (Sijil Pelajaran Malaysia, SPM) level.
- Obtain at least a grade C in Islamic studies subjects (e.g., Al-Syariah, Hifz Al-Quran) and in three other SPM subjects (including Malay language - Bahasa Melayu).
- Satisfy any interview or screening requirements imposed by the university.

Applicants progressing from the IIUM Centre of Foundation Studies are also expected to secure at least a B grade in the Introduction to Psychology course, in addition to meeting the general criteria outlined above.

International applicants

International candidates are required to hold qualifications recognized by IIUM as equivalent to the Malaysian prerequisites. Detailed information regarding admission requirements for international students can be found on the university's website and through its administrative support offices (Academic Management and Admission Division, 2024b).

Fees and Financial Assistance

The program fees are approximately RM 12,000.00 for Malaysian students and RM 71,500.00 for international students (Academic Management and Admission Division, 2024c; 2024d). IIUM offers various scholarships, financial support schemes for eligible students who demonstrate financial need (Finance Division, 2024).

Malaysian citizens can also explore government-funded financing options, such as the Majlis Amanah Rakyat (MARA) and the Perbadanan Tabung Pendidikan Tinggi Nasional (PTPTN), to alleviate the financial burden of higher education.

Academic Support and Student Progression

Student progression in the program is contingent upon sustained academic performance, primarily measured through the accumulation of credit hours and the maintenance of a satisfactory CGPA. A minimum CGPA of 3.0 is recommended, while students whose CGPAs fall below 2.8 receive additional academic support, including guidance and monitoring. If a student's CGPA drops to 2.0, they are placed on academic probation to ensure necessary interventions and academic improvement (Academic Management and Admission Division, 2023).

IIUM fosters an engaging, nurturing, and supportive learning environment through initiatives such as the murid-murabbi (mentor-mentee) system, peer support networks, and access to active student societies (Office of the Deputy Rector (Student Development & Community Engagement, 2025). These initiatives are designed to help students balance their academic pursuits with moral and spiritual values, reflecting the vision of Tan Sri Dzulkifli Abdul Razak, the 6th Rector of IIUM, and preserving the essence of "Leading for Sejahtera Humanising Education."

Collaboration and Partnerships

A strong commitment to local and international engagement is a hallmark of the Department of Psychology at IIUM. Collaborative partnerships with various institutions and organizations underscore the department's resolve to ground psychological scholarships in pragmatic contexts, thereby contributing to the overarching goal of "The Garden of Knowledge and Virtue".

Local partnerships

IIUM actively collaborates with public and private universities, governmental bodies, and non-governmental organizations across Malaysia. These collaborations are instrumental in facilitating academic research, policy consultation, and community-based projects that incorporate the "science of the soul" (Ilm al-Nafs) for social advancement and the betterment of society. Additionally, the department has established partnerships with local communities, including villages, schools of various types (religious, tahfiz, and standard), and refugee support groups—further demonstrating its commitment to serving the public and addressing societal issues with compassion, cultural sensitivity, and psychological expertise.

International partnerships

Beyond Malaysian borders, the Department of Psychology has forged collaborations with universities in Indonesia, Thailand, Pakistan, and other countries. These cross-cultural exchanges foster comparative research, broaden students' global perspectives, and promote international cooperation in the field of psychology. Furthermore, partnerships with international organizations reflect the department's dedication to fostering inclusive and universal perspectives in psychology, in line with the principle of Rahmatan lil Alamin (Department of Psychology, 2023b).

Curriculum

A cornerstone of the Bachelor of Human Sciences in Psychology (Honors) program is the IOK, a process through which Islamic spiritual and ethical values are interwoven with contemporary psychological study and practice. IIUM's Sejahtera Academic Framework (SAF) provides the guiding principles for this harmonization, emphasizing that intellectual development should serve the broader goals of well-being, morality, and community stewardship (Borhan et. al. 2021).

Core Courses

While all courses in the psychology program incorporate elements of the SAF, four courses are particularly central to the Islamization of psychology and the integration of Islamic perspectives into the curriculum (AbdulHamid AbuSulayman Kulliyyah Islamic Revealed Knowledge and Human Sciences, 2023):

History and Philosophy of Psychology. This course delves into the historical development of psychology from both Western and Islamic perspectives, providing a comprehensive understanding of the discipline's evolution and its philosophical underpinnings. It also examines the contributions of Muslim scholars to the understanding of human nature and the mind, laying a foundation for the Islamization of contemporary psychological knowledge.

Science of the Soul I. This course embarks on an in-depth exploration of the concept of the soul ('Ilm al-Nafs), drawing upon Islamic sources, classical thought, and contemporary research to examine the intricate relationship between the soul, cognition, emotion, and physiology. It introduces students to the rich Islamic intellectual tradition concerning the human soul its dimensions and its place in cosmology in the views of Socrates, Plato, Aristotle, Al-Farabi, Al-Ghazali, Ibn Sina and Ibn Bajjah with its multifaceted dimensions.

Science of the Soul II. Building upon the foundations established in "Science of the Soul I," this course delves deeper into Quranic perspectives on human psychology, encouraging students to critically examine conventional psychological theories and juxtapose them with soul-centric models grounded in Islamic traditions. It explores the application of 'Ilm al-Nafs to various areas of psychology, fostering a deeper understanding of human behavior and experience from an Islamic perspective.

<u>Undergraduate Seminar.</u> This course engages students in in-depth analyses of contemporary issues and challenges in psychology through an Islamic lens, fostering critical thinking, problem-solving skills, and the ability to apply psychological knowledge to real-world situations in a manner that is both ethically informed and culturally sensitive.

Islamic Studies Minor

To further enhance their understanding of Islamic principles and their application to various aspects of life, students pursuing the Bachelor of Human Sciences in Psychology (Honors) are required to complete a minor in Islamic studies. This entails taking at least seven courses in areas such as Quran and Sunnah Studies, Fiqh and Usul Fiqh, Usuluddin, and Comparative Religion. The Islamic studies minor ensures that graduates emerge not only with a robust moral compass but also with a nuanced understanding of Islam's intellectual heritage and its relevance to contemporary issues (AbdulHamid AbuSulayman Kulliyyah Islamic Revealed Knowledge and Human Sciences, 2023).

University Required Courses

In addition to the core psychology curriculum and the Islamic studies minor, students are required to undertake university-wide modules, such as Basic Philosophy and the Islamic Worldview, Knowledge and Civilization, and Ethics and Fiqh for Everyday Life. These courses reinforce the ethos of "Tawhidic Epistemology" across all domains of study, fostering a holistic educational experience that integrates intellectual development with ethical and spiritual growth (AbdulHamid AbuSulayman Kulliyyah Islamic Revealed Knowledge and Human Sciences, 2023).

Research Focus and Practical Training

Research conducted within the Department of Psychology at IIUM is deeply aligned with an Islamic epistemological framework, incorporating Quranic, Tawhidic, 'Ilm al-Nafs, and Maqasid (objectives of Islamic law) approaches. As emphasized by the 3rd and 7th Rectors of IIUM, Prof. Emeritus Tan Sri Dr. Mohd Kamal Hassan and Prof. Emeritus Datuk Dr. Osman Bakar, the convergence of divine revelation with empirical inquiry enriches the scope and depth of scholarship, elevating psychological research from a purely descriptive enterprise to a means of moral and spiritual edification (Bakar, 1998; Hassan, 2011). This integration of Islamic perspectives into research methodologies and the interpretation of findings ensures that psychological research contributes not only to the advancement of knowledge but also to the cultivation of ethical conduct and the promotion of human well-being.

Practical training in laboratory settings focuses on cultivating faith (iman) and Islamic character (akhlaq) through hands-on experience and the application of psychological principles in controlled environments. Internships and community service experiences provide students with opportunities to integrate classroom theory with practical engagement, embodying the spirit of "Leading for Sejahtera Humanising Education." Graduates of the program are thus well-prepared to provide culturally and ethically informed psychological services, adapt effectively to diverse work environments, and lead with compassion, wisdom, and a commitment to social responsibility.

Strengths

Strengths of Bachelor of Human Sciences in Psychology (Honors) Program

The Bachelor of Human Sciences in Psychology (Honors) at the Department of Psychology, IIUM, has a strong focus on integrating Islamic perspectives into its psychology curriculum. The department aims to revitalize the Science of the Soul to further enhance the existing frameworks of modern psychology (Rothman & Coyle, 2018). This approach emphasizes the importance of recognizing diverse perspectives, including Islamic and indigenous wisdom, as well as the need to decolonize the field of psychology (Sotillos, 2021).

The department has engaged in an ongoing process of curricular refinement and enhancement, including systematic academic review exercises (Dunn et al., 2007). The program demonstrates several significant strengths. These include a comprehensive perspective that integrates Islamic and scientific knowledge, a robust focus on cultivating students' expertise across basic psychology courses, an emphasis on developing essential technical skills for psychology students, and exposure to the latest developments and specializations within the field.

The Program takes a holistic approach that recognizes the importance of integrating Islamic and scientific perspectives on human behavior and the human psyche. The department has moved away from teaching psychology courses in separation and instead emphasizes a comprehensive integration of Islamic principles through Science of the Soul paradigm and empirical evidence to provide a comprehensive framework for understanding human psychology. In addition, the department has developed two new core courses, the Science of the Soul I and II, which provide a deeper exploration of the Islamic perspective through understanding the role of Soul on the human behavior and mental processes (Daulay, 2014). This approach is a departure from the conventional teaching of psychology courses and reflects the department's commitment to decolonizing the field and considering the Soul element and indigenous sources of knowledge (Kiguwa & Segalo, 2018; Richards, 2011; Vidal, 2011). The new curriculum approach prioritizes the empirical evidence of the psycho-soul perspective and balancing the modern psychology framework with the elements of the soul in explaining human psychology. This comprehensive integration of Islamic and scientific understanding offers a unique and holistic perspective on human behavior and mental processes (Richards, 2011; Vidal, 2011).

Furthermore, the department has recognized the importance of strengthening students' knowledge and intellectual demands in the broad area of basic psychology. Students receiving extensive academic training in the foundational domains of psychology, such as History and Philosophy of Psychology, Ethics in Psychology, Physiological Psychology, Cognitive Psychology, Personality Psychology, Developmental Psychology, Social Psychology, Cross-Cultural Psychology, and Abnormal Psychology. This comprehensive grounding in the core disciplines of psychology is vital, as research has shown that a solid foundation in the scientific underpinnings and theoretical frameworks of the field is essential for developing critical thinking skills and the ability to apply psychological principles effectively (Dunn et al., 2010; Mueller et al., 2020). By equipping students with this broad base of knowledge, the department ensures they have the necessary intellectual tools to engage in more specialized study and research within the field of psychology.

The program also places a strong emphasis on developing students' technical skills in psychology, including academic skills, research methods, psychological assessment, statistics, experimental psychology, counselling technique, and research projects. This focus on equipping students with both theoretical knowledge and practical skills ensures that they are well-prepared to navigate the complexities and demands of the psychology discipline (American Psychological Association, 2011; Naufel et al., 2018; Stoloff et al., 2012), blending the scientific and Islamic perspectives in their approach to understanding and addressing human behavior and mental processes.

Furthermore, the program places a strong emphasis on equipping students with specialized knowledge and exposing them to the latest advancements in the field. The program provides students with opportunities to explore and develop expertise in specific areas of psychology, such as clinical psychology, counselling psychology, organizational psychology, neuropsychology, sports psychology, positive psychology, and more. This exposure to the latest research and best practices in these specialized areas equips students with the knowledge and skills to make meaningful contributions to the field and to address the diverse range of psychological challenges faced by individuals, communities, and organizations (American Psychological Association, 2023; Stoloff et al., 2012).

Lastly, the department's emphasis on strengthening the basic psychology knowledge does not come at the expense of the Islamic perspective. Instead, the program seamlessly integrates the psycho-soul perspective, providing students with a comprehensive understanding of human nature and experience from an Islamic lens, while also grounding their knowledge in the empirical foundations of modern psychology.

<u>Program Growth since Inception.</u> The Bachelor of Human Sciences in Psychology (Honors) has undergone a remarkable evolution since its establishment, transforming it into a comprehensive and highly sought-after degree that continues to attract an increasing number of students. The program has expanded significantly, driven by a clear vision of integrating psychology, Islamic principles, and the concept of the Science of the Soul. This journey demonstrates the program's unwavering commitment to advancing psychological sciences while upholding a foundation in Islamic principles and values. The Department of Psychology at IIUM was established under the AbdulHamid AbuSulayman Kulliyyah of Islamic Revealed Knowledge and Human Sciences, with the aim of harmonizing modern psychological theories and practices with Islamic principles. In its initial years, the department relied on international scholars who were experts in psychology, enriching the program with their extensive knowledge and diverse perspectives. Over time, the department fostered the development of local talent, as alumni advanced through the academic system to become instructors, subject matter experts, and administrators. Currently, the majority of the faculty members are local experts who hold pivotal roles within the department and across IIUM's administration.

The program initially focused on fundamental and methodological courses, integrating Islamic principles throughout its content and assessments. In 2017, following a curriculum review exercise, the program was updated to incorporate emerging fields such as Neuropsychology, Media Psychology, and Community Psychology, while maintaining a strong emphasis on Islamic perspectives. The range of elective courses was expanded, granting students greater flexibility and exposure to new areas of psychology. Based on feedback from students and alumni, the department strategically shifted its focus in the 2023/2024 academic year to re-emphasize technical courses such as research methodology, statistics, psychological assessment, academic skills, and experimental psychology.

This is to ensure graduates remain competitive and skilled, equipping them with a strong foundation for their future careers and postgraduate education. A notable addition to the curriculum was the "Science of the Soul," a course grounded in the Quran, Sunnah, and traditional Islamic literature.

The program achieved full accreditation status from the Malaysian Qualifications Agency (MQA) in 2018, a significant milestone that recognized the department's academic excellence and unwavering commitment to upholding the highest quality standards. In 2024, the department successfully retained its accredited status for another four years during the Program Maintenance Audit conducted by the MQA. This achievement is a testament to the department's consistent quality, its dedication to continuous improvement, and its steadfast commitment to maintaining academic rigor and integrity within its program offerings.

IIUM psychology graduates are highly regarded and sought after by leading organizations across the country. They receive the highest ratings (6-stars rating) from Malaysian employers for their exceptional graduate employability (Talent Bank, 2024), reflecting their excellent preparedness and well-rounded qualities. These graduates are not only recognized for their academic achievements, but also for their ability to seamlessly integrate their psychological expertise with strong Islamic values and ethical principles. Their unique blend of technical skills, critical thinking, and spiritual awareness makes them stand out as exceptional employees who are highly valued by employers for their capacity to contribute meaningfully to the workforce and society at large.

The Department of Psychology at IIUM stands as a model for integrating psychology with Islamic values, adapting to new challenges, and consistently achieving academic excellence. Its graduates are well-prepared to contribute meaningfully to society, embodying ethical and spiritual values in their professional and personal lives.

Key Publications by the Faculty of the Department.

- Dzulkifli, M. A., & Mohd Mahudin, N. D. (2021). Contextualizing Islam in psychological research: Theoretical foundation, current initiatives and way forward. IIUM Press.

- Noor, N. M., & Dzulkifli, M. A. (2012). Psychology in Malaysia: Current research and future directions. Pearson.

- Noor, N. M. (2009). Psychology from an Islamic perspective: A guide to teaching and learning. IIUM Press.

- Ansari, Z. A., Noor, N. M., & Haque, A. (2005). Contemporary Issues in Malaysian Psychology. Thomson.

REVITALIZING THE SCIENCE OF THE SOUL:

Challenges

Reviving the Science of the Soul in the Bachelor of Human Sciences in Psychology (Honors) program presents both opportunities and challenges in aligning academic curricula with Islamic principles. The contemporary discipline of Western psychology has evolved along a trajectory that gradually separated it from the metaphysical and spiritual dimensions of the human psyche, with its foundations rooted in the secularizing forces of the Renaissance, the Scientific Revolution, and the Enlightenment project (Skinner, 2018). This evolution has led to a dissonance between the materialistic and reductionist outlook of mainstream psychology and the worldview of many Muslim students and scholars (Şahin, 2013), contributing to what some scholars describe as the colonization of the psychology discipline (Phiri et al., 2023).

Although the Department of Psychology at IIUM remains steadfast in integrating Islamic perspectives into the teaching, research, and application of psychology, it faces several challenges. Psychologists who attempt to merge Islamic perspectives with Western-originated psychological theories and principles encounter issues such as a declining trend in enrollment, stricter qualification requirements for psychology practitioners, context-specific criteria, limited resources dedicated to the 'Science of the Soul' in psychology, and prevailing attitudes toward research and practice from an Islamic perspective.

Global Trends in Higher Education Enrolment and the Decline in Psychology Intakes

Over the past decade, higher education institutions globally have witnessed a significant decline in student enrolment, reflecting a broader trend shaped by demographic changes, economic instabilities, and evolving career aspirations among younger populations (Dawkins, 2023; Kamssu & Kouam, 2021). In Malaysia, the declining trend in higher education enrolment is evident across various disciplines, including psychology (Jinn et al., 2022; Ministry of Higher Education Malaysia, 2022). Despite the psychology program consistently attracting the highest student intake within the faculty for years, the enrolment of psychology majors has steadily decreased over the last decade (Department of Psychology, 2023a). This concerning decline raises critical questions about the future sustainability of psychology education and its ability to attract and retain students. The intensifying competition from other fields that promise higher employability and more lucrative career paths has posed a significant challenge, as prospective students may be drawn towards academic programs perceived to offer more immediate and tangible career prospects (Arthur, 2002). Addressing this decline in psychology enrolment will require a multifaceted approach, examining the factors influencing student choice and strategically positioning the value proposition of a psychology degree to better align with the evolving aspirations and needs of the younger generation.

Qualifications Required to Practice as a Psychologist

One of the key challenges contributing to the reduced interest in psychology is the stringent qualification requirements for professional practice as a licensed psychologist. To work in this capacity, graduates must complete a master's degree in psychology (Trent, 1993; Taylor & Hardy, 1996), which poses a significant hurdle for students who have only attained a bachelor's degree. This additional postgraduate education requirement effectively bars them from directly entering professional roles within the field, limiting their career advancement opportunities (Taylor & Hardy, 1996). Furthermore, the substantial financial burden associated with pursuing a master's degree, coupled with the perception that psychology may offer less lucrative and rewarding career prospects compared to other academic majors, further discourages many prospective students from pursuing this path (Doran et al., 2016; Szkody et al., 2023). As a result, the psychology field struggles to compete with other disciplines that offer more immediate and attainable pathways to stable and rewarding employment, leading to a concerning decline in student enrolment. Addressing this challenge will require a comprehensive review of the education and qualification structure to ensure greater accessibility and alignment with the evolving career aspirations of the younger generation.

Context-Specific and National Psychologist Association Guidelines

The certification requirements set by national psychologist associations present significant hurdles for psychology graduates (Brown et al., 2004; Reyes et al., 2019). These localized guidelines often restrict the portability and transferability of their qualifications, limiting their mobility and employability prospects in the highly interconnected global job market (Lee, 2013; Parkinson, 2004). For graduates seeking to work internationally, the added burden of meeting the certification criteria mandated by foreign regulatory bodies can incur substantial financial costs and administrative efforts (Arthur, 2002; Calonge et al., 2023). This lack of universal recognition and the narrow applicability of their credentials within specific national contexts diminish the perceived value and versatility of a psychology degree in today's competitive and globalized workforce. The challenge lies in reconciling the diverse national standards and accreditation processes to enable greater portability and recognition of psychology qualifications across borders, empowering graduates to leverage their expertise and skills on a broader international stage.

Limited Availability of Comprehensive Resources in English for the 'Science of the Soul'

The exploration of the 'Science of the Soul' within the discipline of psychology faces a critical and persistent resource gap. Despite the growing recognition and interest in integrating spiritual, metaphysical, and psychological perspectives, comprehensive academic references and scholarly literature on this subject matter, particularly in the English language, remain strikingly scarce (Abu-Raiya & Pargäment, 2010; Iqbal & Skinner, 2021; Saad et al., 2017). This scarcity of comprehensive resources significantly hinders the ability of educators, researchers, and students to fully engage with, develop, and advance this burgeoning field of inquiry (Elzamzamy et al., 2024; Kaplick & Skinner, 2017). Expanding the body of rigorous, accessible, and interdisciplinary literature in widely spoken languages is essential to fostering a deeper and more nuanced understanding of the 'Science of the Soul' and promoting its global relevance and integration within the broader psychological landscape.

Psychologists' Attitudes towards Teaching and Research in the 'Science of the Soul' and Islamic Psychology

Many psychologists' express apprehension and hesitation when engaging in teaching and research with areas like 'Science of the Soul' and 'PPIG' (Iqbal & Skinner, 2021). This anxiety stems from multiple factors, including a lack of familiarity and comfort with unfamiliar subject matter, insufficient academic resources and supporting materials, and the perception that these topics deviate from and challenge the prevailing conventional psychological frameworks and scientific paradigms. There is also concern about the potential misalignment between these alternative perspectives and the dominant scientific worldviews, as well as the challenges in gaining widespread academic recognition and validation for scholarly exploration in these areas. Addressing these anxieties will require targeted professional development and training opportunities to build Muslim psychologists' knowledge and expertise, the dedicated development and curation of comprehensive academic resources, and the establishment of interdisciplinary platforms and collaborative networks that can validate, support, and elevate scholarly inquiry into the 'Science of the Soul' and IP as legitimate and valuable domains of psychological research and practice.

Solutions

Strategic Planning for the Department of Psychology, IIUM

To address the challenges, the Department of Psychology at IIUM is committed to implementing strategic initiatives that respond to current trends while advancing its mission to integrate Islamic perspectives and the

Science of the Soul into the teaching and application of psychology. These strategies aim to enhance accessibility, relevance, and innovation in the department's offerings, ensuring it remains steadfast and responsive to contemporary challenges. The department's strategic direction includes leveraging professional certificates, embedding international standards, integrating Psycho-Soul perspectives with modern psychological demands, and producing resources for the Science of the Soul.

Introducing Professional Certificates in Science of Soul

The department is actively exploring the development of professional certificate programs in Science of Soul, delivered through Open Distance Learning (ODL). Recognizing the decline in full-time student enrollment, the department aims to leverage the growing popularity of online, short-term, and professional courses to broaden its reach. These programs will provide greater accessibility to Science of Soul content, catering to a diverse audience, including working professionals and international students. This initiative aligns with the department's Amanah (responsibility) to disseminate the rich Psychology from Islamic perspectives and the 'Science of the Soul,' ensuring their relevance in understanding human psychology.

Aligning with professional and international standards

To address the increasing demand for specialization in psychology, the department plans to align its curriculum with both local and international professional requirements. By strengthening foundational undergraduate programs and developing master's-level specializations, the department seeks to prepare graduates to meet global standards. This includes embedding international certification requirements into the curriculum and equipping students with the competencies needed for diverse professional roles. Such alignment will enhance the employability of graduates and expand their opportunities to contribute to psychology on a global scale.

Integrating the Soul perspective with modern psychological demands

A key focus of the department's strategic planning is to seamlessly integrate the profound spiritual dimensions of human psychology with the rigorous demands of modern psychological science. This involves a dual emphasis on thoroughly mastering contemporary psychological theories, methodologies, and empirical approaches, while simultaneously embracing and deeply internalizing the rich Islamic principles and values encapsulated within the discipline of 'Ilm al-Nafs (the Science of the Soul). By doing so, the department aims to create a pioneering and unique framework that delicately balances the transformative 'Soul perspective' with cutting-edge, evidence-based psychological practices. This holistic approach will enable the department to cultivate a comprehensive understanding of the human psyche, honoring both its material and transcendent aspects.

Producing foundational references for the Science of the Soul

As part of its long-term strategy, the Department of Psychology at IIUM is embarking on the ambitious task of developing comprehensive, authoritative reference materials for the 'Science of the Soul' and its application in psychology. This far-reaching effort extends beyond simply producing textbooks or journal articles. It involves meticulously conceptualizing the robust theoretical foundations of the 'Science of the Soul,' operationalizing these profound frameworks through rigorous empirical research, and rigorously validating their effectiveness and applicability through extensive evidence-based studies. The ultimate goal is to create pioneering; holistic interventions rooted in Psycho-Soul perspectives that address the multifaceted psychological needs of humanity in a deeply transformative manner. Acknowledging this as a monumental, long-term undertaking, a true Jihad in the academic sense, the department remains steadfastly dedicated to this endeavor, recognizing its immense significance and potential impact. While initial progress has already begun, the department views this initiative as an ongoing, evolving effort that will continue to unfold and mature over the course of many years to come.

The Department of Psychology at IIUM aspires to emerge as a pioneering force in harmonizing soul with contemporary scientific approaches in psychology. By proactively addressing modern-day challenges and cultivating innovation, the department is dedicated to expanding the frontiers of knowledge and shaping the future trajectory of psychology in alignment with its distinctive values and aspirations.

A Road Map for the Department of Psychology

The Department of Psychology at IIUM aspires to establish itself as the hub for revitalizing the Science of the Soul (Ilm al-Nafs), with the goal of enhancing human well-being and effectiveness. This endeavor necessitates a continuous effort to expand the department's content expertise, requiring a multifaceted approach that incorporates both internal and external knowledge sharing, as well as advancement programs. Initiatives such as discourses, dialogues, seminars, and workshops on Psychology from the Islamic Perspective and the Science of the Soul are pivotal for fostering intellectual growth and innovation within the field. These activities not only expand the understanding of these domains but also facilitate the development of a comprehensive Psycho-Soul alternative theory, along with perspectives and models tailored to address human well-being holistically.

By promoting a balanced integration of insights from 'Ilm al-Nafs and modern psychological principles, the department seeks to enhance local acceptance and simultaneously elevate its international reputation. This progress will be supported by innovative teaching methodologies that seamlessly blend traditional Islamic wisdom with contemporary best practices, cutting-edge research that rigorously explores the synergies between 'Ilm al-Nafs and empirically validated psychological frameworks, and empirical evidence that substantiates the tangible value and positive impact of these holistic approaches on human well-being and development. Through this multifaceted strategy, the department aims to establish itself as a leading authority in the field, making significant contributions to the global discourse on the integration of Islamic spirituality and modern psychology.

Strengthening community engagement and collaborations with industry will further cement the practical application of 'Ilm al-Nafs. By forging strategic partnerships with government entities, private organizations, and community stakeholders, the department can establish robust platforms for consultancy, training, and cooperations. These collaborative efforts will bridge the gap between academic theories and real-world practices, allowing for the seamless translation and application of the profound insights from 'Ilm al-Nafs. Through these multifaceted partnerships, the department can expand the reach and influence of 'Ilm al-Nafs, demonstrating its invaluable contributions to advancing holistic human development across diverse contexts and communities. This strategic approach will ensure that the principles and concepts of 'Ilm al-Nafs resonate with and positively impact the lives of individuals, organizations, and society at large.

Attaining greater institutional autonomy is a strategic priority for the department. Enhanced self-governance will empower the department to efficiently manage and execute its strategic plans and initiatives. This streamlined decision-making structure will enable the operationalization of the department's vision to comprehensively and sustainably integrate the principles and concepts of 'Ilm al-Nafs. Autonomy will also facilitate proactive alignment of departmental efforts with the evolving needs of the community, academia, and industry stakeholders.

In summary, the department is committed to advancing its expertise through dynamic initiatives and innovative strategies that reflect the profound insights of Psychology from the Islamic Perspective and the Science of the Soul. By fostering a gradual but deliberate shift from conventional psychological frameworks to 'Ilm al-Nafs, the department aims to enhance holistic wellbeing and contribute to the global discourse on the integration of Islamic wisdom and contemporary relevance within the field of psychology.

Discussion

Student Population and Academic Staffing

The Bachelor of Human Sciences in Psychology (Honors) program at IIUM has demonstrated a steady growth in student numbers over recent academic cycles, despite deliberate reductions in intake during specific years. As of June 2023, the program supports a total of 252 students: 168 from the PSYC1 cohort (cohort 201/171 and below) and 84 from the PSYC2 cohort (cohort 221). This growth reflects the program's commitment to maintaining academic quality and manageable staff workloads.

In 2019, the program strategically recruited eight additional academics (Grade DS45, with Master's degree qualifications) to address the increasing demands of the undergraduate program. For the subsequent two academic years (2019/20 and 2020/21), the student intake was reduced to fewer than 100 students per cohort to ensure a fair distribution of teaching responsibilities among staff members. By 2023, after four academic cycles (2019–2022), the program has achieved a balanced staff-to-student ratio. The ratio is calculated as 252 students divided by 12 undergraduate teaching academics, resulting in a ratio of 1:21, which aligns with international standards for quality education delivery.

Currently, the program has 21 full-time academic staff, 15 of whom are primarily assigned to teach at the undergraduate level. Of this group, nine academics are also responsible for teaching at the postgraduate level, demonstrating the department's multifaceted teaching commitments and its role in advancing both undergraduate and postgraduate education.

While admission rates, graduation rates, and drop-offs are commonly included in discussions of program success, these metrics are not emphasized in this report due to their limited relevance in the context of this discussion. Instead, the focus is placed on current student numbers, academic staffing, and the deliberate measures taken to balance teaching workloads. These factors better reflect the program's ongoing efforts to sustain academic excellence and meet the needs of its growing student population.

Graduate Outcomes and Alumni Feedback

The employability of psychology graduates from IIUM has been consistently tracked through tracer studies conducted within six months of graduation. These studies provide valuable insights into knowledge utilization, employment outcomes, further studies, and the career trajectories of alumni. Between 2020 and 2022, a total of 571 psychology graduates participated in the tracer study. The data reveals the following trends:

- Employed: 353 graduates (62.2%)
- Further Studies: 41 graduates (7.5%)
- Up-skilling Programs: 9 graduates (1.6%)
- Waiting for Placement: 20 graduates (3.5%)
- Exploring Opportunities: 148 graduates (25.4%)

This is further demonstrated by IIUM's recognition in the Talent Bank National Graduate Employability Index. In 2024, IIUM was named one of the Employers' Preferred Universities, highlighting its rigorous academic programs, faculty expertise, and strong industry connections. Specifically, the psychology program achieved a 6-star award, underscoring its effectiveness in preparing graduates for competitive career opportunities.

These outcomes reflect the program's dedication to producing graduates who are academically and professionally prepared, aligning with IIUM's mission to foster holistic and impactful contributors to society.

Faculty Strengths and Expertise

The Department of Psychology at IIUM is supported by a team of qualified and experienced faculty members whose expertise aligns with the program's mission to revive the science of the soul to advance the ummah and humanity holistically. The faculty consists of 21 members, including 15 with doctoral qualifications and six with master's degrees. To ensure continuous professional growth, faculty members participate in monthly seminars and learning halaqas on Islam, Psychology, and the Science of the Soul. These sessions enhance their understanding of psychology from Islamic perspectives and their ability to integrate this worldview into modern psychology.

The department has a strong foundation in Outcome-Based Education (OBE) and remains up-to-date with changes at the Malaysian Qualifications Agency (MQA) level. This ensures the effective implementation of the updated curriculum, including the Psychology Standard 2nd edition, the Code of Practice for Programme Accreditation (COPPA) 2nd edition, and the MQF 2018.

Faculty members bring diverse research interests to the department, addressing various contemporary and societal challenges. Key areas of focus include:

- Islamic Perspectives in Psychology: Islam and Maqasid al-Shariah in psychology, integration of spirituality and religiosity into mental health practices, and mindful parenting.

- Clinical and Counseling Psychology: Cognitive-behavior therapy, person-centered therapy, and participatory action research on community-based approaches for at-risk populations.
- Organizational Psychology: Organizational change and development, leadership in higher education, employee well-being.
- Developmental Psychology: Child and adolescent development, family intervention, parenting, and healthy aging.
- Cognitive and Health Psychology: Neuroimaging, translational neuroscience, obesity research, and emotion regulation.
- Mental Health and Well-being: Anxiety, depression, stress, mindfulness-based interventions, spirituality and mental health, trauma studies, and positive psychology.
- Psychometrics and Assessment: Test development, personality assessment, and higher education admission selection.
- Media and Social Impact: Media effects, countering violent extremism, and community resilience.

Through these research areas and teaching activities, the department contributes meaningfully to advancing the field of psychology while aligning with the program's objectives. Faculty efforts are focused on producing graduates equipped to navigate the complexities of psychological practice in culturally and religiously diverse settings.

Publications on Psychology and Islam by Academic Members in the Past Five Years

Abdul Khaiyom, J. H., Abdul Aziz, A. F., Md Rosli, A. N., Bahari, C. A., & Abdullah, N. S. T. (2022). i-ACT for life: *A prevention module featuring integrated elements of Islamic spirituality and Acceptance and Commitment Therapy (ACT)*. Kulliyyah of Islamic Revealed Knowledge and Human Sciences, International Islamic University Malaysia, Kuala Lumpur.

Abdul Khaiyom, J. H., Abdul Aziz, A. F., Md Rosli, A. N., Bahari, C. A., & Abdullah, N. S. T. (2022). *i-ACT for life: A prevention module featuring integrated elements of Islamic spirituality and Acceptance and Commitment Therapy (ACT) - Practitioner's manual.* Kulliyyah of Islamic Revealed Knowledge and Human Sciences, International Islamic University Malaysia, Kuala

Lumpur.

Abdul Khaiyom, J. H., Abdul Aziz, A. F., Md Rosli, A. N., Bahari, C. A., & Abdullah, N. S. T. (2022*). i-ACT for life (versi Bahasa Melayu): Modul pencegahan dan pengurusan tekanan yang mengintegrasikan elemen Kerohanian Islam dan terapi penerimaan dan komitmen (Acceptance and Commitment Therapy - ACT)*. Kulliyyah of Islamic Revealed Knowledge and Human Sciences, International Islamic University Malaysia, Kuala Lumpur.

Abdul Khaiyom, J. H., Alias, A., Md Rosli, A. N., Abang Abdullah, K. H., Razali, Z. A., Ahmad Basri, N., Mohd Daud, T. I., & Shaharom, M. H. (2023). Clinical preventive approach of Islamic psychology. In *Clinical applications of Islamic psychology*. International Association of Islamic Psychology Publishing.

Abdul Khaiyom, J. H., Bahari, C. A., Abdul Razak, A. L., Fekry Faris, W., Mohamad, M., Abdullah, F., & Zawawi, A. I. (2021). *A manual of spiritual therapy: Islamic perspective*. International Institute of Muslim Unity, IIUM, Kuala Lumpur.

Alias, I. A. (2023). *Inspirasi Risalah Nur dalam menangani penyakit waswas atau OCD. In Inspirasi Said Nursi: Peranan Kerohanian dalam Kehidupan* (pp. 261-289). AHAS KIRKHS & Penerbitan Hayrat.

Alwi Alkaff, Z., & Abdul Khaiyom, J. H. (2021). The role of religiosity and optimism on death anxiety among Singaporean adults during COVID-19. *International Journal of Social Policy and Society, 18(*Special Edition 2021 [S1]), 151-168.

Bahari, C. A., Faris, W. F., & Mohamad, M. (2021). Jalāl al-Dīn al-Rūmī's concept of Ibtilā': Its application to stress management. *Al-Itqan, 5(*1), 5-18.

Basman, A. T., & Sidek, S. (2024). Developing an Islamic psychospiritual module to promote posttraumatic growth among Muslim humanitarian workers in the Philippines: A study protocol. *Asian Journal of Research in Education and Social Sciences, 6(*2), 175-181.

Dzulkifli, M. A., & Mohd Mahudin, N. D. (Eds.). (2021). *Contextualizing Islam in Psychological Research: Theoretical Foundation, Current Initiatives, and Way Forward.* IIUM Press.

Harun, M. F. & Mohd. Taib, M. (2025). 'Putting An Islamic Scholar's Hat on Psychologist': A framework for integrating Islamic concepts into psychological research. *Asian Journal of Islamic Psychology, 2*(1), 1-17. doi.org/10.23917/ajip.v2i1.7812

Hechehouche, O., Dzulkifli, M. A., & Alias, I. A. (2020). The Quranic-based healing through sound and its psychological effect: A review of literature. *IIUM Journal of Human Sciences, 2*(2), 75-80.

Hussin, R., Omoola, S., & Zulkifly, N. I. A. (2022). A SWOT analysis on the concept of spirituality among Muslim support staff in a faith-based higher learning institution in Malaysia. *IIUM Journal of Human Sciences, 4*(2), 1-14.

Ismail, S., Mohamad, M., Abdul Khaiyom, J. H., & Dzulkifli, M. A. (2023). A scoping review of the role of spirituality in dealing with loss and grief among cancer patients. *International Journal of Advanced Research (IJAR), 11*(8), 415-424.

Ismail, S., Mohamad, M., Abdul Khaiyom, J. H., & Dzulkifli, M. A. (2023). The role of 'Stage Theory of Bereavement,' 'Dual Process Model (DPM)' and spirituality in dealing with grief during illness experience in cancer patients. *IIUM Journal of Human Sciences (IJOHS), 5*(1), 50-62.

Jaffer, U., Che Mohd Nassir, C. M. N., Ahmed, M. A., Ahmad H Osman, R., Mohd Darwis, N. H., Mohamad Yusaini, N. S. N., Rusli, S. S., Zul Alam, S. Z., Yusof, M. A. I., & Shahrul, I. S. (2023). Exploring moral development and ethical understanding in children with learning disabilities: A study of teaching ethics and akhlaq in special needs education. *International Journal of Education, Psychology and Counseling, 8*(52), 745-758.

Jaffer, U., Che Mohd Nassir, C. M. N., Ahmed, M. A., Ahmad H Osman, R., Mohamad Asri, M. S., Muhamad, F., Tarmizi, F., & Mohd Idris, N. N. (2023). Exploring morality among orphans: A study of akhlaq and social standards in Pusat Jagaan Hembusan Kasih Sayang. *International Journal of Education, Psychology and Counseling, 8*(52), 773-783.

Jaffer, U., Che Mohd Nassir, C. M. N., Abdul Razak, A. L., Abidin, M. R., Ahmad. H. Osman, R., & Ahmed, M. A. (2022). A biopsychospiritual framework for the investigation of khushu'. *Journal of Pharmaceutical Negative Results, 13*(9), 1522-1529.

Jaffer, U., Che Mohd Nassir, C. M. N., Ahmad H. Osman, R., Abdul Razak, A. L., Allie, N., Ahmed, M. A., Jalaludin, M. A., & Mohd Kadri, N. (2022). The mediating roles of religious and spiritual coping between religiosity, spirituality, and depression among medical and health science students. *European Journal of Molecular & Clinical Medicine, 09*(08), 1209-1223.

Jaffer, U., Che Mohd Nassir, C. M. N., Ahmad H. Osman, R., Abd. Razak, A. L., Allie, N., Ahmed, M. A., Jalaludin, M. A., & Mohd Kadri, N. (2022). The moderating effects of religious and spiritual coping on the relationships of religiosity and spirituality with depression among medical and health science students. *European Journal of Molecular & Clinical Medicine, 9*(8), 28-40.

Jaffer, U., Che Mohd Nassir, C. M. N., Ahmad H. Osman, R., Abd. Razak, A. L., Allie, N., Ahmed, M. A., Jalaludin, M. A., & Mohd Kadri, N. (2022). The relationships of religiosity, spirituality, religious and spiritual coping with depression among medical and health science students. Jisuanji *Jicheng Zhizao Xitong / Computer Integrated Manufacturing Systems, 28*(12), 393-407.

Jaffer, U., Hamidi Izwan, E. S., Azimi, N. D., Mohamad Zaid, R. J., Abdullah, S. N., Che Mohd Nassir, C. M. N., Ahmed, M. A., & Ahmad H. Osman, R. (2024). Dopamine, serotonin, and the pursuit of balance: Neurobiological and Islamic perspectives on motivation–A narrative review. *International Journal of Education, Psychology and Counselling (IJEPC), 9*(56), 997-1012.

Janon, N. S., & Che Izhar, A. (2020). The relationship between religiosity and psychological distress among university students during COVID-19 and Movement Control Order (MCO). *IIUM Journal of Human Sciences, 2*(2), 15-24.

Luthfi, N. I., Alias, I. A., & Mohamad, M. (2023). Religious coping of Malaysian Muslims with high sensory processing sensitivity in facing the loss of loved one(s). *Simulacra, 6*(1), 109-123.

Mohamad, M. (2023). Viewing person-centered counselling from an Islamic perspective. *IIUM Journal of Human Sciences (IJOHS), 5*(1), 39-49.

Misran, R. N., Abdul Khaiyom, J. H., & Razali, Z. A. (2021). The role of religiosity to address the mental health crisis of students: A study on three parameters (anxiety, depression, and stress). *PERTANIKA Journal of Social Sciences and Humanities, 29*(4), 2833-2851.

Md Nasser, N. A., Amri, M. A., Zaid, I., & Abdul Khaiyom, J. H. (2022). Initial construction and validation of the Islamic Gratitude (I-Gratitude) scale. *IIUM Journal of Human Sciences, 4*(2), 52-64.

Mohd Marzuki, Z., Ahmad Fuad, N., Abdul Khaiyom, J. H., Mohd Adnan, N., & Mokhtar, A. (2024). Bibliometric analysis on Islamic spiritual care with special reference to prophetic medicine or al-Ṭibb al-Nabawī. *Intellectual Discourse, 32*(1), 81-114.

Tajul Ariffin, A. H., Abdul Khaiyom, J. H., & Md Rosli, A. N. (2022). Islam, Iman, and Ihsan: The role of religiosity on quality of life and mental health of Muslim undergraduate students. *IIUM Medical Journal Malaysia, 21*(3), 146-154.

Curriculum Accreditation and Internal-External Review

The Bachelor of Human Sciences in Psychology (Honors) at the International Islamic University Malaysia (IIUM) is an accredited program that adheres to the standards of the Malaysian Qualifications Agency (MQA). Key accreditation details include:

Reference Number: MQA/SWA12032

Certificate Number: 26917

Name of Qualification: Bachelor of Human Sciences in Psychology (Honors)

Previously known as: Bachelor of Human Sciences – Psychology (Honors)

Date of Accreditation: Starting 17/07/2018

Institution: International Islamic University Malaysia (IIUM)

Address: Jalan Gombak, 53100, Wilayah Persekutuan Kuala Lumpur

Type: Bachelor's Degree

MQF Level: 6

NEC Field: 0313 (Psychology)

Mode of Study: Full Time

Number of Credits: 125

The program's curriculum development has undergone rigorous internal and external reviews to ensure relevance, alignment with professional standards, and compliance with accreditation requirements. The 231-curriculum structure is a result of feedback from both the full-accreditation audit report in 2018 and earlier reviews.

Internal reviews were carried out by departmental members with expertise in psychology, curriculum design, and educational standards. These reviews assessed the program's academic content, structure, and alignment with the institution's goals. External assessors, experts in developmental and cross-cultural psychology from internationally recognized institutions, contributed additional perspectives. Members of the Board of Studies (BOS), consisting of educational and clinical psychologists with significant academic and professional expertise, as well as contributors to Malaysia's Psychology Programme Standards, further enriched the review process.

The integration of these inputs ensures that the program reflects best practices in psychology while adhering to the Psychology Programme Standards and the MQF (2018). This collaborative approach underscores IIUM's commitment to continuous improvement, producing graduates who meet the demands of a dynamic and diverse field.

Conclusion

The Bachelor of Human Sciences in Psychology (Honors) program at the IIUM exemplifies a distinctive blend of contemporary psychological understanding and the rich Islamic intellectual tradition. Guided by the Tawhidic paradigm, the program emphasizes the Oneness of Allah SWT as the foundation for all knowledge and integrates the Science of the Soul (Ilm al-Nafs) into its curriculum, offering a holistic approach to understanding human behavior and mental processes. This integration reflects IIUM's broader vision of "Leading for Sejahtera Humanising Education," ensuring students graduate with a comprehensive worldview that harmonizes empirical science and Islamic principles.

The program has experienced significant growth since its inception in 1990, with continuous curriculum enhancements informed by rigorous internal and external reviews. These reviews have ensured alignment with the MQF and the Psychology Program Standards, solidifying the program's academic and professional relevance.

Faculty expertise and dedication have further enhanced the program, with research focusing on diverse areas such as organizational psychology, developmental psychology, clinical psychology, and the integration of Islamic perspectives in psychology. Monthly learning halaqah on Islam and psychology enhance the faculty's ability to embed the Islamic worldview into their teaching and research, advancing the program's mission.

Graduate employability data, highlighted by consistent participation in tracer studies, demonstrates the program's success in preparing students for diverse career paths. Most graduates find employment or pursue further studies, reflecting the program's commitment to producing well-rounded professionals equipped with both technical skills and a strong ethical foundation. Recognition from national bodies, including a 6-star ranking in the Talent Bank National Graduate Employability Index, underscores the program's excellence and its alignment with industry expectations.

Looking ahead, the program aims to continue its contributions to the global discourse on psychology by fostering interdisciplinary research, producing foundational resources on the Science of the Soul, and expanding community engagement. By addressing challenges such as declining enrollment and the need for accessible professional qualifications, the department remains committed to ensuring its graduates are well-prepared to navigate the complexities of the modern psychological landscape while upholding the spiritual and ethical values central to Islamic teachings.

This commitment positions IIUM's psychology program as a leader in the field, advancing holistic education that nurtures intellectual, emotional, and spiritual growth for the betterment of humanity.

CHAPTER SIX

POSTGRADUATE DIPLOMA IN ISLAMIC PSYCHOTHERAPIES FOR MENTAL HEALTH

Riphah International University; Islamabad, Pakistan

Mifrah Rauf Sethi, Anis Ahmed & Mujeeb Masud Bhatti

Introduction

Riphah International University (RIU) is currently a leading private higher education institution in Pakistan. RIU is renowned for its strong national presence with a network of campuses spanning both metropolitan and remote cities. Over the recent years, RIU has gained prominence for its unique mission to integrate ethical values in the educational system, particularly those driven by Islamic thought and culture. Since its inception, RIU's leadership has remained cognizant about the global impact of the duopoly formed by Euro-American knowledge paradigms. In recognition of the epistemic imbalance, the university has taken strategic steps to integrate Islamic thought in its true spirit across its curriculum, teaching, research, workplace ethics, and public service. Following the same mission while recognizing the growing prevalence of mental disorders, RIU sought to amplify efforts for addressing mental disorders within Islamic revealed knowledge or where feasible, integrating it with secular psychotherapies. Such approach also reflected an awareness of the limitations of secular psychotherapies in delivering real-world benefits (McGinty et al., 2024), despite efficacy evidence emerging from the West or being replicated in developing nations. It hardly needs emphasis now, as it is well established that secular psychotherapies often fall short in addressing the divine, spiritual and cultural needs of human beings (Haque, 2004; Hussein Rassool, 2024).

Faculty and students at RIU have also shown growing interest in practicing integrated psychotherapies, which has been apparent in their feedback. This interest stems from overstretched resources and limited emphasis on integrating faith in mental healthcare services in Pakistan, both of which hinder the acquisition of practical skills during clinical internships. For example, there are only a few governmental sector psychiatry departments in Pakistan with a lack of trained mental health workforce, guidance manuals and training resources to support practice (World Health Organization, 2020). Even when guidance and training resources are available, service users/patients are unable to get the true benefit because they relate their problems to their faith, and available resources lack any such guidance (Choudhry et al., 2023). Subsequently, this undermines the quality of service delivery. Furthermore, supervisors are not trained in integrated psychotherapies based on Islamic values. Such feedback from faculty (who act as clinical supervisors) and from interns (who are graduate and postgraduate students) has developed a sense of acceptability and inclination towards getting hands-on training on integrated psychotherapies. Therefore, introducing a course where students can learn IP in practice is not only driven by top leadership, but also by faculty, students and service users who have identified this need.

Therefore, in 2022, for the first time in Pakistan, RIU introduced the certified 1-year diploma on Islamic psychotherapies in practice. Currently, the program fills a critical void by offering people with diverse backgrounds an opportunity to deliver Islamically integrated psychotherapies that are both clinically, Islamically and culturally meaningful, thereby ensuring relevance and benefits in real-world settings.

Rationale and Need

Several key challenges faced by those trained in secular psychotherapies or the current approach to IP have prompted the development of this diploma (Badri, 2020; Long, 2014; McGinty et al., 2024). Notable aspects are: i) neglecting revealed sources in addressing mental health despite their clear relevance to human life, ii) rare efforts to integrate faith-based knowledge with secular psychotherapies in the global mental health landscape, iii) limited cultural relevance of secular approaches, iv) significant gaps in training and supervision while practicing integrated Islamic psychotherapies, and v) insufficient emphasis by Islamic psychologists on research and monitoring.

Role of Revealed Knowledge

The secular approach sought to develop a knowledge framework devoid of ideology or presented as value-free. Indeed, it is debatable whether current scientific thought is value-free in true essence; however, the separation of religion from knowledge reduces religion to a private matter. Islam is not merely a religion but a comprehensive way of life that offers divine guidance in addressing mental disorders. Those stakeholders involved in the development of the diploma acknowledge that understanding mental disorders through the lens of the al-Qur'ān and al-Ḥadīth is essential, as this holistic paradigm integrates the various dimensions of human identity, upholds moral responsibility in all spheres of life, and places faith at the core regardless of public or private life (Ahmad, 2013).

Integrating Islamic Faith

There is a growing demand among the public for mental health services that resonate with their values and worldview; however, such efforts have been done rarely. The evidence that non-Muslims have also shown interest in Islamic psychotherapies, and it is not limited to Muslims, is in the work of Islamic psychologists who emerged from Muslim minority countries, and Islamic psychologists have shared their experience of how non-Muslim clients also engage with them (Haque et al., 2016; Khan et al., 2023). Our aim of integrating Islamic teachings into psychotherapy is not to negate secular psychotherapies altogether but rather to enhance divinity, clients' engagement, and clinical effectiveness.

Cultural Relevance

Research has now consistently shown that therapeutic outcomes improve significantly when treatment models are adapted to the client's cultural background. There has been considerable work conducted by academics that may not be considered relevant to IP in its epistemic essence; however, they have aligned psychotherapies with Muslim culture (Mir et al., 2015). Given the scarcity of practice-based work in IP, we adopted a strategic approach, incorporating culturally adapted work while also highlighting its limitations.

Training and Supervision

Despite increasing interest, few formal training programs exist that prepare practitioners to integrate Islamic knowledge into psychological care (Khan et al., 2024). This diploma directly addresses that need, offering rigorous academic and clinical training rooted in Islamic traditions. Furthermore, we also felt that the supervision model/structure for trainee practitioners of integrated psychotherapies has rarely been focused on. In response to this, we aimed to embed manually assisted treatment with dedicated guidance on supervision skills and its format.

Research and Monitoring

Our approach is not only critical of secular approaches but also open to critique of the current understanding and practice of IP in mental health (Haque et al., 2016; Safi, 2014). One of the key limitations of some who have developed integrated psychotherapies is their failure to evaluate the developed approach. This has been overly simplified by saying that knowledge based on revealed Islamic sources cannot be untrue; however, the subtle difference that needs to be understood is that knowledge or psychotherapy based on revealed knowledge is the interpretation of those revealed sources by a human being that can be critically evaluated and evidence of its ineffectiveness is not directed towards revealed sources but towards that interpretation (Ragab, 1999). Therefore, we have attempted to integrate evaluation of psychotherapy's effectiveness in research and practice.

This program, therefore, stands as a timely and essential response to the challenges to both secular and Islamic paradigms of mental healthcare education and service delivery systems.

Historical Overview and Key Contributors

The origins of this diploma trace back to 2019, when the Centre for IP was established following a landmark conference in Lahore, Pakistan, organized by the Riphah Institute of Clinical and Professional Psychology (RICPP). This conference was instrumental in bringing together well-known experts in IP. Stakeholders felt that there is a dire need to build the capacity of postgraduate psychologists to deliver psychological interventions grounded in Islamic revealed knowledge, hence transforming theory into action. Recognizing the need for experienced leadership with mastery in IP, RIU invited Professor Ghoolam Hussein Rasool to establish a platform enabling students to learn practical skills in Islamic psychotherapy. He was later appointed as a course director and consultant to RICPP. In 2022, Professor Rasool became a pioneering force behind the establishment of the first Advanced Diploma in IP and Psychotherapy at RIU, delivered at RICPP, Lahore.

This innovative program was designed by seeking input from psychologists, healthcare professionals and Imams. The course aimed to train professionals in psychology, counselling, healthcare, and social services. It provided an opportunity for learners to critically evaluate secular approaches to psychotherapies, exploring when and how they can be integrated with Islamic approaches, and to develop their capacity to use interventions based on Islamic revealed sources. This program, offered by RICPP, Lahore, was successful, with four students completing the diploma who are now serving as academics and practitioners in the field. Although it presents unique challenges, RIU has been able to sustain the course due to the increasing interest of various academic communities, encouraging feedback from those involved and the strong commitment of leadership.

As mentioned in the beginning, RIU has multiple campuses, most of which house Departments of Psychology, with the central secretariat located in Islamabad. In line with the RIU's vision to enhance outreach and promote inclusivity, the leadership decided to engage all departments in this program. In 2024, the Department of Applied Psychology, Islamabad, launched the second cohort of the Postgraduate Diploma in Islamic Psychotherapies for Mental Health (PGDip) under the leadership of Dr. Saira Khan (Associate Professor of Psychology). The program has since been continued under the stewardship of the current Head of Department, Dr. Mifrah Sethi, who is also an author of this chapter. On the other hand, cross-campus collaboration provided the collective input in refining the course content and delivery, while offering it from the central campus facilitated more efficient administrative processes.

There were some minor revisions made to the course curriculum and admission criteria, including allowing graduates in Islamic Studies with healthcare experience to enroll. The updates also recognized the importance of the task-shifting approach in mental healthcare delivery, emphasizing manually assisted treatments to support students without a mental health background, and placing particular focus on common mental disorders due to their high disease burden (GBD 2019 Mental Disorders Collaborators, 2022). However, the rest of the delivery structure remained unchanged, including mode of delivery (i.e., hybrid), teaching methods and management hierarchy.

Defining Islamic Psychotherapy

Definition and Philosophy

Islamic, or integrated, psychotherapy is defined as a professional relationship between the service provider (the therapist) and the service user (individual having mental health problems), in which they engage in a collaborative dialogue to alleviate symptoms of mental disorders, promote divinity and unity in life, strengthen spiritual growth, and enhance self-awareness and purification. The practice of the service provider is grounded in the theme and essence of Qur'an and Sunnah, and, where appropriate, integrates cognitive, behavioral, and emotional approaches with the understanding of revealed Islamic knowledge (Ahmad, 2013; Rassool, 2021; Rothman & Coyle, 2018). Key conceptual pillars include:

- The human being is understood through the revealed knowledge while focusing on interconnectedness of Nafs (self), Rooh (spirit), Qalb (heart), and Aql (intellect), forming a holistic view of human nature.
- The program also extends to include secular approaches if they are integrated Islamically or culturally adapted for Muslim population including faith-based CBT, mindfulness, schema therapy, and other modalities.
- The goal of therapy includes alleviation of symptoms of mental disorders but also to pursue spiritual and self-purification, unity in life, emotional regulation, and ethical self-development, guided by divine principles.
- The therapist's role is informed by values such as compassion (Rahmah), justice (Adl), sincerity (Ikhlas), and trust in Allah (Tawakkul).

This integrated approach ensures culturally competent, ethically grounded, and spiritually resonant care for people.

Vision, Mission, and Objectives

Vision

To serve as a leading academic program that fuses Islamic knowledge with psychological sciences to advance integrated mental health care.

Mission

To establish a workforce of healthcare providers and academics whose practices are grounded in Islamic ethics and values, therapeutic excellence, and committed to promoting holistic healing through faith-informed psychological practices.

Program Objectives

The program objectives are to develop a cadre of healthcare workforce able to:

- Demonstrate a sound understanding of applied IP and its historical evolution.
- Critically evaluate modern psychological theories and develop an understanding of how and when to integrate them with practices

found/ based in Islamic revealed sources.

- Apply Islamically integrated psychotherapy in clinical settings that enables them to assess mental health problems, identify the relevant treatment, use manuals and guidance to comply with treatment protocol and monitor the progress.
- Conduct scholarly research in Islamic psychotherapies and contribute to academic discourse.
- Uphold ethical standards informed by both Islamic principles and professional guidelines.
- Engage in personal and spiritual growth as practitioners, embodying values essential to both therapeutic and Islamic traditions.

Nature of the Program

Type of Program

The Postgraduate Diploma in Islamic Psychotherapies for Mental Health is a specialised, postgraduate-level qualification. It is not a bachelor's or master's degree, but rather a diploma program designed to provide advanced education and clinical training for individuals with prior academic backgrounds in social sciences, applied health, and Islamic studies with a strong interest and experience in healthcare practice. This program is tailored to equip professionals with the ability to integrate Islamic principles into modern psychotherapeutic practices.

Admission Requirements

Applicants must hold either:

1. A four-year bachelor's degree in Psychology or Applied Psychology or equivalent with at least 50% marks.

OR

2. A four-year bachelor's degree in Social Sciences, Applied Health Sciences, or Islamic Studies with at least 50% marks, along with a demonstrated interest and relevant experience in the applied healthcare sector.

For those falling in the second criterion, preference is given to candidates with prior work experience in any applied healthcare sector. International candidates are encouraged to apply, but documentation confirming the equivalence of their academic qualifications is mandatory.

Duration, Modes of Instruction, and Fee Structure

This one-year program is divided into two semesters and follows a hybrid learning model that includes:

- Live online interactive lectures
- Pre-recorded video content
- In-person classes and discussions
- Supervised clinical placements and role plays

The program is designed to be flexible for working professionals and full-time learners; therefore, classes are scheduled mostly on weekends. Tuition fees are set by RIU. To enhance outreach and engagement, financial support is also available based on merit or need and should be confirmed with the office of financial assistance.

Credit Hours and Progress Evaluation

The program carries a total of 22 credit hours, including 12 credit hours for Semester 1 and 10 for Semester 2. Student performance is assessed through quizzes, exams, written assignments, clinical case reports, and attendance. Students formally appear in the examination twice during the semester, i.e., during the mid-term (midpoint in the semester) and the final term (at the end of the semester). The midterm serves as a formative assessment, providing students with detailed feedback that facilitates preparation for the final exam. The total marks in a course can range from 0 to 100, where 60 marks are required to clear the examination. Notably, a minimum of 75% attendance is required to appear for final examinations.

Graduation Requirements

To graduate, students must complete all academic and clinical components, meet attendance requirements, submit case reports, and pass midterm and final evaluations. Successful graduates receive a certificate in Postgraduate Diploma in Islamic Psychotherapies from RIU, Islamabad.

Faculty Credentials

From the beginning, RIU has established a tradition of inviting faculty who are considered leading experts in their field, and this is no different for the PGDip. In the first batch, we invited well-known Islamic Psychologists, including Professor Ghoolam Hussein Rasool, Dr. Fahad Khan and Professor Muhammad Tahir Khalily, to lead the relevant courses. They remain in touch with RIU and occasionally participate in workshops, seminars, and conferences organized by RIU. Our departments are staffed with a substantial number of faculty members; however, the following are distinguished academics who, in addition to our departmental faculty, contribute to the teaching and supervision of students:

Table 2

Details of the faculty involved in Islamic Psychology Diploma

Faculty	Details
Professor Anis Ahmad	Founding Vice-Chancellor, RIU; Ph.D. (Comparative Religion, Temple University, USA). Former Vice President, IIUI; Founding Dean, Faculty of Revealed Knowledge and Human Sciences, International Islamic University Malaysia; Fellow, University of Sains Malaysia. Former President and Secretary-General, Association of Muslim Social Scientists, USA. Widely published on social, political, psychological and cultural issues, with contributions to major international encyclopedias and journals.
Professor Amber Haque	National Director (Muslim Family Services, ICNA Relief, USA), Ph.D. (Psychology, Western Michigan University, USA), MS (Clinical Psychology, Eastern Michigan University, USA), Non-resident Faculty, CMC, Former Professor of Psychology, IIU Malaysia, United Arab Emirates University, UAE, and Doha Institute for Graduate Studies, Qatar. He has published extensively on Islamic psychology and mental health.
Dr. Alizi Bin Alias	Organizational Psychologist; Ph.D. (Industrial and Organizational Psychology, Universiti Kebangsaan Malaysia), MSc (Applied Psychology, University of Surrey, UK), Bachelors. (Islamic Revealed and Human Sciences, International Islamic University Malaysia). Former Assistant Professor in Psychology, International Islamic University Malaysia; Co-founder, Psychospiritual Institute; published on topics related to IP, organizational psychology, and integration of knowledge, with contributions to international books and journals.
Dr. Jamilah Hanum	Assistant Professor, Department of Psychology, International Islamic University Malaysia; Ph.D (Psychological Medicine, Universiti Putra Malaysia), MSc (Clinical Psychology, Universiti

	Kebangsaan Malaysia), Postgraduate Diploma (Psychology, University of Melbourne). Widely contributed to integrating Islamic spirituality with psychological interventions. Research work focuses on IP, religiosity, and mental health, with contributions to international books and journals.
Zarina Hasseem	Senior Lecturer, International Open University; MA and BA (Psychology, University of the Witwatersrand, South Africa). Also, successfully completed a Postgraduate Diploma in IP from RIU. Experienced in psychometry, counselling, and Islamic-based curriculum development. Author of several books and publications integrating Islamic perspectives with psychological wellbeing.

Institutional Collaboration

The diploma program has been instrumental in developing partnerships within different departments of RIU and also to collaborate with external organizations. The current course curriculum and overall program have been co-developed and are ongoing due to close collaboration among psychology departments and institutes located on different campuses. We have also been able to take on board Tarbiyah, the department at RIU which provides mentoring to faculty and students.

Alongside internal partnerships, we are also able to sign a MOU with Khalil Centre based in the USA. The MOU was agreed by Professor Anis Ahmad (VC, RIU) and Dr. Fahad Khan (Deputy Director, Khalil Centre) in August 2023. The notable aspects of the MOU included co-organizing seminars and workshops for students enrolled in PGDip, facilitating knowledge sharing and exchange through the sharing of published materials, and, where feasible, the Khalil Centre providing mentorship in clinical supervision for students.

RIU is committed to building international partnerships to strengthen the global impact and is currently discussing the renewal of the MOU with the International Islamic University, Malaysia, which was initially signed in 2003.

Curriculum, Strengths, Challenges, and Future Directions

Curriculum

The Postgraduate Diploma in Islamic Psychotherapies includes a carefully structured curriculum with integrated theoretical foundations and applied psychotherapies. The course curriculum is reviewed and updated as needed. Below is a selection of key courses currently offered:

<u>Introduction to IPP.</u> Explores foundations, theory and philosophies of prominent Islamically integrated or culturally adapted psychotherapies models.

<u>Islamic Ethics, Thought, and Culture.</u> Demonstrating epistemological positions of Western thought, a critique of dominant Western thought and how it differs from Islamic thought and epistemology.

<u>Research Methods in Islamic Psychology.</u> Engages students in critically analyzing Western research paradigms and learning research grounded in Islamic tradition. Additionally, we are examining several research methods that aim to integrate Western thought with IP.

<u>Behavioral Therapy for Depression in Muslims.</u> Teaches culturally adapted behavioral activation therapy for treating depression in Muslims using Islamic teachings and spiritual coping.

<u>Islamically Integrated Psychotherapy for Obsessive Compulsive Disorder.</u> Introduces assessment and treatment techniques based on Islamic tradition targeting anxiety and specifically obsessive compulsive disorder.

Research Focus and Practical Training

The diploma emphasizes evidence-based practice and scholarly inquiry. Students are encouraged to build their capacity to critically evaluate scientific research methods and their philosophical position. Further, for the first time, we have included how research has been done in Islamic traditions and also aimed to introduce how research tools can be used to integrate the knowledge. The program also consisted of supervised clinical placements across both semesters. Students handle real cases, submit clinical reports, and practice therapeutic interventions under expert supervision.

Strengths

The key strength of this program is not just to acknowledge the limitation of secular psychotherapies but also to openly recognize that the clinical practice of integrated psychotherapies is at its infancy stage in Pakistan. We are aware that the integration of knowledge in mental healthcare has remained an ambitious goal (Badri, 2020), while the availability of a trained mental healthcare workforce in Pakistan is another challenge (Karim et al., 2004). Never before had the two challenges been conceptualized together; therefore, by doing so, we expanded our program and encouraged people from diverse backgrounds to take admission. For example, individuals with a background in Islamic studies are also eligible to participate, provided they have relevant healthcare experience. The success of this strategy under a task-shifting approach (Hoeft et al., 2018) has been consistently demonstrated over decades of research.

Following the same logic, we recognize that integration is a lengthy process, and we cannot overlook the work that has successfully embedded Islamic teachings into secular psychotherapeutic approaches without delving into epistemological issues. Any such approach may not have followed the pure epistemological methods of adapting the psychotherapies; however, they can be effectively used while acknowledging their limitations and further refining such approaches. Further, this program has a precise focus, i.e. on common mental disorders because of their high disease burden (GBD 2019 Mental Disorders Collaborators, 2022), hence there are specific courses targeting depression, anxiety and OCD to have a considerable impact on practice.

Some other notable strengths include the inclusion of multidisciplinary backgrounds of those involved, weekend classes to encourage professionals to participate, reliance on manuals and guidance tools where possible, and hybrid interaction with the students.

Program Growth Since Inception

Since its launch, the program has grown in visibility, attracting students nationwide and internationally. This is evident in the admission rates; we received a significantly higher number of applications for admission in the second batch. We are able to expand our network of partners and faculty members while ensuring timely updates to the course curriculum.

Faculty Publications in Islamic Psychology (Last 10 Years)

Presented below are selected key publications from our panel of faculty members during their tenure with RIU.

Table 3

Key publications of faculty members during RIU tenure

Lead Author, Year	Title	Journal
Ghoolam Hussein Rasool, 2021	Re-examining the anatomy of Islamic psychotherapy and counselling: Envisioned and enacted practices	Islamic Guidance and Counseling Journal
Jawaria	Development and validation of the Istiqamah Scale for Pakistani Muslim	Journal of Religion and

Zafar, 2025	Adults	Health
Shahid Ijaz, 2017	Mindfulness in salah prayer and its association with mental health	Journal of Religion and Health

Challenges

While outlining the challenges we faced, we contemplate that many of those challenges are global and similar to other programs in IP. The first and foremost challenge was the limited availability of faculty with dual expertise in Islamic scholarship and clinical psychology, which became more intense in combination with skepticism within mainstream academic circles about integrated psychotherapies. There was a lack of therapeutic manuals and practice guidance, along with validated tools (incorporating faith), supervision and monitoring. We found a lack of focused research coupled with insufficient available evidence on the effectiveness of integrated psychotherapies. Finally, there is no system for standard accreditation pathways for integrated psychotherapy training.

Solutions

To address these challenges, the program is actively engaging in faculty development, encouraging collaborative research, and seeking partnerships with International IP institutes. Future steps include:

- Building capacity of our faculty members in integrated psychotherapies by organizing conferences, workshops, seminars, short courses and offering financial support if they attend any such training.
- Building a network of international faculty with mastery in the practice of integrated psychotherapies.
- Making use of manualized treatment along with their practice guidelines to improve treatment fidelity, supervision and monitoring.
- Planning to establish a center for a central research unit focusing on mental health at RIU.
- Encouraging students enrolled in master's to focus their work on developing culturally grounded diagnostic and therapy tools.

Over the next ten years, the roadmap includes:

- Expansion into full Master's and PhD pathways.

- Accreditation by international bodies and IP networks.
- Annual publications in peer-reviewed journals.
- Creation of bilingual (Arabic/English or Urdu/English) training resources.
- Strengthening alumni networks to track impact and employment outcomes.

Discussion

Initial admission rates have been strong, with high student engagement and low dropout rates. Alumni feedback indicates the program has positively impacted professional practice, with many pursuing further studies or applying their knowledge in clinical and community settings. Faculty are highly qualified, with publications contributing to the global discourse on IP. Both internal and external reviews have praised the curriculum's depth and cultural relevance. The program currently awaits national accreditation and is progressing toward recognition from international Islamic psychology associations.

Conclusion

The Postgraduate Diploma in Islamic Psychotherapies represents a pioneering step in integrating clinical psychology with Islamic revealed knowledge. Its unique curriculum, qualified faculty, and clinical rigor set it apart in Pakistan. With strategic planning and continuous innovation, the program is well-positioned to influence Islamic mental health education and practice over the next decade and beyond.

CHAPTER SEVEN

POST GRADUATE CERTIFICATE IN ISLAMIC PSYCHOLOGY

Cambridge Muslim College; Cambridge, UK

Abdallah Rothman, Armaan Ahmed Rowther, Samir Mahmoud, & Khalid Sharif

Introduction

The Cambridge Muslim College (CMC) Postgraduate Certificate of Higher Education (PgCert HE) in Islam and Psychology program (formerly known as the Diploma in Islamic Psychology) represents the outcome of iterative and ongoing efforts over several years to develop a training program rooted in an authentic expression of an indigenous Islamic science of the soul, formulated from the ground-up as opposed to replicating the model of prior intellectual Islamization projects (Rothman, 2021). Its roots can be traced to the pioneering work started by Dr. Malik Badri to develop and teach an academic curriculum of IP at the university level, carried forward through his direct collaboration with Dr. Abdallah Rothman. This collaboration built upon Dr. Badri's early effort to establish one of the first academic IP program at the International Islamic University of Malaysia (IIUM) in Kuala Lumpur in the early 1990s, though Dr. Badri himself acknowledged that this early curriculum more accurately reflected a Western psychology program taught alongside Islamic principles in an effort toward adaptation (M. Badri, personal communication, February 21, 2018).

The creation of academic IP training programs such as these was in response to several growing challenges related to the increasing prevalence of common mental health disorders in Muslim-majority countries and minority or migrant communities (El-Refaay et al., 2025; Sempértegui et al., 2023; Zuberi et al., 2021). One such challenge was the predominance of positivist, materialist frameworks across psychology programs, both at Western universities as well as in Muslim-majority countries. Such frameworks not only excluded traditional Islamic healing practices but also often conflicted with fundamental principles of an Islamic worldview. Moreover, there was rising demand for practitioners who could work across or bridge traditional Islamic and contemporary clinical expertise, maintaining the integrity of both traditions (Ahmad et al., 2023; Hodge et al., 2023; McLaughlin et al., 2022; Shafan-Azhar et al., 2025). Finally, there was mounting evidence that simply overlaying Islamic concepts onto Western psychological theories would be inadequate for connecting Muslim communities meaningfully to modern therapeutic practices (Amri & Bemak, 2012; Badri, 2020; DiClemente & Delaney, 2005; Padela et al., 2012). This approach often results in what has been termed "Muslim psychology," focused primarily on the study of how Muslims think and behave, in contrast to IP grounded in Islamic principles and knowledge from the outset (Rothman & Coyle, 2018). Early attempts at rectifying this problem, including Dr. Badri's efforts in developing the program at IIUM, came out of the dominant intellectual orientation amongst Muslim academics at the time, which was the IOK movement (Al-Attas, 1980; Al-Faruqi, 1987; Safi, 1993). One of the popular arguments within this intellectual project was that academics should first master the Western academic disciplines before seeking to master or draw upon the Islamic sciences (Al-Faruqi, 1987). The program at IIUM was thus limited to Islamization projects that did not necessarily teach an indigenous form of psychology built on the epistemological and ontological assumptions of an Islamic paradigm.

As such, the CMC IP program was the outcome of efforts dating back to 2017 to develop an original curriculum that would first equip students with foundations in an Islamic paradigmatic approach toward human nature and psychology before then critically examining Western psychotherapeutic theories and techniques. Such a structure was based on recognizing the need for students of IP to first "unlearn" reductionist, materialist assumptions as a starting point for reorienting their study of psychology and practice of psychotherapy toward a traditional Islamic foundation. This pedagogical approach reflected an alignment with CMC's commitment to ensuring a holistic and integrative framework for research and education embedded in Islamic epistemological and philosophical traditions. CMC founder Dr. Timothy Winter, also known as Abdal Hakim Murad, has become among the leading Muslim voices in academia in large part due to his agenda of combining authentic Islamic teachings with a broad and deep understanding of modern scholarship and contemporary challenges. With his leadership, CMC has sought to exist in the space between seminary and academic institution, applying conventional university disciplines alongside the traditional Islamic sciences, using reason and revelation to think critically about modern challenges, and thereby "upholding the rich intellectual heritage of Islam in the contemporary world (About Cambridge Muslim College, 2024). From its inception in 2009 CMC included Islamic approaches to counseling in its first program in Contextual Islamic Studies and Leadership with a class on Islamic counseling taught by Sabham Dharmsi. It later hosted an annual weeklong intensive on IP taught by Professor Rasjid Skinner, which would become the precursor and inspiration for the eventual development of the yearlong curriculum for an academic program in IP at CMC.

The development of such a curriculum faced numerous institutional challenges, which highlights the inherent complexity of establishing an authentic Islamic approach within predominantly secular academic landscapes. An early attempt at fulfilling this vision was in 2017 at Al Neelain University in Khartoum, Sudan, whose curriculum in many ways resembled an Islamized Western psychology curriculum, incorporating Islamic concepts but within the more normative academic psychology framework. The attempt was a step closer to Dr. Badri's vision of an indigenous or "bottom-up" IP curriculum, in that the society within which the institution existed was rooted in an Islamic worldview (Kaplick et al., 2021; Rothman et al., 2022). While this allowed for the possibility of an Islamically rooted program, in this case the university administrators, being influenced by their training in Western psychology, were more inclined toward an Islamized approach retaining the Western paradigm of psychology. However, Dr. Badri and Dr. Rothman took on the project with the intention and long-term goal of shaping the trajectory of the program to move more toward an indigenous IP approach over time. During the process of reorienting this program to be closer to a bottom-up IP approach, political unrest in Sudan prevented international students from attending the program in-country and ultimately halted any further program development. Contemporaneously with the program at Al Neelain University, Dr. Malik Badri was invited by Istanbul Sabahattin Zaim University (IZU) to develop an IP masters' program. While the curriculum designed by Dr. Badri and Dr. Rothman for IZU was developed to be more deeply grounded in the

Islamic tradition, it was not adopted due to obstacles related to the more secular expectations of those responsible for review and approval within the Ministry of National Education in spite of strong support from the university rector.

These early experiences underscored entrenched secular biases in academia, even in Muslim-majority contexts, and the need to establish a program that could transcend conventional constraints of a secular model. Such constraints were acutely felt when the CMC Diploma in IP program was initially rejected for curricular validation by the Open University in 2021 as reviewers struggled to categorize it as either an academic psychology program or as an Islamic studies program more closely related to the disciplines of philosophy and theology. In particular, the program's focus on the soul and spiritual purification were considered too far outside the conventional disciplinary boundaries of psychology, leading to recommendations to remove foundational Islamic epistemology in favor of greater focus on cognitive-behavioral techniques and statistical concepts. Such changes ran counter to both the spirit and aims of the program under CMC leadership, and thus the decision was made to move forward with the Diploma in IP at the college without external validation in a manner that would preserve its integrity to a bottom-up and indigenous Islamic approach. This was in alignment with the original vision of Dr. Malik Badri and Dr. Abdallah Rothman, who had assumed the role of Principal of CMC, which allowed for the institutional focus on the development of an IP program (Badri, 1979; Rothman et al., 2022). It was Dr. Rothman's collaboration with a colleague, doctoral student of Shaykh Abdal Hakim Murad (Dr. Timothy Winter) and CMC visiting lecturer Dr. Samir Mahmoud, that helped bring the program to life and create a dynamic and updated approach to the curriculum. Dr. Mahmoud's background in Islamic philosophy and theology complemented Dr. Rothman's background in psychology and counseling, and the two together designed a well-balanced program that combined theological grounding with practical application. Dr. Badri's endorsement of the program as the culmination of his life's work (personal communication, August 15, 2021), and CMC founder Shaykh Abdal Hakim Murad's support for actualizing an IP curriculum based on sound Islamic philosophical and spiritual roots, provided strong impetus and corroboration for the program to continue developing and growing as an unprecedented integrative educational endeavor.

The CMC IP curriculum defines IP through the lens of a traditional Islamic conception of human nature and psychology, one which integrates fidelity to Islamic principles with relevance to contemporary psychological questions and needs. Unlike conventional Islamization approaches that overlay Islamic terminology onto Western secular academic assumptions, the program begins with Islamic ontology and epistemology and the view of humans as inherently spiritual beings whose cognitive, emotional, or behavioral lives cannot be artificially divorced from the soul at their core. This presupposes that Islam offers not only a comprehensive understanding of human psychology but also a pathway for healing and soul development. Rather than approach the Islamic intellectual legacy as a heap of historical writings of only academic interest, the Islamic tradition is approached as a living tradition that can offer much insight into the modern challenges of a post-Enlightenment world.

The CMC IP program's educational aims and objectives are as follows:

1. Articulate classical Islamic philosophical, theological, medicinal, and psycho-somatic paradigms of human psychology.
2. Identify major psychological theories from the 19th century and the development of modern psychology from both secular and spiritual perspectives.
3. Engage critically with modern psychology from an Islamic perspective and related developments in the 20th century.
4. Analyze Islamic and secular models of the self and identify what is distinct about Islamic perspectives of lifespan development, personality and therapeutic approaches.
5. Differentiate traditional Islamic legal, ethical and historical instantiations and realities of cultural and communal psychologies in contemporary contexts.
6. Evaluate innovative approaches to integrating contemporary psychology and classical Islamic psychology in modern contexts.
7. Discern the dynamics of counseling skills within a spiritual orientation informed by the Prophetic model and Islamic ethics.
8. Formulate the development of self-examination practices informed by the Islamic contemplative tradition oriented toward one's own self-transformation.

CMC is very uniquely positioned to achieve these objectives, which require a balance of academic rigor with traditional Islamic authenticity and rely as much on deconstructing students internalized secular assumptions as on conferring new knowledge. CMC's confessional identity allowed it to avoid the type of concessions made by other institutions of higher learning beholden to secular educational standards.

Nature of Program

The CMC program in IP was initially conceived as a diploma requiring nine months of part-time online study with an optional two week in-person experiential summer intensive at the college in Cambridge. It was designed to emphasize Islamic epistemological foundations and psychospiritual development of the practitioner as key priorities, relying on an interdisciplinary team of PhD-level faculty to ensure training would compromise neither academic rigor nor spiritual grounding. Applicants to the program were expected to be individuals seeking to both deepen their understanding of classical IP and engage with contemporary theory and practice, ranging from clinical psychologists, psychiatrists, counselors, etc., who intend practical applications in clinical spaces, community work, and/or coaching. Applicants were required to meet the following minimum criteria for admission:

- A minimum of a BA/BSc or equivalent qualification in any discipline.
- Evidence of professional training or licensing for therapeutic and curative professions.
- Familiarity with foundational Islamic studies and Arabic terminology.
- Proof of English proficiency for non-native speakers, waived if prior degrees were taught in English.

In the initial year offering the diploma, the college received over 200 applications, while subsequent admissions rounds had application numbers consistently between 100-200 (see Table 1). While admissions numbers were presumably higher in the initial few years due to the excitement of the program being the first of its kind on offer, it could also be related to the fact that the college offered a limited number of scholarships to support students from various countries and economies to afford the relatively competitive tuition price of £3,850. The price that was set for the program was based on market rates within the United Kingdom for this type of program with intensive study and small teacher-to-student ratios. The tuition fees cover the administration costs as well as the cost of contracting specialized faculty from all over the world, due to the lack of specific expertise on the subject matter within the college faculty. While CMC aims to provide affordable education with ample scholarship opportunities and does so for its in-person 3-year BA in Islamic Studies, the college does not have any endowment and was not able to sustain scholarships for the IP program after the first two rounds of admissions. However, this has been supplemented by the IAIP through offering a modest number of partial

POST GRADUATE CERTIFICATE IN ISLAMIC PSYCHOLOGY

scholarships from the Fazal Haque Scholarship for Graduate Studies in IP, which is funded by the sales of three IAIP published books.

Table 4

CMC IP Diploma Cohort Demographics by Year

Academic Year	Number of Applications	Number of Graduates	Gender	Age	Region
2024-25	142	28	Female: 23 Male: 4	25 - 58 yrs	North America: 50.00% Europe: 20.00% of which British 13.33% Africa: 13.33% Oceania: 10.00% Asia: 10.00%
2023-24	212	26	Female: 20 Male: 6	22 - 63 yrs	North America: 37.50% Europe: 29.17% of which British 12.50% Asia: 20.83% Oceania: 4.17% Africa: 8.33%
2022-23	195	30	Female: 20 Male: 10	26-66 yrs	Asia: 42.00% North America: 38.00% Europe: 16.00% of which British 10.00% Oceania: 7.00% Africa: 3.00%
2021-22	225	31	Female: 21 Male: 10	22-49 yrs	North America: 44.44% Europe: 40.74% of which British 25.93% Asia: 22.22% Oceania: 14.81% Africa: 3.70%

Graduation requirements include successful completion of all assessments, adherence to minimum live attendance policies (no more than three absences per module), and active participation in all components in the program. The nine-month part-time program is delivered synchronously online over three 11-week terms. Instruction included the following:

- Six hours of live online lectures weekly, held Monday, Tuesday, and Thursday from 1–3 PM (GMT).
- Nine hours of independent study weekly.
- Self-examination practices for psychological and spiritual development.

Faculty Credentials

The program's faculty composition is among its greatest strengths, with all instructors having doctoral level credentials (PhD, MD, ND) in their respective academic fields and also possessing training in areas of traditional Islamic scholarship. This allows students to gain grounding in both Islamic theoretical orientations and their application to modern psychological questions. This is made possible by a faculty that includes theologians and psychologists with expertise in complementary disciplines ranging from Islamic ethics to clinical psychotherapy. The ability to harmoniously integrate instruction in rigorous theory and practical application relies on an approach that transcends the disciplinary boundaries contrived by modern academia.

One illustrative example at the program's outset was the recruitment of Dr. Najah Nadi, a traditionally trained academic with a B.A. in Islamic Studies from Al-Azhar University, M.A. in Religious Studies from Boston University, and D. Phil from the University of Oxford whose research focuses on classical theories of knowledge across philosophy, theology, law, and spirituality. She had previously taught courses on Islamic legal theory, classical logic and ontology, and Islamic spirituality and ethics. The deep relevance of her expertise to a psychology course can only be appreciated through an IP lens that recognizes the centrality of virtue ethics (akhlāq), philosophy (falsafa) and theology (kalām) to an indigenous Islamic understanding of selfhood in both its horizontal (immanent) and vertical (transcendent) forms.

This is similarly applicable to the inclusion of philosophical and theological perspectives from faculty such as Dr. Samir Mahmoud, clinical expertise from psychotherapeutic practice from Dr. Abdallah Rothman, and knowledge of traditional Islamic medicine from Dr. Mazen Atassi. In addition to including a broad range of disciplinary expertise, CMC's global reach and the program's online format facilitated recruitment of leading experts from countries around the world, significantly expanding the pool of qualified instructors: Dr. Rania Awaad, Clinical Professor of Psychiatry at Stanford University School of Medicine and Director of the Stanford Muslim Mental Health & IP Lab; Dr. Mariam Sheibani, Assistant Professor of Islamic Thought at Brandeis University with a PhD from the University of Chicago; and Dr. Yusuf Jha, Specialist in Religious Sciences at the UAE Council for Fatwa with a PhD from University of Nottingham.

Assessment and Measurement of Progress

Student progress is evaluated through diverse assessments tailored to each module's objectives. These include weekly reflective journal prompts, formative essays and summative research papers and presentations. The assessments were designed to measure not only understanding but also the ability to apply IP frameworks to relevant clinical questions. Successful completion of all assessments, live attendance of all classes with up to only three missed classes per module, and active participation are mandatory for graduation. Cohorts are limited to maximum 30 students to ensure close monitoring of learning from instructors and to develop an intimate collegial experience where instructors become familiar with students' strengths and can thereby attune to specific learning needs. In each of the four years the program has run, all students who remain enrolled passed and graduated successfully. On average, two to three students withdrew from the program before the end of the year due to changing life circumstances.

Curriculum

The CMC IP curriculum was designed to guide students through a developmental arc, beginning with foundational Islamic principles before progressing through modern challenges and finally ending with opportunities for application (see Table 2). In the first term (Foundations), the students are led through an exploration of classical sources in three areas: (1) philosophy and theology, which provide a grounding in the epistemology and ontology of the human being from Islamic sources; (2) spirituality, law, and ethics, which provide students with an understanding of how the sciences of moral psychology, ethics (akhlāq), and purification of the self (tazkiyat al-nafs) have traditionally dealt with aspects of what we now term psychology; and (3) Islamic medicine (tibb) and ḥikma traditions, which help students appreciate holistic approaches to health and wellness in the Islamic tradition, in which mind, body, and soul are integral and physical healing is necessarily integrated with approaches to psychotherapeutic growth.

In the second term (Transformations), the curriculum builds upon this foundational knowledge to examine how modern notions of subjectivity have transformed these classical approaches by examining three subject areas: (1) modern subjectivity, which provides students an understanding of the historical context for the shifts in philosophy and ideology with regards to notions of the self; (2) psychology, religion and spirituality, which orients students to the various approaches to psychology and how they compare and contrast to Islamic worldviews; and (3) modern trends in IP, which gives students an overview of the recent and current developments in the emerging field. The goal is to equip students to make sense of modern psychological theories from an Islamic perspective as well as contextualize modern movements within IP over the past century.

Finally, in the third and final term (Integrations), students examine how classical understandings of IP can be put into application across various modes of practice in three areas: (1) Islam, personality and the lifespan, which looks at the nature of the human being and how spiritual conceptualizations impact understandings of trauma and developmental psychology; (2) Islamic law in context, which prepares students to think critically about how the Islamic tradition intersects with modern circumstances; and (3) Islamic psychotherapy and counseling, which orients students to the possibilities of therapeutic applications in mental healthcare, counseling, and community settings. Students participate in group or individual projects and complete case studies that encourage engagement with the challenges and opportunities of applying IP frameworks to clinical and community contexts.

Table 5

CMC IP Program Modules

Module 1: Foundations of Islamic Psychology: Theology, Philosophy & Medicine	
Historical Development of Islamic Psychology:	Traces the development of Islamic theological and philosophical ideas rooted in the Quran, examining their dialogue with other philosophical systems. Covers major figures in Islamic history, theology, and medicine and their contributions to understanding psyche-body integration.
Theological Foundations for the Concept of the Soul/Psyche:	An integrated treatment of core Qur'anic and Prophetic concepts of the nafs/ruh/'aql/qalb, the classical theoretical-methodological approaches to understanding, training, and treating the human psyche, and the spiritual-ethical models for purification and perfection of the soul in pursuit of felicity.

Medical and Social Dimensions of Islamic Psychology:	A focused examination of the **Hikma** tradition's holistic and vitalist medicine and its applications to psychological well-being, its relationships with other ancient medical traditions, and the social dimensions of Islamic psychology and medicine as practiced within communities, institutions, and historical asylums.

Module 2: Transformations of Worldviews: Secular Psychology, Religion and the Revival of Islamic Psychology.

Emergence of the Modern Self:	Traces the philosophical and cultural currents—enlightenment, industrialization, existentialism—that led to new understandings of subjectivity and a "material" or "intensive" sense of self.
Western Psychologies and Spirituality:	Surveys major schools of modern psychology (e.g., Freudian, Jungian, Humanistic, Cognitive) and examines their approaches to religion/spirituality in comparison with Islamic thought.
Contemporary Islamic Psychological Movements:	Explores 20th- and 21st-century Muslim attempts to reconcile or reformulate psychology in light of Islamic theology, highlighting ongoing debates, achievements, and limitations.

Module 3: Integrations of Application in Community: Development, Sociocultural Realities, and Therapeutic Practice.

Lifespan & Personality:	Offers comparative study of Lifespan Development from contemporary and Islamic perspectives, examining human development from pre-conception through death and the afterlife. Explores the concept of *fiṭra* in relation to developmental psychology.
Socio-cultural Contexts:	Examines social psychology understanding of Muslims' lived experiences in modern secular societies, particularly in Muslim-minority contexts, analyzing how cultural, social, political, and economic factors shape Muslim psychological experiences.
Islamic Psychotherapy & Counseling:	Provides understanding of contemporary Islamic psychotherapy and counseling approaches, examining applications of mental health in diverse professional and communal settings.

A cornerstone of the program's pedagogical approach is one of beginning with an 'empty cup' as conceptualized in many spiritual traditions through "unlearning" (takhliyya), namely a structured yet personal journey of introspection to begin recognizing and deconstructing the reductionist or materialist assumptions that are often subtly yet deeply ingrained in mainstream psychology training. This involves critical examination of how modern psychological theories developed within a social and historical context, how they compare to Islamic principles of human nature and psychology, and how such theories and methodologies can be approached with fidelity to an Islamic epistemology and ontology of the human psyche. Rather than discarding prior knowledge, students are encouraged to recontextualize these ideas and their prior training experiences within an IP paradigm, creating space for its integration with modern psychology and psychotherapeutic practice. This process is phased across modules such that students begin with core Islamic philosophical and theological ideas before beginning to engage critically with modern secular frameworks, such that they are prepared to navigate contemporary challenges with clarity and depth. As such, one might understand the CMC IP program's approach to training practitioners as emphasizing a process of cultivation that begins with takhliyya (clearing or emptying the self) before taḥliyya (adorning or beautifying the self). This order of operations helps ensure that students engage from a place of strong theoretical and spiritual grounding, both personally and intellectually. In this way, the program challenges traditional boundaries between academic training and personal development.

Similarly, the CMC IP program's holistic approach addresses critical debates about the feasibility of integrating spiritual development and psychotherapeutic healing, again pushing conventional boundaries between the spiritual (vertical) and the psychological (horizontal) aspects of IP. While some programs and practitioners advocate for the limiting of IP training to cognitive-behavioral methods, the CMC program emphasizes the integral nature of spirituality in understanding psychological distress and healing. Denying the vertical dimension of the psychotherapeutic encounter, including centrality of the qalb (heart) and rūḥ (spirit) to the human psyche, only serves to perpetuate the very secular biases that IP seeks to transcend. Such false binaries also undermine IP's potential to orient clients and patients toward healing rather than merely coping. Without acknowledging Allah as Al-Shāfī (The Healer) and the central importance of the human qalb, including in clinical contexts, therapy risks becoming more superficially focused on the modification of thoughts and behaviors alone, a reductionist goal which belies notions of therapy being Islamic. In contrast, the CMC curriculum trains students in case conceptualizations that address the 'aql, qalb, rūḥ and nafs in an integrated fashion without making simple equivalencies or transposing traditional Islamic terminology onto modern secular frameworks.

The program emphasizes personal and spiritual development

alongside academic rigor. Tools such as self-accounting (muḥāsaba), journaling, self-reflective practices, and personal supervision sessions encourage students' heart-centered growth. The inclusion of fellowship (ṣuḥba) maintains traditional Islamic educational values within a modern format, fostering spiritual growth alongside intellectual development. Throughout these instructional components of the program, guided practice and supervision were incorporated to integrate students' training with traditional Islamic pedagogical and self-refinement. The summer intensive, which was run for the first four cohorts, included paired practice of psychotherapeutic methods and techniques as well as self-development and heart-centered learning. Synchronous or live learning is also heavily emphasized throughout the online portion of the training to foster student engagement that most closely mirrors in-person interactions. As such, lectures are not recorded for dissemination to students, and cohort sizes are capped at approximately 30 students to preserve the opportunity for meaningful interpersonal interactions among faculty and students.

As part of the program's commitment to continuous improvement and research inquiry, a study was conducted by Dr. Rothman and a group from the first cohort of program graduates to investigate the learning journey of students in the subsequent year. The study, entitled Research in Understanding the Heart in Islamic Psychology (RUH-IP), included both periodic quantitative surveys as well as qualitative data analysis of periodic journal entries for self-reflection on personal growth over the academic year (Rothman et al., forthcoming). The results of this small study of 19 participants uncovered four major areas or themes of transformation longitudinally in students: an early emergence of internal struggle, a broadening awareness of the self, engagement in making sense of the self, and finally finding greater coherence and integration toward the conclusion of the program. In the course of this journey, student participants in the study shifted from reports of strong emotions, such as those triggered by insecurities /comparisons or past traumas, toward a greater level of engagement in contemplative practices and centering in the heart. The quantitative measures of the study indicated a broadening of self-awareness from only the cognitive and bodily to also include the heart-centered and spirit-focused self-knowledge from pre- to post-completion of the Diploma in IP Program.

Strengths

The CMC IP diploma program is pioneering in its unabashed acknowledgement of the inherently spiritual nature of the human being in the Islamic tradition and worldview, which is central to its ability to transcend conventional divisions–between the religious and the mundane or the sacred and the profane–to meaningfully explore the clinical and spiritual implications of applying Islamic epistemological principles to contemporary psychological questions or needs. The program's vision of prioritizing a revival of indigenous frameworks, instead of mere adaptation of secular Western models, was in no small part related to the strong endorsement by Shaykh Abdal Hakim Murad, further enhancing the program's credibility in both academic and seminary circles. Shaykh Abdal Hakim described the IP diploma program as "the jewel in the crown of CMC," noting its clear alignment with the college's broader commitment to implementing traditional knowledge to meet modern real-world needs (CMC, 2023, 1:00:00). The program's success has also been evidenced by consistent applicant numbers, receiving an average of almost 200 applications annually. The program also seeks to contribute to the broader field of IP through publications and research, with graduates going on to shape IP practice and research globally. The combination of academic excellence, traditional Islamic authenticity, and practical effectiveness has established the program as a model for IP education. Finally, the program's online format enables global access to top-notch faculty and diverse student cohorts. While the online format presents logistical challenges such as coordinating across time zones, these have been mitigated through a synchronous learning model with strict attendance and participation policies as well as a capped cohort size of 30 students to ensure meaningful interaction and engagement.

The CMC IP program challenges prevailing trends in IP to limit its scope to clinical aspects of "Muslim mental health." It critiques the reductionist approach of separating clinical from spiritual dimensions and posits that truly holistic healing is impossible without acknowledging Allah and the human rūḥ (spirit) and actively engaging with these aspects in applications. The program views IP as a complete understanding of human nature, integrating clinical and spiritual dimensions seamlessly. Without acknowledging the vertical (spiritual) and horizontal (interpersonal) dimensions of existence, it argues, psychological treatment focuses only on coping rather than full, transformative healing.

This perspective is not without its challenges. Critics within traditional scholarship have questioned whether IP programs can appropriately handle deeper spiritual states without the guidance of qualified shuyūkh (traditional Islamic spiritual masters). In response, the program underscores the ethical limitations of practitioners, emphasizing that therapeutic engagement must remain within their training and expertise. Practitioners are encouraged to act as mirrors, facilitating awareness of the spiritual dimension while maintaining clear principled boundaries. This nuanced approach seeks to balance the program's emphasis on spiritual reality with practical ethical considerations, creating a distinct identity within the IP landscape.

Challenges

The CMC IP program, while achieving significant success, has encountered several unique challenges inherent to its pioneering approach and the nascent field of IP. These challenges can be broadly categorized into those related to student expectations, the online learning environment, and the broader perception of IP.

Student Expectations

Expectations vs. Reality. Aligning student expectations with the program's aims has been a key challenge. Many students, particularly practitioners, enroll with the expectation of acquiring qualifications in a specific method of Islamic psychotherapy. However, the program focuses on providing a broad foundation in IP rather than training in a particular therapeutic approach. This has led to a need for clearer communication of the program's objectives and a restructuring of the curriculum to ensure it adequately addresses student needs while maintaining its core focus.

Demand for Immediate Clinical Application. The increasing demand for IP has led to a desire among students for immediate practical application of the knowledge gained in the program to patients and clients. Balancing this demand with the program's emphasis on personal development, self-reflection, and unlearning has required careful consideration and the implementation of strategies such as journaling and personal supervision sessions.

Online Learning Environment

Global Reach and Time Zones. The program's global reach, while a strength in terms of diversity, has presented challenges in coordinating synchronous learning across multiple time zones. Accommodating students and faculty living in regions ranging from the West Coast of the United States to the East Coast of Australia has required strict adherence to live session attendance requirements and careful scheduling, which has in turn impacted the flexibility typically associated with online learning.

Maintaining Engagement and Interaction. Creating a dynamic and interactive learning environment in a virtual setting has been another challenge. The program has addressed this by emphasizing active participation in live sessions, incorporating group activities and discussions, and fostering a sense of community among students despite the online format.

Field of Islamic Psychology

<u>Definitional Ambiguity.</u> The field's immaturity and the lack of a clear consensus on what constitutes IP have posed challenges in communicating the program's unique approach and distinguishing it from other programs and approaches. Addressing this has required a clear articulation of the program's definition of IP and its emphasis on traditional Islamic sciences and the integration of the spiritual dimensions of health.

<u>Engaging with Sufi Tradition.</u> While the program is not exclusively Sufi in its orientation, it acknowledges the significant contributions of Sufi texts and methodologies in the understanding of the human psyche and soul. The diversity of perspectives on Sufism within the broader Muslim community has sometimes manifested as skepticism or resistance, rooted in historical and theological tensions surrounding the role of taṣawwuf (Sufiism) in Islamic scholarship. To address these concerns, the program emphasizes that its approach is grounded in Islamic tradition as a whole, integrating Sufi insights alongside other scholarly perspectives rather than privileging one over another.

<u>Debates on Spiritual versus Clinical Orientations of IP.</u> A key challenge lies in reconciling differing views on the role of vertical (spiritual) and horizontal (interpersonal) dimensions in IP. While some practitioners advocate limiting the therapeutic space to practical, horizontal issues like behavior and cognition, the program emphasizes the indivisibility of spiritual and mundane aspects of human experience. Critics argue that engaging deeply with spiritual dimensions risks encroaching on areas traditionally reserved for qualified spiritual guides (shuyūkh). In response, the program distinguishes between facilitating spiritual awareness and guiding higher spiritual development, emphasizing the former while acknowledging that the latter is more appropriately and ethically reserved for spaces such as the ṭarīqa as opposed to clinical therapeutic practice. This approach still underscores the necessity of reflecting and addressing multiple facets of the human soul in therapy to achieve true healing, rather than merely focusing on coping mechanisms, as conceptualized in the 'iceberg model' of Islamic psychotherapy (Rothman & Coyle, 2020).

Solutions

In the face of diverse programmatic and pedagogical challenges, there also exists immense opportunities for CMC to expand its role in IP education and research to address key gaps in the field, particularly in non-clinical aspects of IP and applications in education, leadership, and community engagement. To this end, as of January 2025 CMC has opened admissions for the fifth cohort to a broader applicant pool by removing the requirement for a professional qualification in psychology or a related field and removing the practitioner training focus. This shift is occurring in hopes of further clarifying that the program is not limited to a particular method or therapeutic approach, instead being designed to ground students in an Islamic paradigm of psychology down to its theoretical foundations. Additionally, the summer intensive that was initially conceived as the practical training element of the program, albeit an optional addition to the core curriculum, is being redesigned to maintain the experiential and self-development focus while making it open and applicable to non-practitioners by removing any clinical training. These changes to the program are intended to address many of the challenges that arose in the program's early development and are a direct result of learning from the experience of running four cohorts and responding to feedback from students, faculty and prospective applicants. The changes also further support the process of program validation by the Open University, in that they align more closely with the program's designation as a Post Graduate Certificate of Higher Education under Theology benchmarks rather than psychology. This also aligns with the College's mission and area of expertise in the field of Islamic Studies. The following solutions reflect the program's commitment to continuous improvement and a dedication to providing a transformative educational experience grounded in Islamic principles while remaining responsive to the evolving needs of students and the field of IP. Additional program improvements made in response to the aforementioned challenges include:

Curriculum Design

Streamlining and Focus. The curriculum has undergone a streamlining process to address the tension between depth and breadth. Non-essential content has been removed, and core modules have been refined to ensure a balance between comprehensive coverage and in-depth exploration of key concepts. This process has involved consolidating modules, clarifying learning objectives, and optimizing the use of contact hours.

Structural and Pedagogical Adjustments. In response to evolving needs, the program has made several structural and pedagogical adjustments to ensure it meets both academic and professional demands. The curriculum has been refined to distinguish its academic focus from therapeutic training, clarifying its role as a theoretical foundation for understanding IP. This change addressed confusion among students about the program's practical applications. The summer program has been restructured to emphasize self-development and heart-centered learning over direct therapeutic techniques, reflecting the program's shift away from clinical training. These adjustments also account for logistical challenges in delivering online education globally, with enhanced synchronous learning strategies and cohort-based engagement to foster a sense of community.

Student Expectations

Enhanced Communication. To better align student expectations with program aims, communication materials have been revised to explicitly state the program's focus on foundational knowledge and personal development rather than training in a therapeutic method. The admissions process now includes open house events and other opportunities for potential applicants to communicate with the admissions department and to clarify and address student expectations and ensure alignment with the program's objectives.

Integration of Experiential Learning. While maintaining its core focus, the program has incorporated more experiential (though non-clinical) learning opportunities to address the demand for practical application. This includes case study discussions, role-playing scenarios, and opportunities for students to apply Islamic psychological principles in their personal and professional lives.

Online Learning Environment:

Structured Flexibility. To mitigate the challenges of global time zones, the program has adopted a structured flexibility approach. While live session attendance remains mandatory, recordings are now selectively provided for students facing unavoidable absences. Additionally, asynchronous discussion forums and online group projects have been implemented to foster interaction and collaboration outside of live sessions.

Cohort-Based Learning. The program has embraced a cohort-based learning model to enhance engagement and interaction. Students' progress through the program as a group, fostering a sense of community and peer support. This model facilitates ongoing discussions, collaborative projects, and the development of deeper relationships among students despite the online format.

Field of Islamic Psychology

Clear Articulation of the Program's Definition. The program has taken a proactive approach to defining its unique position within the broader field of IP. This includes publishing articles and delivering presentations that articulate the program's emphasis on traditional Islamic sciences, the integration of spiritual dimensions of wellbeing, and the importance of personal development. The differences of opinion and approach within the broader field of IP and within the Muslim community regarding the integration of spirituality into IP underscore the importance of clear communication about the program's mission to engage diverse intellectual traditions while fostering a respectful and inclusive learning environment.

<u>Interdisciplinary Dialogue.</u> To address the challenge of balancing the clinical and spiritual, the program has initiated interdisciplinary dialogues with scholars, practitioners, and religious leaders. These dialogues aim to foster a deeper understanding of IP and its implications for clinical practice, personal development, and community well-being.

Discussion

For the first four academic years that CMC has offered the IP program, through academic year 2024-2025, it was delivered as a diploma awarded by the college itself. Thus, the first four graduated cohorts received their diploma certificates from CMC. Those graduates who also completed the summer intensive practical training offered by CMC were then eligible to receive certification from the IAIP, after acquiring the required number of supervision hours. With the shift away from practitioner training, subsequent cohorts, beginning in academic year 2025-26 will no longer be eligible to be certified as practitioners by the IAIP. The program itself remains certified by IAIP, but only as an academic training program, not a practitioner training program. This move is expected to provide more clarity for prospective applicants who are looking more specifically for a practitioner certification program, as well as positioning the program within the IP education landscape more squarely as an academic program in the field of Theology and Religious Studies. This shift further delineates the area of specialty, within the realm of Islamic Studies, as it aligns with CMC's mission, vision, and specialization in theology. This change also has allowed for the program to receive validation, as it is termed in the United Kingdom, as a fully accredited program.

In April of 2025 the program was successfully validated by the Open University (OU) as a Post Graduated Certificate (PGCert) of Higher Education in Islam and Psychology. The academic award is in the discipline of Theology and Religious Studies, using the QAA benchmarks for that discipline. Thus, it is neither a psychology degree nor a practitioner training qualification. While CMC is fully responsible for the design and delivery of the PGCert, graduates of the newly validated program will be awarded their certificates from the Open University. As a part of the validation process the former title of "Islamic Psychology" was not approved by the OU, citing the positioning of the program within Theology and Religious Studies benchmarks, and the title that was approved was "Islamic and Psychology". Admissions are now open to a more diverse pool of applicants and while those with a psychology background are still sought after candidates in fields such as social work, chaplaincy, medicine, leadership and community engagement are encouraged to apply. Given that the original program was predominantly focused on theoretical foundations, this has meant that the new iteration of the program is not much different from the original, in terms of the curriculum and content. The main change overall is the framing of the content to be relevant to a student body with more diverse professional backgrounds, which has more to do with how content is taught than what is taught. However, certain aspects of the curriculum in relation to counseling and psychotherapy have been reoriented more significantly away from therapeutic methods and more toward an overview of important considerations as they relate to non-clinical applications in community mental health and wellbeing.

The evolution of the program in this direction has its advantages and disadvantages. On one hand having a fully accredited IP graduate program is a great achievement for the College and marks a milestone for the development of IP education more generally. There are only a few accredited programs in the world and none with a theological and theoretical focus like this one, offered from a well-respected institution of Islamic Studies Higher Education. On the other hand, the concession of having to give up the title of "Islamic Psychology" and replace it with "Islam and Psychology" is an unfortunate one, given that it does not reflect the actual intention nor content of the program. The title "Islam and Psychology" could further corroborate misconceptions that the project is one of Islamization of Western psychology rather than what it actually is, which is a bottom-up approach to an indigenous "Islamic Psychology". Additionally, it is rather unfortunate that the degree will no longer be awarded by CMC itself and instead will be awarded by the Open University. While these are minor concessions in the grand scheme of things, as they are mere optical considerations, in a field as new and in development as that of IP, perception does have an impact.

While the new direction of the program away from practitioner training may feel like a loss to the already minimal number of practitioner training programs available, that aspect of the program will carry on through Dr. Abdallah Rothman's other projects. As both the Head of IP and Principal of CMC during the first years of the program Dr. Rothman's influence in the practitioner training aspect of the program was due in large part to his vision and area of focus and expertise. Not only was the focus on practitioner training influenced by him, the particular approach to Islamically integrated practice was informed by his own method. The removal of training in a particular therapeutic method was intended to create more clarity and distinguish the program as an academic course of study in theoretical foundations of IP within the larger field of Islamic studies, situated in a theological institution. Dr. Rothman remains as the Head of IP at CMC but has stepped down from his role as Principal heading the college so that he can give more attention to the development of his work in Islamic psychotherapy outside of CMC. In 2025 Dr. Rothman, through his project Dar al Shifaa, launched a practitioner training program in his own Islamically integrated psychotherapy approach called The Shifaa Method. Many alumni of the CMC program, who also completed the summer intensive practical training are continuing on to complete their practitioner training in the Shifaa Method.

The IP program's positioning within CMC presents a unique opportunity for dialogue between the emergent field of IP and the well-established field of Islamic Studies. The development of IP over the past 50 years has tended to lean more toward a clinical focus on psychotherapeutic application. This was a result of the great need in the Muslim community globally for religious grounded mental health services. While this focus needs to continue, it would be of great value to have more efforts in the areas of non-clinical applications of IP, such as education, leadership, social work, and community engagement. Under the guidance of Shaykh Abdal Hakim Murad, one of the most well respected and learned Muslim scholars in the West, there is an opportunity to broaden the scope of IP education to include and be integrated within more traditional subjects in the Islamic sciences. It also presents an opportunity for the exchange of knowledge and perspective of a diverse scholarship, by taking advantage of the expertise of faculty at CMC in areas like theology (kalām), law (fiqh), creed (ʿaqīda), and ethics (akhlaq). As the program has done with the incorporation of scholars like Dr. Najah Nadi, this interdisciplinary collaboration serves to strengthen the knowledge base and deepen the grounding of the subject matter in the traditional Islamic sciences. It is hoped that further efforts to benefit from this opportunity are initiated such as conferences, research projects, and manuscript translation within the research department at CMC.

The Islamic psychology research lab at CMC aims to pioneer studies that bridge classical Islamic knowledge with contemporary psychological challenges. Specific anticipated research projects include comparative studies of Islamic psychological frameworks and modern theories, such as examining parallels between Gestalt psychology and the Islamic concept of the self (nafs) or exploring attachment theory in light of Islamic notions of human nature (fiṭra). The program also seeks to investigate the therapeutic effects of Islamic practices like remembrance (dhikr), prayer (salah), and fellowship (ṣuḥba) on psychological well-being, comparing these to modern secular approaches. These initiatives align with CMC's vision of establishing itself as a leader in developing IP's theoretical foundations and advancing its academic landscape.

Conclusion

As one of the longest running and well-established programs in IP globally, the CMC program has managed to maintain a strong reputation amidst the growing landscape of IP education. This is evidenced by the consistent numbers of enrollment with an average of almost 200 applications each year for five years running, positive feedback from students, and the success of program alumni in continuing on to make contributions in their communities. This demonstrates the soundness of the program design and reasserts that prospective students are looking to learn IP from a bottom-up approach, starting from theological foundations of psychology from an indigenous Quranic framework. Both the inception of the approach to program design and the focus on a truly Islamic paradigm, and thus the success of this program, are due in no small part to the guidance and legacy of Dr. Malik Badri. It is hoped that his soul continues to be honored and elevated through this program and that the graduates are among those who carry on his legacy, inspiring generations to come in the continued development of the contemporary field of Islamic psychology.

CHAPTER EIGHT

GRADUATE CERTIFICATE IN ISLAMIC PSYCHOLOGY

Charles Sturt University; Sydney, Australia

Hanan Dover

Introduction

The discipline of IP has gained momentum since the early 2000 as an important area of study, in both Islamic and non-Islamic regions where mental health professionals seek to serve diverse populations with cultural and religious frameworks that guide their way of life This growth is evident in the expanding body of literature addressing mental health, psychology, and counselling from an Islamic perspective. Notably, in the 1990s, scholars began publishing works on IP, laying the groundwork for the field's development. For instance, Malik Badri considered one of the founding fathers of modern IP, contributed early publications that have been instrumental in shaping contemporary IP. Prior to 2019, there was no accredited tertiary course in IP. There have been various attempts and discussions at IP conferences being held at the IAMP since its inception in 1996, the first being from Amber Haque (2002) publishing a proposed curriculum in IP whilst he was the Head of the Psychology Department, at the International Islamic University in Malaysia (IIUM). It was not until two decades later, in 2020, the ISRA in collaboration with CSU in Australia, established the Graduate Certificate in IP to address this gap, becoming the first university-accredited program in this field in the Western world. The course design and subject content was developed by clinical and forensic psychologist, Hanan Dover. The program's establishment reflects the increasing demand for an alternative understanding to mainstream theories of human behavior and experiences, and for this alternative framework of human psychology to be applied in both counselling and mental health services that resonate with Islamic values and ethical frameworks that underpin IP.

Rationale and Impetus

The interest in the modern field of IP, as we understand it today, was led by the late Professor Malik Badri (1978). His landmark text on The Dilemma of the Muslim Psychologist was the first text in the English language that sought to examine the concerns of the discipline of modern psychology for Muslims and its misalignment with Islamic principles and ethics, and he presented a proposed framework on how Muslims should emancipate from Western notions of human psychology. As the foundational figure in modern IP, Badri (1978) emphasized the importance of the integration of Islamic principles with psychological practice, so that Muslim practitioners do not fall into the lizard's hole.

Whilst his ideas amongst his colleagues at the time was met with fierce resistance in the 1970s given they were predominantly aligned with Western psychological paradigms, it was not until 1997 during the first international conference on 'Counselling and Psychotherapy from an Islamic Perspective' held in Malaysia that there was a wide-spread appreciation of IP, that culminated in the formation of the IAMP was initiated with Professor Malik Badri being a founding member, and President, up until 2016. One of the key objectives of the association since its inception was to introduce a university course in IP. Despite attempts from various Muslim-majority nations to try and reshape their existing psychology curriculums in line with the objectives of trying to 'Islamize' psychology, and publications on how such a curriculum can be proposed (Haque, 2002), there was no complete course in IP. In 2019, Hanan Dover, who at the time was the Vice President of IAMP, sought propose to ISRA a university accredited complete course in IP given their institutional affiliation with CSU in delivering their Islamic Studies Programs. In addition, ISRA, as an organization was uniquely embedded within the grassroots Muslim community in Australia, so the confidence in being able to propose a course in IP to best serve diverse Muslims was encouraging.

The challenges that arose in the development of such a course aimed at providing culturally relevant education for Muslim mental health professionals and enhancing their counselling and therapeutic competence across diverse contexts was that the program was developed in-kind with no available start-up funding at the time, but it had the support from both ISRA and CSU.

Brief History and Key Contributors

The course establishment involved the initial course proposal developed by Hanan Dover contributing her expertise in psychology and specialized interest in IP. She was not affiliated with a university institution at the time but was working clinically in the field of psychology as a psychologist. In collaboration with ISRA, the proposal was to meet the CSU guidelines for the Graduate Certificate in Islamic Psychology. A business case for the course approval was put forward to the Vice Chancellor's Leadership Team in 2019. This involved the proposed four subjects that would form the graduate certificate. Four subjects are not entirely robust, but they were going to be the start to assess for demand for such a course before exploring further options. It was further hoped to ensure that the subjects would not be uniquely Australian but ensure a robust and internationally relevant curriculum to also be suited for international students. The course was designed by Hanan Dover where it was decided that the existing subject already taught as part of the Master's in Islamic Studies program at CSU, 'Essentials in Islamic Spirituality' developed and taught by Associate Professor Zuleyha Keskin would form part of the GCIP. Associate Professor Keskin being an existing staff member of the Islamic Studies Programs at the Centre for Islamic Studies and Civilization (CISAC) with expertise in Islamic Spirituality, would also be the Course Director of the GCIP.

Vision, Mission, and Objectives of the Program

Vision. The vision of the GCIP is to deliver a transformative program that centers Islamic spirituality rooted in theology, as the cornerstone from which the discipline of psychology can emerge. The approach is to reclaim the study of psychology as a spiritually informed human science that also incorporates the emotional and psychological understanding of human behavior and experiences. It seeks to become one of the leading academic and professional programs, empowering academics, mental health professionals, counsellors, educators and community workers to integrate Islamic values within their practice, thereby fostering mental, emotional, and the spiritual well-being for Muslim communities. The program aimed to adopt a framework of holistic mental health within IP, to continue the integrative paradigm psychological and mental health approaches of classical and traditional scholars in mental health care in Islam. Uniquely, the program also aims to be one that is self-transformative for the students to help them understand themselves from an integrative psycho-spiritual framework.

Mission. The mission of the GCIP is to cultivate a new generation of counsellors, chaplains, community workers, mental health workers and practitioners who are religiously informed, culturally competent, and culturally safe to work with Muslims. By educating students on the principles of IP, the program aspires to fill the gaps in current mainstream mental health approaches, addressing the unique spiritual and emotional needs of Muslim individuals and communities. This mission is achieved through an evidence-based curriculum, grounded in theological knowledge, classical Islamic teachings, and modern psychological and counselling research, fostering graduates who can serve diverse communities with integrity and compassion in their working capacities. The mission further emphasizes academic excellence, community engagement, and ethical practice, aligning with CSU's commitment to social responsibility and cultural inclusivity. Through this program, the university aims to contribute meaningfully to the broader discourse on mental health and cultural diversity, showcasing IP as a valuable addition to the mental health field globally.

Objectives. The program's objectives reflect its commitment to providing students with both theoretical and religious knowledge, and practical skills tailored to the unique intersection of Islamic teachings and applied counselling practice. These objectives ensure that graduates are well-prepared to serve their communities, equipped with a deep understanding of both the religious and psychological dimensions of human nature, mental health, human behavior and experiences.

Definition of Islamic Psychology (IP) and Purpose

The GCIP course introduces students to the different approaches Muslim scholars and psychology practitioners have attempted to define IP in the last three decades. The program's definition is built on the recognition that IP is distinct in its ontological and epistemological grounding. Traditional Islamic scholars, such as Al-Ghazali and Ibn Sina, established early frameworks in which mental and spiritual health were interdependent, each influencing and reinforcing the other. In the course, IP is defined as a field of study that incorporates the theological, ethical, and spiritual teachings of Islam into psychological and counselling practice, recognizing human behavior as a holistic interplay of spiritual, biological, emotional, cognitive, behavioral, social, environmental, and socio-political dimensions. This definition aligns with the Quranic view of the human self (nafs) as a dynamic and multifaceted entity, requiring balanced care across all aspects of life, whilst emphasizing the original primordial/innate nature of man (fitrah) as the basis for understanding human nature. It recognizes the human being as a tripartite entity comprised of body (jism), soul (ruh), and intellect (aql) or heart (qalb), with each component working in synergy to achieve mental and spiritual well-being. This approach centers on the understanding of the fitrah as the God-given disposition in every human being, designed to be in harmony with divine guidance, and within its dynamic reality, is the ongoing process of self-refinement and re-orientation towards fitrah.

This definition has also been influenced by leading scholars in the field, such as the late Professor Malik Badri, who advocated for a "decolonization" and "Islamization" of psychology and an acknowledgment of the unique psychological needs within Muslim communities. Badri emphasized that a relevant psychology for Muslims must recognize that healing and self-actualization are achieved through a balanced relationship with Allah (God), the self, and the world. This relationship is understood through the process of tazkiyah (self-purification), a fundamental principle in IP that promotes ethical and moral development alongside emotional and cognitive well-being. This program has adopted this definition of IP to reflect a culturally sensitive and religiously grounded model of human nature and mental health, thereby equipping students to engage with Muslim clients effectively.

Nature of Program

Program Type

Graduate Certificate in IP, a post-graduate university-accredited certificate program.

Admission Requirements

Academic entry requirements include:

- Bachelor's degree (or AQF equivalent) in any discipline from a university or other tertiary education provider.

OR

- Work experience, within the same industry as the course profile, of no less than three years.

Duration, Modes of Instruction, Fees, and Financial Assistance

The program is offered as a full-time study over one year, or part-time study over two years. All classes are delivered online to accommodate diverse schedules and geographical locations.

The total course fee cost for Australian and New Zealand students is $8,984.00AUS or $11,400.00AUS for international students. Each subject fee is $2,246.00AUS. For Australian and New Zealand students or $2850.00AUS for international students. Eligible local students have the option to defer their fees through a government scheme via 'Fee-Help'.

Standard English Language Proficiency (ELP) requirements apply.

Credit Hours and Graduation Requirements

- Completion of relevant tertiary study, or work experience related to the course, may be eligible to receive credit toward the certificate.
- CSU students are responsible to continue to develop skills in English language, literacy and numeracy as appropriate for the discipline to enable participation in the course and graduate prepared to enter the workforce.
- Students must complete the four core course subjects, totalling 32 credit hours, to receive certification. Completion of all assignments, projects, and final assessments is mandatory.

Faculty Credentials

The course instructors comprise professionals with qualifications in either psychology (post-graduate research and coursework) and / or Islamic studies, providing both theoretical knowledge and practical experience in culturally adaptive therapy methods.

Associate Professor Zuleyha Keskin is the Associate Head of School at the CISAC and a lecturer in Islamic Spirituality and Contemporary Islamic Studies. Zuleyha facilitated the development of the Bachelor of Islamic Studies, Bachelor of Islamic Studies (Honors), Master of Islamic Studies, Master of Classical Arabic, and most recently, the Graduate Certificate in IP. Zuleyha has been the Course Director at CSU for these courses since their inception in 2010. Zuleyha's research interests include Islamic spirituality, Inner peace, Islamic theology and ethics, social justice, and women in Islam. She has authored books on inner peace and spirituality and is the Managing Editor of the Australian Journal of Islamic Studies the President of the Australian Association of Islamic and Muslim Studies (AAIMS).

Hanan Dover is the IP Lecturer at CISAC at CSU, and she has published in areas related to psychology and Muslim communities, refugee communities and developed a validated scale that aims to assess Muslim religious reflection. She is also the founder and clinical director of Mission of Hope since 2001 and is the Conference Convenor of the Australian

Muslim Mental Health conferences, Founding member and former Convenor of the Islamic from an Islamic Perspective Interest Group of the Australian Psychological Society (APS). Hanan has been the elected Vice President of IAMP since 2016 and is a on the Board of Trustees of IAMP. Hanan is also one of the founding editors of the Journal of Muslim Mental Health (JMMH). Hanan proposed, planned, and coordinated the first international conference in IP in a Western country in 2001. It was held in Sydney, Australia. This conference was funded by Western Sydney University's School of Psychology. The conference was run for its second year in 2002. She was first invited as an international keynote presenter to the second IAMP Conference held in Sudan by the late Professor Malik Badri in 2004. Since then, she has been invited to present various keynote addresses in IP internationally. Hanan works professionally and clinically as a clinical and forensic psychologist in private practice integrating Islamically-congruent values in the psychological and therapeutic practices when working with Muslim clients.

Partnerships

The program partners via MoU between ISRA and the IAMP to offer students an enriched learning experience. The MoU aims to facilitate access to guest lectures, networking opportunities, and collaborative research. ISRA has collaborated with Mission of Hope hosting the Australian Muslim Mental Health Conference in 2022 and were sponsors of the 2024 conference.

IAMP have been supporters of the Australian Muslim Mental Health Conference in 2022 conference on the theme of IP and the conference in October 2025.

Curriculum

Core Courses and Descriptions

ISL401 Introduction to Islamic Psychology. This course subject introduces students to the historical evolution and core concepts of IP, it's context, definitions and perspectives. Also, a brief history of IP origins from early classical scholars, their worldviews, and its heritage, followed by contemporary perspectives. Perspectives of human nature will be explored from an Islamic perspective whilst drawing on key Islamic constructs to understand the development of human personality and psycho-spiritual growth.

ISL470 Essentials of Islamic Spirituality (pre-existing course subject of the Master's in Islamic Studies Program). This subject addresses the importance of self-development based on the teachings of the Qur'an and hadith (Prophetic narratives). Foundational Islamic spirituality concepts will be covered, such as ihsan (spiritual excellence), ikhlas (sincerity), istiqama (balance) and taqwa (righteousness). These concepts will be discussed alongside ibada (worship) to appreciate the relationship between all these concepts. The spiritual meaning of the five pillars of Islam will also be covered; what each practice signifies; their relationship with one another within the framework of purification of the nafs (ego); and how the five pillars assist in the spiritual development of the practitioner. The importance of the Sunnah (practical teachings of the Prophet Muhammad) in the everyday life of a Muslim will also be discussed, with a particular focus on their application in contemporary times.

ISL402 Islamic Psychology: Human Behavior and Experience. This course subject introduces the fundamental sub-disciplines and theories in psychology and critically evaluates these theories from Islamic perspectives. The sub-disciplines of contemporary psychology including health, behavioral, developmental, personality, social and cognitive psychology are analyzed using the latest research and evidence. The subject also includes Islamic perspectives in relations to human nature, experiences and behavior. Parallels between contemporary psychological perspectives and IP are explored.

ISL403 Applied Islamic Psychology and Counselling. This course subject covers basic counselling interventions to help with mental health concerns using principles of Islamic counselling and psychology. It utilizes current theories, research and culturally competent practices in the delivery of basic counselling interventions to help the healing process. It also explores Prophetic principles of giving counsel and its application. Islamic value systems in relation to mental health issues are explored, considering scriptural, spiritual, ethical, social and cultural contexts. The aim is to develop skills to enable counselling support for the well-being of the diverse Muslim community with an understanding of their spiritual dimensions. This course has a practical component where students are asked to practice the knowledge and skills from the course as part of the subject assessments.

While the program utilizes two core textbooks—Islamic Psychology: Human Behavior and Experience from an Islamic Perspective by Professor Hussein Rassool and Islamic Counselling by the same author as a guide—substantial insights from existing IP literature, and direct professional experiences derived from Islamic counselling practices also form as subject readings that enrich the curriculum significantly.

Strengths, Challenges, and Solutions

Main Strengths

- Uniqueness in the Field: As the only accredited IP university program in the Western world, it sets a precedent for integrating Islamic (religious) perspectives within the discipline of psychological sciences.
- Community-Relevant Curriculum: Developed with direct input from a senior and experienced specialist psychologist Hanan Dover, the curriculum addresses both the scientific and spiritual needs of students and future clients.
- Online-study: The online mode of study allows for international students to enroll and participate in the course.

Program Growth

The program has seen consistent growth since inception, attracting students internationally and garnering attention since it remains the only complete course on IP from an accredited university. It represents a significant step in promoting IP within academic institutions outside of majority-Muslim countries.

Challenges and Solutions

- Challenge: The brief course of four subjects does not allow for entry level accreditation for industry level practice of professional counselling bodies, such as the Australian Counselling Association (ACA).
- Solution: There are current attempts to increase the subjects from four to eight, to try and meet accreditation standards of the ACA, like that already achieved with the Graduate Diploma of Pastoral Counselling at CSU. It is important to note that this program does not qualify any graduate to be a practitioner in IP. It is expected that students seek accreditation and / or license to practice in their respective countries to practice counselling, therapy, etc.

There are also steps to explore a Masters in Islamic Psychotherapy and Counselling Course so that graduates can meet accreditation with the Psychotherapy and Counselling Federation in Australia (PACFA).

- Challenge: Balancing traditional Islamic knowledge with contemporary psychological frameworks.
- Solution: Students are continuously encouraged to study the

Islamic sciences that are offered outside the GCIP course, due to its importance in the field of IP.

Discussion

Program Uniqueness

The program's distinctive value lies in its capacity to cater to both the religious and psychological aspects of basic mental health, providing culturally authentic care models and an introductory framework for ethical practice.

Faculty Publications and Program Development

Rassool, G. H. & Keskin, Z, (2023). Positioning the self (nafs) in psychospirituality, Journal of Spirituality in Mental, 27(1), 1–10.

Dover, H. (2021). IP in Australia: an emerging field, IP Around the Globe, Haque, A & Rothman, A (eds.), pp 24-31, International Association of IP.

Challenges in Islamic Psychology Field

1. Limited resources for the development of IP-focused curricula.
2. Balancing current mainstream ethical standards and Islamic ethical standards in counselling.

Future Roadmap

The program aims to expand further, offering a Graduate Diploma in IP and Counselling. Research initiatives and faculty publications are priority areas, alongside increased partnerships with universities worldwide.

Admission and Graduation Trends

Admissions have grown annually, with high retention rates reflecting student satisfaction.

Table 6

Student Enrolment in the Graduate Certificate in IP Program

Courses	Student Numbers	% Drops off
2022		
ISL401 Introduction to Islamic Psychology	34	20.0%
ISL402 Islamic Psychology: Human Behavior and Experience	23	21.1%
ISL403 Applied Islamic	18	25.0%

Psychology and Counselling			
ISL470 Essentials of Islamic Spirituality	22		16.0%
2023			
ISL401 Introduction to Islamic Psychology	39		15.2%
ISL402 Islamic Psychology: Human Behavior and Experience	19		9.5%
ISL470 Essentials of Islamic Spirituality	18		30.8%
2024			
ISL401 Introduction to Islamic Psychology	36		14.7%
ISL402 Islamic Psychology: Human Behavior and Experience	15		28.1%
ISL403 Applied Islamic Psychology and Counselling	18		25.0%
ISL470 Essentials of Islamic Spirituality	21		54.5%

Table 7

Admission to Program

Year	Applications	Admissions	Admission Rate (%)
2022	66	22	33.33%
2023	51	12	23.53%
2024	45	19	42.22%

Graduates. 2023 – 19 graduates (first year of graduates)

Alumni Feedback. Graduates have reported that the program has improved their practice by deepening their understanding of Islamic perspectives on mental health. Graduates would also like to further their knowledge and practice in this area and are awaiting the Graduate Diploma in IP to be approved by CSU and accredited for practice with a nationally registered association.

Accreditation and Review

The program is regularly reviewed to maintain high academic standards, with accreditation granted by CSU's governing bodies.

Conclusion

Through its defined understanding of IP and a clear mission, vision, and set of objectives, the Graduate Certificate in IP stands as a pioneering effort in culturally relevant mental health education for Muslims that are guided by the Islamic tradition. The program is uniquely positioned to address the growing need for foundational Islamic knowledge that integrates spiritual psychology, psychological sciences, and mental health that serves to offer a unique practice to mental health services that respect and integrate Islamic values. The course curriculum bridges traditional Islamic thought and modern psychology, fostering a nuanced and contextually sensitive approach to mental health.

The aim is to also equip graduates with foundational skills and to also advocate for the broader understanding and application of Islamic principles in psychology and mental health, fulfilling a critical need in today's multicultural and multi-faith societies to serve Muslim communities authentically. This holistic and purpose-driven approach reflects the program's commitment to promoting psychological healing that is both scientifically grounded and spiritually informed, setting a model for future initiatives in IP education worldwide.

Acknowledgements

I would like to acknowledge Associate Professor Zuleyha Keskin in providing the data on student enrolments.

CHAPTER NINE

PSYCHOLOGY AS THE SCIENCE OF THE HUMAN SOUL, COGNITION, EMOTION, AND BEHAVIOR

Avicenna Academy; Yogyakarta, Indonesia

Bagus Riyono

Introduction

The discipline of psychology plays a crucial role in guiding human life. It involves understanding ourselves and the various dynamics that influence our experiences. Currently, mainstream psychological science is predominantly shaped by a Western, secular, and atheistic perspective. This viewpoint regards humans as products of evolution, defining us as human animals. It suggests that humans are continuously evolving, implying that there is no fixed nature of humanity that remains unchanged over time. This belief is not compatible with the Quranic concept of "fitrah" as it is the inherent nature of human beings that is fixed and never change.

An evolutionary perspective on psychology can result in a shifting focus within the field and evolving definitions of mental health. These challenges may mislead the Muslim Ummah in understanding themselves and their social lives. Therefore, as Muslims, we should define psychology according to Islamic teachings found in the Quran and Hadith.

To establish PPIG, we must redefine its purpose, object of study, and methodology. IP seeks to nurture the health of the human soul, emphasizing that life is a journey towards returning to Allah in the hereafter. This approach contrasts with conventional psychology, which is often hedonistic and materialistic, focusing solely on worldly existence.

By adopting a hedonistic approach, we may tend to reject negative experiences and pursue only positive feelings. However, life encompasses both happiness and sadness, as noted in the Quran. IP acknowledges the importance of enduring life's challenges while maintaining our dignity, believing that every experience offers valuable lessons.

This curriculum in IP focuses on the human soul ("nafs"), also referred to as the human heart. Unlike conventional psychology, which has evolved over time—from Freud's exploration of the unconscious to behavioral science's emphasis on observable behavior, and more recently to neuropsychology's focus on the brain—IP consistently places the psyche or soul at the core of its study.

IP employs a multimethod approach that combines observations, psychodynamics, and teachings from the Quran to develop its theories. For instance, Muslim psychologists may begin their work with Quranic studies, integrating their findings with observational data and logical reasoning. This approach is called Maqasid methodology that can serve as a comprehensive framework for advancing psychological theories.

Recognizing the limitations of conventional psychology, this curriculum aims to redefine the discipline from an Islamic perspective, aligning it with the true nature of human beings as creations of Allah. This approach seeks to help psychology students connect more deeply with realities of life and their faith.

Nature of Program

- Type: Certificate
- Admission requirements: The program is available to psychology graduates and other college graduates interested in IP. Registration is conducted online, and applicants must submit their previous transcripts, CV, and a statement of purpose.
- Duration, Modes of Instruction, Fees, and Financial Assistance
    - The program is designed to last for 6 months
    - Instruction will be conducted through a Zoom classroom and

will include lectures, discussions, reading assignments, and paper assignments.

- The program fee for the 6-month duration is 250 USD. A scholarship is available for highly motivated students who are unable to afford the program fee. To apply for the scholarship, the applicant must submit a proposal detailing their motivation to study IP and the limitations of their financial resources.

Credit Hours and Student Progress Measurement

The program is worth nine credit hours. Students must attend all lectures and complete all required assignments to receive a certificate of completion.

Graduation Requirements

To graduate, students must attend at least 85% of the scheduled meetings. They will be required to take midterm and final exams, and they must pass these exams. Additionally, students must submit all required assignments to be eligible for graduation.

Faculty Credentials

The faculty members of the program hold Ph.D. degrees and have a proven record of research and publication in IP.

Curriculum

The philosophy of science. In this discussion, we will explore the various worldviews present within the scientific community, specifically focusing on the materialistic perspective and the Islamic perspective. The Darwinian evolutionary perspective will be examined as one representation of the materialistic viewpoint, with issues related to this perspective illustrated through a video from a documentary. Following this, we will discuss the Islamic worldview as a potential solution to the challenges posed by the materialistic perspective.

The history of science. This topic discusses the development of scientific disciplines over time. A central figure in scientific methodology is Ibn Al-Haytam, who pioneered the experimental method in the evolution of scientific inquiry. He is recognized as the first scientist due to his early work in integrating physical phenomena with mathematics. Ibn Al-Haytam's initial research focused on optics, which inspired Isaac Newton in his development of theories related to the spectrum of light.

The principles of science. Drawing from the wisdom of Ibn Al-Haytam, we can discuss the fundamental principles of science. The primary principle originates from the relationship between human beings and Allah, the Most

Knowing. Since only Allah possesses perfect knowledge of the truth, and all human errors arise from our limitations, humility becomes essential in the pursuit of knowledge. The second key principle of science is that knowledge must be grounded in signs or evidence found within the universe, in the human soul, and in the teachings of the Quran.

The science delusion. The belief that science is the ultimate source of truth can be misleading; this is what we refer to as the "science delusion." It is important to recognize this phenomenon and adopt a critical perspective when claiming what is true. The ultimate truth comes from Allah, while science serves as a discipline to help us understand that truth. When we mistakenly treat science as the sole source of truth, we risk confusion, as scientific discoveries evolve over time. True truth, on the other hand, remains constant and unchanging, regardless of circumstances. It is universal and eternal.

The purpose of life and the purpose of psychological science. In this topic, students are reminded that life extends beyond this world and continues into the hereafter. This understanding is crucial for developing a meaningful life and achieving inner peace. Psychology, as the science of the human mind, aims to promote mental health, which is primarily indicated by a sense of peace in the heart. By recognizing the ultimate purpose of life, individuals will be better equipped to face challenges without succumbing to despair.

The human soul and its dynamics. The human soul is not a mystical entity that exists beyond the body. It is sometimes referred to as the human mind, but this concept extends beyond just cognition. There are four layers of human potential, which represent the modalities of the human soul: sensing, reasoning, empathy, and conscience. These core aspects of the human self, determine how individuals respond to internal and external challenges.

Learning from classical scholars. This discussion will focus on two classical scholars, Abu Zayd Al-Balkhi and Al-Ghazali, who significantly contributed to the fields of psychology and mental health. Their work has influenced contemporary psychotherapy approaches. By exploring the contributions of these classical scholars, students will gain a broader perspective on psychology and its relevance to mental health.

Critical evaluation of Freudianism, behaviorism, and humanistic psychology. This discussion will focus on the core concepts of psychoanalysis, behaviorism, and humanistic psychology, while also highlighting the shortcomings of each perspective. The key figures associated with these three schools of psychology will be introduced, including Sigmund Freud, B.F. Skinner, and Abraham Maslow.

Reconstruction of motivation theories. Motivation, as a key driver of human behavior, has been explained through more than thirty different theories. These theories are grouped into meta-theories of motivation, which encompass five core themes: meaning, freedom to choose, challenge, incentive, and urge. These themes are then incorporated into the human motivation model, which is referred to as a theory of meaning, as all these elements are interconnected and transform into a cohesive sense of meaning.

The dynamics of psychological states. Based on an analysis of risk, uncertainty, and hope, five potential psychological states can be identified that reflect an individual's level of motivation. These states include: (1) learned helplessness, (2) optimum challenge, (3) fatalism, (4) optimum opportunity, and (5) comfort zone. The ideal psychological state is "optimum opportunity," which represents the highest level of motivational energy and individual experience.

Theory of personality. Personality is a fundamental concept in psychology, representing the patterns of behavior and attitudes that an individual exhibits. The anchor personality theory introduced in this course explores traits and tendencies that are adaptable, reflecting the development of the human spirit across time and space. The core argument of this theory is that an individual's personality is shaped by the anchors they choose to embrace. Ultimately, the anchor personality theory suggests that the highest anchor is Allah, which can be attained through virtuous actions.

The principles of life dynamics and mental health. This course serves as a practical guide to mental health by discussing a model of psychological conditions and appropriate responses. The fundamental psychological conditions that all human beings encounter in life are freedom, uncertainty, and vulnerability. These three basic conditions are often referred to as the fundamental laws of psychology. Since freedom, uncertainty, and vulnerability are unavoidable aspects of existence, the way to navigate these conditions is by choosing appropriate responses. The appropriate response to freedom is responsibility, the response to uncertainty is hopefulness, and the response to vulnerability is humility.

Strengths

This program is designed with integrative ideas that connect courses logically and systematically. Each course relates to others in specific ways, meaning that as students' progress in their studies, their knowledge and understanding become increasingly interconnected. A key strength of this program is that the primary reference for developing this understanding is the Al-Qur'an.

Program Growth since Inception

The program began in 2022 and has not yet been evaluated in terms of physical infrastructure.

Faculty IP Publications in the Last Ten Years

Riyono, B. & Intani, Z. F. (2024). *Permasalahan Sensing Mentality dan Penyusunan Instrument Alat Ukur Potensi Dasar Manusia.* ANIMA Indonesian Psychological Journal, 39(1), 163- 182. https://doi.org/10.24123/aipj.v39i1.5501

Riyono, B. (2023). Unveiling the Fundamental Law of Psychology: A Study with "Maqasid" Methodology. *Australian Journal of Islamic Psychology.* In press.

Riyono, B., & Indrayanti. (2023). Pelatihan motivasi risk-uncertainty-hope untuk etos kerja. *Jurnal Intervensi Psikologi, 15*(2), 177-185. https://doi.org/10.20885/intervensipsikologi.vol15.iss2.art7

Riyono, B. (2023). Constructing the Theory of Human Basic Potential Based on Quranic Messages: Study with Maqasid Methodology. Minbar. *Islamic Studies, 16*(2), 449–475. https://doi.org/10.31162/2618-9569-2023-16-2-449-475

Riyono, B. (2024*). Tazkiya Therapy in Islamic Psychotherapy.* Routledge Taylor and Francis Group.

Riyono, B. (2023*). Tazkiya Therapy.* In A. Haque & A. Rothman (Eds.). *Clinical Applications of Islamic Psychology,* (pp. 305-333). International Association of Islamic Psychology.

Riyono, B. (2020). *Motivasi dan Kepribadian.* Al-Mawardi

Challenges

There are two main challenges in implementing this program. The first challenge relates to the prior knowledge of conventional psychology that students have already internalized. This established understanding can be difficult to unlearn, which makes it easier for students without a psychology background to grasp the Islamic perspective. The second challenge involves the educational system, which has largely been developed from a secular viewpoint. As a result, graduates of this program may face difficulties when trying to advance their education to the next level.

Solution

To address the first challenge, a preparatory course should be designed at the beginning of the program to help students unlearn conventional psychology. This course should encourage students to understand the natural phenomena of human life and their own experiences, fostering curiosity without relying on the concepts or terminology of conventional psychology.

In the second step of the course, students will learn from the Quran to explore answers to life's phenomena. This process will help them internalize concepts of human life as expressed in the Quran. By this point, when they revisit the discipline of psychology, they will have a foundational framework to critically evaluate conventional psychology concepts.

The third step involves integrating knowledge from Quranic teachings with existing conventional psychology, guided by Islamic principles as the foundational framework.

This program will collaborate with other established educational institutions, particularly those with an Islamic background, to adapt the curriculum design for other psychology programs. In ten years, it is anticipated that formal psychology study programs will incorporate this current curriculum design.

Discussion

This program is currently in the initiation phase and will only be active throughout the academic year. So far, the drop-off rate is approximately 10%. The admission rate for this program is 250 USD. A scholarship is available for highly motivated students who cannot afford to pay.

One of the alumni from Russia plans to pursue a Ph.D. program. The satisfaction rate for this program stands at 90%. Some students who are professionals in psychotherapy have reported that the concepts introduced in the program are both useful and helpful for their practices. The faculty members all hold Ph.D. degrees and have graduated from universities in the United States. As this is still a new program, there has not yet been any external reviews or accreditation.

The initial challenge of this program involves designing a preparatory course aimed at helping students unlearn conventional psychology. This course will focus on understanding the natural and familiar phenomena of human life, encouraging students to reflect on their own experiences. The goal is to foster a basic level of curiosity without relying on conventional psychological concepts or terminology.

In the second phase, students will explore answers to life's phenomena through the Quran. This will help students internalize the Quranic perspective on human life. When they later engage with traditional psychology, they will have a foundational framework that enables them to critically assess conventional psychological concepts.

The third step involves integrating the knowledge gained from Quranic teachings with existing conventional psychology, framed by Islamic principles.

This program will collaborate with established educational institutions, particularly those with an Islamic foundation, allowing the curriculum to be adapted by other psychology programs. In ten years, it is anticipated that this innovative curriculum will replace existing psychology study programs.

Conclusion

The program titled "Psychology as the Science of Human Soul, Cognition, and Behavior" is distinctive in its purpose, areas of study, and methodology. It is designed around Quranic messages, making it relatable to the Muslim ummah. Additionally, the program integrates key concepts from conventional psychology while positioning Islamic principles as the foundational framework of the discipline.

Feedback from alumni indicates that the knowledge gained from this program is practical, useful, and more accessible to students. Moreover, the program inspires both students and instructors to explore and develop new concepts and applications of psychology based on Quranic teachings.

The next steps will focus on enhancing the program into a more comprehensive psychology curriculum grounded in Islamic principles. The long-term goal is to replace the existing curriculum for psychological studies with a more integrated and thorough program that aligns with the fundamental nature and psychological dynamics of human beings, as outlined in Islamic teachings.

CHAPTER TEN

AL BALAGH ACADEMY'S 4-YEAR ONLINE ISLĀMIC PSYCHOLOGY AND COUNSELLING PROGRAM
with Ongoing Continuing Professional Development in Islāmic Psychology and Psychotherapy

Department of Islāmic Psychology, Psychotherapy, & Counselling,
Al Balagh Academy, Bradford, UK

G. Hussein Rassool

Introduction

Muslims have historically been marginalized in Western academia, particularly in discussions about their religion. Their participation in academic works and debates has been limited. To address this issue, Al Balagh Academy has a bold and transformative vision of becoming the global center in the development of Islāmic thought and knowledge. The academy provides universal access to the best Islāmic education by collaborating with leading Islāmic experts and evolving Islāmic institutions.

Al Balagh Academy aims to establish itself as a center of excellence in Islāmic education and research focusing on contemporary topics and issues affecting Muslims. The academy emphasizes spiritual development as part of the learning process, utilizing diverse pedagogical approaches. By employing these varied teaching methods, Al Balagh Academy equips Muslims with the knowledge, skills, and resources necessary to actively engage in academia and contribute to research, writing, and discussions relevant to Muslims in Western society.

Al Balagh Academy was founded by Shaykh Dr. Rafāqat Rashid, who now serves as the Academic Director, and Mufti Abrar Qasmi, who is the Director.

The Department of Islāmic Psychology and Psychotherapy at Al Balagh Academy focuses on integrating Islāmic principles with contemporary psychological practices. This department offers specialized courses and training programs designed to provide Islāmic with a comprehensive understanding of both Islāmic teachings and modern evidenced-based therapeutic interventions. By drawing from the rich spiritual and psychological insights within the Islāmic tradition, the department aims to equip future therapists, counsellors, Imams, psychologists, clinicians and scholars with the knowledge and skills necessary to address mental health issues within the Muslim community and beyond.

The department is committed to advancing the field of Islāmic psychology and psychotherapy by encouraging research and fostering a community of professionals who are well-versed in both Islāmic scholarship and contemporary psychology. Through its Online 4-Year Islāmic Psychology & Counselling Program and CPD courses, the department seeks to enhance the quality of mental health care in Muslim communities, promoting a holistic approach that respects and integrates cultural and religious values.

Collaboration with institutions

Al Balagh Academy has established strategic partnerships with leading academic and clinical institutions to create a unique platform where traditional Islāmic knowledge meets contemporary education and therapeutic practice. These collaborations are designed to foster an integrated approach to learning and professional growth, ensuring that course participants gain both spiritual depth and academic excellence. Through this network of partnerships, the Academy delivers a wide range of program, foundational, undergraduate and CPD levels, that combine classical Islāmic scholarship with modern academic standards. Course participants benefit from access to an array of enriching resources, including online lectures, interactive workshops, and expert-led seminars across multiple disciplines, equipping them with the tools to thrive both intellectually, clinically and professionally.

Al Balagh Academy has partnered with the UK's Markfield Institute of Higher Education (MIHE), one of the country's most respected Islāmic academic institutions. Through this collaboration, course participants who successfully complete the Online 4-Year Islāmic Psychology & Counseling Program can be fast-track into a UK-accredited BA at MIHE. By opening this route, Al Balagh Academy and MIHE together are providing course participants with a unique chance to pursue advanced Islāmic knowledge while gaining access to further educational, professional, and research opportunities.

On the clinical front, Al Balagh Academy has joined hands with Ihsaan, a specialized Islāmic psychological therapy service, to deliver an innovative Level 1 Online Course in Islāmic Psychology and Counseling. Ihsaan was founded to meet the growing need within Muslim communities, and beyond, for psychological therapies that are both religiously grounded and culturally sensitive, offering an alternative to conventional services that often lack this dimension. By collaborating closely with practicing clinicians and therapists, Al Balagh Academy ensures its program are informed by the latest clinical insights while staying rooted in Islāmic principles, creating a truly holistic approach to mental health and wellbeing.

Undergraduate course in Islāmic psychology and counselling

Al Balagh Academy is now offering a degree-level program in Islāmic Psychology and Counselling, a unique and transformative course designed to meet the growing needs of the Muslim community. Delivered part-time over four years, this program provides course participants with the knowledge, skills, and spiritual grounding to become Muslim counsellors and therapists, Tazkiyah coaches, and Islāmic life coaches.

What makes this program distinctive is its integration of Western psychological theories and techniques with Islāmic principles of mental health, spirituality, and human development. Rather than viewing these two traditions as separate, the course weaves them together to create a truly holistic model of Islāmic counselling and psychotherapy. Course participants are guided not only in acquiring professional competence but also in developing their own spiritual and ethical outlook as future practitioners.

The program is structured across eight semesters, with each semester lasting six months. Modules typically run for 12–16 teaching weeks, giving course participants enough time to absorb and apply their learning while balancing other commitments. With two annual intakes the course has been designed with flexibility in mind. To cater for course participants of different backgrounds, the program offers two distinct tracks. The Standard Track is tailored for those without prior training in psychology or counselling, providing them with the essential foundations of the field. The Advanced Track, on the other hand, is designed for course participants who already hold qualifications in psychology or counselling. These course participants may replace some of the foundational modules with a selection of optional modules, enabling them to deepen their studies in areas most relevant to their professional or academic journey. Course participants must complete at least 120 hours of client work as part of a supervised placement, integrated within the course.

An exciting aspect of this program is the opportunity it opens for further academic progression. The partnership between Al Balagh Academy and MIHE, course participants who successfully complete the Online 4-Year Islāmic Psychology & Counseling Programme (8 semesters) will be eligible for direct advanced entry into Year 2, Semester 2 of either:

- BA in Islāmic Studies, or
- BA in Islāmic Studies with Pastoral Care

This pathway allows course participants to save up to 1.5 years from a standard 3-year UK university degree, while continuing, or after completing, their Islāmic studies at Al Balagh. Through this program, Al Balagh Academy continues its mission to nurture a new generation of professionals who can serve the community with both psychological expertise and deep Islāmic insight.

CPD in Islāmic psychology and psychotherapy

CPD in Islāmic psychology and psychotherapy is essential for merging religious principles with contemporary psychological practices. It ensures that clinicians, academics, and researchers remain updated on the latest research and methodologies that align with Islāmic ethics and values, thereby enabling them to provide culturally and religiously sensitive care. This integration is crucial for effectively addressing the unique needs of Muslim clients.

As the mental health needs within the Muslim community evolve, CPD allows professionals to continuously refine their skills to meet these changing demands. Additionally, CPD plays a vital role in maintaining competence and credibility in the field of Islāmic psychology and psychotherapy. Regular training and education reflect a commitment to professional excellence, ensuring that practitioners adhere to high standards and remain informed about ethical and legal requirements. This dedication is crucial for building trust with clients and preserving the integrity of the profession.

Finally, CPD fosters a culture of research, innovation, and personal growth among professionals. By engaging in ongoing education, practitioners can contribute to the development of new insights and approaches within the field, promoting continuous improvement. This growth not only enhances their own practice but also strengthens the overall impact of Islāmic psychology and psychotherapy within the broader Muslim community.

Islāmic psychology and psychotherapy

Understanding Islāmic counseling and psychotherapy begins with examining the definition of Islāmic psychology, a field that investigates human behavior, cognition, and emotions through the lens of Islāmic beliefs and teachings. Islāmic psychology is defined as "the study of the science of the soul, mental processes, and behavior according to the principles of empirical psychology, rationality, and divine revelation from the Qur'an and Sunnah" (Rassool, 2023b, p. 52). This discipline emphasizes the integration of scientific inquiry with religious principles to achieve a holistic understanding of human nature and behavior.

By combining empirical methods with insights from Islāmic scripture and tradition, Islāmic psychology aims to provide a comprehensive framework for addressing mental health challenges. It recognizes the value of both empirical evidence and spiritual guidance, offering a balanced perspective that promotes well-being within the context of Islāmic teachings. This integration ensures that psychological practices are grounded in science while also aligned with the ethical and spiritual values central to Islām.

Islāmic counseling, or psychotherapy, is defined as "a form of counseling [or psychotherapy] that incorporates spirituality into the therapeutic process and has a faith-based perspective" (Rassool, 2016, p. 193). Rassool (2020, 2025) has further redefined Islāmic psychotherapy and counseling as "an application of interpersonal skills in the development of the self (nafs), intellect (aql), body (jasad), and heart (qalb) based on Islāmic spirituality."

This expanded definition of Islāmic psychotherapy and counseling embraces a holistic approach that acknowledges the interconnectedness of these elements, integrating both psychological and metaphysical dimensions. It emphasizes the comprehensive nature of human experience, highlighting the intricate relationships among these aspects in understanding and treating the self.

Educational philosophy and curriculum development

Authentic Islāmic education should embrace a holistic approach that integrates both acquired knowledge, such as the sciences and humanities, and perennial knowledge rooted in divine revelation (Rassool, 2023a). Unlike the secular and compartmentalized education system that often separates these areas, Islāmic education emphasizes a comprehensive understanding that weaves together intellectual, ethical, and spiritual dimensions.

This integrated concept of education includes not only knowledge (Ta'lim) but also ethical and spiritual nurturing (Tarbiyah) and moral discipline (Ta'dib). Through this approach, Islāmic education aims to cultivate individuals who are intellectually capable as well as morally and spiritually grounded, ensuring a balanced development of the mind, heart, and soul.

The philosophy of Islāmic education seeks to "shape the human being by aligning the three dimensions of sense, mind, and religious faith, based on the belief that harmony among these dimensions can realize human values in practice" (Rayan, 2012). Education for all is a fundamental principle in Islām. However, the pursuit of knowledge is not merely for intellectual gain; it serves as a means for the purification of the soul (Tazkiyah al-Nafs) (Rassool, 2023a).

Notably, there is limited literature on the philosophy of education in Islāmic psychology, with significant contributions primarily from Rassool (2021, 2022). Rassool (2021) has proposed that the goal of Islāmic education in the study of psychology should be:

- To impart Islāmic ethics and sciences that enable Muslim counsellors, therapist, mental health workers and psychologists to develop ethical intelligence.
- To clearly define aims for the professional and personal development of Muslim psychologists in service to the Ummah.
- To provide authentic Islāmic knowledge to Muslim psychologists that leads individuals toward the consciousness of the Creator to obey His commands (Al-Ghazālī).
- To enhance awareness and recognition of the holistic needs (biopsychosocial and spiritual) of both Muslim and non-Muslim patients or clients.

- To improve knowledge and evidence-based intervention strategies required for delivering high-quality counseling and psychotherapeutic care.
- To develop a conceptual framework and curriculum approaches for undergraduate, postgraduate, and CPD programs.
- To cultivate knowledge and skills in Islāmic thought, integrating this into educational programs and teaching practices.
- To apply anthropology and Islāmic teachings, along with the study of Islāmic civilizations, to understand and evolve Islāmic psychology.
- To develop research skills and foster a research-based approach to providing evidence that can effect change in education and therapeutic interventions. (p. 587).

A Vertical and Horizontal Integrated, Embedded Curriculum Model of Islāmic Psychology was developed and implemented by Rassool (2020, 2023a) to facilitate the integration of Islāmic psychology and ethical values within psychological knowledge.

The CDT at Al Balagh Academy, in collaboration with various institutions when appropriate, played a pivotal role in creating and refining the curriculum. This team, composed of experts in Islāmic education, Islāmic psychology, and other relevant fields, worked closely with partner institutions to ensure that the curriculum was both comprehensive and aligned with contemporary educational standards. By leveraging the expertise and resources of these collaborative partners, the team integrated traditional Islāmic teachings with modern pedagogical practices, resulting in a curriculum that is academically rigorous as well as spiritually enriching. This collaborative approach ensured that the curriculum addressed the diverse needs of learners while remaining true to the foundational principles of Islāmic education.

CPD course: Aims, learning outcomes, content, and course team

These courses offer an in-depth exploration of Islāmic psychology and counseling, combining Islāmic teachings with modern psychological practices. Course participants acquire practical skills through case studies and learn to apply Islāmic rulings to real-world mental health scenarios. The curriculum equips course participants to facilitate, guide and treat individuals with psychological disorders from an Islāmic perspective, contributing to the growing field of Islāmic mental health. Tables outline the aims, learning outcomes, and contents for the respective course program.

Table 8

Islāmic counselling and psychology (Level 2): Aims, learning outcomes, contents, course team and duration

Course section	Content
Course aims	The course is designed to enhance course participants' theoretical and practical understanding of Islāmic counselling and psychotherapy, with an emphasis on advanced approaches that support different types of talk therapy. Its goal is to develop therapeutic skills within the Muslim community, so that individuals facing psychological distress can receive effective support. Additionally, it aims to provide professional counsellors with a faith-based, holistic model for their practice.
Learning outcomes	1. Identify and describe the various Islāmic models of Islāmic psychology. 2. Distinguish between culturally relative factors and universal factors in conventional psychology. 3. Describe the therapeutic relationship from an Islāmic perspective. 4. Develop therapeutic skills within an Islāmic framework to support individuals experiencing distress. 5. Examine the management of a diverse range of psychological difficulties, including anger, anxiety, paranormal experiences, psychosis, and depression, from an Islāmic viewpoint. 6. Discuss advanced Islāmic psychological principles that assist those in distress, using case studies for illustration. 7. Analyze the congruence and incongruence of psychological intervention approaches with Islāmic beliefs and practices.
Course contents	• Foundation of Islāmic Counselling and Psychotherapy • Islāmic Counselling and Psychotherapy: From Psychology to Faith • The Fitrah: Nature of Human and Personality Development • Illuminating the Psyche: An Introduction to Psychoanalytic Therapy • Harmony and Dissonance: Jungian Therapy and Islāmic Psychotherapy • Humanistic Therapy: Re-envisioned Through an Islāmic Perspective • Islāmic Insights into Cognitive Behavior Therapy: A Path to Healing the Mind, Soul, and Behavior • Uniting Faith and Therapy: The Islāmic Perspective on Solution-Focused Brief Therapy • Sacred Bonds and Marital Challenges: Islāmic-Oriented Marital Therapy

AL BALAGH ACADEMY'S ONLINE ISLĀMIC IP PROGRAM

	<ul><li>Narrative Therapy Through the Islāmic Lens</li><li>Hope Therapy: Finding Strength in Faith</li><li>Journey Through the Night: An Islāmic Approach to Dream Interpretation</li><li>Mental Health Problems and Psychopathology</li><li>Understanding the Muslim Client and Assessment</li><li>Obsessive Compulsive Disorders and Therapy: Practical Case Studies</li><li>Evil Eye, Jinn Possession, and Black Magic</li><li>Jinn Possession and Psychosis</li><li>Islāmic Models of Resilience and Prevention of Mental Illness</li><li>The Siraat Al-Islāmic Psychotherapy Practice Model</li><li>Case Studies Presentation and Discussion: Dealing with "Possessed Patients" - Practical Case Studies</li><li>Case Studies Presentation and Discussion</li><li>The Future of Islāmic Models of Psychotherapy and Careers in Islāmic Psychology and Counselling</li></ul>This revised version improves clarity and corrects any spelling, grammar, and punctuation errors
Course teams	*Professor G. Hussein Rassool* Professor of Islāmic Psychology Centre for Islāmic Studies & Civilizations CSU, Australia Director of Studies, Department of Islāmic Psychology, Psychotherapy & Counselling *Professor Abdur Rasjid Skinner* Clinical Director, Ihsaan *Dr. Mahbub Khan* Consultant Clinical Psychologist *Dr. Hassam Waheed* Guest Lecturer at Al Balagh Academy *Shaykh Saeed Nasser* Integrative Counsellor *Shaykh Idris Watts* Arabic Teacher *Abdul Hafeez Passwala* Herbalist & Raaqi

Duration of course	24 Live Online Sessions Duration: 6+ Months

Table 9

Addiction Counselling: Islāmic Model – Level 1. Aims, learning outcomes, contents, course team and duration

Course Section	Content
Course aims	This course aims to develop a foundational understanding of nature and scope of addiction in contemporary society. It will examine the physical, social, psychological and spiritual harms caused by addiction to pharmacological substances and addictive activities. It will increase knowledge and understanding of the therapeutic interventions of addictive behaviors from an Islāmic perspective.
Learning outcomes	Develop a greater sensitivity and acceptance of individuals struggling with addiction problems. Examine the basic nature of addictive behaviors. Critically examine the historical, sociological and cultural perspectives of addictive behaviors. Critically evaluate the theories and approaches of addictive behaviors based on existing evidence. Describe the behavioral addictions such as eating disorders, gambling, sex and health problems. Discuss a framework for assessment, risk assessment and screening. Identify the pharmacological and psychosocial interventions in the management of those with addictive behaviors. Discuss the Islāmic methods of intervention strategies in managing addictive behaviors
Course content	Fundamentals of Child Development in Western Psychology Early Childhood Development: Islāmic and Psychological Insights Cognitive Growth and Learning Enhancement Moral and Spiritual Development in Islām Emotional Intelligence and Mental Health in Children Islāmic Principles in Child Rearing and Education Behavioral Management: Islāmic and Psychological Approaches Guiding School-Age Children: A Holistic Approach Ensuring Safety and Promoting Holistic Wellness in Children Islāmic Perspectives on Discipline and Child Behavior Empathy and Compassion in Islāmic Upbringing Adolescent Challenges : Islāmic and Psychological Perspectives Age-Appropriate Islāmic Teachings and Practices

	Parenting in Non-Muslim Countries: Coping with Modern Challenges through Islāmic and Psychological Solutions Effective Communication : Islāmic and Psychological Techniques Reflections and Applications
Course teams	Professor G. Hussein Rassool. Professor of Islāmic Psychology, Centre for Islāmic Studies & Civilizations, CSU, Australia. Director of Studies, Department of Islāmic Psychology, Psychotherapy & Counselling. Dr. Masturah Badzis. Associate Professor at Kulliyyah of Education, International Islāmic University Malaysia, Doctorate in Education (Ed.D.), Child Development and Education, University of Warwick (UK). Linda Bendjafer. Doctoral student in Cognitive Psychology at University of Paris. Clinical Psychologist, Counsellor, French Speaker, Teacher and a Writer. Zulekha Shakoor Rajani. Counselling Psychologist, Mind and Brain Hospital. IP diploma-CMC, Taziyah Therapy-Avicenna Academy, TIIP-Level-1-Khalil Center. M.Sc. Psychology, B.Ed., PGDgC (Guidance & Counseling).
Duration of courses	16 Live Online Sessions Duration: 6+ months

Table 10

Child Psychology: Western Insights and Islāmic Perspectives. Aims, learning outcomes, contents, course team and duration

Course section	Content
Course aims	The aim of the course is to offer a profound understanding of child psychology from diverse perspectives. It examines cognitive development stages, behavioral management, and effective parenting strategies, ensuring a holistic grasp of child growth and nurturing from evidenced-based Western psychological approaches and Islāmic teachings.
Learning outcomes	• Examine the stages of cognitive development in children, informed by both Western psychological theories and Islāmic teachings. • Outline the behavioral management in modifying child behaviors using evidence-based strategies that are aligned with Islāmic principles. • Identify the range of parenting strategies that foster holistic child development, integrating insights from both Western psychology and Islāmic teachings. • Apply child psychology principles in diverse cultural settings, ensuring that their approaches are culturally

	sensitive and relevant.
• Discuss evidence-based psychological practices to child growth and nurturing, balancing them with Islāmic teachings to ensure a well-rounded developmental approach.
• Develop interpersonal skills to provide more effective and empathetic support to children and families by incorporating both Western and Islāmic perspectives on child psychology
Course content	• Fundamentals of Child Development in Western Psychology
• Early Childhood Development: Islāmic and Psychological Insights
• Cognitive Growth and Learning Enhancement
• Moral and Spiritual Development in Islām
• Emotional Intelligence and Mental Health in Children
• Islāmic Principles in Child Rearing and Education
• Behavioral Management: Islāmic and Psychological Approaches
• Guiding School-Age Children: A Holistic Approach
• Ensuring Safety and Promoting Holistic Wellness in Children
• Islāmic Perspectives on Discipline and Child Behavior
• Empathy and Compassion in Islāmic Upbringing
• Adolescent Challenges : Islāmic and Psychological Perspectives
• Age-Appropriate Islāmic Teachings and Practices
• Parenting in Non-Muslim Countries: Coping with Modern Challenges through Islāmic and Psychological Solutions
• Effective Communication : Islāmic and Psychological Techniques
• Reflections and Applications
Duration of courses	16 Live Online Sessions

Duration: 6+ months |

Table 11

The Fiqh of Psychology, Psychiatry, and Counselling

Course section	Content
Course aims	The course aims to provide comprehensive knowledge of key Islāmic principles, rulings, and *Fatawa* related to psychology, psychiatry, and counselling, enabling Islāmic to apply these in real-world mental health scenarios. Through practical insights and case studies, it enhances skills in guiding individuals with psychological disorders from an Islāmic perspective, fostering positive contributions to the field of Islāmic psychology, counselling and psychotherapy.

Learning outcomes	Demonstrate an understanding of the intersection between Islamic fiqh and contemporary psychological concepts, including the legal and ethical considerations in mental health. Analyze the concept of *Ahliyyah* (legal capacity) and evaluate the obligations and responsibilities of individuals with psychological disorders within an Islamic framework. Apply fiqh principles to the understanding and management of common mental health disorders, including depression, anxiety, bipolar disorder, and personality disorders. Evaluate the Islamic legal perspectives on severe mental illnesses, such as psychosis, schizophrenia, and OCD, and discuss their implications for treatment and care. Assess the fiqh-related considerations for neurodevelopmental disorders, including ADHD and autism spectrum disorders (ASD), in both clinical and social contexts. Critically examine Islamic rulings related to substance use disorders, including alcoholism and drug addiction, and their impact on legal and ethical responsibilities. Apply fiqh principles to marriage, divorce, criminal responsibility, and testimony for individuals with psychological or mental health conditions. Analyze the Islamic legal and ethical considerations in psychiatric treatments, including pharmacological interventions, electroconvulsive therapy, and counseling practices. Develop strategies for community support, advocacy, and mental health promotion grounded in Islamic teachings. Reflect on contemporary challenges and future directions in integrating Islamic fiqh with psychological practice, demonstrating critical thinking and ethical decision-making.
Course Overview	The fiqh (Islāmic jurisprudence) related to mental health conditions such as depression, anxiety, bipolar disorder, PTSD, personality disorders, and substance use disorder. Islāmic rulings concerning marriage and divorce for individuals with mental health issues. The Islāmic perspective on reducing stigma surrounding mental health. Treatment interventions for various mental disorders distinguishing between invasive and non-invasive methods. The fiqh regarding *Jinayah* (criminal responsibility), shahadah (testimony and oaths), and psychological disorders. Islāmic rulings pertaining to counseling and therapy practices
Course contents	1. Introduction to the intersection of Islāmic fiqh and psychology. 2. Understanding *Ahliyyah* (legal capacity) and the obligations of individuals with psychological disorders. 3. The fiqh of depression and anxiety disorders. 4. The fiqh of bipolar disorder. 5. The fiqh of post-traumatic stress disorder and personality

	disorders. 6. The fiqh of psychosis, schizophrenia, and severe mental illnesses. 7. The fiqh of OCD. 8. The fiqh of attention-deficit/hyperactivity disorder (ADHD). 9. The fiqh of ASD. 10. The fiqh of alcoholism, drug addiction, and other substance use disorders. 11. The fiqh of marriage and divorce in relation to psychological/mental disorders. 12. The fiqh of *Jinayah* (criminal responsibility) and shahadah (testimony and oaths) concerning psychological/mental disorders. 13. The fiqh of psychiatric treatments, including the use of narcotics and electroconvulsive therapy. 14. The fiqh of counseling practices. 15. The fiqh of community support and advocacy in mental health. *16.* Q&A session and future directions in psychology and Islamic fiqh
Course teams	Shaykh Dr Rafaqat Rashid, traditional Shar'iah scholar, General Practitioner and an international professional trainer and educator. He is the co-founder of al-Balagh Academy and Course Director Al Balagh Academy, UK. Mufti Muhammed Zubair Butt. Chair, Al Qalam, Bradford. Senior Advisor on Islāmic law at the Institute of Islāmic Jurisprudence, Bradford. Lecturer on the Ethics of Transplants and Autopsy at the University of Leeds and is a regular contributor at seminars on Islāmic medical ethics. Mufti Muhammad ibn Adam al-Kawthari, teacher of various traditional Islāmic sciences, and Director and researcher at the Institute of Islāmic Jurisprudence (Darul Iftaa, www.daruliftaa.com.Leicester, UK
Duration of course	16 Live Online Sessions Duration : 4+ months

These courses collectively offer a well-rounded education in Islāmic psychology and psychotherapy, addressing various aspects of mental health and counselling through an Islāmic lens.

Admission requirements for CPD courses

For individuals who already possess formal academic or professional qualifications, direct entry into CPD courses is typically available. These qualifications indicate that the individual has already demonstrated the ability to engage with complex material, complete assessments, and apply their knowledge in a professional context. For those interested in CPD courses who lack formal academic or professional qualifications, possessing strong study skills becomes crucial. CPD courses are designed to enhance knowledge, skills, and competencies in a specific field, and they often require participants to engage with complex material, complete assignments, and apply what they have learned in practical settings. We are envisaging to implement a study skills course in the near future.

Modes of instruction and online structure

The courses utilize a blend of instructional methods, including live online sessions, recorded video lectures, live webinars, discussion forums, and practical assignments, to deliver content effectively. The online structure allows Islāmic to access the ILM Portal upon enrolment, which serves as a central hub for all course materials, announcements, and progress tracking.

The dashboard provides an organized overview of all course components. Each course is divided into modules or units that cover specific topics or themes. These modules typically include recorded video lectures, reading materials, and reflective questions.

To foster engagement, there are interactive elements such as discussion boards and scenarios that encourage course participants to actively participate with the material and interact with one another. Additionally, support resources are available to help course participants access technical support, academic advising, and tutoring services. These resources are designed to assist course participants in overcoming any challenges they may encounter during the courses, including help desks, FAQs, and contact information for support services.

There is a newly updated mobile app designed to maximize learning flexibility by providing seamless access to courses anytime and anywhere. Users can download the app tailored to their device using the following links:

- For Android users: Available on the Google Play Store.
- For iOS users: Downloadable from the App Store.

The app allows users to easily navigate course materials, participate in discussions, submit assignments, and track their progress, offering a convenient and accessible learning experience.

CPD course fees

For CPD courses, fees typically range from £79.99 to £199.99, providing flexible pricing options to accommodate various budgets. Additionally, there are often opportunities to take advantage of significant discounts, making these courses even more accessible. To further ease financial commitment, many programs offer instalment payment plans, allowing course participants to spread the cost over several payments. This approach ensures that financial constraints are minimized, enabling more individuals to invest in their professional growth and development without undue burden.

Al Balagh Academy scholarship

Al Balagh Academy highly values individuals who are committed to pursuing knowledge. Recognizing the significance of education in both personal and professional development, the academy is dedicated to supporting and nurturing course participants who show a strong passion for learning.

To make education more accessible for those who require financial assistance, Al Balagh Academy offers scholarships to eligible applicants. Interested candidates are encouraged to visit the application portal to apply for a scholarship. Once the application is submitted, the Al Balagh Academy team will carefully review it and assess the applicant's eligibility. Applicants can expect a response within 2 to 3 working days, informing them of the outcome and providing further details on the next steps.

Assessment and course grading policy

The course grading policy is designed to ensure that course participants achieve a comprehensive understanding and mastery of the subject matter. To successfully pass, course participants must earn a minimum grade of 40% across all courses. Here's how your performance will be evaluated:

- Weekly Assessment Exams (60% of total points): Throughout the course, the course participants will take approximately 5 to 6 online objective assessments. These assessments are intended to test your understanding and develop your skills. They are crucial for tracking your progress and ensuring you stay on the right path.

- Course Final Examination (40% of total points): The culmination of course participants' learning journey is marked by the course final exam. This decisive assessment evaluates your grasp of the entire course content.

- Achieving a score of 40% or above is essential to pass the course. This balanced approach between regular assessments, and a comprehensive final examination ensures that you not only retain information but also apply your knowledge effectively.

Graduation requirements

Upon successfully completing the course, participants will be eligible to receive a digital certificate of achievement. To qualify for this certificate, the following criteria must be met:

1. Completion of all course modules: Participants must fully engage with all designated course materials, including readings, assignments, and assessments.
2. Minimum passing grade: A minimum grade of 40% is required to be eligible for the certificate of achievement.

Validation and accreditation

Al Balagh courses are designed to provide valuable knowledge and skills, but they do not offer externally accredited or officially recognized qualifications. The course content is developed and refined by Al Balagh's expert team, ensuring that the material is both high quality and relevant. With a growing community of over 40,000 learners, Al Balagh is committed to expanding its reach and impact. The academy's vision is to establish its qualifications as globally recognized through the expertise and dedication of its internal team, rather than relying on formal accreditation or recognition from external institutions. This approach allows Al Balagh to focus on delivering tailored, high-quality education while pursuing its goal of widespread recognition and influence in the field.

Evaluation of CPD courses

Evaluating CPD courses requires a thorough assessment of several key elements to determine their effectiveness and relevance. The course content and structure should be up-to-date, comprehensive, and well-organized, providing a clear and logical progression of information. Instructional methods should employ varied delivery formats and engage participants through interactive activities to enhance learning.

The expertise of instructors is also critical, including their professional qualifications and effectiveness in teaching, which directly impacts the quality of education delivered. Additionally, well-designed assessment and evaluation mechanisms, along with strong participant support and accessible learning resources, are essential to achieving successful course outcomes.

The evaluation process should further consider learning outcomes, such as the extent to which course objectives are met and the practical application of acquired knowledge. The credibility of certifications and the professional recognition of qualifications are important factors for course participants. Furthermore, course participant feedback, gathered through surveys and reviews, provides valuable insights into satisfaction levels and the impact of the course on professional practice.

By systematically examining these components, institutions can ensure their CPD courses provide meaningful and impactful professional development. This evaluation will specifically focus on Level 2 courses in Islāmic Psychology and Counselling offered between 2020 and 2024.

Findings from evaluation of Islāmic Psychology Level 2

The courses attracted a diverse cohort of course participants from multiple countries, highlighting their international appeal (see Figure 1). Although the majority of course participants are from the United Kingdom (UK), this diversity demonstrates that the courses are both accessible and attractive to a global audience. Such an international mix can enhance the learning experience by bringing in different perspectives and cultural insights, enriching discussions and deepening the understanding of psychological concepts.

In the Psychology Level 2 course, the gender distribution (see Figure 4) shows a marked predominance of female course participants, with 74% of participants identifying as women. This pattern reflects broader trends in psychology education, where women typically outnumber men, often representing around 75% of the student body (Clay, 2017).

Figure 3: *Country Wise %*

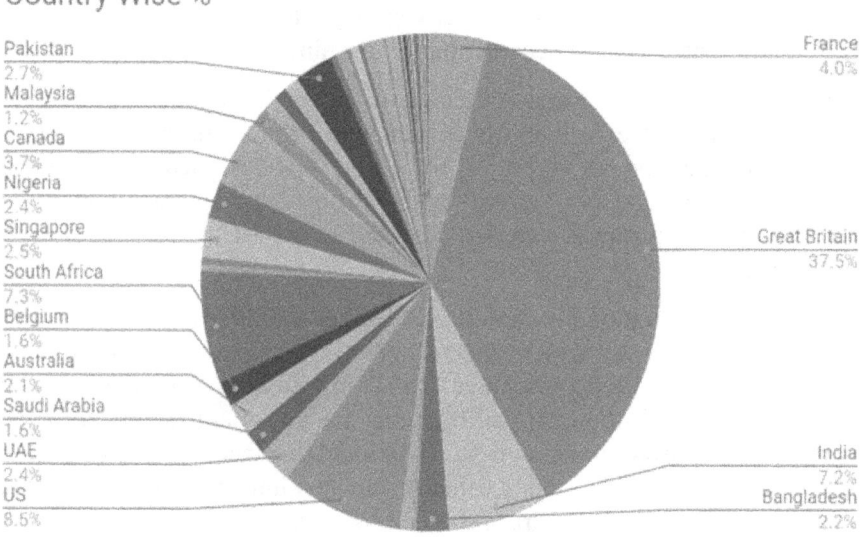

Figure 4

Gender Ratio

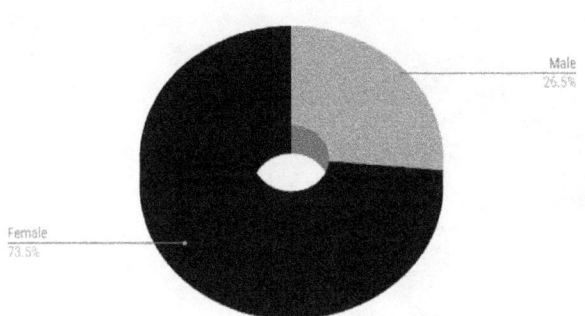

Most course participants rated their initial effort in the course as "Poor" to "Fair" (68%), indicating a moderate level of knowledge at the start (see Figure 5). This suggests that participants generally begin with a basic to intermediate understanding, highlighting the courses' appeal to learners seeking to build upon foundational knowledge.

When examining the course content and structure (see Figure 6), the majority of course participants expressed a positive view of the organization and planning, with 56% agreeing or strongly agreeing that the course was well-structured. To gain a more nuanced understanding, it would be useful to review specific course participants' feedback or comments.

Figure 5

Effort and Learning Outcomes

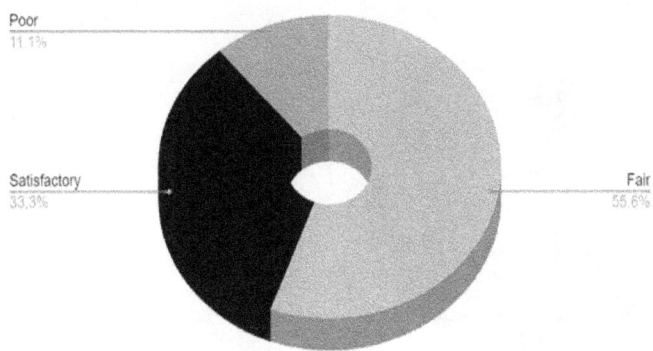

Figure 6

Course Content and Structure

Regarding the evaluation of instructor skills and responsiveness (see Figure 7), the feedback from course participants was overwhelmingly positive. Seventy eight percent (78%) of participants agreed or strongly agreed that the instructors excelled across multiple areas: delivering lectures and demonstrations effectively, presenting material in a clear and well-structured manner, engaging and maintaining student interest, managing live class time efficiently, and being accessible while providing helpful support. This feedback highlights the instructors' strengths and highlights their significant contribution to a positive and engaging learning experience for Islāmic.

Figure 7

Instructor Performance

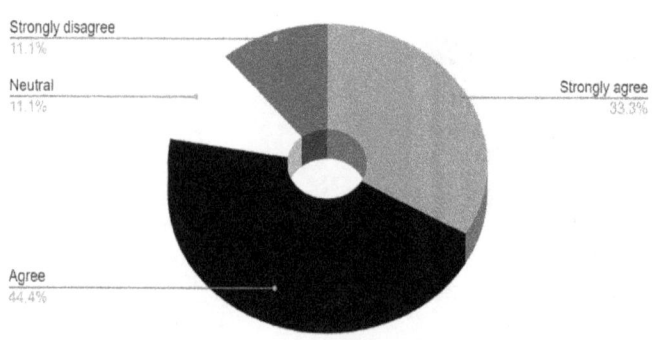

Overall, course participants' satisfaction with the program was highly positive (see Figure 8). Twenty-two percent of course participants (27%) felt the course exceeded their expectations, indicating that a notable portion found it exceptionally engaging, likely due to compelling content, effective teaching methods, or meaningful learning experiences. The majority of course participants (78%) reported that the course met their expectations, demonstrating that the program reliably delivered on its promises and fulfilled course participants' learning needs.

The course was also rated positively for its impact on career development and CV enhancement, with most responses falling under "Agree" or "Strongly Agree." Specifically, 78% of course participants felt that the course content contributed to boosting their careers or strengthening their CVs (see Figure 9). This suggests that the courses are thoughtfully designed to equip course participants with practical skills and knowledge that are directly relevant and valuable in professional settings.

Figure 8

Satisfaction and Overall Course Experience

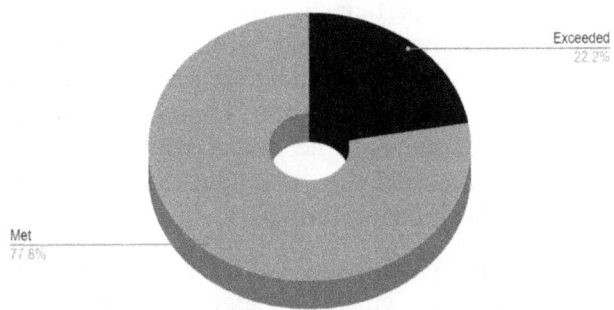

Figure 9

Course content [helped boost your career or CV]

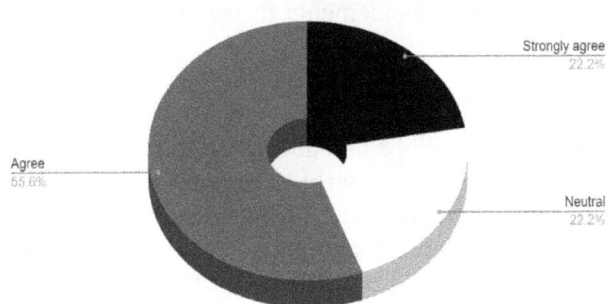

Summary of patterns

Most course participants began the course with a moderate level of knowledge and demonstrated significant improvement by the end. Instructor performance received high ratings from the majority of Islāmic, although some neutral responses suggest variations in expectations regarding teaching styles.

The course effectively retained returning course participants while attracting new learners through targeted marketing efforts. Overall, the course content and instruction proved effective, generating strong interest in future offerings. Course participants expressed satisfaction with the instructors' responsiveness and support, and there was a high level of satisfaction regarding the career relevance of the skills and knowledge gained.

However, the relatively lower scores for "Skill at End" indicate that placing greater emphasis on practical skills and measurable outcomes could further enhance course participants' satisfaction.

A notable portion of course participants (33%) were returning learners from Al Balagh Academy, reflecting strong retention and satisfaction with previous courses. This demonstrates the academy's ability to maintain course participants' interest and loyalty, highlighting that its programs effectively meet course participants' needs and expectations. The positive trend in returning course participants highlight the quality and effectiveness of the academy's educational offerings.

Additionally, some course participants (11%) enrolled through direct marketing, showing the success of email campaigns and promotional advertisements. Nearly all course participants expressed interest in enrolling in further courses at Al Balagh Academy, indicating overall satisfaction and a strong desire to continue their learning journey.

In summary, the data analysis provides valuable insights into the strengths and areas for improvement in the Psychology Level 2 course, offering clear guidance for future enhancements to better support course participants learning and engagement.

Challenges

To further enhance the course, it would be valuable to collect more detailed feedback from course participants, particularly those who felt the course merely met their expectations. Understanding their perspectives can help identify areas for improvement and ensure that a greater number of course participants have an exceptional learning experience in the future.

While gender imbalance and international diversity offer many benefits, they also present certain challenges. It is important to ensure that course content and teaching methods are inclusive and accessible to all participants, regardless of gender or cultural background. This may include providing additional support for participants facing language barriers or adapting to different cultural learning styles. Efforts to encourage more male participants to enroll could also help balance the gender ratio and enrich classroom interactions.

Course modifications: Integrate the latest research and best practices in Islāmic psychology and counseling. Include case studies and practical applications to enhance learning outcomes. Increase the number of live, interactive sessions and group discussions to make the course more engaging. Maintain comprehensive documentation of course structure, content, and assessment methods. Ensure that the curriculum meets required competencies and learning outcomes and is regularly reviewed and updated to comply with accreditation standards and industry best practices.

Digital accessibility: Ensure that online resources are fully accessible by adhering to web accessibility guidelines (e.g., WCAG). Provide materials in multiple formats, such as audio or large print, and offer additional support like sign language interpreters, note-takers, and assistive technology.

Developing a study skills program: Design a program to support participants with lower academic preparedness. Offer preparatory courses to build foundational skills in reading, writing, and critical thinking. Conduct workshops on time management, note-taking, exam preparation, and effective study techniques. Pair participants with mentors to provide guidance throughout their studies and develop individualized learning plans to address specific academic needs while tracking progress.

A Road map for the next ten years

Al Balagh Academy aspires to become a leading global institution in Islāmic education, psychology, and counselling. To realize this vision, the academy plans to expand its curriculum to include advanced Islāmic studies, address contemporary issues, and develop interdisciplinary programs. Efforts will also focus on obtaining accreditation from recognized educational bodies, enhancing the credibility and recognition of its programs. These initiatives aim to ensure that course participants receive a comprehensive and respected education in Islāmic studies.

To enhance online learning, Al Balagh Academy intends to invest in state-of-the-art platforms with interactive features and has already launched a mobile app to provide flexible access to course materials. The academy also aims to broaden its global reach by offering courses in multiple languages. In addition, regional learning centers will be established to facilitate face-to-face instruction, while hybrid programs will combine online coursework with in-person sessions to enrich the overall learning experience.

Support for course participants with disabilities will be a priority, ensuring that all learning environments are inclusive and accessible. Faculty development will be emphasized through CPD, research opportunities, and support for publication, maintaining high teaching standards and contributing to the fields of Islāmic sciences, psychology, psychotherapy, and allied health and social care disciplines.

Course participants support services will include mentorship programs, study skills workshops, and career guidance to assist learners in their academic and professional journeys. The academy will also explore technological innovations, such as artificial intelligence (AI) and virtual reality (VR), to personalize learning experiences and create immersive educational environments.

Moreover, Al Balagh Academy encourages course participants to engage in community service initiatives that benefit both Muslim and non-Muslim communities, including charity work, educational workshops, and social outreach programs. The academy will foster a sense of community and maintain strong alumni engagement, promoting the practical application of Islāmic principles in real-world contexts. Ultimately, Al Balagh Academy is committed to providing accessible, authentic knowledge and skills that benefit both the *Ummah* and the wider global community.

Faculty IP publications in the last ten years

Hassem, Z., Ismail, S., Vad Walla, N., & Rassool, G. Hussein. (2025). *Working with crisis and trauma from an Islāmic perspective. 1st Edition.* Focus Series on Islāmic Psychology & Psychotherapy Routledge.

Rassool, G. Hussein. (2025). *Islāmic Counselling & Psychotherapy.* 2nd Edition. Routledge.

Rassool, G. Hussein. (2025). *Treating Addictive Behaviors from an Islāmic Perspective. 1st Edition.* Focus Series on Islāmic Psychology & Psychotherapy. Routledge.

Rassool G. Hussein. (2025). *Exploring the Intersection of Islāmic Spiritual and Psychotherapy: Healing the Soul.* Springer

Aboul-Enein, B. H., Rassool, G. Hussein., Benajiba, N., Bernstein, J., & Mo'ez Al-Islām E. Faris (2025). *Contemporary Islāmic*

Perspectives in Public Health. Cambridge University Press.

Rassool, G. Hussein. (2025). *Spiritual Integration in Islāmic Psychotherapy: Unveiling the Therapist's Soul.* Focus Series on Islāmic Psychology & Psychotherapy. Routledge.

Latif, J., Dockrat, S., & Rassool, G. Hussein. (2024). *Integrating Spiritual Interventions in Islāmic Psychology A Practical Guide. First Edition.* Focus Series on Islāmic Psychology & Psychotherapy. Routledge.

Rassool, G. Hussein., & Benmebarek, Z. (2024). *Revaluation des concepts et des pratiques du counseling et de la psychothérapie Islāmique.* Doi:10.13140/RG.2.2.31278.73285.

Rassool, G. Hussein. (2023). *Integrated Research Methodologies in Islāmic Psychology. 1st Edition.* Focus Series on Islāmic Psychology & Psychotherapy. Routledge.

Rassool G .Hussein. (2023). *Islāmic Psychology: The Basics.* Routledge.

Rassool, G. Hussein. (2023). *Advancing Islāmic Psychology Education: Knowledge Integration, Model, and Application. 1st Edition.* Focus Series on Islāmic Psychology & Psychotherapy. Routledge.

Rassool, G. Hussein., Nawaz, J., Latif, S., & Mudassar, U. (2023). Development and Psychometric Evaluation of a Scale for Measuring the Conception of Islāmīc Psychology. *Pakistan Journal of Clinical Psychology, 22*(2), 69-79

Rassool, G. Hussein. (2023).Critical Reflections on Current Status of Scholarship in Islāmic Psychology – Challenges and Solutions. *Australian Journal of Islāmic Studies, 8*(3), 37-54.

Shabir, R., Latif, S., & Rassool, G. Hussein. (2023). Fear of COVID-19, Obsessive Compulsive Symptoms and Psychological Well-being: Moderating Role of Harm Avoidance Behaviors among Adults in Lahore, Pakistan. *Pakistan Journal of Professional Psychology: Research & Practice (PJPPRP), 14*(2), 43-55.

Ahmad, S.M., Rassool, G. Hussein., & Nawaz, K. (2023). A National Survey of Islāmic Psychology Content in Psychology Programs in Pakistan. *Bahria Journal of Professional Psychology, 22, (2)*14 - 26.

Rassool, G. Hussein., & Iakhin, F.F. (2023). *Islāmic Psychology in the Commonwealth of Independent States: Current Status, Trends and Prospects,* in Elmira Muratova & Elmira Akhmetova, Muslims of Central Eurasia since the 19th Century. Baku, Azerbaijan: Idrak Public Union, (pp. 217-244).

Rassool, G. Hussein ., & Keskin, Z. (2023).Positioning the Self (Nafs) in Islāmic Psycho-Spirituality. *Journal of Spirituality in Mental Health.* DOI 10.1080/19349637.2023.2264848.

Owens, J., Rassool, G. Hussein., Bernstein, J., Latif, S., & Aboul-Enein,

B., (2023). Interventions using the Qur'an to promote mental health: A systematic scoping review. *Journal of Mental Health, 32*(4),842-862.

Rassool, G. Hussein., Nawaz, K., Latif, S, & Mudassar, U. (2023). Prevalence of Depression, Anxiety and Stress during COVID-19 among Frontline Workers. *Journal of Islāmic International Medical College, 18*(2), 121-127.

Rassool, G .Hussein. (2023).Spirituality and Psychology: Integration of knowledge Rationale, Realities, Prospects and Challenges. *Journal of the British Islāmic Medical Association, 13,* 5. https://www.jbima.com/

Rassool, G. Hussein., & Khan, W,N.A. (2023). *Hope in Islāmic Psychotherapy. Journal of Spirituality in Mental Health,* DOI: 10.1080/19349637.2023.2207751

Qayyum, H., Latif, S., & Rassool, G. Hussein. (2023). Anxiety in Online Classes, Learning Style and Student's Satisfaction Among University Students in Current Pandemic of COVID-19. *Pakistan Journal of Psychological Research, 38* (1), 97 110.

CHAPTER ELEVEN

ISLAMIC PSYCHOLOGY CERTIFICATE

Académie Islam & Psychologie; Paris, France

Ali Habibbi

Introduction

The field of IP is expanding globally; however, the French-speaking world is lagging in this area. This underdevelopment is surprising, especially given the large French-speaking regions that are home to millions of Muslims across various continents. Many countries are part of the French-speaking community, and a significant number of French-speaking Muslims do not speak English or Arabic. This language barrier limits their access to training opportunities available in those languages.

IP is largely unfamiliar in the French-speaking world, which is significantly shaped by the French interpretation of secularism. This interpretation is framed as a philosophy that dismisses the influence of religion on individuals. Instead of fostering inclusivity by safeguarding individuals and their beliefs, it becomes exclusive by imposing a single, narrow model of social behavior that all members of society are expected to adhere to.

Given the current situation and the urgent need for French-speaking Muslims to be understood, acknowledged, and supported, the AIP has undertaken the responsibility of promoting IP. Their objective is to educate and train individuals who are interested in this approach.

In 2023, AIP launched two certification programs in IP, initiated by Dr. Ali Habibbi, PhD in Clinical Psychology and Psychopathology, and a researcher at ISTAC-IIUM.

The first program, composed of two one-year long levels, is designed for mental health professionals who want to specialize in IP. The second program spans two years and is intended for non-mental health professionals seeking training in this field.

Additionally, a program titled "Awareness of Mental Health" was developed specifically for Imams and religious leaders.

Nature of Program

The **Islamic Psychology Certificate**, offered online by *AIP* in collaboration with the *ISIP* and the *Al-Balkhi Institute*, is a two-tier program—an initial 12-month level followed by a 10-month advanced level—created specifically for licensed psychologists, psychiatrists, and psychotherapists. The program provides both theoretical and practical insights into IP by examining and redefining traditional academic concepts from a Quranic perspective. This innovative approach deepens our understanding of human nature and psychology, grounded in the principles of the Islamic tradition.

Instruction is delivered online on weekends through a blend of live sessions and pre-recorded materials, offering flexibility for working professionals. Level 1 consists of 150 hours of classes taught by various instructors, a 100-hour internship, and a tuition fee of €2,000. Level 2, the Practical Training in the NAFSI Approach, is open to those who have earned the Level 1 certificate and extends over 10 months, featuring 210 hours of instruction with Dr. Ali Habibbi, a five-day residential seminar in Marrakesh in collaboration with Maristan Aïcha, and a 100-hour internship, with a tuition fee of €3,000.

Upon completing the program, students will receive a certificate. Their understanding of the course objectives and engagement will be assessed through various methods, including class discussions, essays, presentations, group projects, exams, and online quizzes. Assessment may also involve critical dialogues and require active participation in supervision sessions. Additionally, students must write and defend a dissertation or scientific article of at least 15 pages.

ISLAMIC PSYCHOLOGY CERTIFICATE

Curriculum Level 1

This certificate aims to provide students with a comprehensive understanding of IP, allowing them to apply this knowledge in various settings—ranging from clinical environments to community contexts—thus enhancing their professional and personal practices.

Unit 1: Founding of Islamic Psychology

This unit examines the origins of IP by tracing its history and development up to the modern era. It highlights the significant contributions of Muslim scholars from the 8th to the 14th centuries, emphasizing their impact on contemporary mental health practices. The course also addresses the philosophical influences and epistemology of IP, providing a solid foundation for a deeper understanding of the discipline.

Unit 2: Islamic Foundations

This unit focuses on essential Muslim beliefs and practices, examining their relevance to health and well-being. It covers topics such as Muslim rights, Islamic jurisprudence related to health, and the spiritual psychology of the soul. The aim is to provide participants with a comprehensive understanding that enhances their clinical practice.

Unit 3: Decolonizing the Social Sciences

This critical unit explores the influence of Western psychology and its cultural implications while advocating for a decolonized approach to the field. Participants are encouraged to reassess Western frameworks and incorporate Islamic perspectives that effectively blend faith with contemporary psychological concepts.

Unit 4: Modern Islamic Psychology

This unit examines contemporary trends in IP, emphasizing the relationship between modern psychology and Islamic principles. It addresses ethical considerations, deontology in Islamic psychotherapy, and research methods specific to the field, equipping students to tackle psychological challenges with a spiritually informed perspective.

Unit 5: Psychopathology

In-depth exploration of psychiatric disorders and their treatment through the lens of IP is covered in this unit. Topics include post-traumatic stress disorder, the psychopathology of possessions, and the

Islamic approach to common mental disorders.

Unit 6: Clinical Approaches

This unit focuses on therapeutic interventions, including clinical approaches such as NAFSI therapy (*Niyya and Acceptance for the Empowerment of the Fiṭra through Active Islamic Spirituality*, developed by Ali Habibbi), Islamic Cognitive Behavioral Therapy (CBT), and specific techniques. It also emphasizes research and practical applications in clinical settings.

Unit 7: Nutrition, Health and Addiction

Exploring the connection between diet, mental health, and prophetic medicine, this unit presents an Islamic viewpoint on nutrition and its effects on psychological well-being. Participants will learn about specific dietary practices and their influence on both mental and physical balance. It also focuses on managing addictions from an Islamic perspective, exploring treatment models and spiritual therapeutic interventions to help patients overcome their addictions.

Unit 8: Sexology, Ethics and Intimacy

This unit delves into the challenges of human sexuality in clinical practice through the prism of Islam. It covers marital intimacy, sexual disorders, sexual education, modesty, shame, sexual violence, and the construction of sexual identity from a therapeutic and ethical perspective.

Unit 9: Mental Health, the Unseen and the Occult

This unit explores psychic manifestations related to the unseen, spiritual beliefs and disorders perceived as supernatural. It offers clinical and theological frameworks to distinguish between pathology, religious symbolism, and spiritual reality, while proposing a framework for ethical intervention.

Unit 10: Family and Relationship Dynamics

Addressing modern family and relationship challenges, this module provides strategies for couples and family therapy, conflict management, and understanding domestic violence. It pays particular attention to the needs of gifted children and families with members on the autism spectrum.

Unit 11: Supervision

This module provides students of IP with hands-on experience, allowing them to apply their knowledge under expert supervision while engaging in case study discussions and receiving constructive feedback on their practice. Emphasizing the integration of Islamic principles into therapeutic interventions, the course also nurtures ethical and professional development. A mandatory 100-hour clinical or community internship must be completed in a community setting—such as a mosque, association, school, or Islamic center—enabling students to serve disadvantaged populations, gain professional experience, and collaborate with local religious leaders.

Unit 12: Final Project and Dissertation

Students will undertake a research project or dissertation, gaining new skills in research methodology, data analysis, and academic writing. The course includes opportunities for project presentations, constructive feedback, and preparation for the final defense of the dissertation. Each module is designed to offer a comprehensive and practical understanding of various aspects of IP, enhanced by a spiritual and ethical perspective.

Curriculum Level 2

This program is composed of week-end 9 sessions in addition to a weekly course. It seeks to form qualified practitioners to accompany patients through the NAFSI approach. Each session is designed to combine targeted instruction, cross-readings of disorders, case studies, guided therapeutic practice, and self-reflective work, while honoring the foundations of the Islamic tradition and meeting the contemporary demands of therapeutic practice.

Here are the themes of the sessions: Anxiety & Panic, Anger & Reactivity, Depression & Despair, Self-Image & Shame , Attachment & Dependency, Addiction & Lack of Self Control, Crisis of Faith & Confusion, Trauma & Post-Trauma, Burnout & Inner Emptiness.

It is followed by a Residential Seminar in Marrakech at Maristan Aïcha, 5 days of in-depth learning, integration, and group work.

Strengths

The teaching team consists of 13 international experts from various fields, including psychiatry, psychology, sociology, religious studies, philosophy, Islamology, and dietetics. Level 2 trains students in a unique approach to psychotherapy (NAFSI) under the close supervision of Ali Habibbi.

The program offers flexible learning options, featuring live classes on weekends and access to recorded sessions. This makes it ideal for professionals and students who need to balance personal obligations with their professional development.

This is the only certificate in IP available in French, making it accessible to all French-speaking Muslims who do not speak other languages.

The certificate in IP intended for mental health professionals is taught by the following instructors:

1. Dr. Ali Habibbi, Psychologist
2. Pr. Hussein Rassool, Professor of Psychology
3. Dr. Zoubir Benmebarek, Psychiatrist
4. Dr. Samah Jabr, Psychiatrist
5. Mestari Nassima, Psychologist
6. Wahiba Bahhou, Psychologist
7. Hanane Afellah, Dietician-Nutritionist
8. Dr. Tayeb Chouiref, Islamologist
9. Sofiane Meziani, researcher-PhD student in philosophy
10. Sofiane Driouch, Imam
11. Fatma Mamouni, Psychopathologist
12. Léa Pourcelot, Neuropsychologist
13. Dr. Anaïs Massot, Historian of the Middle East

Selected publications

G. H. Rassool, Psychology Professor

Rassool, G.H., Khan, W.N.A. (2024). Hope in Islāmic psychotherapy, *Journal of Spirituality in Mental Health*, 3, 243-248. https://doi.org/10.1080/19349637.2023.2207751.

Rassool, G.H., Latif, L., Dockrat, S. (2024). *Integrating Spiritual Interventions in Islamic Psychology: A Practical Guide.* Taylor & Francis.

Rassool, G.H. (2023). Critical Reflections on Current Status of Scholarship in Islamic Psychology–Challenges and Solutions, *Australian Journal of Islamic Studies*, 8(3), 37-54.

Rassool, G.H., Kalsoom, N., Latif, S., Mudassar, U. (2023). Development and psychometric evaluation of a scale for measuring the conception of Islamic psychology, *Pakistan Journal of Clinical Psychology*, 22(2), 69-79. Retrieved from https://www.pjcpku.com/index.php/pjcp/article/view/191

Rassool, G.H., Keskin, Z., (2023), Positioning the self (nafs) in Islāmic psycho-spirituality, *Journal of Spirituality in Mental Health*, 1-10. Advance online publication. https://doi.org/10.1080/19349637.2023.2264848

ISLAMIC PSYCHOLOGY CERTIFICATE

Ali Habibbi, Dr in Clinical Psychology and Psychopathology

Habibbi, A. (Upcoming publication). *Developing a Systemic Integrative Curriculum in Islamic Psychology, in Advancing the Clinical Practice of Islamic Psychology Through Education and Research.* Hamad Bin Khalifa University (HBKU), Doha, Qatar.

Habibbi, A. (Accepted). A Qur'an-Centered Therapeutic Approach to Addiction Using the NAFSI Model. *Journal of Muslim Mental Health.*

Habibbi, A. (2025). *La Psychologie Islamique.* Édition Al Bayyinah.

Habibbi, A. (2023). *La gestion des conflits.* Édition Al Bayyinah.

Anais Massot, Dr in History of the Middle East

Massot, A. (To be Published). The tariqa Naqshbandiyya-Khalidiyya in Damascus: Actors of the Socio-political Changes during the Ottoman Tanzimat Reforms. *Journal of the History of Sufism.*

Massot, A. (2016). Ottoman Damascus During the Tanzimat: The New Visibility of Religious Distinctions, in *Modernity, Minority, and the Public Sphere: Jews and Christians in the Middle East,* ed. S.R. Goldstein-Sabbah, H.L. Murre-van den Berg. Leiden : Brill.

Massot, A. (2012). Modernization, Communal Space and Inter-Confessional Conflicts in Nineteenth- Century Damascus. *Syrian Studies Association Bulletin,* vol. 17, n°2.

Massot, A. (2023). Review of Rana Abu-Mounes, *Muslim-Christian Relations in Damascus amid the 1860 Riot, The Journal of Ecclesiastical History* 74, no. 1: 211–12.

Massot, A. (2023). Review of Ussama Makdisi, *Age of Coexistence: The Ecumenical Frame and the Making of the Modern Arab World, Archives de sciences sociales des religions.*

Massot, A. (2018). Review of Heather Sharkey, *A History of Muslims, Christians and Jews in the Middle East»,* *Syrian Studies Association Bulletin,* vol. 23, Issue 1.

Zoubir Benmebarek, Psychiatrist

Benmebarek, Z., (2022). Mental health law in Algeria: new amendments, old concerns, *BJPsych International,* 19(1), 21–24. https://doi.org/10.1192/bji.2021.14

Benmebarek, Z. (2017). Psychiatric services in Algeria, *BJPsych International,* 14(1), 10-12. https://doi.org/10.1192/s2056474000001598

Tayeb Chouiref, Islamologue

Chouiref, T. (2012). Social justice and education of the soul in Islam: Al-

Ghazālī's approach, *Religions: A Scholarly Journal*, 2, 127-135. https://doi.org/10.5339/rels.2012.justice.19

Challenges

Lack of Official Recognition

IP is not widely acknowledged within mainstream mental health systems. This lack of recognition may pose challenges for the acceptance of certificates by academic and professional institutions.

Cultural and Religious Resistance

Some mental health professionals may be skeptical or hesitant to incorporate a religious perspective into their clinical practice, particularly in regions where secularism is prevalent, such as in some French-speaking countries.

Limited Resources for Supervision

Finding skilled and experienced supervisors in IP can be challenging, especially for participants located in remote areas or regions where this discipline is not well developed.

Lack of Teaching Materials in French

Developing high-quality teaching materials in French may be difficult, as most existing resources on IP are primarily available in Arabic or English.

Balancing Theory and Practice

Achieving an effective balance between theoretical learning and the practical application of the concepts taught can be challenging, particularly in an online format where direct interaction is limited.

Solutions and roadmap

Strengthening Official Recognition (2025-2026)

Objective: Integrate IP into mainstream mental health systems.

Actions:

- Establish partnerships with recognized universities and academic institutions for co-accreditation.
- Organize international symposiums and conferences on IP to raise awareness among mental health professionals.
- Develop academic publications in reputable journals to legitimize the discipline.

Strategies to Overcome Cultural and Religious Resistance (2025-2027)

<u>Objective.</u> Promote the acceptance and integration of IP in secular and diverse environments.

<u>Actions.</u>

- Launch awareness campaigns targeting mental health professionals to highlight the benefits of incorporating religious perspectives into clinical practices
- Develop an inclusive discourse that underscores the commonalities between IP and the humanistic and ethical principles of Western psychology.
- Create specialized program units that address the impact of secularism and religious beliefs on clinical practice, preparing graduates to respond to objections professionally.

Development of Supervision Resources (2025-2028)

<u>Objective.</u> Ensure adequate supervision for students by establishing a network of qualified supervisors.

<u>Actions.</u>

- Identify and train local supervisors in IP through a specialized training program.
- Set up an online supervision system utilizing video conferencing technology to connect students with qualified supervisors, regardless of geographical location.
- Create an international network of supervisors and mentors in collaboration with recognized institutions and experts in the field.

Production and Dissemination of Educational Materials in French (2025-2029)

<u>Objective.</u> Create a library of educational resources in IP that is accessible in French.

<u>Actions:</u>

- Launch a project to translate and adapt key resources in IP, collaborating with specialized translators and experts in the field.
- Encourage the creation of new publications in French, such as manuals, articles, and case studies, by offering grants for research and writing.

- Develop an online platform dedicated to disseminating these resources, providing easy and free access for students and professionals.

Strengthening the Balance Between Theory and Practice (2024-2030)

Objective. Provide students with a comprehensive education that combines both practical and theoretical training.

Actions:

- Integrate practical internships into the certificate program in partnership with clinics and Islamic mental health centers.
- Develop online simulations and practical workshops that allow students to apply theoretical concepts in realistic scenarios.
- Regularly evaluate the program's content and adjust the balance between theory and practice based on student feedback and developments in the field.

Discussion

As we prepare for the launch of the IP Certificate, it is important to recognize the challenges and opportunities that lie ahead. This innovative program, set to launch in 2024-2025, represents a significant step in promoting IP within the French-speaking community. Designed for state-certified psychologists, psychiatrists, and psychotherapists, the program uniquely integrates Islamic principles with modern psychological practice, distinguishing it from other available certifications.

Moving forward, it is crucial to continually develop and adapt the program based on student feedback and advancements in the field. By offering high-quality training, the IP Certificate will not only meet the expectations of mental health professionals but also contribute to the recognition and evolution of IP as a respected discipline in both academic and clinical settings.

Conclusion

The IP Certificate for the 2024-2025 academic year marks a significant advancement in the education and training of mental health professionals by integrating an Islamic perspective into their practice. This unique program, offered in the French-speaking world, aims to address the growing mental health needs of French-speaking Muslims. It provides both theoretical and practical approaches that are deeply rooted in Islamic principles.

However, several challenges have been identified, particularly concerning official recognition, cultural resistance, supervision, and teaching materials. These issues require careful attention and strategic solutions. The proposed roadmap offers a solid framework to overcome these obstacles and ensure the program's sustainability and success. (For reference: https://www.islam-psychologie.com/certificat-psychologie-islamique

ISLAMIC PSYCHOLOGY COUNSELLOR CERTIFICATE

Introduction

IP is gaining considerable interest in the French-speaking Muslim community. However, not everyone exploring this field is a qualified health professional. Some may be therapists, coaches, nurses, or individuals looking to support and help Muslims without committing to the extensive training required to become a psychologist or psychiatrist.

To meet the growing demand for counselling training among non-mental health professionals and to prevent potential issues stemming from misinformation, Ali Habibbi developed a two-year online program in October 2024.

This 24-month program trains certified counselors in IP. It combines clinical psychology, psychopathology, Islamic studies, and mediation techniques, equipping students to offer effective and culturally relevant psychological support for Muslims facing various challenges in their lives.

Nature of Program

To enroll in the program, students must possess a high school diploma, as the program is intended for a wide audience.

Upon completion of the program, students will receive a certificate. Their assessment will occur through various methods, including class discussions, essays, presentations, group projects, exams, and online quizzes. Additionally, students are required to participate in supervision sessions and write and defend a dissertation or a scientific article that is at least 15 pages long. Each assignment will be graded.

Admission requirements

The classes are conducted online on weekends, offering a blend of live sessions and pre-recorded content for greater flexibility for working individuals. Participants will receive over 200 hours of lessons from various instructors and will complete 100 hours of internship. The total cost of the training program is €2900.

This program is developed in partnership with the ISIP and the Al-Balkhi Institute in the USA.

Curriculum

Unit 1: Introduction to Islamic Psychology

This course introduces the fundamental concepts of IP, examining human nature through the lens of Islamic teachings. Students will explore the history and evolution of discipline and understand how it contrasts with Western psychology.

Unit 2: Foundations of Islam

This course explores the fundamental principles of Islam, including its religious beliefs, practices, and ethical values. Students examine how these elements affect mental and spiritual well-being, particularly focusing on the relationship between spirituality and mental health.

Unit 3: Introduction to General Psychology

This course introduces the principles of modern psychology, focusing on human development theories, personality theories, and fundamental concepts of psychopathology. Students will develop a general understanding of key psychological approaches and theories, as well as a clear distinction between Islamic and Western perspectives.

Unit 4: Biological Basis of Psychology

This course explores the neurobiological basis of human behavior, including brain structures and functions, and the impact of biological factors on behavior and mental health. Students will learn how genetics, hormones, and neurotransmitters influence psychological processes.

Unit 5: Nutrition and Health

This module explores the connection between diet, mental health, and prophetic medicine, providing an Islamic perspective on nutrition and its influence on psychological well-being. Participants will learn about specific diets and how they affect mental and physical balance.

Unit 6: Psychopathology

This course covers common mental disorders, including their symptoms, diagnoses, and assessments. Students examine various treatment approaches, incorporating an Islamic perspective on mental health and healing.

Unit 7: Child and Adolescent Psychology

This course explores the psychological development of children and teenagers, emphasizing key stages of cognitive, emotional, and social growth. Students learn to recognize the specific challenges faced during these developmental ages.

Unit 8: Family Dynamics and Systemic Therapy

This course explores theories of family dynamics and family therapy techniques. Students delve into practical case studies to understand how external interventions can help resolve conflicts and strengthen family relationships.

Unit 9: Islamic Counseling

Students study counseling theories and techniques with a focus on their application within an Islamic context. The course emphasizes strategies for providing effective support while honoring Islamic beliefs and values.

Unit 10: Addiction

Students explore various forms of addiction, including both behavioral and substance-related addictions. The course emphasizes the risk and protective factors linked to addictions, as well as prevention and treatment strategies based on Islamic principles and concepts derived from revealed sources.

Unit 11: Supervision

This unit offers practical experience for students of IP, enabling them to apply their knowledge under the guidance of experts. Students engage in case study discussions and receive constructive feedback on their practice. The focus is on integrating Islamic principles into interventions while fostering ethical and professional behavior.

Unit 12: Final Project and Dissertation

Students will undertake a research project or dissertation that will help them develop their skills in research methodology, data analysis, and academic writing. The course includes project presentations, constructive feedback, and preparation for the final defense.

Each module is designed to offer a thorough and practical understanding of various aspects of IP, enhanced by a spiritual and ethical perspective.

Strengths

Accessibility for Non-Mental Health Professionals

This program addresses a significant gap by providing specialized training for individuals interested in IP, without requiring prior mental health education. This accessibility opens the door to a diverse range of counselors who can better serve the needs of French-speaking Muslims.

Holistic and Integrated Approach

The program combines elements of clinical psychology, psychopathology, Islamic sciences, and mediation techniques, offering comprehensive training that addresses mental, emotional, spiritual, and physical well-being.

Flexible Learning Options

Offered in a 24-month online format, this program allows students to take courses on weekends, making it ideal for those with work or other commitments. The combination of live weekend classes and pre-recorded content provides excellent flexibility.

Islamic Perspective on Key Topics

Each unit integrates an Islamic perspective on subjects such as nutrition, psychopathology, and family dynamics. This unique approach equips students with specific skills that cater to the cultural and religious needs of Muslim communities.

Instruction by International Experts

By collaborating with recognized institutions such as ISIP and the Al-Balkhi Institute, along with participation from an international team of educators, the program ensures high-quality training rooted in the latest research and best practices in IP.

Practical Training and Supervision

The program includes supervised practical sessions, allowing students to apply their knowledge in real-world settings. This hands-on experience is crucial for developing applicable and ethical skills for their professional careers.

Focus on Family Dynamics and Systemic Therapy

The unit dedicated to family dynamics and systemic therapy is especially relevant as it addresses the specific needs of Muslim families. It provides strategies to strengthen relationships and resolve conflicts within the framework of Islamic values.

Attention to Addiction

The inclusion of addiction training from an Islamic perspective is a significant advantage for counselors, enabling them to address addiction issues in a culturally and religiously sensitive manner.

Islamic Counseling Unit

This unit emphasizes techniques and strategies aimed at providing support that respects clients' beliefs and values, thereby enhancing the effectiveness of counseling within Muslim communities.

Instructors

Dr. Ali Habibbi, Psychologist

Pr. Ghulam Hussein Rassool, Psychology Professor

Dr. Zoubir Benmebarek, Psychiatrist

Mestari Nassima, Psychologist

Wahiba Bahhou, Psychologist

Kerkri Hafsa, Psychologist

Hanane Afellah, Dietician-Nutritionist

Sofiane Driouch, Imam

Linda Bendjafer, Psychologist

Léa Pourcelot, Neuropsychologist

Dr Anaïs Massot, Historian of the Middle East

Key publications

Benmebarek, Z. (2022). Mental Health Law in Algeria: New Amendments, Old Concerns. *BJPsych International*, 19(1), 21–24. https://doi.org/10.1192/bji.2021.14

Benmebarek, Z. (2017). Psychiatric Services in Algeria. *BJPsych International*, 14(1), 10–12. https://doi.org/10.1192/s2056474000001598

Habibbi, A. (in prep). Developing a Systemic Integrative Curriculum in Islamic Psychology, in Advancing the Clinical Practice of Islamic Psychology Through Education and Research. Hamad Bin Khalifa University (HBKU), Doha, Qatar.

Habibbi, A. (in press). A Qur'an-Centered Therapeutic Approach to Addiction Using the NAFSI Model. *Journal of Muslim Mental Health.*

Habibbi, A. (2025). La Psychologie Islamique. Édition Al Bayyinah.

Habibbi, A. (2023). La gestion des conflits. Édition Al Bayyinah.

Rassool, G.H., Khan, W.N.A. (2024). Hope in Islamic Psychotherapy.

Journal of Spirituality in Mental Health, 3, 243–248. https://doi.org/10.1080/19349637.2023.2207751

Rassool, G.H., Latif, L., Dockrat, S. (2024). Integrating Spiritual Interventions in Islamic Psychology: A Practical Guide. Taylor & Francis.

Rassool, G.H. (2023). Critical Reflections on the Current Status of Scholarship in Islamic Psychology: Challenges and Solutions. *Australian Journal of Islamic Studies*, 8(3), 37–54.

Rassool, G.H., Kalsoom, N., Latif, S., Mudassar, U. (2023). Development and Psychometric Evaluation of a Scale for Measuring the Concept of Islamic Psychology. *Pakistan Journal of Clinical Psychology*, 22(2), 69–79. Retrieved from https://www.pjcpku.com/index.php/pjcp/article/view/191

Rassool, G.H., Keskin, Z. (2023). Positioning the Self (Nafs) in Islamic Psycho-Spirituality. *Journal of Spirituality in Mental Health*, 1–10. Advance online publication. https://doi.org/10.1080/19349637.2023.2264848

Challenges

Professional Differentiation and Recognition

Counselors trained in IP who lack a background in mental health may face challenges in gaining recognition from health institutions and potential employers. Clearly defining their roles, capabilities, and limitations in comparison to qualified psychologists or psychotherapists can be difficult.

Ethical Supervision and Responsibility

Students without prior training in mental health may struggle to manage complex situations or recognize their limitations. It is crucial to establish clear guidelines to prevent inappropriate interventions and avoid situations that could be harmful to clients.

Access to Professional Opportunities

Graduates of this program may encounter difficulties in securing professional opportunities or gaining acceptance within conventional mental health frameworks. The recognition of their certification outside the religious context may also pose significant challenges.

Cultural Resistance and Skepticism

Counselors trained in IP might experience resistance from Muslim communities and skepticism from mental health professionals regarding the effectiveness and legitimacy of non-professionals practicing this discipline.

Developing and Maintaining Educational Quality

ISLAMIC PSYCHOLOGY CERTIFICATE

As the program is designed for a diverse audience with varying levels of prior knowledge, it can be challenging to maintain high educational standards tailored to each student's needs. Ensuring that all participants acquire adequate practical and theoretical skills is essential.

Solutions

Professional Differentiation and Recognition (2025-2026)

Objective. Establish clear recognition of the role of counselors in IP.

Actions :

- Collaborate with mental health organizations to define and establish clear professional boundaries for trained counselors.
- Develop additional certifications in collaboration with universities or recognized organizations to enhance the credibility of the certificate.
- Create a support and resource network for graduates to facilitate their integration into mental health organizations.

Ethical Supervision and Responsibility (2025-2027)

Objective. Ensure that counselors practice ethically and responsibly.

Actions.

- Introduce specific training modules focused on professional ethics and the limitations of practice for counselors.
- Establish a mandatory supervision system where counselors in training receive guidance from experienced professionals.
- Create a specific code of ethics for IP counselors, outlining clear guidelines for situations that require referral to qualified mental health professionals.

Career Development (2025-2028)

Objective. Increase career opportunities for graduates.

Actions:

- Create partnerships with community centers, Muslim associations, and NGOs to integrate counselors into community support programs.
- Develop an online platform dedicated to placing graduates in suitable roles, facilitating networking and connections with

potential employers.

- Organize networking events and conferences to enable graduates to connect with mental health professionals and recruiters.

Cultural Resistance and Skepticism (2025-2030)

Objective. Reduce resistance and skepticism toward IP among non-health professionals.

Actions:

- Launch awareness campaigns to inform Muslim communities and mental health professionals about the value and effectiveness of IP.
- Publish case studies and research demonstrating the effectiveness of IP counseling conducted by program graduates.
- Build alliances with religious leaders and influencers to legitimize and promote the role of IP counselors within communities.

Development and Maintenance of Educational Quality (2025-2029)

Objective. Ensure a high level of quality in teaching.

Actions.

- Establish a teaching assessment committee to regularly adapt and update the program based on student needs and developments in the field.
- Introduce continuous assessments and gather student feedback to refine educational content and teaching methods.
- Develop interactive teaching tools and online resources to enhance learning, including practical case simulations and online workshops.
- This roadmap will address the identified challenges and help consolidate the reputation and effectiveness of the IP Counselor Certificate in the long term.

Discussion

As we prepare to welcome the first class of students for the 2024-2025 academic year, several key elements deserve special attention. The admission rate will be a crucial indicator of interest in this innovative program among non-mental health professionals. To manage potential dropouts, we must proactively identify and address barriers that may prevent some students from completing their training.

The experience and qualifications of the faculty will also be critical to the success of the program. Additionally, examinations will play a vital role in assessing students' progress, ensuring that graduates are well prepared to provide psychological support in line with Islamic values.

The accreditation of the program is a crucial step toward ensuring the official recognition of the certificate, both academically and professionally. This recognition will open doors for future graduates, providing them with career opportunities in a variety of professional settings.

Conclusion

The launch of the IP Counselor Certificate for the years 2024-2025 is an ambitious initiative with significant potential. Its goal is to train non-mental health professionals in the necessary skills to provide counseling to Muslims while respecting their religious and cultural specificities. The preparation process, which includes developing the program, selecting instructors, and establishing rigorous evaluation mechanisms, has been completed to ensure an enriching educational experience that meets high academic standards.

The learning process of this inaugural cohort will be closely monitored, as it will help determine the program's future direction. The success of this first year could not only validate the importance of the certificate but also encourage the expansion of IP within the French-speaking world. Going forward, it will be crucial to continue developing and refining the program based on student feedback and to seek accreditation for broader recognition of its graduates.

This program is set to create new opportunities for non-mental health professionals by equipping them with the tools needed to provide culturally relevant psychological support to the French-speaking Muslim community.

CHAPTER TWELVE

CERTIFICATE IN ISLAMIC COUNSELING

Aligarh College of Education; Aligarh, India
Akbar Husain

Introduction

The demand for mental health services has significantly increased in a large country like India, coinciding with a growing awareness of the benefits of religious and spiritual practices. Islamic beliefs, practices, and values can help individuals address deficiencies, ailments, and dysfunctions, leading to personal growth and improved well-being. It is essential to have faith in one's ability to heal through reading the Qur'an and Hadith, engaging in prayer, and cultivating moral values.

Islamic counseling places a strong emphasis on spiritual elements guided by the Qur'an and Sunnah. From an Islamic perspective, human thoughts and behaviors are the result of interactions between the soul (al-nafs), the heart (al-qalb), the spirit (al-ruh), and the intellect (al-aql). Our fitrah influences these components and contributes to our personality.

During a Board of Studies meeting on October 21, 2023, the Department of Islamic Studies at Aligarh Muslim University (AMU) in Aligarh, India, announced the introduction of two new undergraduate courses: Islamic Counseling and IP. These courses will be available starting in the 2024-2025 academic session.

Rationale and impetus

There is an urgent need for counselors trained in Islamic principles in various settings, which motivates the creation of this course. IP utilizes a conceptual and methodological framework to explore, describe, and explain psychological phenomena, drawing directly from Quranic principles. The reasons for introducing this course are diverse and multifaceted.

Firstly, it highlights the importance of a certificate program in today's context. Secondly, it offers an integrative and practical model for the field of IP, applicable in both research and training. Thirdly, it discusses how psychologists, counselors, social workers, and scholars of Islamic Studies who specialize in IP can assist individuals in coping with physical and psychological illnesses. Lastly, it acknowledges that the field of Islamic Counseling is transforming into a professional domain.

The aim of this program is to redefine the foundational concepts of IP and establish their relevance in contemporary psychology. To achieve this, we will systematically explore two interconnected questions: What is IP, and why is it necessary? Current research in this field often emphasizes its theoretical, conceptual, and practical aspects. Additionally, understanding the Quran is frequently used to test predictions and hypotheses derived from its teachings. In IP, psychological assessments of religious beliefs, attitudes, and personality traits are considered the gold standard.

A key assumption is that religious and spiritual phenomena can be effectively studied using correlational methods. Another assumption is that Islamic therapeutic or counseling interventions can significantly alleviate people's suffering. These assumptions can lay the groundwork for developing theories or models in IP that explore how individuals and communities think, believe, and act.

The primary aim of Islamic psychological research is to better understand people's behavior, emotions, and experiences, both on an individual level and within groups. As a result, many Muslim psychologists concentrate their studies on aspects such as personal faith, religious attitudes, and levels of religiosity, while often adhering to established models of personality and self. Islamic practices—such as prayer, fasting, and meditation—are conducted individually and collectively, and there are

CERTIFICATE IN ISLAMIC COUNSELING

compelling practical and scientific reasons for their significance in promoting physical, mental, and spiritual well-being.

The Certificate Course in Islamic Counseling aims to develop this field as a conceptual and methodological approach to advancing psychological science.

Names of the key people who established the program

Professor Akbar Husain was primarily responsible for establishing the program at AMU and other organizations in India by organizing the orientation program and delivering several lectures.

1. Islamic Psychology & Counselling. A.M.U., Aligarh. July 16-19, 2018.
2. 12 lectures in one week at Orientation Program on Counselling Interventions (Islamic counseling) organized by the Malappuram Centre and Department of Psychology, Aligarh Muslim University. February 4-7, 2019.
3. Lectures on Islamic Counseling in the International Course on Islamic Psychology: From Knowledge and Research to Practices. Faculty of Psychology and Social Cultural Sciences, Universitas Islam Indonesia, December 16, 2019.
4. Orientation Program on Islamic Counseling and Psychotherapy Organized by Institute of Objective Studies, Aligarh Chapter, September 16-22, 2020.
5. Islamic Counseling for the Prevention and Management of Coronavirus Discussion Pandemic. The 2nd International Intensive Course on Islamic Psychology. Department of Psychology, Islamic University of Indonesia, November 14, 2020.
6. The Institute of Objective Studies, Aligarh Chapter, organized a lecture of Prof. Akbar Husain, Department of Psychology, Aligarh Muslim University, Aligarh on February 21, 2022, which was presided by Professor Azizuddin Khan, IIT Bombay. Prof. Husain spoke on "Islamic Practices and Psychotherapy in Clinical Setting,"
7. Islamic Counselling Intervention. SIO Headquarters, Delhi, May 28, 2022.
8. Islamic Practices in Clinical Setting. The 7th IAMP conference continuing the legacy of Prof. Malik Badri: The founding father of modern Islamic Psychology (5-8 February 2022)
9. Islamic Practices and Psychotherapy in Clinical Setting. Institute of

Objective Studies Aligarh Chapter, February 21, 2022.

10. Islamic Counselling. Shobai Islami Maashra, Markaz Jamat Islami Hind, New Delhi. February 19, 2022.
11. Islamic Counselling. Al-Barkaat Institute of Islamic Research and Training, Aligarh. June 3, 2024.
12. Islamic Counselling Interventions. Al-Barkaat Institute of Islamic Research and Training, Aligarh. June 8, 2024.

How does your program define IP?

Our program defines IP as the scientific study of human thoughts, feelings, behaviors, and experiences through an Islamic lens. There is often a distinction between the methods typically used by psychologists to achieve a holistic understanding of human behavior and those employed by Islamic-based psychologists. By utilizing Islamic approaches, individuals can experience changes in their cognitive, emotional, and behavioral aspects.

Vision, Mission, and Objectives

The program aims to introduce both theoretical and practical knowledge of IP, enhancing awareness and the effectiveness of Islamic practices. It also seeks to shift from mere education to professional practice.

It is also envisioned that Islamic counseling programs will benefit both students and parents. In the job market, diploma courses can provide valuable insights into both short- and long-term professional opportunities. These courses can enhance job training prospects as well.

Islamic practices and counselling can significantly support young adults by promoting their well-being and helping them develop a sense of purpose in their lives. This sense of purpose can be further strengthened through participation in religious activities that involve selfless service to others.

Objectives

1. Provide essential knowledge of Islamic Counseling as a profession.
2. Offer practical insights necessary for understanding client behaviors.
3. Develop professional skills in students from Psychology, Education, Social Work, and Islamic Studies through targeted training.

To meet the goals of the diploma course, it is crucial to train competent students who can work in diverse settings. Both government and nongovernment organizations should acknowledge the importance of Islamic Counseling in tackling mental health challenges.

The program objectives are derived from the writings of Maulana Ashraf Ali Thanvi as outlined by Haque (2024):

1. Develop an understanding of the dynamics between the heart, soul, and intellect. It is essential to balance these three fundamental elements for the purification of the heart.
2. Cultivate self-will and effort to achieve good moral character, as personal qualities are key to improving one's circumstances. Thanvi emphasized that it is not just religious rituals that create change; rather, it is enhanced knowledge, thoughts, and actions that truly make a difference for individuals.
3. It is important to understand both the overt and subtle divine laws (Sharia), as gaining only overt knowledge is insufficient for meaningful change. Only by exploring the deeper meanings can one attain higher realities and improve one's psychological state.
4. Focus on changing both thoughts and actions. Thanvi stressed that finding peace should not be the primary goal, as it is not entirely within one's control. However, by changing one's mindset and engaging in righteous actions in accordance with the traditions of the Prophet (SAW), peace will naturally follow.
5. Maintain regular contact with the counselor until your issues are resolved.

Duration of the Course

Academic Year (eight months)

Intake. 20 students (This course will be run when a minimum of ten students will take admission).

Minimum Qualifications. A master's degree in Psychology, Social work, Islamic Studies, Education, or M.Ed. with at least 55 % marks from the recognized University or College.

Admission Procedure

Admission will be through a written test consisting of the following:

1. General Mental Ability (reading comprehension, verbal and numerical reasoning as measured by standardized psychometric tests), academic performance test scores, self-report inventories, interviews. Psychometric tests include the WAIS, and Raven's

Matrices. Academic performance is measured by GPA and standardized test scores. Self-report is assessed through measures of cognitive and emotional self-regulation.

2. Awareness and interest in the area of Counselling

    70 + 30

    Total = 100

An admission test will be conducted if we receive application more than the number of seats (20), otherwise candidates will be selected on the basis of merit, i.e. marks obtained in M.A / MSc. Examinations.

Admission Fee

As per University/College Rules.

Organization of the Course: Four Months Teaching

Table 12

Organization of the courses

Sr. No.	Papers	Exam Marks	Sessional Marks	Total Marks
1.	Introduction to Counselling	75	25	100
2.	Islamic Counselling	75	25	100
3.	Islamic Practices	75	25	100
	Total			**300**

Practical: 2 Months (At least four Psychological Tests based on the Quranic concepts)

Exam Marks	Sessional Marks	Total Marks
75	25	100

12 Case studies and Presentations (Students, Addicts, Family, etc.): 100

Internal Assessment: 50

External Assessment: 50

CERTIFICATE IN ISLAMIC COUNSELING

Total = 100

Grand Total = 500

Internship. Satisfactory completion of 2 months of internship under a 'Senior qualified Clinical Psychologist / Counselor. During the period of internship, the students are required to do the case work / counseling of at least ten cases. Trainees will be attached to educational institutions, rehabilitation centers and hospitals.

Medium of Instruction. English

Attendance. 75% attendance is mandatory (10% exemption on grounds of illness subject to production of a medical certificate)

Qualifying Marks. Minimum 50 % marks on each paper and 50% in practical and Case Work

Declaration of Results and Award of Division

a. Candidates who pass individually on each paper securing the prescribed minimum marks in theory and practical's separately and also at the University/Council Examination and internals separately will be declared to have passed the examination and completed the course satisfactorily.

b. Those who secure 75 % and above on an average will be declared as passed in 1st Class with distinction.

c. Those who secure an aggregate of 60% and above but less than 75% on the aggregate (based on both internal and external) will be declared to have passed the examination in the First division.

d. Candidates who have passed in all the papers both theory and practical and also secured an average of 50% and above, but less than 60% (based on both internal and external) will be declared to have passed the examination in Second division.

e. The procedure for requirement and completion of the course in case of those who are unable to take the exam. or fail will be governed by the prescribed University rules.

Faculty Credentials. Ph.D. in Counseling/Ph.D. in Clinical Psychology, Ph.D. in Social Work

Thorough understanding of the Quran and Sunnah

Strengths

- Main program strengths and what makes it unique
- To develop professional competency in the area of Islamic Counseling

Challenges

- Placement of Trainees
- Getting accreditation from the professional body
- Job in the government sector

Solutions

- Specific to the challenges mentioned above
- At this stage it is difficult to provide road map for the next ten years.

Note: The above-mentioned points cannot be discussed before starting the program.

Conclusion

Islamic counselling operates within a framework that is deeply rooted in Islamic beliefs and practices. It incorporates techniques and approaches derived from the Quran, Sunnah, and Hadith while adhering to Islamic ethics. Professionally, Islamic counseling aligns with the core tenets of Islam, focusing on helping clients make positive changes in their lives.

The nature and scope of Islam as a religious worldview, along with the debates surrounding Islamic counseling, often advocate for a departure from Western counseling theories. Instead, the emphasis is placed on applying Islamic principles to counseling practices, which promotes the integration of spiritual aspects. This approach encourages Muslim counselors to develop psycho-spiritual methodologies based on Islamic teachings that facilitate positive transformation in their clients.

By exploring Qur'anic verses, the Sirah of the Prophet, his traditions, and the biographies of his companions, counselors can derive valuable insights for implementing effective counseling processes. These sources provide a foundational reference for developing a professional approach to Islamic counseling.

The proposed certificate course aims to integrate innovative theoretical and methodological psychological approaches, enhancing the understanding of individual and societal phenomena. This, in turn, will contribute to the development of healthier and more sustainable societies in the future.

CHAPTER THIRTEEN

AN ISLAMIC APPROACH TO ISLAMIC PSYCHOLOGY AND PSYCHOLOGICAL THERAPIES

Ihsaan Therapeutic Services; Bradford, UK
Rasjid Skinner

Introduction

The Part 1 course was first taught in 2001 and has been running 1 to 3 times a year since then. It was designed in response to requests by Muslim therapists (e.g., Clinical Psychologists, Dynamic Psychotherapists, and Counselors) who were experiencing a dissonance between their sense of fitra and what they had been taught from mainstream 'Western' Psychology.

An additional Part 2 course was introduced in 2017, but its syllabus was substantially revised in consultation with the late Professor Malik Badri for subsequent courses. In response to demand from psychological therapists, the focus on the Part 2 course is more practice-focused and deals with a specific area of clinical work.

The understanding of IP is taken from Skinner's 1989 paper (republished 2018), Traditions, Paradigms and Basic Concepts in IP. Key principles and vocabulary are largely derived from Al-Ghazali, particularly as interpreted by Gianotti (Gianotti,) but Kuhn's (Kuhn, 2015) and Enriquez's (Enriquez, 1990) approach to understanding cultural paradigms in psychology are also foundational.

IP is defined as the psychology that rests on Islamic Paradigms and is thus distinguished from 'the filter approach' and the Islamicisation of Psychology (Kaplick & Skinner 2017).

Purpose

The ultimate object of the combined Part 1 and Part 2 courses is to produce a cadre of psychological therapists competent to work from an Islamic framework in both the diagnosis and treatment of psychological disorders, with both Muslims and Non-Muslims.

The Part 1 course is predominantly theoretical and aims to enable students to understand the different paradigms underlying 'Western' and 'Islamic' Psychology, to critique mainstream 'Western' Psychology and Psychiatry with confidence, and to apply an Islamic understanding in the formulation of case material.

The Part 2 course is more clinically focused, involving the application of IP principles in particular areas of clinical practice.

Accreditation

The course is not accredited by a government entity. This is not required in the UK.

Part 1 and Part 2 courses were accredited by the IAIP during Professor Badri's lifetime and are expected to be accredited by the UK Association for Islamic Psychology, which is shortly to be incorporated.

Qualified therapists who have completed the Part 1 and Part 2 courses are encouraged to enroll for supervision work as recommended supervisors, on whose 'ijaza' they can apply to the National Association to be accredited as 'Islamic Psychological Therapists'.

Course Level

Both courses are at the post-graduate level, but Part 1 is open to undergraduates. Entry to Part 2 is generally restricted to those with 'mainstream' qualifications in therapies or undertaking such training.

Course Content

Part 1.

- The cultural niche of 'Western' Psychology
- Western' and 'Islamic' paradigms
- Islamic Models of the Self
- Key Islamic psychological concepts
- Psycho-spiritual dynamics
- Particular Islamic diagnostic principles
- The useful and the toxic in 'Western' and the other traditions of psychology
- Specific Islamic therapeutic interventions (e.g., the use of the Names, diet, the Sunnah sports)
- Fiqh issues
- Dealing with the occult

Part 2. The humor and traditional Islamic medicine (Tibb): including diet and some herbal medicines.

IP applied in specific clinical areas, e.g., treating psychoses, mass trauma, complex traumatic reactions, family and couple therapy, pornography and other addictions, different categories of OCD, dream analysis, and Islamically nuanced psychodynamic therapy and CBT

Recommended Literature

Badri, M. (2016). *Dilemma of Muslim psychologists.*
Dajani, S. (2023). *Sufis and Sharī'a: The Forgotten School of Mercy.* EUP.
Gianotti, T. J. (2001). *Al-Ghazālī's Unspeakable Doctrine of the Soul: Unveiling the Esoteric Psychology and Eschatology of the Iḥyā'.* BRILL.
Kaplick, P. M., & Skinner, R. (2017). The evolving Islam and Psychology movement. *European Psychologist, 22*(3), 198–204. https://doi.org/10.1027/1016-9040/a000297
Skinner, R. (2018). *What is Islamic Psychology? An Introduction.* Ihsaan Website (Ihsaan.org.uk).

Class Projects

There are no examinations, essays, or assignments, but an emphasis on formulating case studies in small groups.

Comparison with Other Courses

The Part 1 course has been run in Turkey (Zaim University) and Pakistan (IIU, Islamabad) with contributions from Malik Badri and Abdullah Rothman.

The course has some content in common with the courses devised by Hooman Keshavi and the Al Kalil Centers.

Duration. Both Part 1 and Part 2 are 5-day residential courses. The number of students for each course is capped (in the UK) at 24, with an optimum of 18. Courses are face-to-face, not online.

Enrollment Trends. Courses are generally oversubscribed from their inception. About 20% of students came from outside the UK.

Course Fees. Course fees are around USD 700, excluding the cost of overnight accommodation.

Instructors. Course organizer and principal instructor, Rasjid Skinner, Consultant Clinical Psychologist.

Other regular instructors.

- Hakim Shahid Bukhari - Hakim
- Dr Samir Dajani - Islamic Scholar
- Dr Mahbub Khan - Consultant Clinical Psychologist
- Dr Rabia Malik - Systemic Family Therapist
- Sheikh Shah Nawaz - Islamic Scholar and Psychodynamic psychotherapist
- Dr Rufus May - Consultant Clinical Psychologist
- Sheikh Sayeed Nasser - Islamic Scholar and Integrative Psychotherapist
- Dr Abdul Wali Wardak – Consultant Clinical Psychologist
- Sheikh Idris Watts – Islamic Scholar and Counsellor

Student Satisfaction

Students have consistently rated the teaching quality and utility of the courses between 'Very Good' and 'Excellent'. The majority rated 'Excellent'.

Concluding Comments

Without the financial resources and university backing to operate training 'from scratch' in Islamic Psychological therapy, we think the training format we operate in the UK, i.e., providing intensive, high-quality, short, and affordable courses to psychological therapists with 'mainstream' qualifications, is probably the best way of meeting the demand for IP-based psychological therapy.

We are, however, considering changing the format of the Part 2 course- from 5 residential days to a series of 1 day and weekend events on specific clinical topics. This would allow more time for practical training and allow students to select topics most relevant to their area of clinical practice. However, this format would be less attractive to foreign students and more expensive to organize - and student feedback suggests students enjoy and benefit from the discussions that develop in a residential course. The jury is still out.

We are aware that our courses could reach far more people and be much cheaper to deliver if they were 'online,' but we are convinced that quality clinical training can only be delivered 'face to face.'

CHAPTER FOURTEEN

ISLAMIC PSYCHOLOGY AT STANFORD UNIVERSITY

Stanford University Muslim Mental Health and Islamic Psychology Lab

Palo Alto, California, USA

Huda Naeem & Rania Awaad

Introduction

The IP course at Stanford University, referred to as PSYC144 for undergraduate students or PSYC244 for graduate students, is offered annually in the Spring quarter jointly by the Department of Psychiatry under the School of Medicine and by the Center for CSRE (cross-listed as CSRE 144A) under the School of Humanities and Sciences. The course was first offered in 2020 with Dr. Rania Awaad as the instructor, making the Spring 2025 quarter the sixth year it has been taught. The goal of its creation was to rewrite an otherwise Eurocentric narrative around the history of psychology as the Western world currently understands it. As the first IP course offered in any Western psychology program taught annually as part of the mainstream curriculum at a secular university by a core faculty member, this course aimed to bring Muslim voices and perspectives from Islamic heritage into the psychological field. The course highlights the landmark contributions to the fields of psychiatric and mental health care and places a heightened emphasis on the extensive involvement of Islamic civilization in this field of science.

At the time of the course's conceptualization, the Muslim Mental Health and IP Lab, formerly known as the Muslim Mental Health Lab, at Stanford University was rebranded to encompass research in the field of IP. While Muslim Mental Health and IP are overlapping disciplines, each involves distinct specializations in both contemporary research and historical study. With this additional label added to the Lab's focus, Dr. Awaad collaborated with Lab members to bring the framework of this course to the attention of Stanford's administration. The courses' curriculum is a stark difference from the standard psychology courses offered in Western academic settings; the class focuses on addressing psychological principles and psychopathology from the ground up, tying in elements from the Holy Quran and the Sunnah and principles of historical Islamic intellectualism and tradition to teach and facilitate the creation of frameworks of psycho-spiritual healing for Muslim communities.

This course facilitates an in-depth understanding of behavioral science in both the historical and contemporary Muslim world. It begins with an exploration of Islamic epistemology, focusing on key issues such as the relationship between secular and sacred sources of knowledge and the mind-body dilemma as seen from both Islamic and Western psychological perspectives. By examining the foundational distinctions between Islamic and Western psychologies, this course examines holistic models of health and pathology, bringing in principles of transformation that lead to positive character reformation as understood by both frameworks.

A key focus of this course is to compare Islamic and Eurocentric methodologies and examine the ontological structure of the human psyche in both frameworks. Students are expected to gain a deep understanding of psychopathological conceptualizations in Islamic and Western mental health care traditions while investigating the healing systems built within them. It touches on the historical fact that the first psychiatric wards were founded in the Muslim world, consequently rooting a significant portion of the world's first medicalized psychiatric treatments in the historic Muslim world. The course fosters an appreciation of the Islamic intellectual heritage as it relates to contemporary behavioral science, calling for a comparison between the Islamic mental health care tradition and modern standards of care to uncover and create approaches directly curated to heal all aspects of an individual's psychological and spiritual self.

This course addresses the resurgence of IP as a response to the limitations of Eurocentric mental health care models, specifically their misalignment with treating diverse populations. Students analyze and critique dominant mental health discourse, understanding where they hold room for improvement in addressing the needs of Muslim patient populations. The course delves into the importance of culturally tailored treatments for minoritized communities and the need to integrate Islamic concepts, interventions, and perspectives into modern psychological frameworks and psychotherapeutic interventions. Crafted using integral research and knowledge obtained by and advocated for by leading scholars such as Dr. Malik Badri, known as the father of IP (Rothman et al., 2022), Dr. Rasjid Skinner, Dr. Abdallah Rothman, Dr. Hooman Keshavarzi, and Dr. Awaad herself, this course delivers a well-rounded and extensive study into the core concepts of IP.

Nature of Program

The IP course is a four-credit seminar-style course taught every Spring semester and is available to both undergraduate and graduate students. The course is structured to include lectures, group discussions, guest speaker presentations, and student-led presentations, primarily in an in-person format with occasional Zoom sessions. The course is open to all matriculated undergraduate and graduate students at Stanford who wish to enroll. By being offered jointly in the Departments of Psychiatry and Humanities and Sciences at Stanford, this course is open to all undergraduate and graduate students rather than limiting it to specific student populations or programs. Current standard tuition rates apply for both undergraduate and graduate students, and financial aid is applicable based on University policies. Auditing is permitted for matriculated undergraduate and graduate/professional students, postdoctoral scholars, visiting scholars, Stanford faculty, and Stanford staff, with the consent of the instructor, department, and the Office of the University Registrar (Auditing a Stanford Course | Stanford University Bulletin, 2024). All auditors are expected to engage with the materials as fully as any other student attending the course.

To succeed in the course, timely completion of assignments is required, ensuring that work matches the expected comprehension of the material taught in the course. Additionally, meaningful input and participation are expected for both virtual and in-person class sessions. The course is graded on attendance, three quizzes, weekly reading reflections, a midterm paper and presentation, and a final presentation.

During the course, students are expected to complete a selection of required readings, using those readings to participate meaningfully in course assignments and class-wide discussions, as well as writing short reflections on key ideas from each reading to build upon the material learned during classes. Reflections are meant to include connections students make between course materials and other personal or contemporary events, questions they may have, or general thoughts they have about the material. Assigned readings include chapters from the Maristāns and Islāmic Psychology: A Historical Model for Modern Implementation (Routledge, 2024) and the Applying Islamic Principles to Clinical Mental Health Care: Introducing Traditional Islamically Integrated Psychotherapy textbook (Routledge, 2020), also referred to as the "TIIP textbook," journal articles by leading experts in the field, including Dr. Malik Badri. Through the required assignments and readings, students have the opportunity to engage with specific aspects of Islamic traditions in mental health care. Students are assigned a paper and presentation in which they are expected to report their findings on a Maristan or a hospital in the historic Islamic world. Additionally, students are required to interview a community scholar, a Muslim mental health specialist, an advocate, or a community leader to gain an understanding of their work and perspectives on mental health within Muslim communities.

Dr. Rania Awaad, M.D., teaches the course. She is a Clinical Professor and the Director of the Stanford Muslim Mental Health and IP Lab under the Department of Psychiatry and Behavioral Sciences at Stanford University. She also serves as the President of the Muslim mental health community nonprofit, Maristan—a key community partner of the Lab. She is also the Associate Chief of the Division of Public Mental Health and Population Sciences and Co-Chief of the Diversity and Cultural Mental Health Section. Dr. Awaad is a Senior Fellow at the Yaqeen Institute for Islamic Research and the Institute for Social Policy and Understanding (ISPU). She has previously served as the founding Clinical Director of Khalil Center-San Francisco and a Professor of Islamic Law at Zaytuna College. In addition to her medical studies, Dr. Awaad holds degrees in classical Islamic studies and certifications (Ijazat) in the Qur'an, Islamic Law (Shari'a), and other subfields of Islamic Sciences.

In addition to being offered by the Departments of Psychiatry and Humanities and Sciences, the IP course is also listed as a component of the Sohaib and Sara Abbasi Program in Islamic Studies, which is offered by the Global Studies Department at the School of Humanities and Sciences. There is not currently an established Islamic Studies major or minor at Stanford, but approval is pending. Once the formal courses of study are approved, PSYC 144 is set to be an offering in the Abbasi Program's final curriculum and will be cross-listed with their course codes (Islamic Studies, 2025).

Due to the course's focus on the historical and contemporary foundations of IP, it is currently cross-listed by the CSRE Department, also under the School of Humanities and Sciences, as CSRE 144A. Students working towards a major or minor in CSRE can register for this course using the departmental course code, allowing it to be applied as a degree-specific elective or towards a self-designed CSRE subplan (Center for Comparative Studies in Race & Ethnicity, 2023).

Strengths

This course offers a well-rounded and dynamic experience by combining multiple factors that ensure it is uniquely curated. Through expert-led instruction, diverse and knowledgeable perspectives from key guest speakers, and institutional support, this course provides an unparalleled experience in IP within the secular Western world. Students gain a thorough understanding of the course content, with these strengths contributing to the course's credibility, maintaining its academic rigor and relevance to the growing and evolving discipline of IP.

Expert-Led Instruction

The course is taught by Dr. Awaad, an internationally acknowledged leader in Muslim mental health and IP. Through her experience establishing Muslim mental health clinics and creating tailored training programs for clinicians and community leaders, she has been a founding member of the movement towards curated tools for Muslim mental health and spiritual wellness, particularly in areas where Muslims are minoritized and marginalized. Alongside her work in Muslim mental health, she is passionate about uncovering the historical roots of mental health care from the Islamic tradition. In addition to her extensive experience in psychiatric practice, teaching, and Islamic studies, she is an affiliate faculty of IP at the CMC and The Islamic Seminary of America, where she teaches courses that connect principles of IP with contemporary counseling and cultural nuances, contributing to the growth and mentorship of the next generation of IP scholars and practitioners.

Dr. Awaad has been an author of several IP publications, many of which have been products of the Stanford MMH&IP Lab. Some of her most recent IP publications include:

Awaad, R., & Nursoy-Demir, M. (2024). *Maristāns and Islāmic Psychology: A Historical Model for Modern Implementation (1st ed.)*. Routledge. https://doi.org/10.4324/9781003329589

Awaad, R., & Ali, S. (2023). *The original self-help book: Al-Balkhi's 9th-*

century "Sustenance of the body and soul".. *Spirituality in Clinical Practice, 10*(1), 89–98. https://doi.org/10.1037/scp0000310

Awaad, R., Nursoy-Demir, M., Khalil, A., & Helal, H. (2023). Islamic Civilizations and Plagues: The Role of Religion, Faith and Psychology During Pandemics. *Journal of Religion and Health, 62(*2). https://doi.org/10.1007/s10943-023-01765-z

Awaad, R., Conn, Y. S., Kolkailah, N., El-Haddad, H., Ali, S., & Fereydooni, S. (2022). From Alchemy to Psychiatry: A Glimpse into the Ethics and Mental Health Practices of Tenth-Century Muslim Physician Abū Bakr al-Rāzī. *Harvard Review of Psychiatry, 30*(5), 323–326. https://doi.org/10.1097/HRP.0000000000000347

Rothman, A., Ahmed, A., & Awaad, R. (2022). The contributions and impact of Malik Badri: Father of modern Islamic psychology. *American Journal of Islam and Society, 39*(1-2), 190–213. https://doi.org/10.35632/ajis.v39i1-2.3142 .

Keshavarzi H, Khan F, Ali B, Awaad R. (Eds.) *Applying Islamic Principles to Clinical Mental Health Care: Introducing Traditional Islamically Integrated Psychotherapy.* New York, NY, USA: Routledge; 2021. doi:10.4324/9781003043

Awaad R., Mohammad A., Elzamzamy K., Fereydooni S., Gamar M. "Mental Health in the Islamic Golden Era: The Historical Roots of Modern Psychiatry" in Moffic HS, Peteet JR, Hankir AZ, Awaad R. (Eds.) Islamophobia and Psychiatry: Recognition Prevention and Treatment. Cham Switzerland: Springer; 2019. Chapter 1, Pg. 3–19. doi:10.1007/978-3-030-00512-2

Awaad, R., & Ali, S. (2016). A modern conceptualization of phobia in al-Balkhi's 9th-century treatise: Sustenance of the Body and Soul. *Journal of Anxiety Disorders, 37,* 89–93. https://doi.org/10.1016/j.janxdis.2015.11.003

Awaad, R., & Ali, S. (2015). Obsessional Disorders in al-Balkhi's 9th-century treatise: Sustenance of the Body and Soul. *Journal of Affective Disorders, 180,* 185–189. PMID: 25911133

Guest Speakers and Diverse Perspectives

With Stanford University serving as the global academic hub for research on Muslim mental health and IP, the course offers students a unique opportunity to gain hands-on experience by visiting community partner sites and hearing from esteemed guest speakers. The guest speakers are key scholars who have made significant contributions to revitalizing the traditions of IP and its application in the contemporary world. These scholars, practitioners, and academics have penned extensive works that serve as the foundation of modern IP principles, including material featured in the required readings of this course, which reflects the revolutionary nature of this course. Students have the chance to hear from the founders of the contemporary revitalization of IP and connect the learned content from this course to the individuals who were part of its conception.

Dr. Rasjid Skinner, PhD, a Psychologist in the UK and the founder of Shifa Clinic, is a pioneer in the field of IP. Throughout his extensive career, which has spanned over 40 years, Dr. Skinner has made a wide and prolific set of academic and practical contributions to the teaching and practice of IP and Muslim mental health care. In particular, he has contributed extensively to how concepts rooted in Islamic tradition can inform and tailor psychological practice, particularly for Muslim clients (Biographies – Ihsaan Therapeutic Services, Bradford, 2017). Students have the remarkable opportunity to hear from Dr. Skinner, connect their readings of his work to his explanations and insights, and ask questions to receive direct answers from one of the foremost experts in IP.

Dr. Abdallah Rothman, PhD., is the head of IP at CMC and founder of Dar al-Shifaa, a private psychotherapeutic organization focused on Dr. Rothman's approach of healing inspired by Islamic principles of holistic care (About – Dar Al-Shifaa (2025), and the Executive Director of the International Association of IP. He has done integral work on the intersection between mental health practice and Islamic spirituality (Abdallah Rothman | CMC, 2023). Dr. Rothman's invitation to the course as a guest speaker provides students with the opportunity to learn his uniquely integrative approach to IP firsthand, thereby enhancing their understanding of spiritually integrated mental health care tools and practices.

Dr. Hooman Keshavarzi, Psy. D., an Illinois-based licensed clinical psychologist, Founding Director of the Khalil Center, and Program Director of the College of Islamic Studies at Hamad Bin Khalifa University in Qatar, is another prominent figure in the fields of Muslim mental health and IP (Dr. Hooman Keshavarzi, 2025). Dr. Keshavarzi has also contributed to writing required reading material for this course. Namely, he is a primary contributor to the required TIIP textbook, making his guest contribution an opportunity for students to interact with a core founder of the material on which the course is built.

Shaykh Dr. Asim Yusuf, MD., is a specialist in Islamic metaphysics, psychology, and spirituality and one of the most senior English-speaking scholars in the UK. Dr. Yusuf is considered a leading authority in IP, the head of the Nur-al-Habib Foundation —a community organization focused on holistic education and social welfare —and the executive chair of the British Board of Scholars and Imams. He has developed a framework for the systemic integration of classical Islamic approaches with mental health and several Islamically indigenous working models of psychotherapy (About Us, 2015). He is also a primary contributor to the course required TIIP textbook.

Occasionally, the guest speaker sessions are recorded and posted on YouTube. In the past, the general public has had opportunities to attend Zoom sessions of the class featuring guest speakers, as information posted on the Stanford MMH&IP Lab Instagram page has made the class a medium for sharing information beyond the students enrolled in the class, adding to its unique and distinctive modality. Additionally, in recent years, non-student Stanford affiliates, such as interns or fellows, have audited the course, increasing its accessibility and the availability of uniquely offered IP knowledge from the source beyond Stanford students.

Recognition and Institutional Support

Dr. Awaad proposed the formation of this course by demonstrating that it fulfills the general education breadth requirement for undergraduate students at Stanford University, specifically the "Ways of Thinking/Ways of Doing" ("Ways") requirement. Upon inception, the course was approved to be an option for the Ways 'Exploring Difference and Power' (EDP) graduation requirement for Stanford students. This allows any undergraduate student to choose to take the class, regardless of their major, to fulfill this portion of the Ways requirement for graduation, leading to a diverse group of students enrolling in the course.

In addition to the Ways designation, the course has been selected as a Cardinal Course by the Haas Center for Public Service at Stanford University and can contribute four credits to the 12-credit requirement necessary for the Cardinal Service Notation on student transcripts, recognizing significant public service activities throughout their undergraduate careers. Through this designation, the course has also been able to receive funding for each cycle it has been taught, allowing all guest speakers to receive an honorarium for their time.

In the past, the Cardinal funds have also been used for students to work with the Bay Area Muslim Mental Health Community Advisory Board (Awaad, Obaid, et al., 2023; Ali et al., 2023), a community-based participatory approach comprised of Muslims living in the San Francisco Bay Area, California, working to address the mental health needs of local Muslims in the community. Students were able to interview members of the board and identify gaps in the implementation of IP in the community, including program accessibility, community education efforts, and available clinical resources. These funds allowed students to connect to local advocacy work in Muslim mental health and IP implementation, providing insight into areas where growth and support are needed.

Challenges

During the conceptualization and development of the course, the main challenge was obtaining approval to make it a consistently offered course that fulfilled a Ways requirement. This process entailed significant dialogue between Dr. Awaad and the Stanford administration. Ultimately, the course was approved to start in 2020, which, coincidentally, was the first year of the COVID-19 pandemic. The first session of the course was taught online, which set the ground for the modality to be adaptable throughout future semesters and have a mix of in-person and online sessions. Over the years that the course has been taught, Dr. Awaad has not encountered any additional significant challenges.

Solutions

Dr. Awaad hopes this course will continue as a core curriculum offering at Stanford. As she continues to teach the course, Dr. Awaad would like to connect with professors who teach other psychology courses at Stanford University, combining expertise and knowledge from various experiences. Alongside that engagement, she hopes that this course will influence other educators to reexamine their curriculums and adjust their courses to incorporate the material taught in this course.

On a larger scale, she hopes that this course will facilitate a ripple effect, carrying IP across the Western world. She hopes to see the principles of IP through this course and other contemporary IP efforts, challenge Eurocentric academic perspectives and be integrated into practical mental health treatment applications. She sees this course and the Stanford MMH&IP Lab as crucial components in a larger pipeline. The process begins with the Lab, which is a hub and powerhouse for research on Muslim mental health and IP. The pipeline progresses to the IP course and then to Maristan, a community-facing service-providing organization, transitioning from theory and research to academic education and ultimately to the broader community, thereby facilitating the creation of informed communities and well-rounded researchers and clinicians within Muslim communities and beyond. Her ultimate goal in this pipeline is to launch a full Maristan, a complete institution serving as a center of mental and spiritual healing for the diverse and underserved Muslim community, a core contributor to the translation of IP principles into contemporary clinical implementation.

Discussion

Dr. Awaad's course is highly acclaimed at Stanford University and in the broader community of Muslim mental health professionals, both current and budding. Stanford University is accredited by the Western Association of Schools and Colleges, Senior College and University Commission (WSCUC), which means it meets high educational standards and undergoes continuous evaluations to maintain its accreditation. Additionally, the psychiatry department at Stanford University has been a leading department among universities in the United States and is recognized as a powerhouse for innovative and groundbreaking research in the social and behavioral sciences. The high standards and academic excellence that underpin this accreditation, as well as the acclaim of the Stanford Department of Psychiatry, are evident in the instruction of the IP course.

The most recent offering of this course involved interviewing each guest speaker using a set of specific questions related to the history of the IP field, such as the challenges they anticipate as the popularity of the framework increases in the future. Using this information, the Stanford MMH&IP Lab obtained approval from the Stanford Internal Review Board (IRB) to conduct a qualitative analysis for a scholarly paper on the perspectives and conceptualizations of experts in the field of IP. Alongside this opportunity, students have also been able to submit their Maristan midterm papers towards an eventual collation of essays, which will be transformed into a book about Maristāns on the historical global stage, allowing students to be part of this collective book project(s).

Conclusion

Stanford University, recognized as the hub for Muslim mental health and IP research, offers this groundbreaking course to provide students with an immersive learning experience in these fields. Through the unique synthesis of guest lectures, participation in field visits to community partner sites, and contributions to interactive group discussions, students gain firsthand exposure to the growing space of Muslim mental health. This course is designed to cultivate a comprehensive understanding of these topics. As the first annual IP course offered at a secular Western academic institution as part of its mainstream offerings, this course plays a pivotal role in introducing IP principles into institutions and clinics that typically follow Eurocentric frameworks and standards of care. This course showcases the work and voices of key figures in the Muslim mental health and IP disciplines, creating opportunities for student engagement and growth, community participation, and addressing deficiencies in current psychotherapeutic treatment for diverse Muslim communities.

A key feature of this course is its engagement with leading scholars and practitioners in the fields of Muslim mental health and IP. Students can learn from experts who have dedicated their careers to addressing the unique psychological and spiritual needs of Muslim communities. These insights provide a valuable foundation for understanding the historical roots, theoretical bases, and practical applications of IP in clinical and community-based settings.

Beyond academic learning, this course fosters student engagement, community involvement, and professional growth. By facilitating direct involvement with local community organizations and clinical practitioners, students are encouraged to critically assess gaps in existing mental health treatments and propose solutions that integrate faith-based approaches with psychotherapeutic tools. In doing so, the course empowers future mental health professionals, researchers, and advocates to develop culturally responsive interventions that address the diverse needs of Muslim populations within the secular Western stage and beyond.

CHAPTER FIFTEEN

UNIFYING PERSPECTIVES: MERGING CONTEMPORARY AND ISLAMIC PSYCHOLOGY IN UNIVERSITY CURRICULA IN PAKISTAN

Shifa Tameer-e-Millat University, Islamabad, Pakistan

Muhammad Tahir Khalily, Neelam Ehsan, Fatima Khuram, & Tamkeen Saleem

Introduction

In an era characterized by rapid global transformation, societies are experiencing shifts in values, habits, and beliefs that significantly influence human behavior (Abramson & Inglehart, 2009). As psychology aims to understand these behaviors, its theoretical foundations—primarily rooted in Western thought—dominate the discipline (Greenfield, 2013). Emerging in the aftermath of World War I, Western psychology adopted a secular approach, positioning itself as a scientifically rigorous field that distanced itself from cultural and religious frameworks (Steinmetz, 2022). While this orientation has contributed to the development of the field, it has also marginalized non-Western perspectives, including Islamic views on the mind, behavior, and mental health. The legacy of colonialism and the secularization of academic institutions continue to shape education systems globally, particularly in formerly colonized regions such as Pakistan (Khan, 2023). This Western influence has markedly affected the design of psychology curricula, favoring a secular and individualistic interpretation of human behavior over more holistic and culturally embedded understandings. In contrast, the history of Islamic civilization, especially during its Golden Age, offers a narrative where science and religion were harmoniously integrated (Renima et al., 2016).

IP, known as "ilm al-nafs" (the science of the self), dates back to the early Islamic period and presents a rich, scientifically grounded tradition for comprehending the human condition. Figures such as al-Balkhi, who in the 9th century conceptualized mental health conditions akin to OCD, exemplify the depth of early Islamic thought in psychology (Awaad & Ali, 2015).

In recent decades, scholars have actively worked to revive IP, advocating for its incorporation into modern academic frameworks to provide culturally relevant and contextually appropriate psychological care, particularly for Muslim populations (Badri, 1979; Saleem & Khalily, 2021). This chapter investigates the efforts of academics involved in integrating IP with contemporary psychology in Pakistani universities. By exploring the challenges and benefits of merging these two perspectives, it aims to propose strategies for effectively incorporating IP into university curricula.

The Secularization of Psychology and the Islamic Alternative

The historical separation between science and religion in the West, which peaked during the Renaissance, has had a profound impact on various academic disciplines, including psychology (Karlson, 2017). This divide, rooted in the tension between the Church and scientific inquiry, led to the secularization of knowledge and the exclusion of religious perspectives from scientific fields. Psychology emerged as a distinct discipline in the late 19th century, adopting this secular orientation. Influential figures such as Sigmund Freud and Alfred Adler promoted theories that were often critical of religion (De Jesus Cortes, 1999).

In contrast, the Islamic tradition has long embraced a more integrated approach to knowledge. During the Islamic Golden Age (8th-14th centuries), scholars did not view science and religion as conflicting. Islamic civilization fostered advancements in various fields, including medicine, astronomy, mathematics, and psychology, all within the framework of Islamic thought (Saliba, 2006). This holistic approach to knowledge facilitated the development of a rich body of psychological theory and practice that was deeply informed by the Islamic worldview.

The divergence between Western and Islamic perspectives on psychology became more pronounced during the colonial era when Western education systems were imposed on many Muslim-majority societies. This imposition disrupted the indigenous knowledge systems of these regions, including IP, leading to the widespread adoption of Western psychological theories and practices. Consequently, many contemporary psychology programs in Muslim-majority countries, such as Pakistan, continue to prioritize Western approaches over their own rich intellectual traditions (Khan, 2023).

The Emergence of Islamic Psychology

In the modern era, one of the most prominent advocates for integrating Islamic principles into psychology is Professor Malik Badri, often referred to as the father of modern IP. Trained in the West, Badri recognized the limitations of applying Western psychological models to Muslim patients without taking their cultural and religious contexts into account (Badri, 1979). His groundbreaking work, "The Dilemma of Muslim Psychologists," critiques the uncritical adoption of Western psychology by Muslim practitioners and calls for the development of a distinctly Islamic approach to understanding mental health and behavior.

Badri's work laid the foundation for the contemporary movement of IP, which has gained momentum in recent decades. Initially focused on cultural sensitivity and the adaptation of Western psychological models for Muslim populations, this movement has evolved into a broader effort to establish IP as a legitimate scientific discipline in its own right. Today, IP aims to align psychological principles with Islamic teachings, offering a more holistic approach to mental health that incorporates spiritual concepts such as Tazkia Nafs.

Approaches to Integrating Islamic and Contemporary Psychology

There are two primary approaches to integrating IP with contemporary psychology. The first approach advocates for a complete separation between the two disciplines, arguing that IP, with its unique ontological and epistemological foundations, should be regarded as a separate field of study. Proponents of this view suggest that IP should be housed within departments of Islamic Studies, while contemporary psychology remains within the broader discipline of psychology (Rothman et al., 2022).

The second approach, which this chapter supports, calls for the integration of Islamic principles into the broader framework of contemporary psychology. This model advocates for preserving those aspects of modern psychology that align with Islamic teachings while decontextualizing or modifying elements that diverge from the Islamic worldview. In this approach, psychology departments would adopt an IP framework, providing students with a more comprehensive understanding of human behavior that encompasses both scientific rigor and spiritual insight (Khalily, 2024).

To explore the integration of IP into contemporary psychology curricula, a study was conducted at the Department of Clinical Psychology at Shifa Tameer Millat University in Islamabad. This study employed a qualitative exploratory approach, conducting semi-structured, in-depth interviews with 15 faculty members from the Departments of Psychology at the International Islamic University and Shifa Tameer-e-Millat University in Islamabad, Pakistan. Participants were selected through purposive sampling based on their expertise in both Islamic and contemporary psychology.

The interviews aimed to capture participants' perspectives on the integration of IP into university curricula. Questions were developed based on a thorough literature review and pilot interviews, focusing on key themes such as the relationship between Islamic and contemporary psychology, pathways to integration, and the challenges and facilitators of such integration. The responses were analyzed using thematic analysis via NVIVO-12 Plus software, identifying six principal themes: (1) definitions of IP, (2) recognition of contemporary psychology, (3) the relationship between the two fields, (4) pathways to integration, (5) barriers and facilitators, and (6) recommendations for future integration.

The thematic analysis revealed several important insights into the integration of IP with contemporary psychology. Participants emphasized the need for a more inclusive curriculum that reflects the diversity of human experiences, particularly in Muslim-majority societies. They also highlighted the potential benefits of integrating IP into university programs, including fostering cultural sensitivity, promoting ethical responsibility, and nurturing well-rounded psychologists.

Key barriers to integration included resistance from faculty trained in Western psychological models, a lack of resources and expertise in IP among faculty, and challenges in developing interdisciplinary collaborations. However, participants also identified several facilitators of integration, such as increasing awareness of the importance of cultural and religious perspectives in psychology, promoting faculty development in IP, and supporting research initiatives in this field.

To establish IP on a robust foundation, it is recommended that an academic curriculum of IP be introduced at the graduate and postgraduate levels within mainstream psychology courses and degree programs.

Framework for Curriculum Development in Pakistani Institutions

Over the past decade, there has been significant research exploring the validity of faith-based counseling and psychotherapy, along with innovations within this field. This has led to a growing recognition of IP as a comprehensive approach to understanding human behavior, aiming to bridge the gap between IP and contemporary psychology. Many academic institutions in Muslim countries have initiated a paradigm shift by incorporating IP perspectives into their curricula.

Pakistan is not an exception to this trend. The historical development of IP in Pakistan has transformed over time, initially referred to as "Muslim Psychology" and evolving into a distinct field known as "Islamic Psychology." This emerging discipline has long been integrated into various educational institutions, albeit under different names, all rooted in Islamic teachings. These institutions have offered relevant courses, organized conferences, developed psychological tests, and published empirical research, all contributing to curriculum development in IP (Saleem & Khalily, 2021).

Several universities in Pakistan have specifically included state-of-the-art IP curricula in their undergraduate programs. However, this initiative is still in its foundational stages, primarily because many Muslim psychologists have not been trained in IP and are uncertain about their beliefs and practices (Skinner, 2019). The dissonance experienced by these psychologists is often attributed to the belief that psychology is a purely logical discipline and should not be connected with faith through the heart (Qalb). Despite this secular perspective held by many Muslim psychologists, there has been a notable interest in academia and research among scholars and educational leaders to study IP in terms of theory, research, and practice. Many academic institutions in Pakistan have actively worked to counter stereotypes attached to IP. Proponents argue that incorporating the concepts of the soul (Ruh) linked to the heart (Qalb) and spirituality (Tazkia) into the understanding of self (Nafs) has produced a more meaningful model, which is an emerging necessity in this field of knowledge.

However, this does not mean that IP will be exclusively taught in degree programs. In fact, Western approaches to psychology still dominate the course curricula across psychology degree programs in Pakistan, a reality that many recruiting agencies accept. The IP course is designed to be systematically introduced as a complementary course alongside the foundational models of contemporary psychology, which include theories and perspectives from secular approaches, supplemented by other disciplines and evidence-based clinical practice drawn from global Western psychology curricula.

Current Trends of Islamic Psychology in Curriculum Development and Practice

Recognizing the urgent need for an integrated conceptual framework, several Pakistani universities have initiated the process of holistic curriculum development. This aims to decolonize psychological knowledge in both undergraduate and postgraduate curricula, providing students with a comprehensive understanding of the subject matter. To achieve this, the preparation and development of IP courses for various levels undergo a thorough review process. This process assesses the needs of the relevant field and develops course content that fulfills the intended objectives. Consequently, most course curricula are based on a systematic integration of fundamental Islamic knowledge and psychological science.

In this context, Rasool's (2009) principles for designing and developing courses—specifically, setting clear aims and objectives while aligning them with desired learning outcomes—are largely followed. However, there is still a need for greater sophistication regarding the breadth and depth of the subject matter. Many renowned scholars and professors have contributed significantly to the curriculum development of IP. While there are numerous influential figures, a few key psychologists deserve special mention. These include Prof. Dr. Anis, Prof. Dr. Mah Nazir Riaz, Prof. Dr. Farhana Jehangir, Prof. Dr. Muhammad Tahir Khalily, Dr. Tamkeen Saleem, Dr. Neelam Ehsan, Dr. Kehkasha Arouj, Dr. Ghazala Fazal Dad, Dr. Shahid Ijaz, Dr. Fatima Khurram, and Prof. Dr. Ziasma Haneef.

As mentioned earlier, the rationale behind this integration is to bridge the gap between contemporary psychological perspectives and culture-specific domains. This aims to foster critical thinking and raise awareness regarding the practical aspects of psychology. It is argued that an all-inclusive perspective on the subject matter enhances the practical application of psychological knowledge.

The framework of IP as a course in the current educational model is not limited to a single degree program. Many universities have introduced IP as a core course across various undergraduate, graduate, and postgraduate programs. It is typically offered as a core course alongside contemporary psychological models, or in some cases as an elective, within the respective degree programs. The foundational framework for this subject is consistently similar across almost all degree programs, as it critically integrates the fundamental principles of Islam with contemporary psychological sciences. Consequently, the current curriculum for "Islamic Psychology" in most degree programs is designed holistically, incorporating essential elements of Islam alongside established psychological knowledge.

At the undergraduate level, the course content of IP includes an introduction to the historical roots of psychological knowledge based on the contributions of early classical Muslim philosophers in the field of Ilm-ul-Nafs (the science of the soul), as well as mental health concepts, practices, and behavior shaping. Additionally, the curriculum covers concepts of human personality and behavior as derived from the Quran and Sunnah, integrating these with contemporary psychological principles. A significant portion of the course also addresses basic Islamic principles and ethics relevant to typical human behavior shaping. At this level, the current course content of IP aims to develop an educational model based on the IOK as proposed by Al-Faruqi (1988). Notably, the five pillars of Islam, as outlined in Al-Faruqi's framework, are integral to the course aims and objectives of the majority of curricula.

In contrast, the curricula for postgraduate psychology programs build upon previous coursework, focusing on the vertical and horizontal integration of IP and Islamic disciplines with contemporary psychological models, as described by Rasool (2021). The primary objective of these curricula is to foster an understanding among students of the cosmological framework of Islam and the structure of humanity within this context, while aligning it with the scientific understanding of human psychological functioning. Furthermore, to address the need for an Islamic perspective in mental health practice, these programs enable students to apply their learning in practical clinical psychological work. The model is structured to help students comprehend the psychological impact of various dimensions of Islam, such as Iman (Faith) and Ihsan (Excellence), in order to better understand the conceptualization of mental health and psychopathology within an Islamic framework. This understanding then informs the development of indigenous, Islamically integrated psychotherapeutic techniques, as well as adaptations of Western psychological models. This integration of classical Islamic knowledge with modern Western theories is based on the principles of integrated curricula as noted by Shoemaker (1989) and Shafi (1985), as referenced in Rasool (p. 591).

On the other hand, few postgraduate course curricula have gone beyond the basic concept outlined in Al-Faruqi's (1988) model by incorporating not only the fundamental principles of Islam but also emphasizing Islamic policies in relation to teaching and learning. In fact, such models can pave the way for curriculum development that reflects core Islamic perspectives while also integrating the scientific nature of contemporary psychology. More specifically, these models can be seen as part of an educational development program primarily based on recent research and publications in the field of IP.

The applied nature of the subject, which addresses both the contextual and cultural aspects of understanding human behavior and incorporates contemporary psychological theories, makes this field particularly unique and enriching. This uniqueness is amplified when viewed in light of current trends supported by scientific research evidence. A significant portion of the course content at the postgraduate level is derived from this research. Consequently, by adopting scientist-practitioner models, crucial issues related to the cultural dimensions of human behavior can be explored through scientific research, providing confirmatory evidence.

Important evidence regarding the cultural aspects of human behavior is presented alongside contemporary psychological perspectives. These advancements are not confined to one area of psychology; rather, they encompass major applied psychology domains, such as psychological assessments, psychotherapies, understanding the self from spiritual perspectives, morality, spiritual wisdom, Tazkia (purification of the soul), intention and consciousness, the maladies of the Nafs (self), remedies for the Nafs, clinical supervision, and character development. While this list can be extensive, from an educational standpoint, this type of learning process emphasizes understanding subject matter through scientific evidence, and enhances the practical development of cognitive, affective, and psychomotor skills (Madani, 2016).

An essential component in designing and developing these curricula is highlighting procedures for the periodic evaluation of courses. This evaluation is vital to determine whether the proposed course curricula are being successfully implemented. In this context, Berghout's model of Islamization emphasizes the importance of program feedback. According to Rasool (2021), feedback or program evaluation is a critical aspect that involves monitoring, implementing, and evaluating degree programs that have integrated IP curricula into their study schemes.

Therefore, understanding the crucial role of curriculum evaluation in maintaining quality and essence is necessary. Many Pakistani universities have undergone multiple periodic course revisions. The aim of these evaluations and updates is to refine and enhance the courses at various levels, incorporating input from experts in the relevant fields to maintain high standards of teaching and learning. Consequently, in line with updated course objectives and outcomes, several important areas have been included in the course curricula, all while preserving the core components of Al-Faruqi's basic model of Islamic principles in the majority of the courses.

Revamping Islamic Psychology Education

In Pakistan, the journey of Muslim psychology began at GCU Lahore and the University of Peshawar, where the first course on IP, titled "Muslim Psychology," was exclusively offered to students. Later, the Department of Psychology at one of these universities integrated this course into its master's curriculum. In 2002, after the restructuring of the University Grants Commission and the establishment of the HEC of Pakistan, initiatives were introduced to enhance the quality of higher education. As part of these efforts, the National Curriculum Revision Committee for Psychology convened in Lahore in 2006 to evaluate the content, aims, and objectives of the discipline. This resulted in the introduction of Muslim psychology as an optional subject for eighth-semester students, contingent on the availability of qualified instructors. Some university departments made it a compulsory course, while others offered it as an elective.

Numerous Islamic psychologists have contributed to the establishment of IP as a distinct discipline within the realm of contemporary psychology. Various university departments began integrating current perspectives on the subject into their curricula. Notably, the IIUI has made significant progress in promoting IP. In 2007, Professor Dr. Malik Badri was invited to lead the psychology department in alignment with the university's objectives. Consequently, a three-credit course on Muslim psychology was introduced as an optional course in the bachelor's program and made compulsory in both the Master of Science and doctoral programs.

In 2015, a pivotal advancement in course development occurred with the founding of the Riphah Institute of Clinical and Professional Psychology (RICPP) in Lahore. Led by Prof. Dr. Anis Ahmed, Vice Chancellor of RIU, in consultation with Prof. Dr. G. H. Rasool and Prof. Dr. Muhammad Tahir Khalily, the institute aimed to create a comprehensive educational program for psychologists in Pakistan, enhancing their ability to address various psychosocial issues faced by individuals and communities.

A significant turning point in the evolution of Muslim psychology into IP occurred during a five-day certified course on IP, organized by Prof. Dr. Muhammad Tahir Khalily in January 2019. This course, conducted in collaboration with the IAIP and featuring Dr. Abdullah Rothman and Prof. Rasjid Skinner, focused on Islamic approaches to psychology and psychotherapy. In September 2019, the Center of Islamic Psychology and the Tarbiyah Department offered a six-month certified course in IP, facilitated by G.H. Rassool from the United Kingdom, which attracted students and faculty members from across Pakistan, providing them with a deeper understanding of IP.

The Department of Clinical Psychology at Shifa Tameer-e-Millat University is dedicated to transforming psychological education and practice in Pakistan by focusing on the de-colonization and Islamization of psychological knowledge. This approach aims to create an effective framework for addressing psychological issues and understanding human beings from Islamic perspectives. The department offers a dual framework that allows for a more holistic understanding, diagnosis, and treatment of mental health, fostering an environment where individuals can find solace in both faith and science.

A transformative initiative by the Department of Clinical Psychology was the organization of a three-day course on Traditionally Integrated IP in June 2022. This course, led by Dr. Fahad Khan and Dr. Hooman Keshavarzi and organized by Prof. Dr. Muhammad Tahir Khalily in collaboration with Khalil Center, paved the way for the establishment of IP programs and courses. The curriculum design has been approved and is now being taught in the department as major subjects.

Table 13

Curriculum Development of IP across Educational Levels

Level of Education	Program Offered	Course Code	Course Title	Curricula Designed	Curricula Approved	Course Offered	Credit Hours
Undergraduate	Bachelors of Science in Clinical Psychology (BSCP)	CPIP 4003	Islamic Psychology (Foundation)	Fall 2022	Spring 2023	Fall 2024 to BSCP 5th Semester	03
Post Graduate	Masters of Science in Clinical Psychology (MSCP)	CPIP 6023	Islamic Perspectives in Psychopathology & Psychotherapy	Spring 2024	Fall 2024	Spring 2025	03
Post	PhD in	CPP	Islamic	Fall	Spring	Fall	03

Graduate	Clinical Psychology	T 8013	Perspectives of Integrated Psychotherapy	2022	2023	2023	
Diploma	Post Magistral Diploma in Clinical Psychology (PMDCP)	CPIP 5013	Islamic Perspectives in Mental Health & Psychopathology	Fall 2022	Spring 2023	Spring 2023	03

The department offers a range of courses that encompass both traditional and contemporary psychology. These courses emphasize Islamic perspectives, integrating cultural and religious contexts into clinical psychology. This approach gives students a unique advantage in understanding patients from an Islamic psychological viewpoint. Each course is specifically designed according to educational levels and approved timelines, with clearly defined credit hours allotted. To translate IP knowledge into practice, the following efforts have been made at Shifa Tameer Millat University (STMU).

IP-Integrated Psychology Clinic in a University Setting

We are pleased to announce that the Department of Clinical Psychology at Shifa Tameer-e-Millat University is the first university in Pakistan to establish an Islamically integrated psychological care service on its campus. This achievement has been made possible by the grace of Allah and the vision of the university's higher management, particularly the esteemed Vice Chancellor, Prof. Dr. Muhammad Iqbal Khan, and Dr. Muhammad Tahir Khalily, Professor of Clinical Psychology and Dean of the Faculty of Social Sciences.

The Shifa Psychological Service Clinic (SPSC) was established under the leadership of Prof. Dr. Muhammad Tahir Khalily, with guidance from Dr. Tamkeen Saleem, the Head of the Department of Clinical Psychology. Both are accomplished scholars in the field of IP.

The clinic is part of a larger multi-disciplinary healthcare center known as the Shifa University Center for Health (SUCH).

Mission

The Shifa Psychological Services Clinic serves as a center for training, services, and research. Our mission at SPSC includes the following objectives:

1. To provide professional training for students enrolled in various degree programs within the Department of Clinical Psychology.
2. To offer high-quality, affordable, and evidence-based psychological services to individuals in the STMU community and the general public.
3. To conduct clinical research, particularly aimed at developing contextualized, Islamically-grounded solutions for mental health issues affecting individuals and the broader population.
4. To engage in community activities that promote the overall health and well-being of individuals.

Values

The values driving our work at Shifa Psychological Services Clinic are:

- ايمان | Faith: All work within SPSC is Islamically-grounded and –compliant.

- خدمت | Service: The purpose of the clinic is to serve the needs of the people of Pakistan. This value is reflected in conscientious financial policies and in community mental health projects.

- كمال | Excellence| احسان in Arabic: The services delivered upholds industry standards and principles of practice.

- تعاون | Collaboration : The clinic model is interdisciplinary with medical care available along with psychological service delivery. We operate collaboratively, sharing knowledge and resources with other services within SUCH.

- تحقیق | Evidence based: The practices used within the clinic are empirically validated and we aim to be an evidence-based and evidence-generating enterprise. Furthermore, research conducted will focus on finding contextualized, Islamic, holistic solutions to the mental illness crisis.

These values are reflected in the code of conduct for clinic staff and practitioners, particularly regarding guidance for interacting with members of the opposite gender, maintaining dignified professional behavior, and adhering to the highest ethical standards of practice. We have a zero-tolerance policy for backbiting, gossip, bullying, harassment, and other behavioral issues. We encourage our team to embody Prophetic mannerisms in their care and interpersonal interactions.

Services

The center has been providing care to students, faculty, and staff at the Park Road Campus, Shifa Tameer-e-Millat University, free of charge since February 1, 2024.

We aim to open the clinic to the public in the coming weeks, offering minimal morning service rates to ensure access to quality care. Evening and weekend services will be introduced after six months at competitive market rates. In line with the clinic's values, we offer the possibility of generous needs-based discounts that can be requested by the patient or recommended by the clinician.

The clinic is equipped to deliver psychological care to adults, adolescents, and children. We have established a specialized child therapy area, equipped with therapeutic materials to address the needs of children experiencing various psychological issues. Additionally, the clinic features designated areas for group therapy and individual therapy, allowing clinicians to provide care in a variety of formats.

The clinic offers a range of specialized assessment services, including:

1. Neurodevelopmental disorders
2. Neurodegenerative disorders
3. IQ and intellectual assessments
4. Psychoeducational assessments
5. Personality assessments
6. Psycho-diagnostic assessments, focusing on the maladies of the Nafs

Additionally, the clinic provides Islamically integrated therapies, such as Schema Focused Therapy, Narrative Exposure Therapy, and Community Reinforcement Approach, along with contemporary treatment strategies for neurodevelopmental disorders.

The model of care at Shifa Psychological Services Clinic is holistic and includes lifestyle modifications, wellness tips, and psychological and spiritual techniques aimed at improving the mental health of clients.

Practitioners and Staff

Careful selection has led to a diverse team capable of providing mental health services for adults, children, and adolescents. The team consists of highly qualified clinicians with PhDs or relevant certifications. It is led by the renowned Consultant Clinical Psychologist, Dr. Uzma Masroor, who has a special interest in Islamically integrated therapy.

The clinical team is well-trained to provide psychological care to individuals across different age groups. Additionally, the staff is equipped with skills in de-escalation techniques and has undergone intensive clinical supervision to manage any potential crises effectively.

Supervision

The clinical team holds weekly supervision meetings, which take the form of Grand Rounds attended by departmental PhD students. These sessions provide an excellent opportunity for students to learn from experienced clinicians and receive feedback on cases, as well as engage in collaborative treatment approaches.

The practitioners follow a structured clinical supervision framework, which assigns levels based on developed competencies and years of experience. This system promotes the development of specialized skills and establishes a tiered training structure: the Consultant supervises the senior clinicians, who in turn oversee the clinicians in the tier below them, and they supervise the students. The Consultant reviews and oversees all tiers during the weekly clinical supervision meetings.

Regarding the SPSC model: One of our goals in establishing this clinical service on a university campus in Islamabad, Pakistan, is to demonstrate the feasibility of setting up a successful, Islamically integrated psychological care setting in urban environments, specifically catering to the nation's diverse youth. When IP is taught or applied in practice, a common concern arises about its applicability to clients with varying levels of religiosity. We have been achieving positive results with college students, who exhibit differing degrees of religious commitment.

Challenges and Barriers

1. Limited awareness and understanding of IP among faculty and institutions may result in hesitation or resistance to its integration.
2. Curriculum changes require time, effort, and departmental support, which may slow down the process of integration.
3. A shortage of qualified faculty with expertise in IP complicates course delivery and guidance in this field.
4. Balancing IP with accreditation requirements can be a challenge.
5. There is a perception that IP is limited or culturally restricted, which may hinder its acceptance. Some individuals fear that it offers limited employment opportunities and lacks access to resources.

6. Resistance may arise from traditionally trained professionals who view IP as a deviation from established practices or as ethically challenging due to its religious elements, despite the fact that Islamic ethics closely align with professional standards.

Benefits of Integration

1. Enhances cultural sensitivity and fosters an inclusive learning environment.
2. Provides a holistic perspective that connects spiritual, psychological, and social dimensions.
3. Encourages critical thinking and promotes deeper evaluation of various psychological frameworks.
4. Prepares students to deliver culturally competent care in diverse settings.
5. Opens up pathways for innovative mental health approaches that benefit diverse populations.
6. Fosters dialogue, mutual respect, and appreciation among different cultural and religious perspectives.
7. Broadens students' exposure to global perspectives, preparing them to work effectively in multicultural environments.

Conclusion

In conclusion, integrating IP with contemporary psychology offers a valuable opportunity to create a more inclusive, culturally relevant, and comprehensive psychology curriculum. This integration not only enhances students' understanding of human behavior but also addresses the increasing demand for culturally sensitive mental health services that resonate with diverse populations, particularly in Muslim-majority societies and among Muslim minorities worldwide.

By bridging the gap between Western-centric psychological models and the rich, culturally rooted perspectives of IP, this approach provides a holistic view of mental health that acknowledges the spiritual, ethical, and social dimensions often highlighted in Islamic teachings. This dual framework supports the development of psychologists who are not only technically skilled but also culturally aware and ethically responsible. They can approach psychological issues with an understanding that aligns with their clients' values, beliefs, and experiences.

The strategies outlined in this chapter—including the development of inclusive courses, fostering faculty expertise, promoting interdisciplinary collaboration, providing Islamically integrated clinical care, and encouraging research in IP—are essential steps toward achieving this integration. These efforts help to address key barriers such as limited resources, faculty shortages, and resistance from traditionally trained professionals, ultimately creating an academic environment that nurtures openness, mutual respect, and an appreciation for diverse viewpoints.

Ultimately, a psychology curriculum that is both diverse and inclusive benefits not only students but society as a whole. By preparing future psychologists to operate in multicultural and multi-faith environments, universities contribute to a broader global understanding of mental health and well-being. This comprehensive approach can inspire innovative methods of mental health care, foster empathy and understanding across cultural boundaries, and promote a more nuanced and ethical framework for psychological practice. By doing so, the field of psychology can better address the challenges of a globalized world, providing individuals and communities with mental health support that is both effective and meaningful within a broad cultural context.

CHAPTER SIXTEEN

INTRODUCING ISLAMIC PSYCHOLOGY COURSES
at Two Centers of the Islamic Psychology Association & the Comprehensive Center for Counseling, Growth, and Empowerment (CCGE) in Qom and Mashhad, Iran.

Hamid Rafiei-Honar & Masood Azarbayejani

Introduction

Despite the availability of formal courses in psychology and Islam at Universities of the Islamic Republic of Iran and research centers, establishing a true "Islamic psychology" demands further efforts in curriculum development, resources, methodologies, and teaching staff. To address these needs, some active organizations in the country have recently initiated quarterly courses focused on IP. Two significant initiatives in this area, in which the authors of this chapter have been actively involved, are highlighted.

The first initiative is the "Comprehensive Course in Islamic Psychology" (CCIP), and the second is the "Seasonal School in Islamic Psychology"

(SSIP). The CCIP was initially developed and launched by the Islamic Psychology Association (IPA) under the title "Level 1 Islamic Psychology Training" during 2018-2019, followed by its Level 2 or supplementary course in 2023 (IPA, 2025). Meanwhile, the first SSIP was organized by the Comprehensive Center for Counseling, Growth, and Empowerment (CCGE) of Astaan Quds Razavi in February 2018, with subsequent schools conducted in September and February of 2019 (website of CCGE, 2025).

Since its inception in 2004, the IPA has attracted several hundred psychologists with backgrounds in Islamic studies from seminaries, enabling it to offer educational programs for students. Furthermore, the growing interest among students in Islamic studies motivated these two centers to design such courses. The authors of this chapter, who played an integral role as designers and instructors of these programs, define IP as the science of studying the 'Nafs' and its functions. This field aims to explore and establish laws or norms that ensure mental health and foster a fulfilling life across individual, family, and social dimensions, aligned with the divine objectives set by God for humanity (Rafiei-Honar & Azarbayejani, 2021).

Course Goals

Short-term goals

•　Acquaint students, professors, and researchers with IP's general principles.

•　Introduce the academic community and educate individuals to the works, findings, and results of IP.

•　Showcase the potential of IP in comparison with the findings of mainstream psychology.

•　Equip psychologists with additional knowledge and skills based on Islam, enhancing their effectiveness within Islamic cultural contexts.

Long-term goals

Enhancing the standing of IP as a formal major in public universities across the country. Establishing standards for Islamic-based counseling and treatments in decision-making organizations like the Psychology System Organization. Promoting IP's findings in society to improve mental health and foster a well-being centered on monotheism.

Regarding the nature of the institutions organizing these courses, it is important to note that they are held by non-profit centers and are not directly affiliated with government bodies. The IPA operates as a subsidiary of the Qom Seminary, a recognized official religious institution in the country. Additionally, Astaan Quds Razavi, based in Mashhad, Iran, is a bonyad responsible for managing the Imam Reza shrine (the burial site of the eighth Imam of the Twelver Shiites) and various other affiliated institutions (Rafiei Honar & Azarbayejani, 2025).

Course Level

To enroll in the comprehensive IP course or the seasonal IP school, individuals need at least a master's degree in psychology or a related field such as counseling, religious education, or educational sciences. The first CCIP course was attended by twenty people, while around forty individuals joined the second course. In the SSIP courses, a total of sixty graduate and doctoral psychology students took part (Rafiei-Honar & Azarbayejani, 2021). Although these courses do not confer an official government degree, they offer participants certificates of completion that hold value for inclusion in their academic resumes for clinical and educational centers.

Through these courses, attendees gain a thorough understanding of the difference between IP and mainstream psychology, learning about models and theories specific to IP. This knowledge encourages academic participants to explore IP in their research endeavors and thesis writing for future degrees. Meanwhile, social activists among the participants are motivated to share the insights of IP with the public, aiding in its dissemination and development.

Courses and Student Evaluation

This section outlines the core focus of two specific courses and their respective evaluation methods.

CCIP Courses. The CCIP encompasses five distinct courses. Table 1 provides an overview of each course's title, characteristics, and recommended resources.

Table 14

Overview of CCIP Courses: Titles, Syllabi, and Suggested Resources

	Course title	Syllabi	Resources
1	Fundamentals and Generalities of Islamic Psychology	• Overview of Islamic Psychology: Challenges and Objectives • Historical Evolution and Progress of Islamic Psychology • Use of Anthropological,	Shojaei, M. (2015). Islamic psychology (basics, history and territory) [Persian]. Qom: AMIU Kayyani, Arani, M. (2018). Psychology in the Quran: Foundations and Applications [Persian]. Qom: RIHU Shojaei, M. (2019).

		Epistemological, and Value-Based Principles to Address Issues in Islamic Psychology • Interconnections between Islamic Psychology and Other Islamic Disciplines, including Jurisprudence, Principles, Ethics, Mysticism, and Philosophy	Psychology in Quran and Hadith [Persian]. Qom: RIHU Narooei, R. (2022). Fundamentals of Islamic Psychology [Persian]. Qom: IKERI
2	Methodology of Islamic Psychology	• Methodological Foundations of IP Methodological Models in IP • Core Principles of Psychological Assessment within IP • Approaches for Creating Treatment Protocols Based on IP	Pasandideh, A. (2019). The method of psychological understanding of religious texts [Persian]. Mashhad: CCGE Nooralizadeh Mianaji, M. (2017). Method of modeling psychological concepts and structures from Islamic texts (Quran and Hadith) [Persian]. Qom: IKERI Salarifar, M., Azarbayejani, M., & Rahimi-Nejad, A. (2011). Theoretical Foundations and Psychometrics of Religious Scales [Persian]. Qom: RIHU
3	Development and Personality in Islamic Psychology	• Understanding the fundamentals and concepts of growth and development, with dimensions rooted in Islamic teaching • Exploring growth through the insights of Muslim thinkers • Introducing a model of growth shaped by Islamic teachings	Biriya, Nasser et al. (1995) Developmental Psychology with a View to Islamic Sources, Tehran: SAMT Bashiri, A. & Heidari, M. (2017). Personality theories with a view to religious sources [Persian]. Qom: IKERI Shojaei, M. (2024). Personality psychology with an Islamic approach, [Persian]. Qom: AMIU

		• Analyzing the emergence, development, and characteristics of personality as guided by Islamic sources • Examining behavior motivation according to Islamic sources • Assessing growth and personality metrics based on Islamic principles	
4	Psycho-pathology in Islamic Psychology	• Basics of Psychopathology in Islamic Texts • Understanding Psychopathology through Muslim Scholars • Categorization of Psychopathology According to Islamic Teachings • Analysis and Interpretation of Psychopathology in Islamic Literature	Janbozorgi, M., & Ansari, H. (2024). Psychopathology with cultural considerations [Persian]. Qom: RIHU Manteqi, Morteza (1991). Etiology and Treatment of Mental Illnesses in the Islamic Realm, Tehran: ACECR Abu-Torabi, A. (2007). Critique of normative criteria in psychology in the Light of Islamic Sources [Persian]. Qom: IKERI Rafiei Honar, H. (2021). Lecture on Psychopathology with an Islamic Approach. Qom: IAP
5	Counseling and Therapy in Islamic Psychology	• Fundamentals of Psychological Change and Reconstruction in Islamic Sources • Core Principles and Techniques of Psychotherapy and Counseling in Islamic Teachings • Healing Strategies and Practices in	Janbozorgi, M., & Gharavi, S. M. (2018). principles of psychotherapy and counselling: an Islamic approach. 2nd eds [Persian]. Tehran: SAMT and RIHU Janbozorgi, M. (2019). Spiritually multidimensional psychotherapy: a God-oriented approach [Persian]. Qom: RIHU

		Islamic Contexts • Individual and Interpersonal Therapeutic Guidelines with an Islamic Perspective	Narooei, R. (2017). The Theory Islamic Self-Discovery for treatment of OCD [Persian]. Qom: IKERI Rafiei-Honar, H. (2016). Psychology of self-control with an Islamic attitude [Persian]. Qom: IKERI

SSIP Courses. The SSIP offers four distinct course titles. Table 2 introduces these courses, their characteristics, and recommended resources.

Table 15

Overview of SSIP Courses: Titles, Syllabi, and Suggested Resources

	Course title	Syllabi	Resources
1	Philosophy of Islamic Psychology	• Definition, importance, goals, and related concepts of the philosophy of mind and psychology • The subject and goals of IP • Methodology in IP • Relationship between understanding the "Nafs" and psychology • Perfection and happiness of the Nafs as the highest human goals in desirable psychology	Azarbayejani, M. (2021). Philosophy of Psychology [Persian]. Qom: RIHU. Mario Bunge & Ruben Ardila (1987). Philosophy of Psychology, translated and criticized by Zare'an, M.J. et al.(2013) Qom: RIHU Hassani, S.H., and Mousavi, H. (2018). Sadra's Anthropology of Action, Qom: RIHU
2	Method of Psychological Understanding of Religious Texts	• Exploring the process of analyzing religious concepts, focusing on methods and stages of conceptualization using verses and narrations as a foundation • Recognizing the interrelated system of concepts within the Quran and Hadith • Deriving psychological guidelines from Islamic	Pasandideh, A. (2019). The method of psychological understanding of religious texts [Persian]. Mashhad: Astaan Quds Razavi Nooralizadeh Mianaji, M. (2017). Method of modeling psychological concepts and structures from Islamic texts (Quran and Hadith)

		sources in a cohesive, thematic, and systematic approach	[Persian]. Qom: IKERI
3	Evolution of Islamic Psychology in Iran and the World	• Gaps and limitations of contemporary historiography in psychology • The role of religion in ancient Greek psychological thought • Contributions of Muslim thinkers to the development of psychological knowledge • The history of modern IP in the 19th century • The current status of IP and its future prospects	Shojaei, M. (2015). Islamic psychology (basics, history and territory) [Persian]. Qom: AMIU Gharavi, S. M., & Azarbayejani, M. (2012). A look at Islamic psychology [Persian]. (M. Forghani, A. Sheikh Shojaei, & N. Nouri, (Eds.). Qom: RIHU. Rafiei Honar, H. (2018). Lecture on history of Islamic psychology. Qom: IAP
4	Treatment Protocols and Psychological Interventions with a Religious Approach	• Understanding the fundamentals of clinical interventions in the Islamic context • Key principles and methods of psychotherapy and counseling within the Islamic framework • Various forms of clinical interventions adopted in Islamic practices • An overview of the principles, stages, and methods involved in God-oriented spiritual therapy	Janbozorgi, M., & Gharavi, S. M. (2018).principles of psychotherapy and counselling: an Islamic approach. 2nd eds [Persian]. Tehran: SAMT and RIHU Janbozorgi, M. (2019). Spiritually multidimensional psychotherapy: a God-oriented approach [Persian]. Qom: RIHU Sadeghi Seresht, A. (2019), Development of Psychological Interventions (Stages and Development Method), Qom: RIQH

Note. The evaluation method for all the courses introduced is divided into two parts: 20 percent from class activities during the semester and 80 percent from the final exam. The course content is based on the teacher's lesson plans for each course.

Duration, Credit Hours, and Tuition Fees

The CCIP spans 100 hours, with each course covering 20 hours in ten 2-hour sessions, offered over one academic semester. Meanwhile, the SSIP features intensive courses lasting three days per season, totaling 24 hours of instruction across twelve 2-hour sessions. The tuition fee for the CCIP is approximately $40, whereas the SSIP costs about $10.

Registration details are announced through a call on the IPA website and via the information channel of the CCGE each semester or at the start of each academic year. Course start times vary based on reaching a minimum enrollment of 15 participants. Participation is entirely optional, as these courses are extracurricular and are held outside the formal education system of government centers. They welcome individuals from across the country and abroad who are familiar with Persian. Courses are available both in person and online, with details posted on the organizing centers' websites.

Instructors for these courses typically include faculty members from official universities in the country. Many have defended various Islamic models and ideas within psychology and have published scientific works and research articles. According to the organizing centers, student satisfaction rates exceed 95 percent, showcasing the effectiveness of these courses (Rafiei Honar & Azarbayejani, 2025).

Limitations and Prospects

The main limitation of these courses is the lack of practical and executive attachments. This means that the courses are mostly presented in a theoretical and conceptual manner, and due to the intensive nature of the courses, participants have fewer opportunities for practical experiences in developing treatment protocols or implementing treatments during the training course. However, there has been progress with the introduction of operational and internship courses that offer supervised practical experiences in research and treatment, guided by professors. Looking ahead, it appears that the coming decade in Iran will witness a domestic surge in the development and expansion of this training approach, potentially extending to other countries. The authors of this chapter hope to establish IP training courses at an international level, collaborating with global centers and leveraging online training opportunities.

ISLAMIC PSYCHOLOGY PROGRAMS IN THE ISLAMIC REPUBLIC OF IRAN

Shahed University, Tehran, Iran

Masood Azarbayejani & Hamid Rafiei-Honar

Introduction

Education is one of the most essential social institutions, with a history that spans several millennia. It plays a crucial role in transmitting norms, values, and beliefs to new generations. Education not only promotes and expands knowledge within society but also facilitates the application of that knowledge among its members. Additionally, it fosters the conditions necessary for creativity and skill development in students, ultimately contributing to a better quality of life.

Universities, as institutions of higher and postgraduate education, hold a unique and significant position in advancing a developed society. They do more than generate scientific knowledge, create wealth, and apply various technologies for the benefit of humanity; they also provide meaning in life. Fourth-generation universities have particularly emphasized this mission. They view the institution not just as a platform for the commercialization of knowledge but as a meeting point for diverse segments of society. Their goals include achieving a transcendent educational experience, promoting practical reasoning and ethics, advocating for justice, challenging injustice, and serving as venues for aesthetic exploration (Lyotard, 1982; Readings, 1996; Berne, 2000).

Recognizing the essential role of religion in fulfilling the needs for spirituality, moral values, and aesthetic experiences when interacting with natural phenomena as divine signs, religion can be a crucial resource for achieving the objectives of fourth-generation universities. Among various faiths, Islam might be particularly effective due to the spiritual depth of its teachings and its focus on rationality and learning.

IP is a significant movement within the spiritual framework of psychology. It strives, on one hand, to describe, analyze, explain, predict, and manage behavior and psychological processes to enhance mental health and adaptability. On the other hand, it seeks to attain spiritual well-being and holistic happiness in both this life and the hereafter. This approach is rooted in beliefs about creation and resurrection, as well as a transcendent way of living (Azarbayejani, 2023, Haque & Rothman, 2021;

Janbozorghi,2021; Nelson, 2009).

Consequently, the field of IP can make a significant contribution to realizing the goals of the fourth-generation university, as affirmed by the Holy Quran.

« ... قَدْ جَاءكُم مِّنَ اللهِ نُورٌ وَكِتَابٌ مُّبِينٌ يَهْدِي بِهِ اللَّهُ مَنِ اتَّبَعَ رِضْوَانَهُ سُبُلَ السَّلَامِ وَيُخْرِجُهُم
»مِّنَ الظُّلُمَاتِ إِلَى النُّورِ بِإِذْنِهِ وَيَهْدِيهِمْ إِلَى صِرَاطٍ مُّسْتَقِيمٍ«

(Al-Ma'idah, 15-16)

"There has come to you from Allah a light and a clear Book, by which Allah guides those who seek His pleasure to the paths of peace, and by His command, He brings them out of darkness into light, guiding them to a straight path."

In recent years, particularly in this century, we can analyze the development of IP using a meta-synthetic approach informed by various Muslim psychologists (Kaplick & Skinner, 2017). The historical evolution of this field, especially in the Islamic Republic of Iran, can be divided into four stages: preparation, refinement, comparison, and establishment (Rafiei-Honar, 2018).

Since the foundational period (2001-present), we have seen the emergence of Islamic theories and models that address various topics, including personality, motivation, psychotherapy, psychometrics, mental health and hygiene, family dynamics, religious psychology, positive psychology, social psychology, and developmental psychology. Additionally, many Islamic psychological scales and questionnaires are used as measurement tools, and a variety of Islamic psychological protocols are implemented in counseling and psychotherapy clinics.

During this period in the Islamic Republic of Iran, we have witnessed a significant increase in scientific production, including several hundred books, master's theses, and doctoral dissertations. In addition, more than ten scientific quarterly journals and magazines have been launched, focusing on the intersection of Islam and psychology. Numerous scientific conferences and symposiums have also facilitated discussions among academic scholars on IP (Rafiei-Honar & Azarbayejani, 2021, in Haque & Rothman, 2021).

These initiatives, particularly the creation of scientific content, have laid the groundwork for establishing educational programs in this area. According to the "Higher Education Planning Office" of the Ministry of Science, Research and Technology of the Islamic Republic of Iran (https://prog.msrt.ir), there are currently 37 psychology majors and 12 counseling majors offered at various academic levels across the country's universities and scientific centers. Among these 49 majors, 9 are university programs, which include 2 undergraduate majors, 6 master's degree majors, and 1 doctoral degree major. Additionally, there are 2 seminary programs specifically related to the fields of Islam and psychology, with level 3 equivalent to a master's degree and level 4 equivalent to a doctoral degree.

Islamic Psychology Discipline

The field of "Islamic Psychology" focuses on the study of psychology through an Islamic lens, highlighting coherence and purity in its methodologies. It was developed at the master's level by a group of Islamic psychologists within the Psychology Commission of the Specialized Council for the Development and Promotion of Human Sciences. This field has been officially approved by the Ministry of Science, Research and Technology.

The development of Islamic psychology is driven by several key factors:

Addressing the Theoretical Gap

This field was established to provide psychological theories rooted in Islamic and religious perspectives.

Enhancing Mental Health

IP aims to expand the understanding of mental health by integrating ethics, faith, and spirituality.

Integrating Science and Religion

By combining scientific inquiry with religious teachings, IP creates a foundation for advancing knowledge in this area.

IP is defined as the scientific study of human behavior, emotions, thoughts, and spiritual matters grounded in Islamic principles, assumptions, and goals derived from the Quran and Hadith. Its aim is to describe, explain, predict, and manage these aspects to promote human health and happiness in both this world and the hereafter.

The main objective of this curriculum is to ensure mastery of the fundamentals, teachings, and concepts of IP as articulated in primary Islamic texts and by Muslim scholars. Additionally, it seeks to cultivate the ability to conduct research and apply this knowledge within Muslim cultures.

This educational program has the following objectives:

1. To introduce the Islamic perspective on various psychological issues and topics.

2. To establish a foundation for training educators and researchers in the field of IP.
3. To enhance psychological knowledge with an Islamic orientation and spiritual perspective.
4. To establish foundational principles for developing methodologies in IP.
5. To implement findings from IP research in alignment with societal needs.

The Master's degree in IP requires a total of 32 credits, which are divided into three categories: 12 specialized credits, 16 elective credits, and 4 thesis credits. Students typically complete the program over the course of five semesters and must successfully defend their thesis.

To gain admission, candidates must pass an entrance examination that assesses their proficiency in several areas. These include specialized Arabic language skills for interpreting religious texts, understanding the Quran and Hadith, psychology, psychological teachings found in the Quran and Hadith, and the philosophy of psychology.

Additionally, students may need to complete around 20 credits of remedial (prerequisite) courses to strengthen their foundational knowledge in IP. This requirement is particularly important for those who come from non-psychology backgrounds, as they may need additional prerequisite units to qualify for admission.

The core courses are organized into three categories: specialized, elective, and thesis, as outlined in the following tables:

Table 16

Titles of the specialized and elective syllabus in IP

Row	Specialized Syllabus	Number of Units
1	Fundamentals of IP 1 (Knowledge of Science)	2
2	Fundamentals of IP 2 (Knowledge of Nafs)	2
3	The methodology of understanding the Qur'an and Hadith	2
4	Psychometrics of religious concepts	2
5	Social psychology with an attitude towards Islamic sources	2
6	Mental health in Islam	2
7	Thesis	4
	Elective Syllabus	
1	Advanced research method	2

IP PROGRAMS IN THE ISLAMIC REPUBLIC OF IRAN

2	Advanced inferential statistics	2
3	Developmental psychology from the perspective of Islam	2
4	Anthropology from the perspective of Islam and psychology	2
5	Motivation and Emotion in the Light of Islamic Sources	2
6	Psychopathology in the Light of Islamic Sources	2
7	Theories of psychotherapy in Islamic sources	2
8	Moral Psychology in the Light of Islamic Sources	2
9	Psychology of religion & spirituality	2
10	Positive psychology in the Light of Islamic Sources	2
11	Personality psychology in the Light of Islamic Sources	2
12	Religious Science	2

Tables 17 and 18 introduce the skills, abilities, and competencies expected of graduates of the IP field, according to the courses offered to them:

Table 17

Role, ability and general competence expected from graduates

No	General skills, competencies and abilities	Related Courses
1	Ability to understand the shortcomings and limitations of contemporary psychology and its differences from IP	Fundamentals of Islamic Psychology 1 and 2, Anthropology from the Perspective of Islam and Psychology
2	Ability to conduct research in psychological fields and the ability to write scientific articles	Advanced inferential statistics, advanced research methodology
3	Familiarity with common language and literature in psychological knowledge	Personality psychology, psychopathology, developmental psychology

Table 18

Role, ability and special competence expected from graduates

No	Special skills, competencies and abilities	Related Courses
1	Analyzing the psychological issues of society from an Islamic perspective	Social psychology in Islamic sources, developmental psychology from the perspective of Islam, anthropology from the perspective of Islam and psychology
2	Ability to provide	Mental health in Islam, psychopathology

	psychological services in the field of prevention and treatment of mental disorders with an Islamic approach	with a view to Islamic sources, psychotherapy theories in Islamic sources
3	Skills in presenting religious propaganda and principles of religious education with a psychological approach	Developmental PPIG, personality psychology with a view to Islamic sources, moral psychology with a view to Islamic sources, positive psychology with a view to Islamic sources
4	The ability to measure and evaluate the psychological and spiritual state of individuals in society using religious assessment and measurement tools	Psychometrics of religious concepts, psychology of religion and its criticism, personality psychology with an approach to Islamic sources, advanced research methods, advanced inferential statistics
5	Psychological response to religious problems and doubts	Fundamentals of Islamic Psychology 1 and 2, Methodology of Understanding the Quran and Hadith, Psychology of Ethics with a View to Islamic Sources, Positive Psychology with a View to Islamic Sources

In this program, students are introduced to over one hundred new sources in the field of IP that form the basis of the syllabus. The courses place special emphasis on spiritual and ethical approaches, particularly in areas such as philosophical psychology (Ilm an-Nafs) and the systematic understanding of the Quran and Hadith. Students are encouraged to engage in critical thinking and rational analysis while examining various topics, and the use of experimental methods in psychological research is emphasized.

This subject is being offered for the first time at Shahed State University in Tehran, and Baqir al-Uloom University in Qom, a non-governmental institution, is also seeking approval to offer it. Public universities provide this program free of charge, while private ones typically charge around $3,000. Although the program is primarily conducted in person, remote participation is available with coordination from the university. Additionally, students from other universities can enroll by passing an entrance exam.

In this field, instructors are psychologists who possess a strong understanding of Islamic sciences. The aim is not only to introduce students to the scientific foundations of IP but also to integrate practical aspects of this discipline into daily life, promoting the development of an Islamic lifestyle. IP offers various career opportunities, both now and in the future, including:

1. Counseling and Psychotherapy: Graduates can pursue careers in psychological clinics, family counseling centers, and hospitals.
2. Education and Teaching: There are opportunities for teaching at universities and schools as professors or educational consultants.
3. Research and Investigation: Graduates can engage in research and work at centers focused on IP.
4. Employment in Government Organizations: Positions are available in sectors related to mental health, welfare, and social affairs.
5. Cultural and Social Development: Graduates can contribute to cultural and social programs that promote Islamic values.

Recommendations

To promote and accelerate the global recognition of IP as a scientific discipline, especially in Muslim countries, the following key initiatives are proposed:

Exchange of Ideas

Facilitate the sharing of successful experiences and ideas in the training of IP programs.

Periodic Conferences

Organize regular conferences to observe and disseminate effective practices from different countries within this field.

Theoretical Foundation

Establish a foundation for theorizing and modeling issues in IP, particularly within doctoral research.

Methodological Focus

Enhance attention on specific methodologies pertinent to IP to advance this discipline.

International Associations

Develop and expand international IPA to foster collaboration, especially concerning educational initiatives.

Resource Compilation

Prepare, compile, and expand essential resources and textbooks for IP curricula at undergraduate, graduate, and doctoral levels.

Translation of Textbooks

Translate IP textbooks into the languages required by Islamic countries and Muslim populations in other regions.

Collaborative Endeavors

Set aside ethnic, religious, racial, and gender differences to facilitate cooperation and collaboration.

Diversity and Pluralism

Embrace diversity and pluralism in theoretical perspectives and practical models within the Islamic paradigm.

Dialogue with Modern Psychology

Engage in logical and scientific dialogue with mainstream psychology and strive to establish and advance academic disciplines in IP.

Collaboration with Knowledge Centers

Collaborate with official psychological institutions, such as the American Psychological Association (APA), to introduce the objectives and framework of IP and seek formal recognition from these organizations.

Conclusion

The Islamic Ummah and the broader Islamic world have reached a level of intellectual and scientific maturity that paves the way for the reconstruction of a new Islamic civilization, reminiscent of the early centuries of Islamic history. IP exemplifies this civilizational approach, as it facilitates a positive interaction between modern humanities and Islamic principles. This interaction enables Muslim scholars to develop Islamic humanities through a new meta-synthesis. Over the past three decades, Muslim psychologists in the Islamic Republic of Iran have made significant strides in formulating, presenting, and legitimizing IP as a distinct discipline grounded in Islamic principles. They have successfully implemented this discipline in reputable universities.

CHAPTER SEVENTEEN

CERTIFICATE IN ISLAMIC THEORETICALLY ORIENTED COUNSELING
Graduate-level Courses in Islamic Psychology

Istanbul Sabahattin Zaim University; Istanbul, Türkiye

Ayşe Kaya Göktepe

Background

During the 19th-century modernization of the Ottoman Empire, the Halkalı Agricultural and Baytar Mekteb-i Ali was established on the plots of land belonging to the Sultan Bayezid II Foundation. Its mission was to teach agricultural techniques, instill a sense of responsibility, promote production ethics, and encourage public service. This institution educated and later employed Mehmet Akif Ersoy, the poet of the İstiklal Marşı (Turkish National Anthem), fostering a spirit of knowledge and working in the service of the community.

In 2010, IZU was established on this historic campus and later transferred to the İlim Yayma Foundation, reflecting a shared commitment to public service and education. The university is named after Sabahattin Zaim (1926–2007), a professor and pioneer in Islamic economics and labor economics in Türkiye. He embodies his academic and practical legacy, focusing on the intersection of national and religious values since the 1950s (Çakır, 2025). The university features seven faculties, 22 PhD programs, and 78 Master's programs (36 non-thesis/ 42 thesis). Notable programs include those rooted in Islamic ontology and epistemology, such as Islamic Economics and Finance, Islamic Law, and Economics.

The Faculty of Islamic Sciences (FIS) was founded on May 15, 2012, to nurture scholars who can understand and interpret Islam's enduring principles in the context of contemporary human and social realities. The Faculty is rooted in a civilization emphasizing tawhid/the oneness of existence, knowledge, and values. The curriculum aims to revive the intellectual and spiritual depth of Islamic thought, exploring its theological, philosophical, and historical dimensions in a manner that resonates with the needs of modern society. The Faculty views Islamic civilization as a historical legacy and a vibrant tradition that continues to shape meaning and morality across different times and places.

The Department of Foundational Islamic Sciences emphasizes the principles of faith, worship, and ethics derived from the Qur'an and Hadith. The Department of Islamic History and Arts examines how Islamic values have been expressed in various historical and cultural contexts. The Department of PRS explores the intellectual and existential dimensions of belief and practice, offering graduate-level courses such as IP.

IZU's mission is to educate virtuous and exemplary individuals who embody the values of our civilization, generate scientific knowledge, serve humanity, and are well-prepared to shape the future. The university envisions becoming an internationally recognized research institution distinguished by its academic and physical infrastructure, producing highly sought-after graduates. Furthermore, it aims for its publications to serve as valuable reference sources and to lead in specific areas, aspiring to rank among the top five foundation universities.

Malik Badri, a modern IP movement pioneer, worked at IZU between 2017 and 2021. Although there is not yet a standalone program in IP, the Psychology of Religion and Spirituality Lab is currently being established. This lab aims to support academic research and foster collaboration in IP.

Nature of The Program

IP courses are offered through the Master's program in SCG and Master's and PhD programs in PRS. The SCG program is designed to train professionals with theoretical and practical knowledge in psychology, enabling them to integrate spirituality into therapeutic contexts. This program is grounded in ethical principles and focuses on developing skills in scientific research and writing.

Following successful international models, the SCG program prepares experts to meet the rising demand for spiritual counseling services in Türkiye. While emphasizing general competencies in spiritual counseling, the program is framed within an Islamic context that reflects Türkiye's religious background. Course topics include psychological counseling within Islamic civilization and the intersection of medicine and spirituality, drawing from Islamic ontology and epistemology.

The PRS Master's Program provides an interdisciplinary curriculum that examines the individual, social, and intellectual dimensions of religion through the lenses of philosophy, psychology, sociology, and history. By integrating classical Islamic thought with modern social sciences, the program equips students with theoretical and methodological tools in various areas, including Islamic philosophy, logic, the psychology of religion, and the sociology of religion. A distinctive feature of the program is the course titled "Basic Concepts of Islamic Psychology," which explores psychological theories rooted in the Islamic tradition. This course offers a critical engagement with Western psychology, providing historical, conceptual, and epistemological insights drawn from Islamic intellectual heritage, and frames psychological issues and solutions within an Islamic perspective.

In 2019, IZU launched the Counseling from an Islamic Theoretical Orientation Certificate Program in collaboration with the IAIP, under the leadership of Malik Badri. This intensive 5-day course was designed for mental health professionals and students, introducing them to Islamic perspectives on psychology and Counseling. It combined theoretical foundations with practical approaches to addressing mental distress.

The program included lectures, discussions, and experiential sessions led by Malik Badri, Rasjid Skinner, and Abdallah Rothman. At the conclusion of the course, participants received a joint certificate from IZU and IAIP. The objectives of the program were as follows:

- Distinguish between culturally relative and universal factors in Western psychology.
- Identify and describe the Islamic models of the self.
- Describe the therapeutic relationship from an Islamic perspective.
- Identify the therapeutic aims and objectives of IP and Counseling.
- Explore various Islamic perspectives on mental health diagnosis.

- Describe Western therapeutic approaches and their applicability to Muslims.
- Apply Islamic psychological principles in diagnosis and treatment using case studies.

Admission Requirements

Applicants for the certificate program must submit the following documents: an application form, a high school diploma or student certificate, a transcript, a passport or Turkish ID (for residents), and a passport-sized photo. All documents must be translated into Turkish or English and certified by a notary or consulate.

To be considered for a 100% scholarship, applicants must also provide valid SAT or YÖS scores, a letter of intent, and reference letters.

Graduate students admitted to thesis tracks with a minimum ALES score of 55 may be eligible for research assistantships and YÖK scholarships. Thesis students complete 30–36 ECTS, while non-thesis students complete 24–30 ECTS, plus a seminar or project. A preparatory module offers an additional 8–12 ECTS.

Faculty Credentials

The PRS Master's Program benefits from a diverse faculty that includes four professors, five associate professors, and two assistant professors, all internationally recognized in philosophy, religious studies, and Islamic thought. The academic staff holds graduate degrees in various fields, such as religious education, hadith, mysticism, religious psychology of religion, clinical psychology, and social services. This diversity ensures interdisciplinary teaching aligned with each lecturer's expertise.

In the SCG Master's Program, faculty members specialize in theology, Islamic sciences, psychology, and Counseling. Students receive supervision and gain valuable experience through experiential learning approaches. The Counseling from an Islamic Theoretical Orientation Certificate Program, launched in 2019 under the guidance of Malik Badri, Rasjid Skinner, and Abdallah Rothman, was one of the first programs of its kind, effectively combining theory and practical application.

Between 2021 and 2024, the FIS produced 210 scholarly works, comprising 60 articles, 52 books, 57 book chapters, 40 conference papers, and one project. This output reflects a strong institutional vision emphasizing collective achievement over individual accomplishments. Between 2018 and 2020, Malik Badri, who taught IP courses for psychology students, organized an IP Summer School that was also open to students from outside the university. In 2018, he also pioneered a two-day IP conference featuring distinguished scholars and contributors in the field, including Hussein Rasool, Rania Awaad, Mustafa Merter, Abdallah Rothman, Yasien Mohamed, Hooman Keshavarzi, Süleyman Derin, Rasjid Skinner, Yusuf Jha, and Carrie York Al-Karam. In 2019, he launched a five-day certificate program titled Counseling from an Islamic Theoretical Orientation, leading the way in IP counseling training. These initiatives positioned IZU as a hub where researchers interested in IP can unite and impact the contemporary scientific world.

2019

Effects of Religious Participation on Social Inclusion and Existential Well-Being Levels of Muslim Refugees and Immigrants in Turkey Cetin, Mehmet Article International *Journal For The Psychology Of Religion Volume: 29* Issue: 2 Special Issue: SI Pages: 64-76 Published: APR 3, 2019

Machouche, S., Bensaid, B., Ahmed, Z. Kemanusiaan (2019*). Crossroads between Islamic spirituality and the instruction of science. Volume 26*, 2019, Pages 23-45

2022-23

Bahcecioglu Turan G.; Yildiz E.; Özer Z. The Effects of Strength of Religious Faith on Post-Traumatic Growth in Patients with Epilepsy. *Epilepsy and Behavior* Article 10.1016/ J.Yebeh. 2023. 10934

Özer Z.; Aksoy M.; Turan G.B. The Relationship Between Death Anxiety and Religious Coping Styles in Patients Diagnosed with Covid-19: A Sample in The East of Turkey Omega (United States) Article 10.1177/ 00302228 211065256

Partnership With Other Programs or Institutions

The Erasmus+ Student Mobility Program, coordinated by IZU's International Office, supports international academic exchange and provides grants to students studying across Europe. IZU has agreements with 48 universities in Malaysia, the United States, the United Kingdom, Indonesia, and Jordan. Partnerships with the IAIP and the American Islamic College include joint research, academic visits, and events, such as the 2019 IP Certificate Program in collaboration with IAIP.

Curriculum

IZU offers various graduate-level courses in IP. Descriptions of these courses are given in the table below. The approach to IP presented in the courses at IZU is a discipline grounded in the ontological and epistemological foundations of the Qur'an and Sunnah and informed by the classical Sunni tradition. It constructs its understanding of human nature (fiṭrah) and the inner faculties of the self—such as the soul (rūḥ), intellect ('aql), nafs, and heart (qalb)—through the lens of divine revelation and prophetic teachings. Ontologically, it views the human being as a creation of God whose existence is defined by the dynamic balance between inner and outer dimensions. Epistemologically, it emphasizes that human access to knowledge and moral truth is mediated through revelation and rational inquiry, with revelation as the ultimate source of guidance. IP integrates spiritual teachings and traditional psychological insights within this framework to foster mental and emotional well-being. Consistent with the classical Sunni paradigm, the therapeutic strategies it proposes seek to cultivate inner harmony and moral excellence aligned with the ethical and spiritual vision of the Qur'an and Sunnah.

Table 19

IZU Graduate Course Structure and Outcomes in Islamic Psychology

	Graduate Program	Description of The Course	Outcomes of the course
FDB506- Basic Concepts in Islamic Psychology	Philosophy and Religious Sciences, MA	This course offers an in-depth exploration of the theological, theoretical, and practical foundations of IP; traces its historical evolution; engages with advanced Master's level readings on core theories and applied practices in the field; and hones students' ability to apply theological concepts appropriately across both classical and contemporary case scenarios.	**IP and Methodology:** To give students an in-depth understanding of IP's scope, topics, and methodology. **Decolonization and the Islamic Human Model:** Examines the decolonization of psychology and the reconstruction of the human model in terms of Islamic ontology and epistemology. **Historical and Theoretical Development:** It enables students to understand the historical development of IP and the essential thinkers and practices of the Ottoman period. **Qur'an and Sufi Psychology:** It helps them to learn the basic concepts of human psychology and Sufi psychology in the Qur'an. **Modern Islamic Psychotherapy**: Equips

CERTIFICATE IN THEORETICALLY ORIENTED COUNSELING

			students with the ability to examine Islamic psychological counseling methods (TIIP, IIP).
FDB 604 – Psychology of Sufism	Philosophy and Religious Sciences PhD	This course examines the intersection of psychology and Sufism, concentrating on the psychological aspects of mystical tendencies and Sufi practices. Students will explore the fundamental concepts of Sufism, its spiritual and psychological practices, and the impact of mystical experiences on human development (seyr al suluq). Topics include the relationship between mysticism and psychology, the psychological processes involved in mystical experiences, and the role of spiritual guidance in Sufi traditions.	• Understand and explain the relationship between Sufism and IP. • Illustrate and compile the elements of the relationship between Sufism and IP. • Distinguish between religious and mystical experiences. • Comprehend the processes of personality and self-reconstruction in Sufi Psychology. Identify the principles of spiritual guidance in Sufism based on the relationship between the Sheikh and the disciple as spiritual authorities. • Understand the processes of rebirth through self-analysis by examining examples from Sufi personalities.
MDR 535 – Counseling and Guidance Practices in Islamic Civilization	Spiritual Counseling and Guidance MA	This course explores counseling and healing approaches that developed historically from the founding period of Islamic civilization to the Ottoman healing tradition. It examines counseling practices in the Qur'an, Sunnah, hadith, and Sufi sources, qalb-aql-nafs-ruh models, tazkiyah (self-training) teachings, and healing	*Theological and Theoretical Background:* To enable students to understand IP's theological, theoretical, and practical foundations. *Awareness of Historical Development:* To comprehend the historical course of psychological Counseling and mental health services in Islamic civilization, especially in the context of classical period thinkers and institutions.

		treatment methods. The course offers a comparative perspective with modern psychotherapy theories and techniques (Cognitive Behavioral Therapy, Psychodynamic, Humanistic Approach, etc.). It discusses how traditional Islamic methods and current scientific therapeutic practices can be integrated. Through case studies, group work, and experiential practice, students develop counseling and psychotherapy skills that are culturally sensitive, grounded in religious references, and follow ethical principles. Through academic literature review and practical application during the course, participants can transfer theoretical knowledge in IP to clinical and Counseling settings.	*Theories and Approaches:* To learn about human models and psychotherapeutic approaches developed in IP. *Methodological Competence:* To gain the ability to analyze the methodology of IP, the basic concepts of the Qur'an, and Sufi psychology. *Modern Practices:* To introduce contemporary Islamic-oriented psychological counseling methods (TIIP, IIP) and to evaluate how these methods are integrated with traditional knowledge. *Critical Thinking and Analysis:* To critically evaluate the relationship between modern psychology and Islamic thought and to gain the ability to analyze models developed as an alternative to Western-centered psychology. *Application Skills:* To gain the ability to apply Islamic psychotherapy models in the light of historical accumulation and theoretical knowledge, in line with current case studies.
MDR 537 - Islamic Spirituality and Sufism	Spiritual Counseling and Guidance MA	This course examines the origins and evolution of Sufism by surveying its earliest practitioners, major orders, founders, and foundational concepts. It then explores how	*Defines* the basic concepts of Islamic spirituality in a narrow and broad sense. *Describe* the historical origins and key developmental stages of Sufism, including its earliest practitioners and

CERTIFICATE IN THEORETICALLY ORIENTED COUNSELING

		Tasawwuf (Sufism) has been transmitted to the present day, illustrating enduring principles through case studies of historical and contemporary Sufi movements.	foundational schools. *Analyze* major Sufi orders' teachings and institutional structures and their founding figures. *Explain* their evolution and trace core Sufi concepts (e.g., dhikr, maʿrifa, tawḥīd). *Interpret* the influence of Sufi culture on subsequent intellectual, artistic, and religious movements up to the present day.
MDR XXX- Tibb Al-Ruhani	Spiritual Counseling and Guidance MA	This course explores the holistic Islamic tradition of Tıbb-ur-Ruhānī ("spiritual medicine"), examining how classical scholars addressed both material and spiritual dimensions of human health. Topics include human nature (fiṭrah), body, soul, heart, common spiritual afflictions (fear of death, heart maladies), and remedies from Prophetic medicine, Sufism, ethics, and the IOK. Students will analyze key concepts, including heart health, mental well-being, spiritual needs, and the role of ethical virtues in promoting spiritual well-being. The course emphasizes that spiritual health and moral virtues are deeply intertwined, with virtues such as patience, gratitude, and humility playing a vital role in maintaining mental and spiritual balance. Tıbb al-Ruhānī, distinct from physical medicine, addresses the human	*Understands* the relationship between psychology and religion in Islamic tradition. *Makes comments* about the approach of Islamic tradition to human nature/structure (Fıtrat). *Gains knowledge* of psychological studies produced from Islamic tradition in the past and today. *Recognizes* Muslim scholars and their theories that have contributed to psychology, psychiatry, and psychological Counseling. *Understands* the approaches of Islamic thinkers to mental illness and health.

	existence beyond the body, incorporating spiritual, philosophical, ethical, and psychological dimensions. By connecting these concepts with Islamic theology, philosophy, and Sufism, the course provides a comprehensive framework for understanding and addressing human well-being.

Strengths

The program is setting up a Psychology of Religion and Spirituality (PRS) lab, where students can conduct research projects. The construction of the laboratory commenced in 2025 and is still in process. It focuses on research projects in IP. The lab aims to adopt an interdisciplinary approach to psychological research within the context of religion, specifically Islam. Beyond clinical psychology, it examines the psychological effects of Islamic beliefs, practices, and experiences on individuals and society within various subfields, including social, cultural, developmental, and cognitive psychology. Embracing a critical and reflective approach that challenges ontological and epistemological assumptions prioritizes the generation of need-based, evidence-driven knowledge. In this regard, the laboratory aims to develop innovative research models that adhere to scientific principles while being mindful of the specific needs of Muslim populations. The objective is to contribute to advancing academic knowledge and developing psychological approaches that address societal needs, specifically within an Islamic framework.

ISIP Türkiye established the ISIP student club in 2021, which now has approximately 305 members at IZU. The club was established to unite university students from various fields interested in IP, promoting collaboration and advancing the IP movement in Türkiye through ISIP Türkiye, which has approximately 1,500 members in WhatsApp groups and over 10,000 views on its YouTube videos. Since its official launch on October 9, 2024, the club has organized events such as 'Meeting Tea with IP, Emotion Awareness Collage Workshop from Islamic Perspective, Fıtrat-Based Psychological Self-Care, Curiosities About the Act, Master's Degree Process in Turkey and Abroad, Fasting: Spiritual Balance and Spiritual Counselling, They organized various academic events, such as an

IP reading colloquium with Assist. Professor Ayşe Kaya Göktepe and workshops to comprehend the classical works of al-Ghazali with Professor Suleyman Derin. Brotherhood Iftar with ISIP Team, and others, with 305 participants, successfully met its objectives.

One of the key strengths of IZU was having Dr. Malik Badri as an IP professor from 2017 to 2021. He taught IP to psychology students during his tenure and organized the IP Summer School twice, open to external applicants. In addition, he organized the IP Conference in 2018, hosting prominent global academics who have significantly contributed to the field. Furthermore, he offered the first Islamically Oriented Counseling certificate program in 2019, in collaboration with IAIP.

Publications

A few publications from our program include Dr. Malik Badri's (2021) Emotional Aspects in the Life of the Prophets, which analyzes the emotional lives of the prophets. It is a book of contemplation and exploration into the emotional lives of the prophets, examining God's wisdom in shaping their physical, psychological, and spiritual makeup from childhood to suit the trials of prophethood He would place upon them. It is a cognitive lesson on how to enter the world of the prophets, combining a precise scientific understanding of psychology—tested according to Qur'anic standards and vision—with faith rooted in the emotions of love, awe, and hope, thereby harmonizing the cognitive, practical, and emotional dimensions. At the same time, Badri's compilation, Cultural Adaptation and Islamization of Psychology, provides a theoretical framework for the cultural adaptation of modern psychology to Islamic values (Badri, 2017a).

Badri co-authored the Trilingual Dictionary of Psychiatry and Psychology (Dictionary Annafssany), which strengthens the terminological infrastructure of education regarding terminological clarity and interdisciplinary communication (Badri, 2017b). In particular, the Qur'anic-based spiritual intelligence proposal by Bensaid et al. (2014) supports the theoretical basis of the program by structuring the relationship between IP and the cognitive-emotional domain.

Kaya-Göktepe's translation of Malik Badri's commentary on Abu Zayd al-Balkhî's The Sustenance of the Soul emphasizes historical continuity by drawing attention to the Islamic roots of cognitive behavioral approaches (Al-Balkhi, 2025). Finally, Kaya-Göktepe's (2025) paper examines the therapeutic impact of classical Turkish music not solely through the structure of its modal system (makams) but more significantly through the spiritual and moral training undergone by the mutrıb (performer) within the framework of the meşk system (traditional Turkish education system of music). It argues that this pedagogical and ethical formation, rooted in the Sufi tradition of the shaykh–murid relationship, constitutes the essential foundation of the meşk system that enables music to serve as a healing medium in Ottoman Sifahanes. Much like the process by which a modern psychotherapist must undergo their inner analysis before guiding others, the mutrıb (music player) must also experience a transformative journey ethically and spiritually, which enables them to transmit not merely sound but soul-level resonance through the music (Kaya-Göktepe, 2025).

Discussion

IZU has pioneered interdisciplinary graduate programs that combine psychological counselling, classical Islamic sciences, and spiritual care. The Master's in Spiritual Counselling & Guidance and MA & PhD in Philosophy and Religious Sciences offer a unique focus that aims to combine modern psychological methods with the intellectual heritage of Islam. However, the interdisciplinary nature that distinguishes these programs also poses significant theoretical, practical, and institutional challenges, such as bringing together different epistemological traditions, overcoming language barriers arising from classical texts, linking academic training with professional standards, and constructing a distinctive identity in IP.

The academic qualifications, strengths, the studies carried out in IP at IZU, and the mission of the university are presented above. Although the presence of Malik Bedri, who is considered the founder of IP, at IZU is undoubtedly a turning point, it is also a fact that some limitations may slow down the momentum in this field. These issues will be addressed in detail below, and the discussion section will present strategic approaches to the current challenges of the department, solutions to these challenges, and opportunities for inter-institutional collaboration.

Challenges of the Program

The main challenge of the Master's programs in Spiritual Counseling & Guidance and Philosophy and Religious Studies lies in their interdisciplinary curriculum, which combines psychological counseling, Islamic thought, and spiritual care. Balancing modern psychological methods with classical Islamic sciences demands a high level of multidisciplinary competence. The differing philosophical foundations of these two fields pose additional challenges for students and Faculty.

Although there is a scientific preparatory program for students holding BA and BS degrees in different scientific disciplines aimed at increasing their knowledge in religious sciences/psychology, it extends the duration of education and creates an academic burden. Students without a religious background often struggle in theology courses due to differences in knowledge levels, which may deter applicants from non-religious disciplines.

IP courses are included in these programs. However, the lack of a dedicated master's program hinders the development of a specialized identity and the in-depth exploration of Islam-based therapeutic models. In Türkiye, the term "psychology of religion" is often associated with Islamic content, potentially leading to the lack of an independent title for "Islamic Psychology." While the Certificate Programme in IP offers a general framework in a short-term and intensive structure, it falls short in practical skills and mentorship, making applying learned knowledge in professional settings challenging.

Strategic Suggestions for the Institutional and Pedagogical Development of Islamic Psychology Training Programs

It is evident that interest in IP has increased significantly in the past decade. However, challenges remain due to the lack of a universally accepted definition, the dominance of Westernized scholarship, and the utilization of classical sources in Arabic, Persian, and Ottoman Turkish is impeded by the language barrier. Badri (2020) noted that these issues can be addressed through interdisciplinary approaches and East-West academic collaboration. For IP to be recognized as a distinct field, well-structured MA and PhD programs must be established. Academic representation is essential for developing practical models and modalities for therapists, as well as for attracting researchers considering an academic career in this area.

While it is valuable to include courses on IP in existing postgraduate programs, creating an independent curriculum that comprehensively addresses the theoretical foundations, methodological approaches, and practical dimensions of the field is crucial for both academic depth and the formation of a professional identity. Current IP programs usually integrate research methods from modern psychology along with knowledge from Islamic sciences, such as Hadith, Sirah, and Tafseer. However, while the approach of IP aims to synthesize insights from both domains, it is often covered in isolated courses rather than through an integrated curriculum.

Furthermore, there is an urgent need to develop a hybrid methodology specific to IP, as it combines distinct ontological and epistemological foundations. This methodology should integrate scientific research methods with principles derived from Islamic legal theory (usul al-fiqh). Since classical texts are primarily written in Arabic, Persian, and Ottoman Turkish, students must also learn these languages. Additionally, since contemporary psychological research is predominantly conducted in English, proficiency in academic English is essential.

Collaboration with public institutions is vital to ensure that graduates of IP programs have clear career paths and a positive social impact. Official roles such as "spiritual counselor" or "Islamic psychological counselor" should be formally defined within sectors such as health, education, and religious services. In Türkiye, no official definition existed; only those recognized as spiritual counselors can apply their IP knowledge in professional settings. Furthermore, most accredited therapy models in psychology originate from Western cultures and are based on Western epistemology and ontology.

The establishment of international accreditation boards is imperative to ensure the proper oversight of applications of IP in the field. These boards would pave the way for global accreditation by providing representative offices in various countries. Like the American Psychological Association (APA), International Association of Islamic Psychologists conduct studies on accreditation of master's and doctoral programs in IP as well. These programs should adhere to specific standards to prevent the field from becoming marginalized, helping to integrate diverse elements, such as cultural interpretations and procedural differences.

Conclusion

The PRS and SCG Master's programs at IZU exemplify the essence of IP by blending rigorous scientific methods with classical Islamic sciences. These programs provide applied case analyses and structured mentorship, forging a hybrid approach that combines fiqh-based epistemology with modern research practices.

To firmly establish IP within academia and practice, and to translate these strengths into lasting social impact, IZU should launch dedicated MA and PhD programs in IP. These programs should be seamlessly integrated with existing certificate offerings and complemented by partnerships with public and private practice sites.

Such strategic expansion will create clear career pathways for graduates, foster a homegrown group of specialists, and meet the urgent demand for qualified spiritual counselors, educators, and therapists. This will ensure both the academic rigor of the field and its relevance in the real world.

With its extensive collection of original IP manuscripts and active collaborations with leading international scholars in Türkiye, IZU is exceptionally well-positioned to establish a standalone, independent IP program. The university libraries and other libraries in Istanbul contain original manuscripts of foundational texts, providing ready access to primary sources and the latest literature on IP. Furthermore, the Psychology of Religion and Spirituality Laboratory maintains strong collaborations with prominent IP scholars abroad, making IZU a guardian of tradition and a global hub for research and practice.

References

Abdul Rahim, N.M. (2005). Construction of an intelligence test based on Ibn-al Jawzi's book on intelligence. Unpublished PhD thesis, University of Khartoum.

Abdulhamid AbuSulayman Kulliyyah Islamic Revealed Knowledge and Human Sciences. (2023). *Study Plan for Bachelor of Human Sciences in Psychology (Honors) (Cohort 231xxx onwards)*. International Islamic University Malaysia. Retrieved from: https://kulliyyah.iium.edu.my/ahaskirkhs/wp-content/uploads/sites/7/2023/09/PSYC-231-Study-Plan-.pdf

Abdullah, S. (2002). Islamic Counseling and Psychotherapy: Trends in Theory Development. Retrieved January 10, 2009, from World Wide Web: http://www.cresentlife.com/articles/htm

Abdullah, S. (2007). Islam and counseling: models of practice in Muslim communal life. *Journal of Pastoral Counseling, 42*.

Abi-Hashem, N. (2007). The agony, silent grief, and deep frustration of many communities in the Middle East: Challenges for coping and survival. In P.T.P. Wong & C. J. Wong (Eds.), *Handbook of multicultural perspectives on stress and coping* (pp. 457-486). New York: Springer.

About – Dar al-Shifaa. (2025). Dar-Al-Shifaa.com. https://dar-al-shifaa.com/about/

About Us. (2015). Nur Al-Habib Foundation. https://education.nuralhabib.org/pages/about-us

Abramson, P., & Inglehart, R. F. (2009). Value Change in Global Perspective. In Google Books. University of Michigan Press.

Abu Hatab, F. (1992). Nahw wijha Islamiyya l-'ilm al-nafs (Towards an Islamic Paradigm for Psychology). *AlMuslim AlMuasir, 62*, 135–184.

Abu Hindi, W. (2002). *Nahw tibb nafsi Islami* (Towards an Islamic psychiatry). Nahdet Misr Publishing Group.

Abu-Raiya, H., & Pargament, K. I. (2010). Empirically based psychology of Islam: Summary and critique of the literature. *Mental Health, Religion & Culture, 14*(2), 93–115. https://doi.org/10.1080/13674670903426482

AbuSulayman, A.H. (1993). Crisis in the Muslim Mind. *International Institute of Islamic Thought*, Herndon, VA.

Academic Management and Admission Division. (2023). *Student academic performance evaluation (undergraduate) regulations 2021*. International Islamic University Malaysia. Retrieved from: https://division.iium.edu.my/amad/wp-content/uploads/sites/2/2023/11/SAPER-2021-as-of-24-Feb2023-496th-Senate-Meeting.pdf

Academic Management and Admission Division. (2024a). *IIUM Catalogue 2024*. International Islamic University Malaysia. Retrieved from https://photos.iium.edu.my/flip/ijazah/

Academic Management and Admission Division. (2024b). *Bachelor degree programs –International*. International Islamic University Malaysia. Retrieved from https://division.iium.edu.my/amad/admission-2/

Academic Management and Admission Division. (2024c). *Bachelor degree program Malaysian local student. International Islamic University*

Malaysia. Retrieved from: https://division.iium.edu.my/amad/wp-content/uploads/sites/2/2024/08/2.1.2-UG-Local-same-rate-11.pdf

Academic Management and Admission Division. (2024d). Bachelor degree program international and permanent resident. *International Islamic University Malaysia*. Retrieved from: https://division.iium.edu.my/amad/wp-content/uploads/sites/2/2024/08/2.4.2-UG-International-After-Discount-Sem-1-2024-2025.pdf

Achour, M., Grine, F., Mohd Nor, M. R., & Mohd Yusoff, M. Y. Z. (2015). Measuring religiosity and its effects on personal well-being: a case study of Muslim female academicians in Malaysia. *Journal of religion and health, 54*(3), 984-997.

Ahmad, A. (2009). Global ethics, environmentally applied: An Islamic view. In King-Tak Ip (Ed.), *Environmental ethics: An intercultural perspective* (pp. 93–112). Rodopi.

Ahmad, A. (2012). Islamization of knowledge: A futurist perspective. In I. Yusuf (Ed.), *Islam and knowledge: Al-Faruqi's concept of religion in Islamic thought*. I.B. Tauris.

Ahmad, A. (2013). A global ethics for a globalized world. *Policy Perspectives*, 63-77.

Ahmad, F., AlZeben, F., Kattan, W., Alyahyawi, H. Y., & Hassan, A. N. (2023). Prevalence, Correlates, and Impact of Psychiatric Disorders and Treatment Utilization Among Muslims in the United States: Results from the National Epidemiological Survey of Alcohol and Related Conditions. *Community Ment Health J, 59*(8), 1568-1577. https://doi.org/10.1007/s10597-023-01145-7

Ahmadi, A. A. (1983). *Fitrah: Islamic psychology foundation [Persian]*. Tehran: Amirkabir Publishing House.

Al-Faruqi, I. R. (1989). Islamization of Knowledge: General Principles and Work Plan, *International Institute of Islamic Thought*, Herndon, VA.

Al-Attas, M. N. (1980). The concept of education in Islam. Muslim Youth Movement of Malaysia Kuala Lumpur.

Al-Attas. S, M. N. (2001). *Risalah Untuk Kaum Muslimin*. Kuala Lumpur: ISTAC.

Al-Balkhi (2025). *Ebu Zeyd El-Belhî Psikolojik Sağlığın Korunması Risalesi 9. Yüzyıl Hekiminden Bilişsel Davranışçı Terapi*. (A. Kaya-Göktepe, Trans.) Mahya. Original Source: The Sustenance of the Soul (trans. M. Badri). IIP.

Al-Faruqi, I. R. (1987). Islamization of knowledge: General principles and work plan. *International Institute of Islamic Thought*.

Al-Faruqi, I. R. (1989). *Islamization of knowledge: General principles and work plan* (2nd ed., rev. & expanded; A. A. AbuSulayman, Ed.). International Institute of Islamic Thought.

Al-Ghazali, A. H. (2010). *The marvels of the heart* (W. J. Skellie, Trans.). Fons Vitae. (Original work published circa 1100)

Al-Ījī & Taşköprizade (2018). *Risalah al-Akhlāq*. Kuwait: Dar al-Deyaa.

Ale-Ishaaq, M. (1990). *Islam and Psychology* [Persian]. Qom: Al Ishaaq Publisher.

REFERENCES

Ali, S. S., Mahoui, I., Hassoun, R., Mojaddidi, H., & Awaad, R. (2023). The Bay Area Muslim mental health community advisory board: evaluation of a community based participatory approach. *Epidemiology and Psychiatric Sciences*, 32, e7.

Al-Krenawi, A., & Graham, J. R. (1997). Spirit possession and exorcism in the treatment of a Bedouin psychiatric patient. *Clinical Social Work Journal*, 25(2), 211-222.

Al-Najjar, A. (2002). *Al-Tasawwuf al-Nafsi* (Psychological Sufism). General Egyptian Book Organization.

Al-Qardawy, Y. (1979). *Al-Ibadah fie al-Islam*. Beirut: Muassasah al-Risalah.

Alsharif, N. Z., Galt, K., & Kasha, T. (2011). Health and healing practices for the Muslim community in Omaha, Nebraska. *Journal of Religion & Society. Supplement*, 7, 150-168.

Alyas, A. (2021). The establishment and growth of Islamic psychology in Malaysia. In A. Haque and A. Rothman (Eds.), *Islamic Psychology Around the Globe*, International Association of Islamic Psychology, Seattle, WA.

American Psychological Association. (2011). Principles for quality undergraduate education in psychology. *American Psychologist*, 66(9), 850–856. https://doi.org/10.1037/a0025181

American Psychological Association. (2023). Emerging trends in psychology for 2023. *American Psychological Association.* https://pages.apa.org/2023-trends-in-psychology/

Amri, S., & Bemak, F. (2012). Mental health help-seeking behaviors of Muslim immigrants in the United States: Overcoming social stigma and cultural mistrust. *Journal of Muslim Mental Health*, 7(1), 43-63.

Ansari, Z. A. (1992). Quranic Concepts of Human Psyche. New Delhi: Institute of Objective Studies.

Ansari, Z. I. (2006). *Towards understanding the Qur'an: Abridged version of Tafhim ul Qur'an by Sayyid Abul A'la Mawdudi.* The Islamic Foundation.

Arif, S. (2023). Rethinking the concept of Fiṭra. *American Journal of Islam and Society (AJIS)-Volume 40 Issues 3-4*, 40(3-4), 77-103.

Arthur, N. (2002). Preparing students for a world of work in cross-cultural transition. *Australian Journal of Career Development*, 11(1), 9–14. https://doi.org/10.1177/103841620201100104

Asy Syaikh, A. B. (2015). *Fathul Majid: Syarh kitab at-tauhid.* Jakarta: Darul Haq.

Auditing a Stanford Course | Stanford University Bulletin. (2024). Stanford.edu. https://bulletin.stanford.edu/academic-polices/enrollment/auditing

Awaad R, Obaid E, Kouser T, Ali S. Addressing Mental Health Through Community Partnerships in a Muslim Community (2023).*Psychiatry Serv*. 74(1):96-99. doi: 10.1176/appi.ps.202100505. Epub 2022 Sep 6. PMID: 36065581.

Awaad, R., & Ali, S. (2015). Obsessional Disorders in al-Balkhi's 9th century treatise: Sustenance of the Body and Soul. *Journal of Affective Disorders*, 180, 185–189. https://doi.org/10.1016/j.jad.2015.03.003

Awaad, R., & Ali, S. (2016). A modern conceptualization of phobia in al-Balkhi's 9th century treatise: Sustenance of the Body and Soul. *Journal of Anxiety Disorders*, 37, 89-93.

Awaad, R., & Ali, S. (2023). The original self-help book: Al-Balkhi's 9th century "Sustenance of the body and soul". *Spirituality in Clinical Practice, 10*(1), 89.

Awaad, R., Nursoy-Demir, M., Khalil, A., & Helal, H. (2023). Islamic civilizations and plagues: The role of religion, faith and psychology during pandemics. *Journal of Religion and Health, 62*(2), 1379-1393.

Awaad, R., Obaid, E., Kouser, T., & Ali, S. (2023). Addressing mental health through community partnerships in a Muslim community. *Psychiatric Services, 74*(1), 96-99.*Biographies – Ihsaan Therapeutic Services, Bradford.* (2017). Ihsaan.org.uk. https://ihsaan.org.uk/team/biographies/

Awaad, R. (2024). *Islamic Psychology, Spring 2024 Syllabus*. Courses | Muslim Mental Health & Islamic Psychology Lab | Stanford Medicine

Azarbayejani, M. (2023) Spiritual Health, Research Institute of Hawzah and University (RIHU).

Azarbayejani, M., Ahmadi, M., Gharavi, S. M., Salarifar, M., Narooei, R., Rafiei-Honar, H., et al. (2020). General details of the program and the title of the master's degree courses in Islamic psychology. Committee on Psychology and Religion in the Special Working Group on Psychology of the Council for the Transformation and Promotion of the Humanities of the MSRT of IRI [Persian-Unpublished], Unofficial Publication.

Badri, M. (1979). The Dilemma of Muslim Psychologists. MWH London Publishers.

Badri, M. (1996). Counseling and psychotherapy from an Islamic perspective. *Al-Shajarah: Journal of the International Institute of Islamic Thought and Civilization (ISTAC), 1*(1&2), 159–175.

Badri, M. (2002). The Islamization of Psychology its "why", its "what", its "how" and its "who". An article presented at the Islamic perspective of psychology inaugural conference organized by The Australian Society of Islamic Psychology. *Australia: University of Western Sydney.*

Badri, M. (2016). The Dilemma of Muslim Psychologists. London: MWH London Publishers.

Badri, M. (2017a). Cultural Adaptation and Islamization of Psychology: A Book of Collected Papers.

Badri, M. (2017b). Human Behavior Academy, Manchester. Dictionary Annafssany: Psychiatry and Psychology (Arabic, English, and French Dictionary of psychiatric and psychological terms), The Arab Federation of Psychiatry and the Arab Foundation of Psychological Sciences.

Badri, M. (2020). The Islamization of psychology: Its "why," its "what," its "how," and its "who." *International Journal of Islamic Psychology, 3*(1), 22–33. https://doi.org/10.33182/ijip.v3i1.1486

Badri, M. (2021). Emotional Aspects In The Life Of The Prophets: Psychological Revelations And Reflections. Istanbul S. Zaim University.

Bakar, O. (1998). *Classification of knowledge in Islam: A study in Islamic philosophies of science.* Cambridge: The Islamic Texts Society.

Bakhtiar, L. (2019). *Quranic psychology of the self: A textbook on Islamic moral psychology.* Chicago, Kazi Publications.

REFERENCES

Bastaman, H. D. (2005). Dari KALAM Sampai Ke API: Psikologi Islami Kemarin, Kini, Esok. *Jurnal Psikologi Islam, 1*(1), 5-16.

Bazzi, T., & Azarbayejani, M. (2023). The Ethical Responsibility of Elderly Care in Islamic Doctrine (Scope and Territory. *Quarterly Scientific Journal of Applied Ethics Studies, 19*(2), 37-64.

Bearn, G. C. (2000). Pointlessness and the University of Beauty. In P.A. Dhillon & P. Standish (Eds.), *Lyotard: Just Education,* pp. 230-256. Routledge.

Bensaid, B., Machouche, S. B. T., & Grine, F. (2014). A Qur'anic framework for spiritual intelligence. *Religions, 5*(1), 179-198.

Berghout, Abdul Aziz (2011) Values and education within the framework of Islamization of knowledge. In: Islamization, Ethics and Values in Science and Technology. IIUM Press, International Islamic University Malaysia, pp. 3-15. ISBN 9789670225821

Borhan, L., Azman, A. W., Mat Ghani, G., Abdullah, M. F., Abdul Rahman, Z., & Yusoff, Z. M. (2021). Sejahtera Academic Framework: Humanising Education for Rahmatan lil-Alamin Post-COVID 19 Disruption. *Gombak: International Islamic University Malaysia.*

Brown, D. T., Benson, A. J., Walker, N., Sternberger, L., Lung, D. S., & Kassinove, H. (2004). A systemic view of higher education and professional psychology: Implications of the Combined Integrated model of doctoral training. *Journal of Clinical Psychology, 60*(10), 1091–1103. https://doi.org/10.1002/jclp.20036

Cakir, C. (n.d.) Zaim Sabahattin, TDV Encyclopedia of Islam https://islamansiklopedisi.org.tr/zaim-sabahattin (Accessed April 22, 2025)

Calonge, D. S., Shah, M., Aguerrebere, P. M., Abdulla, N., Connor, M., Badr, M., & Blakemore, E. (2023). Should I stay or should I go? International students' challenges and opportunities to secure employment in their host country after graduation: A scoping review using PRISMA. *Journal of Applied Learning & Teaching, 6*(2), 1–24. https://doi.org/10.37074/jalt.2023.6.2.20

Cambridge Muslim College. (2023, August 10). Islamic psychology graduation ceremony 2023 [Video]. YouTube. https://www.youtube.com/watch?v=36EQoEVmAvk

Cambridge Muslim College. (2024). About Cambridge Muslim College. Retrieved May 15 from https://www.cambridgemuslimcollege.ac.uk/about/cmc

Cambridge Muslim College. (2025). Islam & Psychology. https://www.cambridgemuslimcollege.ac.uk/programmes/ipd/

Center for Comparative Studies in Race & Ethnicity. (2023). Stanford.edu; Stanford University. https://ccsre.stanford.edu

Choudhry, F. R., Khan, N., & Munawar, K. (2023). Barriers and facilitators to mental health care: A systematic review in Pakistan. *International Journal of Mental Health, 52*(2), 124-162.

Ciftci, A., Jones, N., & Corrigan, P. W. (2013). Mental health stigma in the Muslim community. *Journal of Muslim Mental Health, 7*(1), 17-32.

Clay, R.A. (2017). Women outnumber men in psychology, but not in the field's top echelons July/August. *Monitor in Psychology, 48,* 7.

Coşkun Çakır, "Zaim, Sabahattin", Retrieved April 22, 2025. TDV İslâm Ansiklopedisi, https://islamansiklopedisi.org.tr/zaim sabahattin

Daulay, N. (2014). Islamic education in the study of Islamic psychology. *Ar-Raniry: International Journal of Islamic Studies, 1*(2), 193–208. https://doi.org/10.20859/jar.v1i2.11

Dawkins, M. C. (2023). Declining enrolments—A call to action! *Issues in Accounting Education, 38*(1), 9–18. https://doi.org/10.2308/issues-2023-001

De Jesus Cortes, (A. (1999). Antecedents to the Conflict Between Psychology and Religion in America. *Journal of Psychology and Theology*, 27(1), 20-32.

Department of Psychology. (2023a). *Undergraduate curriculum review and development* [Unpublished manuscript]. Department of Psychology, AbdulHamid AbuSulayman Kulliyyah of Islamic Revealed Knowledge and Human Sciences, International Islamic University Malaysia.

Department of Psychology. (2023b). *Collegiate professionals.* International Islamic University Malaysia. Retrieved from: https://psychologyiium.wixsite.com/website/collegiate-professionals

DiClemente, C. C., & Delaney, H. D. (2005). Implications of Judeo-Christian Views of Human Nature, Motivation, and Change for the Science and Practice of Psychology. *In Judeo-Christian perspectives on psychology: Human nature, motivation, and change.* (pp. 271-308). American Psychological Association. https://doi.org/10.1037/10859-014

Doran, J. M., Kraha, A., Marks, L. R., Ameen, E. J., & El-Ghoroury, N. H. (2016). Graduate debt in psychology: A quantitative analysis. *Training and Education in Professional Psychology, 10*(1), 3–13. https://doi.org/10.1037/tep0000102

Dunn, D. S., McCarthy, M. A., Baker, S. C., Halonen, J. S., & Hill, G. (2007). Quality benchmarks in undergraduate psychology programs. *American Psychologist, 62*(7), 650–670. https://doi.org/10.1037/0003-066x.62.7.650

Dunn, D. S., Brewer, C. L., Cautin, R. L., Gurung, R., Keith, K. D., McGregor, L. N., Nida, S. A., Puccio, P., & Voigt, M. J. (2010). The undergraduate psychology curriculum: Call for a core. In D. F. Halpern (Ed.), *Undergraduate education in psychology: A blueprint for the future of the discipline* (pp. 47–61). American Psychological Association.

Ekman, P., & Goleman, D. (2007). *Knowing our emotions, improving our world: A conversation with Paul Ekman and Daniel Goleman.* More Than Sound Productions.

Elmahdi, M. (1990). *Al-'ilaj al-nafsi fi daw' al-Islam* (Psychotherapy in light of Islam). Dar Elwafaa.

Elmahdi, M. (2002a). *Mustawayat al-nafs* (Dimensions of the psyche). Dar El-Bitash.

El-Refaay, S. M., Kenny, C., & Weiss, S. (2025). Depression and Anxiety Among Arab Individuals in the United States: A Meta-analysis. *J Immigr Minor Health, 27*(2), 329-350. https://doi.org/10.1007/s10903-024-01648-9

REFERENCES

Elsdörfer, U. (2007). *Medizin, Psychologie und Beratung im Islam: Historische, tiefenpsychologische und systemische Annäherungen*. Königstein: Helmer.

Elzamzamy, K., Bader, R. K., & Bircan, F. B. (2024). Contemporary scholarship on classical Islamic psychology. *Journal of Muslim Mental Health, 18*(1), 4-44. https://doi.org/10.3998/jmmh.6025

Enriquez, V.G (1990) *Indigenous Psychology*, Diliman.

Finance Division. (2024). Scholarship and financial assistance available at IIUM. International Islamic University Malaysia. Retrieved from https://division.iium.edu.my/finance/scholarship/

GBD 2019 Mental Disorders Collaborators. (2022). Global, regional, and national burden of 12 mental disorders in 204 countries and territories, 1990-2019: a systematic analysis for the Global Burden of Disease Study 2019. *The Lancet Psychiatry, 9*(2), 137-150.

Gianotti, T. J. (2001). *Al-Ghazālī's Unspeakable Doctrine of the Soul: Unveiling the Esoteric Psychology and Eschatology of the Iḥyā'* (Vol. 104). Brill.

Goleman, D. (1996). *Emotional intelligence: Why it can matter more than IQ*. Bantam Books.

Greenfield, P. M. (2013). The changing psychology of culture from 1800 through 2000. *Psychological science, 24*(9), 1722-1731.

Hamid, R. (1977). Reflections on a balanced Islamic personality. In *From Muslim to Islamic: Proceedings of the First Symposium on Islam and Psychology* (Vol. 1).

Hanson, M. (2025). *Average Cost of a Master's Degree*. Retrieved on June 4th, 2025, from https://educationdata.org/average-cost-of-a-masters-degree

Haque, A. (1983). An Interview with B.F. Skinner. The Ninth Annual Convention of Applied Behavioral Analysis, May 23, Milwaukee, Wisconsin. URL: https://academia.edu/resource/work/1163884

Haque, A. (1996). Cognitive Restructuring of Muslim Psychologists Towards Developing a Firm Faith: A Prerequisite for Islamization of Psychology. *Islamic Thought and Scientific Creativity, 7*(4), 100-108.

Haque, A. (1997). National Seminar on Islamization of Psychology: Seminar Report, *Intellectual Discourse*, 5:1, 88-92.

Haque, A. (1998a). International Seminar on Counseling and Psychotherapy: Conference Report, *American Journal of Islamic Social Sciences*, 15:1, 153-157.

Haque, A. (1998b). Psychology and religion: Their relationship and integration from an Islamic perspective. *American Journal of Islam and Society, 15*(4), 97-116.

Haque, A. (2000). Psychology and Religion: Two Approaches to Positive Mental Health. *Intellectual Discourse*, 8(1), 81-94.

Haque, A. (2001a). Interface of Psychology and Religion: Trends and Development. *Counseling Psychology Quarterly*, 241-253.

Haque, A. (2001b). Psychology and Religion: Indicators of integration. *North American Journal of Psychology, 3*(1), 61-76.

Haque, A. & Masuan, K. A. (2002). Religious psychology in Malaysia. *International Journal for the Psychology of Religion*. 12:4, 277-289.

Haque, A. (2002). Psychology of Religion: Analyzing Religious Development, Orientation, and Negative Social Behaviors. *Indian Social Science Review,* 4(1), 25–42.

Haque A. (2002). Proposed Syllabus in Islamic Psychology. An article presented at the Islamic perspective of psychology inaugural conference organized by The Australian Society of Islamic Psychology. Australia: University of Western Sydney. Proposed Syllabus for Islamic Psychology

Haque, A. (2004). Psychology from Islamic perspective: Contributions of early Muslim scholars and challenges to contemporary Muslim psychologists. *Journal of Religion and Health,* 43(4), 357–377. https://doi.org/10.1007/s10943-004-4302-z

Haque, A. (2004). Religion and Mental Health: The Case of American Muslims. *Journal of Religion and Health. 43*(1), 45-58.

Haque, A. & Mohamed, Y. (Eds.). (2005). Psychology of Personality: Islamic Perspectives. Cengage Learning Asia.

Haque, A. (2005). Mental health concepts and program development in Malaysia. *Journal of Mental Health,* 14:2, 183-196.

Haque, A. (2006). Review of the Book: Counseling and Psychotherapy with Arabs and Muslims: A Culturally Sensitive Approach, by M. Dwairy. *Journal of Muslim Mental Health, 2,* 101–106.

Haque, A. (2007). Preserving cultural identity in the 21st century: Challenges to the Emirati youth. *Journal of Social Affairs, 24*(94), 13–31.

Haque, A. (2007). Psychotherapy and Soul-Searching: Responses to Spirituality Roundtable, *Psychoanalytic Perspectives.* 4(2). 49-58.

Haque, A. (2008). Culture-bound syndromes and healing practices in Malaysia. *Journal Of Mental Health, Religion, and Cultur*e. 11:7, 685-696.

Haque, A. and Keshavarzi, H. (2014). Integrating traditional healing methods in therapy: Enhancing cultural competence in working with Muslims in the West. *International Journal of Culture and Mental Health.* 7(3), 297-314.

Haque, A., Khan, F., Keshavarzi, H., & Rothman, A. E. (2016). Integrating Islamic traditions in modern psychology: Research trends in last ten years. *Journal of Muslim Mental Health, 10*(1).

Haque, A. (2018). Integration of Psychology and Theology. Guest lecture, Faculty of Theology, Aligarh Muslim University, Aligarh, India. Integration of Psychology and Theology

Haque, A. & Rothman, A. (Eds.). (2021). *Islamic Psychology Around the Globe.* International Association of Islamic Psychology. Seattle, WA.

Haque, A., & Mohamed, Y. (Eds.). (2022a). Psychology of Personality: Islamic Perspectives. International Association of Islamic Psychology, Seattle, WA.

Haque, A. (2022b). Islamic Counseling Mental Health Series Booklet 3, ICNA Relief, Muslim Family Services. Booklet3_ICNAS-compressed.pdf

Haque, A. (2023). Integrating Thanvi's counseling techniques in therapies. In A. Haque & A. Rothman (Eds.), *Clinical Applications of Islamic Psychology*

REFERENCES

(pp. 157–175). International Association of Islamic Psychology. Seattle, WA.

Haque, A. (2024). Integrating Thanvi's Counseling Techniques in Therapies. In A. Haque & A. Rothman (Eds). Clinical Applications of Islamic Psychology. IAIP Publishing, Seattle, USA.

Haque, A., Miri, S. J., Hassem, Z., Ismail, S., Akram, A., Di Bello, A., Elhawary, Y., Shadicky, Z., Salee, M. H., Aboobaker, S., Saragih, N. H., Saber, D., Bey, R., Fayyaz, F., & Benmebarek, Z. (2024, Feb. 7-8). Global survey of IP programs. *First Islamic Psychology Conference.* Hamad Bin Khalifa University, Doha, Qatar.

Haque, A. (2025). Shah Wali Ullah Dehlavi: Spiritual faculties, human dispositions, and self-transformation. *International Journal of Islamic Psychology, 8*(1), 25–41.

Haque, A. May 22, 2025. Islamic Psychology in the 21st Century [Keynote address], 3rd International Conference, Riphah International University, Islamabad, Pakistan. Islamic Psychology in the 21 st Century

Hassan, M. K. (2011). *Voice of Islamic moderation from the Malay world.* MPH Publishing. International Islamic University Malaysia. (2024a). *Background.* https://www.iium.edu.my/v2/background-2024/

Higher Education Commission (HEC). (2006). Revised Curriculum of Psychology for BS (Hons) 4-Year Program and MS (Hons) 2-Year Program. Retrieved from: https://www.google.com/url?sa=t&source=web&rct=j&url=h-ps://hec.gov.pk/english/services/universities/RevisedCurricula/Documents/2005-2006/ City%2520Regional-2006.pdf&ved=2ahUKEwj5krWTj-7uAhXSolwKHZmT CxkQFjABegQIGhAC&usg=AOvVaw1uYMPtJP82f PAveokAUER0

Hodge, D. R., Zidan, T., & Husain, A. (2023). How to Work with Muslim Clients in a Successful, Culturally Relevant Manner: A National Sample of American Muslims Share Their Perspectives. *Soc Work, 69*(1), 53-63. https://doi.org/10.1093/sw/swad048

Hoeft, T. J., Fortney, J. C., Patel, V., & Unützer, J. (2018). Task-sharing approaches to improve mental health care in rural and other low-resource settings: a systematic review. *The Journal of Rural Health, 34*(1), 48-62.

Hosseini, S. A. (1985). A Preliminary Study of the Principles of Islamic Psychology [Persian]. Mashhad: Astaan Quds Razavi.

Husain, M.G. (1996). Psychology and Society in Islamic Perspective, New Delhi: Institute of Objective Studies.

Husain, A., Nazam, F., & Khatoon, Z. (2018). *Manual: Islamic Counselling.* New Delhi: Global Vision Publishing House.

Husain, A. (2021). *Quranic Guidance, Therapy & Islamic Counselling Interventions.* New Delhi: Qazi Publishers & Distributors.

Husain, A., & Fakhr, R. (2023). *Religious and Spiritual Counselling.* New Delhi: Global Vision Publishing House.

International Islamic University Malaysia (IIUM). (2024b). *Philosophy.* https://www.iium.edu.my/v2/philosophy-2024/

International Islamic University Malaysia. (2024c). *Vision and mission.* https://www.iium.edu.my/v2/vision-and-mission-2024/

Iqbal, N., & Skinner, R. (2021). Islamic psychology: Emergence and current challenges. *Archive for the Psychology of Religion, 43*(1), 65–85. https://doi.org/10.1177/0084672420983496

Islamic Studies. (2025). Stanford.edu; Stanford University. https://islamicstudies.stanford.edu

Janbozorgi, M. (2021). Spirituality Multidimensional Psychotherapy, A God-oriented Approach. Research Institute of Hawzah and University (RIHU)

Jinn, L. C., Zaman, I. A. K., Zakaria, S., Mahali, S., & Aleng, N. A. (2022). Analysing the undergraduate enrolment pattern in Malaysian public universities using statistical methods. *Journal of Mathematical Sciences and Informatics, 2*(2), 1–16. https://doi.org/10.46754/jmsi.2022.12.001

Kamssu, A. J., & Kouam, R. B. (2021). The effects of the COVID-19 pandemic on university student enrollment decisions and higher education resource allocation. *Journal of Higher Education Theory and Practice, 21*(12), 143–153.

Kandaswamy, D. (2007). *Islamic ways of managing stress. Seven ways to deal with stress.*

Kaplick, P. M., & Skinner, R. (2017). The Evolving Islam and Psychology Movement. *European Psychologist, 22*(3), 198–204. https://doi.org/10.1027/1016-9040/a000297

Kaplick, P., Loucif, A., & Rüschoff, I. (2021). Islamic Psychology in Western Continental Europe: A top down approach. Islamic psychology around the globe, 324-349.

Karim, S., Saeed, K., Rana, M. H., Mubbashar, M. H., & Jenkins, R. (2004). Pakistan mental health country profile. *International Review of Psychiatry , 16*(1-2), 83–92. https://doi.org/10.1080/09540260310001635131

Karlson, T. (2017). PARSE. Parsejournal.com. Retrieved from https://parsejournal.com/article/the-idea-of-theuniversity-and-the-process-of-secularisation

Kaya- Göktepe (2025). Music Therapy and the Psychology of Religion: Exploring Soul Harmony in Ottoman Sifahanes. IAPR Conference 19-22 Aug 2025, Birmingham, UK

Keshavarzi, H., & Haque, A. (2013). Outlining a psychotherapy model for enhancing Muslim mental health within an Islamic context. *International Journal for the Psychology of Religion, 23*(3), 230-249.

Keshavarzi, H., & Khan, F. (2018). Outlining a case illustration of Traditional Islamically Integrated Psychotherapy (TIIP). In C.Y. Alkaram (Ed.), Islamically integrated psychotherapy: Uniting faith and professional practice. Pp. 175-207. Templeton Press.

Keshavarzi, H., Khan, F., Ali, B., & Awaad, R. (Eds.). (2020). *Applying Islamic principles to clinical mental health care: Introducing traditional Islamically integrated psychotherapy.* Routledge. https://www.mentalhealth.org.uk/your-mental-health/about-mental-health/what-are-mental-health-problems https://www.islam-psychologie.com/certificat-conseiller-psychologie-islamique

REFERENCES

Keshavarzi, H., Harfi, S., Elzamzamy, K., Khan, F., & Kaban, E. (2022). *The Islamic Workbook for Religious OCD (Waswasa): A Guide for Overcoming Intrusive Thoughts and Compulsions.* Claritas Books.

Keshavarzi, H., Aycan, S., Altinisik, E., Khan, F., & Elzamzamy, K. (2024). *The Islamic Workbook for Managing Anxiety,* Khalil Center. The Islamic Workbook for Managing Anxiety - Khalil Center

Keshavarzi, (2025). Khalil Center. https://khalilcenter.com/staff/dr-hooman-keshavarzi

Khalifa, O.H. (2001). Experimental Psychology in the Arab-Islamic Heritage: Arab Foundation for Studies and Publishing, Beirut.

Khalili, S. (2008). *Psychologie, Psychotherapie und Islam - Erste Entstehungsphasen einer Theorie aus islamischer Psychologie.* VDM Verlag.

Khalily, M.T. (2024). Maladies and Remedies of the Nafs. International Students of Islamic Psychology, Bing Videos

Khan, F., & Keshavarzi, H. (2023). Theoretical foundations and clinical applications of traditional Islamically integrated psychotherapy. In P. S. Richards, G. E. K. Allen, & D. K. Judd (Eds.), *Handbook of spiritually integrated psychotherapies* (pp. 193–212). American Psychological Association. https://doi.org/10.1037/0000338-010

Khan, F., Aycan, S., & Keshavarzi, H. (2023). *Clinical Applications of Traditional Islamically-Integrated Psychotherapy (TIIP) Model: Case of a Turkish female.* In Haque A. & Rothman A. (Eds.), *Islamic Psychology Around the Globe* (pp. 61- 90). International Association of Islamic Psychology. Seattle, WA.

Khan, F., Keshavarzi, H., Ahmad, M., Ashai, S., & Sanders, P. (2023). Application of Traditional Islamically Integrated Psychotherapy (TIIP) and its clinical outcome on psychological distress among American Muslims in outpatient therapy. *Spirituality in Clinical Practice. 12*(2), 147 – 160. Retrieved from: https://doi.org/10.1037/scp0000350

Khan, F. (2025). Islamic Psychology: The Missing Link in Muslim Mental Health. In A. Haque (Ed.), *Muslim Mental Health in North America* (pp. 95-116). Muslim Mental Health Consortium, Department of Psychiatry, Michigan State University.

Khan, S. (2023). The iron dome of Eurocentrism: a decolonial reconnaissance of academic imperialism in Pakistan. *Third World Quarterly, 1*(1), 1–16. https://doi.org/10.1080/01436597.2023.2216644

Khan, S. H., Khalily, M. T., & Hussain, B. (2024). Effectiveness of indigenously developed clinical supervision in therapeutic setting. *Journal of Professional & Applied Psychology* , 5(2), 184–190. https://doi.org/10.52053/jpap.v5i2.260

Khatib, M. A. & Shennan, A.M. (2003). Introduction to Psychology. *The Open University of Sudan Publications.*

Kiguwa, P. & Segalo, P. (2018). Decolonizing psychology in residential and open distance e-learning institutions: Critical reflections. *South African Journal of Psychology,* 48(3), 310–318. https://doi.org/10.1177/0081246318786605

Koenig, H. G., & Shohaib, S. A. (2014). Muslim beliefs, practices, and values. In *Health and Well-being in Islamic Societies: Background, Research, and Applications* (pp. 27-41). Cham: Springer International Publishing.

Kuhn, T.S (2015). The Structure of Scientific Revolutions, University of Chicago Press.

Langgulung, H. (1983). *Teori-teori kesihatan mental: Perbandingan psikologi modern dan pendekatan pakar-pakar pendidikan Islam.* Kajang, Malaysia: Penerbit Pustaka Huda.

Langgulung, H. (1989). Research in psychology: Toward an ummatic paradigm. In International Institute of Islamic Thought (IIIT) (Ed.), *Toward Islamization of disciplines* (pp. 115-130).

Lee, K. C. (2013). Training and educating international students in professional psychology: What graduate programs should know? *Training and Education in Professional Psychology,* 7(1), 61–73. https://doi.org/10.1037/a0031186

Long, W. (2014). Critical reflections on the islamicisation of psychology. *Revelation and Science,* 4. https://journals.iium.edu.my/revival/index.php/revival/article/view/104

Lyotard, J. (1982). Presenting the unpresentable; the sublime. *Artforum.*

Madani, R. H. (2016). Islamization of Science. *International Journal of Islamic Thought, 9,* 51-63.

Magid, M. (n.d.) 'Counselling couple', Rahmaa Institute. Online at www.rahmaa.org/counseling/family counseling-couple/. Originally: Islamic Society of North America, www.isna,net (accessed October 15, 2014).

Mahmoud, A. (1990). *Nahw dustur 'amal li-'ulama' al-nafs al-muslimin* (Towards an Operational
Constitution for Muslim Psychologists). *Rabitat Al-Tarbiya Al-Haditha, 23,* 144–117.

Majariyya, A., Shalabi, A., Al-Shinnawi, U., Ziyada, K., Morsi, S., Anwar, A., Abd Al-Ghaffar, G., Abu Al-Makarim, F., Idris, M., Abd Al-Wahhab, N., Abd Al-Tawwab, N., Hanafi, H., Husain, N. A., Al-Sayyid, A. M., Farag, T. S., & Mahmoud, A. S. (2011). *'Ilm al-nafs fi al-turath al-Islami* (Psychological sciences in the Islamic heritage) (Vol. 4). Dar Al Salam/International Institute of Islamic Thought.

Malaysian Qualifications Agency. (2024). *Malaysian Qualifications Framework (MQF)* (2nd ed.). Malaysian Qualifications Agency.

Malaysian Qualifications Agency. (2025). *Malaysian Qualifications Register: Bachelor of Human Sciences in Psychology (Honors) [Previously known as Bachelor of Human Sciences Psychology (Honors)].* Retrieved from https://www2.mqa.gov.my/mqr/english/epapariptaAA.cfm?IDAkrKP=16877

McGinty, E. E., Alegria, M., Beidas, R. S., Braithwaite, J., Kola, L., Leslie, D. L., Moise, N., Mueller, B., Pincus, H. A., Shidhaye, R., Simon, K., Singer, S. J., Stuart, E. A., & Eisenberg, M. D. (2024). The Lancet Psychiatry Commission: transforming mental health implementation research. *The*

REFERENCES

Lancet. Psychiatry, *11*(5), 368–396. https://doi.org/10.1016/S2215-0366(24)00040-3

McLaughlin, M. M., Ahmad, S. S., & Weisman de Mamani, A. (2022). A mixed-methods approach to psychological help-seeking in Muslims: Islamophobia, self-stigma, and therapeutic preferences. *J Consult Clin Psychol*, *90*(7), 568-581. https://doi.org/10.1037/ccp0000746

Merter, M. (2014). *Psikolojinin üçüncü boyutu nefs psikolojisi ve rüyaların dili* (1st ed.). The Third Dimension of Psychology, the Psychology of Nafs and the Language of Dreams. Kaknüs Yayınları.

Merter, M. (2016). *Dokuz yüz katlı insan: Tasavvuf ve benötesi psikolojisi.* Nine Hundred Layers of a Human; Sufism and Transpersonal Psychology. (15th ed.). Kaknüs Yayınları.

Ministry of Higher Education Malaysia. (2022). *Higher Education Report: Malaysia.* UNESCO National Commission.

Mir, G., Meer, S., Cottrell, D., McMillan, D., House, A., & Kanter, J. W. (2015). Adapted behavioural activation for the treatment of depression in Muslims. *Journal of Affective Disorders*, *180*, 190–199. https://doi.org/10.1016/j.jad.2015.03.060

Mitha, K. (2020). Approaches from the Islamic Golden Age. *Journal of Muslim Mental Health*, *8*(3), 105-120.

Morsi, S. (1983). *Al-Nafs Al-Mutma'inna* (The peaceful soul). Maktabat Wahba.

Mueller, J., Taylor, H. K., Brakke, K., Drysdale, M., Kelly, K., Levine, G. M., & Ronquillo-Adachi, J. (2020). Assessment of scientific inquiry and critical thinking: Measuring APA goal 2 student learning outcomes. *Teaching of Psychology*, *47*(4), 274–284. https://doi.org/10.1177/0098628320945114

Murken, S., & Shah, A. A. (2002). Naturalistic and Islamic Approaches to Psychology, Psychotherapy, and Religion: Metaphysical Assumptions and Methodology—A Discussion. *The International Journal for the Psychology of Religion*, *12*(4), 239–254.

Muslim Mental Health and Islamic Psychology at Stanford. (n.d.). Muslim Mental Health & Islamic Psychology Lab. https://med.stanford.edu/mmhip.html

Mustaqim, A. (2024). *Tafsir ekologi: Relasi eko-teologis Tuhan, manusia, dan alam.* Bantul: Damai.

Naufel, K. Z., Appleby, D. C., Young, J., Van Kirk, J. F., Spencer, S. M., Rudmann, J., & Richmond, A. S. (2018). The skillful psychology student: Prepared for success in the 21st-century workplace. *American Psychological Association.* https://www.apa.org/careers/resources/guides/transferable-skills.pdf

Nelson, J. M. (2009). Introduction to psychology, religion, and spirituality. In *Psychology, Religion, and Spirituality* (pp. 3-41). New York, NY: Springer New York.

Noor, N. M. (Ed.). (2009). Psychology from an Islamic Perspective: A Guide to Teaching and Learning. IIUM Press.

Office of the Deputy Rector (Student Development & Community Engagement). (2025). *Student clubs & societies.* International Islamic University Malaysia. Retrieved from: https://odrsdce.iium.edu.my/student-clubs-society/

Padela, A. I., Killawi, A., Forman, J., DeMonner, S., & Heisler, M. (2012). American Muslim perceptions of healing: key agents in healing, and their roles. *Qual Health Res*, *22*(6), 846-858. https://doi.org/10.1177/1049732312438969

Parkinson, S. (2004). Training and practicing standards for educational psychologists in the Republic of Ireland. *School Psychology International*, *25*(4), 439–454. https://doi.org/10.1177/0143034304048778

Phiri, P., Sajid, S., & Delanerolle, G. (2023). Decolonising the Psychology Curriculum: A Perspective. *Frontiers in Psychology*, *14*. https://doi.org/10.3389/fpsyg.2023.1193241

Rafiei-Honar, H. (2018*). Self-Regulation Therapeutic Pattern for Depression Based on Islamic Sources: Conceptual Modelling, Treatment Protocol Development, Feasibility, and Reviewing its Preliminary Results.* PhD Thesis [Persian-Unpublished]. Qom: IKERI.

Rafiei-Honar, H. & Azerbaijani, M. (2021). Islamic Psychology in Iran: Past, Present and Future (2021). In *A. Haque & A. Rothman, Islamic Psychology Around the Globe*. IAIP, Seattle, WA.

Rafiei-Honar, H., & Azarbayejani, M. (2023). Islamic psychology in Iran: Past, present, and Future. *Journal of Islamic Psychology*, *9*(18), 47-82.

Rafiei Honar, H., & Azarbayejani, M. (2025). Lived experience of designing and holding the training courses of CCIP & SSIP. Written by Hamid Rafiei Honar, faculty number of the Islamic Sciences and Culture Academy (ISCA).

Ragab, I. A. (1999). On the methodology of islamizing the social sciences. *Intellectual Discourse*, *7*(1). https://doi.org/10.31436/id.v7i1.309

Rahmanto, S. W., Fachrunisa, R. A., & Suseno, B. (2024). Khushoo in Salah: An overview of Nafs (Islamic psychological perspective). *Asian Journal of Islamic Psychology*, 8-14.

Rania Awaad, MD | Stanford Medicine. (2021). CAP Profiles. https://med.stanford.edu/profiles/Rania_Awaad

Rassool, G. H. (2009). *Alcohol and drug misuse: a handbook for students and health professionals*. Routledge.

Rassool, G. H. (2015). Cultural competence in counseling the Muslim patient: Implications for mental health. *Archives of Psychiatric Nursing*, *29*(5), 321-325.

Rassool, G. Hussein. (2016). *Islāmic Counselling: From Theory to Practice*. Oxford: Routledge.

Rassool, G. H. (2018). *Towards the Development of a Theoretical Framework and Model of Islamic Psychotherapy and Counselling: Challenges and Opportunities*. (Unpublished paper).

Rassool, G. Hussein. (2020). Cognitive Restructuring of Psychology: The Case for A Vertical and Horizontal Integrated, Embedded Curriculum Model for Islāmic Psychology. *Islāmic Studies, 59*(4),477-494.

Rassool, G. Hussein., (2020). Towards a redefinition of Islāmic Psychotherapy and Counselling. Lecture at Al-Balagh Academy. *Islāmic Counselling and Psychology-Level 2*. July 2020.

REFERENCES

Rassool, G. H. (2021). Re-examining the anatomy of Islamic psychotherapy and counselling: Envisioned and enacted practices. *Islamic Guidance and Counseling Journal,* *4*(2), 133–143. https://doi.org/10.25217/igcj.v4i2.1840

Rassool, G. Hussein. (2021). Decolonizing Psychology and Its (dis) contents, in G. Hussein Rassool. *Islāmic Psychology: Human Behavior and Experiences from an Islāmic Perspective.* Routledge (pp. 583–601).

Rassool, G. H., & Luqman, M. M. (2022). *Foundations of Islamic psychology: From classical scholars to contemporary thinkers.* Routledge. Retrieved from: https://doi.org/10.4324/9781003181415

Rassool, G. Hussein. (2023a). *Advancing Islāmic Psychology Education: Knowledge Integration, Model, and Application.* 1st Edition. Focus Series on Islāmic Psychology & Psychotherapy. Routledge.

Rassool, G. Hussein. (2023b). *Islāmic Psychology: The Basics.* Routledge.

Rassool, G. H. (2024). Exploring the intersection of Islāmic spirituality and psychotherapy. *Cham: Springer.*

Rassool, G. H. (2024). Islāmic counselling and psychotherapy: An introduction to theory and practice. Routledge.

Rassool, G. Hussein. (2025). *Islāmic Counselling and Psychotherapy: From Theory to Practice.* 2nd *Edition.* Oxford: Routledge.

Rayan, S. (2012)., Islāmic Philosophy of Education. *International Journal of Humanities and Social Science, 2*(19), 150-156

Readings, B., & Marsden, G. M. (1996). The University in Ruins. *Nature, 382*(6588), 219-219.

Renima, A., Tiliouine, H., & Estes, R. J. (2016). The Islamic Golden Age: A Story of the Triumph of the Islamic Civilization. *The State of Social Progress of Islamic Societies,* 25–52. https://doi.org/10.1007/978-3-319-24774-8_2

Reyes, A., Tureson, K., Arias, J., Peraza, J., Gonzalez, D. A., Lerner, D., & Santos, C. (2019). Barriers and concerns regarding board certification in clinical neuropsychology: A program evaluation. *Archives of Clinical Neuropsychology,* *34*(7), 1304-1304. https://doi.org/10.1093/arclin/acz029.71

Riaazi, H (1981). Education based on Islamic Psychology [Persian]. Tehran: Ganjineh (Treasure).

Richards, G. (2011). *Psychology, religion, and the nature of the soul: A historical entanglement.* Springer.

Riyad, S. (2004a). *Ilm al-nafs fi al-Quran al-Karim* (Psychology in the Holy Quran). Iqraa Establishment for Publishing and Distribution.

Riyad, S. (2004b). *Ilm al-nafs fi al-hadith al-sharif* (Psychology in the Hadith tradition). Iqraa Establishment for Publishing and Distribution.

Rothman, A., & Coyle, A. (2018). Toward a framework for Islamic psychology and psychotherapy: An Islamic model of the soul. *Journal of Religion and Health, 57*(5), 1731–1744. https://doi.org/10.1007/s10943-018-0651-x

Rothman, A., & Coyle, A. (2020). Conceptualizing an Islamic psychotherapy: A grounded theory study. *Spirituality in Clinical Practice, 7*(3), 197.

Rothman, A. (2021). Developing a Model of Islamic Psychology and Psychotherapy: Islamic Theology and Contemporary Understandings of Psychology (1st ed.). Routledge. https://doi.org/10.4324/9781003104377

Rothman, A., Ahmed, A., & Awaad, R. (2022). The Contributions and Impact of Malik Badri. *American Journal of Islam and Society, 39*(1-2), 190–213. https://doi.org/10.35632/ajis.v39i1-2.3142

Rothman, A. | *Cambridge Muslim College*. (2023, October 12). Cambridge Muslim College | Faith in Scholarship. https://www.cambridgemuslimcollege.ac.uk/aer/

Rothman, A., Mamat, Z., Dean, S., & Khan, I. (book forthcoming). Examining practitioner's educational experience in an Islamic psychology training program: A mixed-methods feasibility study.

Riyad, S. (2004a). *'Ilm al-nafs fi al-Quran al-Karim* (Psychology in the Holy Quran). Iqraa Establishment For Publishing & Distribution.

Riyad, S. (2004b). *'Ilm al-nafs fi al-hadith al-sharif* (Psychology in the Hadith tradition). Iqraa Establishment for Publishing & Distribution.

Rüschoff, I., & Kaplick, P. M. (2018). Integrating Islamic Spirituality into Psychodynamic Therapy with Muslim Patients. In C. York Al-Karam (Ed.), *Islamically integrated psychotherapy: Uniting faith and professional practice* (pp. 127-151). West Conshohocken, PA: Templeton Press.

Saad, M., Medeiros, R. de, & Mosini, A. C. (2017). Are we ready for a true biopsychosocial–spiritual model? The many meanings of "spiritual." *Medicines, 4*(4), 79–85. https://doi.org/10.3390/medicines4040079

Safi, L. (1993). The quest for an Islamic methodology: The Islamization of knowledge project in its second decade. *American Journal of Islamic Social Sciences, 10*(1), 23-48.

Safi, L. (2014). *The foundation of knowledge: A Comparative study in Islamic and western methods of inquiry*. Retrieved from: https://books.google.com/books?hl=en&lr=&id=WitcCgAAQBAJ&oi=fnd&pg=PA15&dq=the+foundation+of+K+n+o+w+l+e+d+g+e+safi&ots=fEf1Eq47eq&sig=yQseD6RJlv4XcaosPQWMvc6YtRg

Şahin, A. (2013). Reflections on the possibility of an Islamic psychology. *Archive for the Psychology of Religion, 35*(3), 321–347. https://doi.org/10.1163/15736121-12341270

Salem, M. O. (2009, January 13–15). An Islamic theory for the mind (p. 83). *The 5th SELF International Biennial Conference, Book of Abstracts*, Al Ain, UAE.

Salem, M. O. (2010). Integrating spiritual techniques into psychotherapy—Islamic model (p. 129). *Proceedings of the 1st International Conference of Saudi Psychiatric Association*, Al Khobar, Saudi Arabia.

Saleem, T. & Khalily, M. T. (2021)., A Journey from Muslim Psychology to Islamic Psychology in Pakistan. In *A. Haque & A. Rothman (Eds.), Islamic Psychology Around the Globe*. International Association of Islamic Psychology. 213-227. Seattle, WA.

Saliba, G. (2006). Essay Review: Islamic Science at its Best: In Synchrony with the Heavens: Studies in Astronomical Timekeeping and Instrumentation in

REFERENCES

Medieval Islamic Civilization, i: The Call of the Muezzin, in Synchrony with the Heavens: Studies in Astronomical Timekeeping and Instrumentation in Medieval Islamic Civilization, ii: Instruments of Mass Calculation. *Journal for the History of Astronomy, 37*(2),233–238. https://doi.org/10.1177/002182860603700209

Sempértegui, G. A., Baliatsas, C., Knipscheer, J. W., & Bekker, M. H. J. (2023). Depression among Turkish and Moroccan immigrant populations in Northwestern Europe: a systematic review of prevalence and correlates. *BMC Psychiatry, 23*(1), 402. https://doi.org/10.1186/s12888-023-04819-4

Shafan-Azhar, Z., Suh, J. W., Delamain, H., Arundell, L. L., Naqvi, S. A., Knight, T.,…Buckman, J. E. J. (2025). Psychological Therapy Outcomes and Engagement in People of Different Religions. *JAMA Netw Open, 8*(4), e254026. https://doi.org/10.1001/jamanetworkopen.2025.4026

Shafii, M. & Shafii, M. (1985). *Freedom from the Self: Sufism, Meditation and Psychotherapy*. Human Sciences Press.

Shennan, A.M. (2002). The Islamic Religious Character Scale: Development and Psychometric Properties. A preliminary study in a Sudanese sample. *Tafkur, 4*(1).

Shoemaker, B. J. E. (1989). Integrative education: A curriculum for the twenty-first century. *OSSC Bulletin, 33*(2), n2.

Skinner, R. (2018). Traditions, paradigms, and basic concepts in Islamic psychology. *Journal of Religion and Health, 58*(4), 1087–1098. https://doi.org/10.1007/s10943-018-0595-1

Skinner, R. (2019). Traditions, paradigms and basic concepts in Islamic psychology. *Journal of religion and health, 58*(4), 1087-1094.

Skinner. A.R. (2025, February 16). Al Balagh Academy. https://www.albalaghacademy.org/ustaad/professor-abdur-rasjid-skinner/

Smith, R. (1997). *The norton history of the human sciences*. W. W. Norton.

Sobron, S., Jinan, M., & Taufik, T. (2017). *Islam and Ipteks*. Surakarta: Muhammadiyah University Press.

Sotillos, S. B. (2021). The decolonization of psychology or the science of the soul. *Spirituality Studies, 7*(1), 18–37.

Steinmetz, C. H. D. (2022). Psychology of Coloured People: A Critical Note to the Dominance of Euro-American-Oriented Psychology over the Psychology of Non-Western Countries. *Advances in Social Sciences Research Journal, 9*(3), 179–198.https://doi.org/10.14738/assrj.93.12035

Stoloff, M. L., Curtis, N. A., Rodgers, M., Brewster, J., & McCarthy, M. A. (2012). Characteristics of successful undergraduate psychology programs. *Teaching of Psychology, 39*(2), 91–99. https://doi.org/10.1177/0098628312437721

Suseno, B. (2024). Muslim prayer (Salah), and its restorative effect: Psychophysiological explanation. *Asian Journal of Islamic Psychology*, 1-7.

Szkody, E., Hobaica, S., Owens, S., Boland, J., Washburn, J. J., & Bell, D. (2023). Financial stress and debt in clinical psychology doctoral students. *Journal*

of Clinical Psychology, 79(3), 835–853. https://doi.org/10.1002/jclp.23464
Taha, A.H., & Salama, A.H. (2006). *Strategies of educational and psychological stress*. Jordan: First version, Dar Al-Fikr.
Taha, Z.B. (1995). Psychology in Arab-Islamic Heritage. University of Khartoum Publishing House, Sudan. The International Institute of Islamic Thought (IIIT). *Behavioral Sciences and Methodology, Part 2*, Washington.
Talent Bank. (2024). Employability ratings (6-star ratings): By field of study (Psychology). https://www.talentbankgroup.com/eca#university
Taufik, K,.R., Ibrahim, R., Abdullah, H., & Widhiastuti, H. (2024). Preserving Qur'an through blind eyes: Self-regulation of blind people in memorizing the Qur'an. *Journal of Disability & Religion, 28*(1), 1-12.
Taufik, T., & Ibrahim, R. (2020). Making sense of disaster: Affinity to god as a coping strategy of Muslim refugees in Central Sulawesi. *Journal of Loss and Trauma, 25*(1), 61-73.
Taufik, T., Dumpratiwi, A. N., Prihartanti, N., & Daliman, D. (2021). Elderly Muslim wellbeing: Family support, participation in religious activities, and happiness. *The Open Psychology Journal, 14*(1).
Taufik, T., Prihartanti, N., Daliman, D., Karyani, U., & Purwandari, E. (2023). Be alone without being lonely: Strategies to improve quality of life for an elderly Muslim living in nursing homes. *Current Psychology, 1*, 1-7
Taylor, R. D., & Hardy, C. A. (1996). Careers in psychology at the associate's, bachelor's, master's, and doctoral levels. *Psychological Reports, 79*(3), 960–962. https://doi.org/10.2466/pr0.1996.79.3.960
Thanvi, A. A. (1936). *Talimat*. Idara-e-Ashrafia.
Thoyibi, M., & Ngemron, M. (1996). *Psikologi Islam*. Muhammadiyah University Press.
Trent, J. T. (1993). Issues and concerns in master's-level training and employment. *Journal of Clinical Psychology, 49*(4), 586–592. https://doi.org/10.1002/1097-4679(199307)49:4<586::AID-JCLP2270490417>3.0.CO;2-C
Utsaimin, M. B. (2004). *Syarh Tsalatsatil Ushul*. Riyadh: Daar at Thuraya.
Utsaimin, M. Ş. (2023). *Syarah aqeedah al washitiyah Asy Syaikh al Islam Ibn Taimiyah*. Jakarta: Darul Haq.
Vahab, A. A. (1996). An Introduction to Islamic Psychology. New Delhi: Institute of Objective Studies.
Vidal, F. (2011). *The sciences of the soul: The early modern origins of psychology*. The University of Chicago Press.
Website of the Academic Center for Education, Culture and Research (ACECR) (2025). Available at: https://acecr.ir/en
Website of the Al-Mustafa International University (AMIU) (2025). Available at: https://miu.ac.ir/
Website of the Comprehensive Center for Counseling, Growth and Empowerment (CCGE) of Astan Quds Razavi (2025). Available at: https://moshavere.razavi.ir/
Website of the Imam Khomeini Education and Research Institute (IKERI) (2025). Available at: http://qabas.iki.ac.ir

REFERENCES

Website of the Islamic Psychology Association (IPA) (2025). Available at: www.Islamicpa.com

Website of the Organization for Researching and Composing University Textbooks in the Islamic Sciences and the Humanities (SAMT) (2025). Available at: https://samt.ac.ir/en

Website of the Psychology and Counseling Organization (PCO) of I.R. Iran (2025). Available at: https://pcoiran.ir

Website of the Research Institute of Hawzah and University (RIHU) (2025). Available at: http://rihu.ac.ir

Website of the Research Institute of Quran and Hadith (RIQH) (2025). Available at: www.riqh.ac.ir

What is accreditation? (2023). Accreditation; Stanford University. Retrieved from: https://wasc.stanford.edu/what-accreditation

World Health Organization. (2020). *Mental Health Atlas 2020 Country Profile: Pakistan.* World Health Organization.

York Al-Karam, C. (2018). *Islamic Psychology: Towards a 21st Century Definition and Conceptual Framework. Journal of Islamic Ethics.* Brill Publications.

York Al-Karam, C. (2020). *Islamic Psychology: Expanding Beyond the Clinic.* Peer reviewed article in *Journal of Islamic Faith and Practice. Volume 3.* 111-120.

York Al-Karam, C. (2021). *Islamic Psychology in the United States.* Book chapter in *Islamic Psychology Around the Globe.* In A. Haque and A. Rothman (Eds.). International Association of Islamic Psychology.

York, C. (2024). *Living Islamic Psychology: Portrait of a Muslim American Psychologist.* In *Spirituality in Clinical Practice ®* special issue on psychologists of faith working in a secular profession. March 2024. American Psychological Association.

York, C. (2025). *Introduction to Islamic Psychology.* Retrieved on June 5th, 2025, from https://myui.uiowa.edu/my-ui/courses/details.page?id=851872&ci=170950

Yusoff Zaky Yacob (1977). *Saikologi Remaja.* Kota Bharu: Sharikat Dian Sdn. Bhd.

Yusoff Zaky Yacob (1986). *1001 Masalah Jiwa Manusia* – Jilid 1.Kota Bharu: Dian Darulnaim Sdn. Bhd

Yusoff Zaky Yacob (1989). *1001 Masalah Jiwa Manusia* – Jilid 2. Kota Bharu: Dian Darulnaim Sdn. Bhd

Zarabozo, J.M. (2008). Hadith No. 7', in, Vol.1, Denver, CO: Al-Basheer Company for Publications and Translations, Commentary on the Forty Hadith Of al-Nawawi pp. 397-415.

Zuberi, A., Waqas, A., Naveed, S., Hossain, M. M., Rahman, A., Saeed, K., & Fuhr, D. C. (2021). Prevalence of Mental Disorders in the WHO Eastern Mediterranean Region: A Systematic Review and Meta-Analysis. *Front Psychiatry, 12,* 665019. https://doi.org/10.3389/fpsyt.2021.665019

APPENDIX

A GUIDE TO ISLAMIC PSYCHOLOGY PROGRAMS
Chapter Invitation

Rationale

In recent decades, Islamic Psychology has emerged as a field of interest in many parts of the world. However, the nature and extent of the existing programs and practices are not readily available. Compiling all structured IP programs from universities and organizations would provide a comprehensive guide for stakeholders and promote discipline at the international level.

Chapter Contents

To maintain consistency, please use the following outline. The authors can add extra information in the discussion section. It is encouraged that the program coordinator author the chapter. If this is not possible, the program head or coordinator should be the coauthor.

Chapter Title: Program name, followed by the institution, and author(s).

Introduction

- Background and context
- Rationale and impetus
- Brief history with names of the key people who established the program
- How does the program define IP and why?
- Vision, missions, and objectives

Nature of Program

- Type (bachelor's, Master's, diploma, or certificate)
- Admission requirements
- Duration, modes of instruction, fees, and financial assistance
- Credit hours or other ways of measuring student progress
- Graduation requirements
- Faculty credentials
- Partnership with other programs or institutions

Curriculum

- List of courses with descriptions (max five lines each)
- Please do not include the entire curriculum
- Describe research focus and practical training, if available

Strengths

- Main program strengths and what makes it unique
- Program growth since inception
- Faculty IP publications in the last ten years. List a maximum of five most recent publications in APA Style. If not in English, please provide a translation for an international audience.

Challenges

- Main challenges (maximum five) in bullet points or small paragraphs

APPENDIX

Solutions
- Specific to the challenges mentioned above
- A road map for the next ten years, not exceeding 500 words

Discussion
- Admission rates, graduations, and drop-offs
- Alumni feedback and survey on knowledge utilization, employment, further studies, etc.
- Faculty strength, qualifications, and IP publications
- Internal and external reviews
- Accreditation
- Other

Conclusion
- Summarize by addressing the significant points, implications, and future directions.

Timeline and chapter length

The proposed timeline for chapter submission is **December 31, 2024.** Chapter length is expected to be under 5,000 words, including references, if any.

Islamic Psychology Courses

Please adhere to the provided template for consistency. Authors should have at least a master's level education, with at least one author holding a doctoral degree in psychology.

Proposed chapter template

- Name of Suggested IP course, module, or program
- Rationale for an independent course, module, or program
- Definition of IP and the suggested program in the Islamic context
- Describe historical works and their basis in Islamic sources
- Objective of the course, module, or program
- Program prerequisites, and requirements, if any, with rationale
- Curriculum structure with a component of practical training

- o Include research methodology, qualitative and quantitative measures, a research project, ethical issues, etc.
- o Chapter deadline and word limit: **December 31, 2024, 3,000 words max.**

Editor email: amberhaque@yahoo.com

www.ingramcontent.com/pod-product-compliance
Lightning Source LLC
Chambersburg PA
CBHW020453030426
42337CB00011B/94